D1388008

FIVE HUNGARIAN
WRITERS

FIVE
HUNGARIAN
WRITERS

D. MERVYN JONES

OXFORD
AT THE CLARENDON PRESS
1966

Oxford University Press, Ely House, London W. 1

GLASGOW NEW YORK TORONTO MELBOURNE WELLINGTON
CAPE TOWN SALISBURY IBADAN NAIROBI LUSAKA ADDIS ABABA
BOMBAY CALCUTTA MADRAS KARACHI LAHORE DACCA
KUALA LUMPUR HONG KONG

PRINTED IN GREAT BRITAIN

PREFACE

THESE essays are an attempt to introduce the reader to five of the major figures in Hungarian literature before 1849. 'Introduce', because no previous acquaintance is implied; no knowledge of the Magyar language is presupposed and all quotations are given in translation. I have, however, also printed complete poems and many other verse quotations in the original Hungarian. It is in the original that poetry is to be found, not in my translations; these aim solely at providing what I understand to be the meaning. Some Hungarian poems have been most successfully rendered into English verse, but those which lend themselves readily to verse translation are a minority; it seemed, therefore, best to use prose throughout. In selecting my quotations I have tried above all to illustrate the writer's development, even at the cost of excluding much that an anthology of his best work would have to contain.

In electing to write essays on individual writers, rather than a general history of Hungarian literature, I have been influenced by a desire to attempt first to give the reader a more complete idea of the men and their works than would be possible in a survey of the whole field. At the same time, individuals cannot be discussed without some reference to their background, and I have prefixed to the essays an Introduction sketching the history of Hungarian literature to 1849. I have also included some brief notes in the Index, where I have tried to explain certain individual words, such as the titles of Hungarian county officials, for which there is no exact English equivalent. The subjects of these notes are marked in the text by an asterisk (*). I have also included a brief, non-technical guide to the pronunciation of the Magyar language.

The problem of finding suitable English equivalents is particularly acute with proper names. It finally seemed simplest to make no attempt to anglicize any Hungarian Christian names, as by no means all correspond to common English names; I have also left personal names in their Hungarian order, with the surname preceding the Christian name, as if in an index. Some Hungarian names consist simply of a surname and a Christian name; others (the names of nobles) are tripartite, the surname being preceded by a geographical name, the provenance or seat of the family.

I have not supplied a bibliography, which would be irrelevant for the non-specialist (to whom the book is primarily addressed) and superfluous for the specialist, though I have written some footnotes and given certain references with the latter in view. I must, however, gratefully acknowledge my especial indebtedness to the work of *Arany and Klaniczay on Zrínyi; of Gálos, Király, and Zolnai on Mikes; of Gyulai, Horváth Károly, Lukácsi, Balassa, and Tóth on Vörösmarty; of Ferenczi, Lukinich, Sőtér, and Voinovich on Eötvös; of Endrődi, Ferenczi, Hatvany, Illyés, and Pándi on Petőfi; and of Horváth János, Pintér, and Szerb on everything. The new Hungarian Academy literary history unfortunately appeared too late for me to use it.

I have left till the end of this preface the particular pleasure of recording my personal obligations—to the Rector and Fellows of Exeter College, Oxford, and to the Warden and Fellows of St. Antony's College, Oxford, for their great generosity in electing me to the Fellowships which I held while this book was being written; to Mr. D. M. Davin and his colleagues at the Clarendon Press; and to all others who have helped me, especially to those who have read, and enormously improved, my essays: Mr. Raymond Howard-Gordon, Dr. C. A. Macartney, Professor John Mac-Queen, Mr. S. Weinstock (who has guided my Hungarian studies from the beginning), and my mother, Mrs. G. A. Jones.

D. MERVYN JONES

CONTENTS

GUIDE TO HUNGARIAN PRONUNCIATION

a   as in English 'want' (not as in 'hand'): a vowel only slightly more open than short 'o' in English.

á   the same sound as in French 'à', only long. More open than 'a' in English 'father'.

b   as in English.

c   = 'ts', with the two consonants pronounced as closely together as possible.

cs   = English 'ch' in 'church'. This sound is in fact occasionally spelt 'ch' in Hungarian proper names.

cz   = (Hungarian) 'c', for which it is an archaic spelling now surviving only in proper names.

d   as in English.

e   as in English 'send', but an open vowel, with no suggestion of an 'é' sound. It is in fact the same vowel as French 'è', only short.

é   as in French, only long. It is the same vowel as 'ai' in English 'rain' as pronounced by a Scotsman.

eö   = (Hungarian) 'ö', of which it is an archaic variant found only in proper names, e.g. 'Eötvös'. The 'e' is not pronounced.

f   as in English.

g   always hard, as in English 'go'.

gy   = English 'd'+'y'—the first sound in English 'due' or French 'Dieu'. To be pronounced without any trace of the English 'j' sound.

h   as in English.

i   the same vowel as (Hungarian) 'í', only short. Not the English short 'i' as in 'is'.

í   = English 'ee' as in 'seen'.

j   = English 'y' as in 'yet'.

k   as in English.

l   as in English.

ly   = English 'y' as in 'yet'. Final 'ly' = French 'l' *mouillé*; thus the last syllable of 'Kodály' is pronounced like French 'aille'.

m   as in English.

n   as in English.

ng as in English 'finger'. (Not as in 'sing'; the 'g' is always pronounced.)

ny = English 'n'+'y' (as in 'vineyard') or French 'gn'.

o the same vowel as (Hungarian) 'ó', only short. Not the English short 'o' as in 'box'.

ó the pure long 'o', as in English 'pole' as pronounced by a Scotsman.

ö the same vowel as German 'ö', only short: French 'eu' as in 'peu'.

ő the same vowel as (Hungarian) 'ö', only long.
These two vowels, Hungarian 'ö' and 'ő', do not occur in English, but if the English word 'further' is pronounced with rounded lips, the vowels produced will approximate closely to the Hungarian 'ő' and 'ö', in that order.

p as in English.

r as in English, only very slightly rolled (not guttural).

s = English 'sh' as in 'ship'.

sz = English 's' (cf. 'Liszt').

t as in English.

ty = English 't'+'y'—the first sound in English 'tune'.

u as in English 'push', or short 'oo' as in 'book'.

ú = long English 'oo' as in 'moon'.

ü = French 'u' (short).

ű the same vowel as (Hungarian) 'ü', only long.

v as in English.

w (only in foreign words) = 'v'.

x (only in foreign words) as in English. Initial 'x' too is pronounced as 'ks', not as 'z'.

y final 'y' in proper names (e.g. 'Vörösmarty') = (Hungarian) 'i'. Otherwise 'y' is used only in foreign words (e.g. 'yacht'), except for its occurrence in 'gy', 'ly', 'ny', and 'ty'. In pronouncing these sounds, care must be taken not to make the 'y' a vowel; thus 'könyv' (= 'book'), 'nagy' (= 'great'), for instance, are monosyllables.

z as in English.

zs = English 's' in 'leisure', 'pleasure'; French 'j' in 'je'.

All Hungarian vowels are pure; there are no diphthongs.

Double consonants are given their full value in pronunciation. For instance, Hungarian 'kk' = English 'kc' in 'bookcase', with a slight pause on the doubled consonant.

Double 'cs' is spelt 'ccs'.

,, 'gy' ,,   'ggy'.

,, 'ly' ,,   'lly'.

,, 'ny' ,,   'nny'.

,, 'sz' ,,   'ssz'.

,, 'ty' ,,   'tty'.

All Hungarian words, however many grammatical suffixes they may possess, are accented on the first syllable.

INTRODUCTION

THE history of Hungarian literature begins with the gradual emergence of Magyar alongside Latin as a literary language, as a vehicle for the written word. Although the Gospel was preached in the vernacular in the reign of Hungary's first Christian king, the king who was later canonized as St. Stephen (reigned 1000–38), and in spite of a rich store of folk-tales and songs, of history and legend, the oldest surviving written texts in the Magyar language are versions of Latin originals, the *Funeral Oration* (*Halotti Beszéd*) of *c.* 1200, and in verse, the beautiful *Lament of Mary* (*Ó-Mária Siralom*) of *c.* 1300. These show the language in a state of development which indicates that they had a long line of predecessors now lost; and Magyar manuscripts could be lost all too easily. In 1241–2 Hungary had been completely devastated by the Tartars and about half its population killed. In addition, contempt for the 'barbarian' Magyar language was widespread, and many surviving codices, including that containing the *Lament of Mary*, have been mutilated.

Nevertheless, conditions became more and more favourable for the rise of Hungarian literature. The growing number of foreign visitors to Hungary created a demand for Latin–Magyar glossaries; the compilation of these in turn led to the expansion of the language, strengthening its position as a vehicle for literature. Nuns who did not know Latin acquired religious works written in Magyar; the surviving Magyar *Legend of St. Margaret* and *Legend of St. Francis*, for instance, were both produced for convents. Then about 1430 the first surviving Magyar translations of parts of the Bible were completed.

Secular literature in Hungary, however, remained oral till the Renaissance. Hungary's Renaissance was the most glorious period in her history; King *Mátyás (Matthias Corvinus, reigned 1458–90) made Buda probably the principal centre of Renaissance culture outside Italy. The 'Corvina' library was one of the finest collections of manuscripts in Europe; the Royal printing-press was set up in Buda as early as 1473. The King presided over an intellectual life which attracted scholars of European standing. In the Bishop of Pécs, Janus Pannonius (1434–72), Hungary had one of the greatest Latin poets of the century. His elegies are inspired by a truly spontaneous personal feeling; an outstanding example is the pathos of *On his illness in camp* (*De se aegrotante in castris*). His Italian education in no way weakened his devotion to his country; *Matthias King of Hungary to the Italian poet Antonius Constantius* (*Matthias Rex Hungarorum Antonio Constantio Poetae Italo*) expresses the same determination to defend the homeland, if necessary alone, as we find in Zrínyi (ch. 1) and Petőfi (ch. v).

The culture of the court of King *Mátyás was primarily Italian, but literature in Magyar did not die; court bards sang of the King's mighty deeds and founded a lasting literary tradition. A century later Sir Philip Sidney wrote in his *Apologie for Poetrie*: 'In Hungary I have seen it the manner at all feasts, and other such meetings, to have songs of their ancestors' valour; which that right soldierlike nation think the chiefest kindlers of brave courage.'

2

In 1526, thirty-six years after *Mátyás' death, his kingdom, now suicidally divided by social injustice, was transformed by the Turkish victory at Mohács into a country threatened with extinction. Not only was the kingdom divided; the physical destruction and above all the tragic depopulation, by both slaughter and enslavement, constituted an irreparable disaster; but Hungarian literature survived.

Two months after the battle of Mohács, a young Protestant scholar named Sylvester János (*c.* 1504–*c.* 1553) enrolled as a student at Cracow University, where in the following year he helped to produce the first printed book in the Hungarian language. In 1539 appeared his Hungarian grammar, which standardized the language and thereby decisively raised its status. Two years later he published the first complete translation of the New Testament into Hungarian, with a preface *To the Hungarian People* (*Az magyar nipnek*) written in Hungarian elegiacs, a most convincing demonstration that the vernacular was ideally suited to the classical dactylic metres. Sylvester's career illustrates the forces which kept Hungarian literature alive: the invention of printing, the standardization of the language, which printing assisted, and the Reformation, which, though it

I

ZRÍNYI (1620–1664) * HEROIC EPIC

I

THE defence of Szigetvár, in south-west Hungary,[1] by Count
Zrínyi against Suleiman the Magnificent in 1566 is one of
the greatest among the many actions which stand as symbols
of the Hungarian resistance that defended Europe from the Turk
in the sixteenth century. The Sultan had launched what was to
be his last expedition against Hungary, to prevent the Emperor
Maximilian II from gaining control of Transylvania. In spite of
the danger, the Imperial generals would not move; their armies
stood by while the defenders of Szigetvár faced the Turks alone.
Inspired by Zrínyi's leadership they resisted for over a month,
accounting for some 20,000 Turks—eight times their own numbers
—before resistance became impossible and Zrínyi led all his men
into a final sortie.

Ten years earlier, too, in the summer of 1556, Szigetvár had
been besieged, though by a less formidable Turkish force, under
Ali, the Pasha of Buda. On this occasion the Hungarians, commanded by Horváth Márk, though obliged to abandon the town,
held out unaided in the fortress for seventy-seven days; and eventually disaffection among his subordinate commanders caused the
Pasha to raise the siege.

The gallantry of Horváth and his men was sung by the bard
Tőke Ferenc, 'not for pleasure, but for love of the men of Sziget',
who gave him first-hand information. He is essentially a chronicler,
concerned to give the full facts; he describes in detail the geographical situation of Szigetvár, names the fallen. His style is crude
and often prosaic; Hungarian poetry is still in its earliest stages,
and Tőke is by no means the greatest of his kind. Yet he has something of the grandeur which often accompanies artlessness, and has
brought out the universal significance of his subject, its place in
the unceasing struggle between Christian and heathen, its value as
a testimony to Hungarian unity and loyalty.

[1] The poets commonly call the place simply 'Sziget'; 'vár'='fort'.

B

The second siege, too, was honoured, in the same year as the action itself, by an anonymous bard who, though he clearly knew Tőke's poem, made his own much shorter (344 lines against Tőke's 628) and approached his subject far more as an imaginative artist. His style is as unpolished as his predecessor's; but he paints a moving picture of the human suffering entailed by the siege, especially by the desperate and tragic preparations for the final sortie. On the Turkish side, too, he vividly portrays the shame of the Sultan at his initial failures, and his desperation at the loss of so many of his best soldiers, which resulted in his own death; and, though giving relatively few historical facts, the poet rightly felt the importance of the siege as marking the peak of Turkish power in Hungary. In addition, Zrínyi's heroism was celebrated by poets in other languages; by fellow Croats, notably Krnarutić, and in Latin by the Transylvanian Saxon humanist Schesaeus, also (in 1587) by the Hungarian students at Wittenberg in a collection of Latin poems.

But all earlier literature on the siege has been overshadowed, almost as completely as Homer has overshadowed his predecessors, by the epic written in the winter of 1645-6 by the hero's own great-grandson and namesake, Zrínyi Miklós. Zrínyi was, however, not only an epic poet, not only his hero's descendant, but a hero himself, who already at the age of twenty-five, when he wrote his masterpiece, had fought the same enemy in the same country as his ancestor. It is as if we had an epic on the First Crusade by Richard Cœur de Lion.

Born in 1620, the descendant of an outstanding family, the poet was brought up, and made his home, at Csáktornya[1] in the Mura-köz (Medjumurje), the strip of land between the Mura, the Drave, and the former Austrian frontier. Twenty-five miles to the north-east he could see the Turkish fortress of Kanizsa, which Austrian feebleness had delivered into the hands of the Turks in 1600, to become the base for organized raids over the whole district. The situation was essentially the same as in Suleiman's time, but now the Hungarian outposts were much less well organized; Vienna neglected to pay them and they were often reduced to living off the land; morale sank, their literature, which had flourished in the previous century and produced in *Balassi one of the greatest of Hungarian lyric poets, declined. Finally, though Turkey was now

---

[1] Now Čakovec in northern Yugoslavia.

weak, Vienna strictly forbade any attacks on the invaders, preferring to concentrate its energies on the Thirty Years War.

Such was the situation when Zrínyi took over his estates from his
guardian, Cardinal *Pázmány, in January 1637, and settled at
Csáktornya with his younger brother Péter. His childhood early
developed his capacity to assume responsibility and take decisions.
He lost both his parents and his uncle before he was seven, then
his isolation was intensified by the deaths of a succession of his
guardians. Moreover, monastic orders had sought to acquire part
of the family estates, and the Court was trying every means short
of force to stop the export of cattle to Italy from the port of Bakar
(near Fiume), which was owned by the Zrínyis and so escaped the
Austrian customs.

The Muraköz, too, was not only a richly fertile region, but of
prime strategic importance; it stood between Turkish-controlled
territory and Styria, and, for the Hungarians, was the only link
between Croatia and those parts of Transdanubian Hungary not
under Turkish occupation. Zrínyi quickly saw this and, acting on
what he saw, soon won the respect and fear of the Turks. The
Dutch scholar Jacobus Tollius, who visited Csáktornya in 1660,
saw a picture of the first exploit of the future poet, in which he
turned round to decapitate a Turk who was pursuing him and had
grabbed his coat.[1] By 1640 we find the Pasha of Kanizsa complaining to the Austrians of raids reaching to Kanizsa itself, including
the theft of the Pasha's own horses, and it was clear that Zrínyi
was effectively ending the impunity which Austrian policy had ensured for the Turks. Vienna, however, far from supporting the
Zrínyis, tried repeatedly to bring them to heel, while the Turkish
attacks continued, causing widespread destruction and misery,
which the poet vividly described to the King in a letter of 14 April
1642. But when Zrínyi got marching orders, it was to fight not
Turks but Swedes; only in 1645 did the King yield to his representations that the situation in the Muraköz demanded his and his
brother's presence. Unity is strength, and Zrínyi rightly calculated
that the combined forces of the Christians who were fighting one
another were strong enough not only to defend Hungary (and so
Europe), but to move over to the offensive and drive out the Turk
once for all. He followed closely current events from the *Mercurio*
of his Venetian friend Vittorio Siri; he had an equally thorough

[1] Cf. p. 59.

knowledge of the past, and his library, which Tollius described as 'outstanding' (insignem), contained every work of importance on Hungarian history, together with many on Turkey and eastern Europe. Zrínyi had read how Turkey could be defeated in Achille Tarducci's *Il Turco Vincibile in Ungaria* (The Turk in Hungary can be conquered), published in 1579; and now Turkey was still weaker. Her defeat at Candia in 1645 showed that. The period following his service in the Thirty Years' War was also a critical one in Zrínyi's private life. He became engaged in June 1645 to a Croat lady, Maria Eusebia Drasković, and married her on 11 February 1646; but she had been already engaged to another when he first sought her hand in 1639, and there had been a possibility that he too might marry another. It was in these years that he first turned to poetry.

He was already exceptionally well read, though he had found his schooling, in Graz and Vienna, anything but congenial. By the autumn of 1634 he had had enough, and we find him complaining of swollen knees, which a foreign tour would certainly cure, whereas school and university would make them steadily worse. His poor health was, however, clear also to impartial observers, and in July 1635 the King approved the foreign tour on which Zrínyi had set his heart.

Italy was the obvious destination; apart from the universal reasons for going there, there were commercial and family connexions with Venice, where an ancestor of Zrínyi's had been made a patrician in 1314, and where he still had relatives. He set out in April 1636 and spent eight months in Italy. We know no details of his visit, but he was certainly received in audience by Pope Urban VIII, who gave him a copy of the Latin poets. No doubt it was in Italy, too, that he acquired his intimate knowledge of Italian poetry, especially Tasso and Marino.

Zrínyi's early poems are five in number; one, *The Huntsman and Echo*, is addressed to 'Julia', the others to 'Viola'. Of the latter, two are entitled *Idilium*, the first with the sub-heading 'In which a huntsman complains of Viola's cruelty': the third, *Fantasia Poetica*, is a dialogue between a shepherd, Titirus, and Viola, in the course of which Viola passes from cursing her lover, his fields, and his flocks, to yielding to his verses and accepting his love: the fourth is a *Lament of Ariadne* (*Arianna sírása*).

In the *Lament of Ariadne* the poet tells us that he is at work on an epic: 'I am singing of Mars with his weapon of wrath, to forget the love that torments me', and this passage, together with the opening of the epic itself,[1] may be taken in conjunction with the similarity of Zrínyi's own position to that of the huntsman and later to that of Titirus, to justify the inference that all these poems are autobiographical. The Idylls and the *Fantasia* may thus be assigned to the period immediately preceding the poet's engagement in June 1645, the *Fantasia*, in which Viola finally renounces Licaon in favour of Titirus, being the latest. *Ariadne* is shown by the autobiographical references it contains to come after the *Fantasia*; the epic is under way, and Viola is now not cruel but treacherous. It will then have been written later, probably before the end of 1645, prompted by some trouble between the poet and 'Viola' during their engagement. *The Huntsman and Echo*, addressed to 'Julia', is less accomplished than the Viola poems and probably earlier.

These poems are scarcely masterpieces; they are overlong, repetitive, and heavy with classical allusions, though the *Fantasia* and *Ariadne* show that the poet is learning conciseness. They also retain some of the artificiality of the pastoral convention; but Zrínyi strikes out on his own from the beginning, and the hero of the first Idyll is no wistful shepherd in Arcady but a huntsman 'ranging the forests of the Drave' who is keeping for his Viola a pair of lynx cubs. Moreover, even where Zrínyi is most plainly indebted to his Italian models, he is no mere adapter. For instance, the opening words of the Second Idyll, 'Kegyetlen, hová futsz?' (Cruel one, whither dost thou run?) are almost a literal translation of the beginning of Marino's *La Ninfa Avara* (*The Avaricious Nymph*): 'Crudel, crudele, e dove / si veloce ne vai?' (Cruel, cruel one, whither dost thou depart so fast?) Then Marino's 'Fuggi forse e paventi / questo, che in man mi vedi, arco leggiadro' (Perhaps thou art fleeing in terror at this light bow that thou seest in my hand) (4–5) has given Zrínyi the opening line of his third stanza 'Talán félsz ijamtól, kit hordozok velem?' (Perhaps thou fearest the bow I am carrying). But whereas Marino continues 'Non è già questo di Diana l'arco (7) . . . non è l'arco d'Amor (11) . . . Questo è l'arco di Febo' (14) (This is not the bow of

---

[1] 'I who before with youthful spirit sported with the sweet verses of love, struggled with the cruelty of Viola, now sing, in the louder poetry of Mars, of arms and the knight. . . .'

Diana, ... it is not the bow of Love, ... This is the bow of Phoebus),
Zrínyi goes straight to the point, in the lines immediately following the preceding quotation: 'Cupido ija az, kiben nincs kegyelem. /
Nyilamnak nincs hegye, nincs mérges szerelem / Ijamban, de vagyon
csak tűled félelem' (This is the bow of Cupid, in which there is no
mercy. There is no head on my arrow, no wrathful love in my bow,
but there is only fear of thee). From now on in the poem, with rare
exceptions like a reference to Daphne, Zrínyi is quite independent.
In the *Fantasia Poetica*, however, Zrínyi is a mature poet. He is
here working within the pastoral convention, in the literal sense,
but it is in no way an encumbrance. The opening lines may be
based on an idea which can be traced through *Balassi and Petrarch
to Virgil, but they are poetry in their own right:

> The huntsman takes his rest, when the sun goes down; the shepherd
> lies down when he comes home; the ploughman eats merrily, when his
> work is done; but I like a madman, like a bat at eventide, range the
> forests, because great grief smites me.[1]

The characters may have classical names and indulge in mythological allusion; but much of the poem is written in the style of
Hungarian folk-song. There is far less repetition than in the Idylls,
and the verse is delightfully varied, providing a striking contrast
to the four-line Alexandrine stanza in which they are written, and
perfectly reflecting the changes in Viola's mood from the little
vixen who hurls this furious patter-passage at her lover:

> Hasten from me, for your verses are to me a sharp dagger, the hoar-
> frost to the flower, the stone to the wheat, the hook to the fish, the snare
> to the bird, the net to the beast, the rot to the sheep, an arrow to my
> heart, grief[2] to my spirit, a plague to my life.[3]

[1] Titirus

Az vadász elnyugszik,
Ha az nap lemegyen;
Az juhász lefekszik,
Hogyha haza megyen;

Szántó vigan észik,   5
  Dolga végben megyen:
Én penig, mint bolond, mint esti
  denevér,
Járom az erdőket, mert az nagy
  bánat vér.   (Stanza 1)

[2] The text has the anomalous 'to my grieving spirit'; possibly the poet
meant to put 'Bú kedvemnek' (grief to my spirit).

[3] Fuss tűlem, verseid mert nekem
       éles tőr,   55
   Dér virágnak,
   Kű buzának,
   Horog halnak,
   Lép madárnak,

Háló vadnak,   60
Métély juhnak,
Nyil szűvemnek,
Bus[2] kedvemnek,
Mirigy életemnek.   (10)

to the true love of the last stanza:

> So be it, my sweetheart, as you wish, for your lovely verse has swayed me. Henceforth I will be your servant, your companion and your love, your sweet flower.[1]

The last of this group, the *Lament of Ariadne*, is less successful. Besides reverting to a stock mythological theme, it is awkwardly constructed; although it opens in the first person, we soon realize that we are listening not to Ariadne but to the poet himself, who has been betrayed by his Viola, and now invites her to listen to a lament of Ariadne which he will sing. Yet whatever criticisms can be made of this poem as a whole, here too there are moments of sheer beauty.

These early works, then, are uneven, but Zrínyi has learnt the essentials of his art; he can assimilate his reading and apply it to the expression of his personal feelings. The future is full of promise.

2

The hero-poet now turned to epic, and his subject lay ready to hand. We could have assumed that his great-grandfather was continuously in his thoughts, if the ample proof furnished by the margins of his books had not been forthcoming; Zrínyi of Szigetvár was a hero of popular legend, and his heroism was obviously relevant to the situation of the poet's own day. Zrínyi did not, however, compose his epic to inspire his countrymen, but 'for pleasure', as he said in his preface to his poems when he published them in 1651.

The basic plot is quite simple. During Suleiman's invasion of Hungary, a series of brilliant and successful attacks on his armies, launched by Zrínyi from Szigetvár, causes him to change his route and give the capture of Szigetvár priority over all other operations, using his full force. The final result cannot now be in doubt; the defenders are first compelled to abandon the town and withdraw to the fort; then further resistance becomes impossible and Zrínyi leads all his men into the final sortie. The story thus has not only a heroic quality, but a definite shape; Hungarian

---

[1] Ugy légyen, édes szűvem, az mint akarod,
Mert engemet az te szép versed meghajtott.

Immáron ezután lészek te szolgálód,   165
Társod és szeretőd, és te szép virágod. (24)

successes, which we know must be temporary, are followed by a
reversal of fortune, the Turks regaining the upper hand and captur-
ing the fort in the final climax. The heroism, and the shape, are
essential to an epic.

In spite of these vital assets, however, Zrínyi's theme presented
exceptional difficulties. First, he was writing from the point of
view of the vanquished. Certainly, in the *Iliad* we often see events
from the Trojan point of view, our sympathies are often with
Hector; but the subject of the *Iliad* is not the fall of Troy. Zrínyi's
theme, however, is the action itself, the successful Turkish siege of
a fortress which had defeated the enemy on a previous occasion.
Secondly, although the Sultan had died during the siege, the
Hungarian resistance had not immediately altered the course of
events; indeed in the eighty years that had elapsed the situation
had remained in essentials the same. How, then, could the poet
exalt the defeated above their conquerors, and also give his subject
a universal significance?

These problems are solved at one stroke by Zrínyi's religious
conception of his theme; the action is initiated by God Himself.
The Hungarians are not walking in the way of Christ; they are
fickle, idolatrous, rent by mutual discord and strife. This is their
gratitude for the benefits He has conferred on them; He brought
them out of Scythia, as He did the Jews from Egypt, and settled
them in Pannonia, a fair land flowing with milk and honey, and
made them invincible knights: He sent them the gift of the Holy
Spirit and brought them to Christianity through His Son: He
gave them holy kings, peace, and honour. But now He realizes
that He has nourished ungrateful vipers in His bosom, and will
cause them to be subjugated by the Turks until they recognize
that they have abandoned their Lord and repent. So He summons
the Archangel Michael, and orders him to go down into Hell and
dispatch a Fury to arouse the wrath of the Sultan against the
Hungarians. Here we see the God of the Old Testament, stern,
terrible, inexorable. 'I am that great God of vengeance', He says
(I. 19),[1] and Michael's attempt to intercede for the good Hungarians,
and to ask if it is really the divine purpose that they should be
smitten along with the wicked, is met by rebuke and threat; whereupon the Archangel says no more but sets out on his mission.

---

[1] References are to canto and stanza (the poem is written in four-line Alexandrine stanzas).

Already we can see the fruits of Zrínyi's wide reading; God's speech enumerating the sins of the Hungarians recalls a poem of the sixteenth-century Calvinist pastor Szkhárosi Horvát András, *The Curse (Az átokról)*, an application to the Hungarians of Moses' curse in Deuteronomy XXVIII; and Zrínyi's conception of the Turks as the instrument of divine punishment on Hungary had been formulated also by Károlyi Gáspár, who produced the first complete translation of the Bible into Hungarian (and was, like Szkhárosi Horvát, a Calvinist pastor) in his work *Two books on the causes of the good and evil fortunes of all countries and kings*.[1] Foreign literature, too, has played its part; in Tasso God initiates the action by sending Gabriel to Goffredo with God's command that Jerusalem be liberated. So with Allecto, the Fury whom Michael dispatches to Suleiman; Juno uses her to sow the seeds of war in *Aeneid* VII, and in Canto IX of *La Gerusalemme Liberata* she incites the Sultan Sulimano to take up arms against the Crusaders. In Zrínyi she assumes the form of Suleiman's dead father Selim, just as in Tasso she disguises herself as an old man, and as Cruelty in Marino's *Strage degli Innocenti* (*Slaughter of the Innocents*) assumes the form of Herod's dead brother to instigate the King against the Innocents. The part played by Allecto and the nether powers recalls also the Latin hexameter poem of Alan of Lille (twelfth century), the *Anticlaudianus*, which was printed several times in the seventeenth century. But what matters is Zrínyi's power to assimilate his reading and combine it with original elements, such as Michael's plea.

The exposition of the subject in religious terms is completed in the last two cantos, XIV and XV. In XIV the Turkish sorcerer Alderán rouses all the spirits of Hell against the Hungarians, inaugurating the proceedings with a sacrifice of twelve Christian boys. The nether powers who now rise up, being almost entirely classical in origin, seem somewhat incongruous, though the sonority of the names is not the least important part of the effect. The last of them, however, is relevant indeed—Mahomet's son-in-law, Hazret Ali, who pronounces the heathen doomed:

In Sziget there dwell not such Christians as the leaves of the Koran can harm, or the spirits of Hell or shroud: they have a God greater than Mahomet.

---

[1] The translation of the Bible was published in 1590, the *Two books* in 1563.

He concludes: 'I see that they are far dearer to God than those who before were disunited; they too shall fall, but woe unto your blood!' (XIV. 64)

In the last canto Zrínyi, addressing his men before the final battle, tells them that Hungary's sins have been expiated; then God is seen again, in a very different aspect. His divine glory and radiance are now described at length in a passage which stands in the strongest possible contrast not only to the immediately preceding canto, but also to the opening episode of the poem, which began abruptly with the words 'The great Almighty looked on to earth'. Now God orders the music of Heaven to be silent, and the hosts of Cherubim and Seraphim to assemble. He tells them that the men of Sziget are fighting for Him, but that the spirits of Hell have risen in hate against them and must be driven back into the depths; then He sends Gabriel down at the head of the heavenly host, to rout the evil spirits and bring the souls of the knights of Sziget to Heaven. Gabriel and the angels obey the divine command with a 'great happiness' which is the direct antithesis of the cowed silence with which Michael had set out on his mission in Canto I. Gabriel reaches Sziget, where he finds Zrínyi ready to meet his end, praying to God, and heartens him; then the angels attack the legions of Hell, which seize Alderán and drag him down with them. We shall thus read of Zrínyi's final sortie knowing that the Hungarians are victorious before God.

As with the opening, there are obvious parallels in other epics; the confrontation of the heavenly and nether powers may have been suggested by the account of the siege of Saguntum in Book II of Silius Italicus' *Punica*, which Zrínyi had certainly read; Alderán is a descendant of Tasso's Ismeno, and God sends down Michael to rout the evil spirits Ismeno has stirred up (IX. 58); in the final battle (XVIII. 92) Michael reveals to Goffredo the hosts of Heaven fighting by his side. The conveying to Heaven of the souls of Hungarian soldiers killed in battle against the Turk is found in the bard *Tinódi, also in the Wittenberg-album. Like all great artists, Zrínyi knew the work of his predecessors.

The impact of the tremendous episodes which begin and end Zrínyi's epic is not in any way lessened by the fact that the events related have their natural as well as their supernatural causes. Suleiman is influenced not only by Allecto but by a letter from his general Arszlán in Buda, assuring him of victory, because of the disunity, imprudence, and lack of military talent among the Hungarians; the final battle is brought on by fire as well as by the spirits summoned by Alderán. These passages relate the beginning and end to the rest of the poem, from which they might appear divorced if the action were wholly on a supernatural plane. To achieve this, however, the natural parallels to the supernatural events must, as Zrínyi has seen, not be overstressed.

God appears as a speaking character only in the first and last cantos—an economy which magnificently strengthens the structure of the poem. The danger of anthropomorphism is avoided, by the two memorable lines which follow God's command to Gabriel: 'Thus He spoke, not with tongue and not with speech, but with radiant divine will' (xv. 33). Otherwise He intervenes only rarely, to direct the course of particular events, as when He turns Suleiman's attention from Eger to Szigetvár (III); but the poet, and the Hungarians, are continually aware of His presence and purpose. An essential part of that purpose, however, the turn of the fortunes of battle in favour of the Turks, is worked out without His direct intervention. It is by his treatment of this change of fortune that Zrínyi gives his epic a middle as well as a beginning and an end.

We know that the Hungarians must perish; but first they achieve an unbroken run of successes so great that by the opening of VIII Suleiman is in despair and, at least to himself, admits defeat. But already a shadow has fallen over the Hungarian camp by the death of the hero Farkasics. His leader speaks a moving lament over him, with reflections on the changeability of Fortune, and the brevity of human life:

Water, fire, earth, and the great heavens last for long: Man, their master, for the twinkling of an eye; stone walls, great towers, for many centuries: Man, who made them, for an hour.[1]

Already the atmosphere is changing. When the proem to IV warned us that in spite of Zrínyi's successes Fortune still had power over him: when, in v, Zrínyi, knowing that he would never leave Sziget alive, sent his son away to safety, tragedy still lay in the future. Now for the first time it becomes part of the present; then

---

[1] Víz, tűz, föld, és nagy ég tartanak sokáig: Kűfalok, nagy tornyok sok száz esztendeig:
Ember, ezek ura, egy szempillantásig;   Ember, ki csinálta ezeket, óráig. (VII. 45)

in IX two heroes of the fighting which follows the death of Farkasics go out on a night raid and do not return. The proem to X, like that to IV, describes the fickleness and cruelty of Fortune, but with the all-important addition of the definite statement that she *has now* changed, and has ceased to show goodwill towards Sziget. And in X. 7 ff. we are told that Zrínyi, seeing that the whole town of Szigetvár has been burnt down and that the Turkish cannon have destroyed a tower of the fortress, wisely decided to abandon the town and transfer all his forces to the fortress. This solves also the problem created for the poet by the long series of repeated Turkish attacks of which the historical siege consisted; he avoids the monotony and gloom inherent in their detailed narration, while yet remaining true to history, by describing briefly their results, *after they have taken place*. The centre-piece of the structure of the poem, however, is the night raid itself.

A night raid as a feature of heroic epic goes back to the *Iliad* (Book X), where, however, the treatment is not at all heroic or tragic; it was Virgil who first conceived his night raid as a tragedy. What Zrínyi has done is to present his raid, implicitly, as the turning-point of the whole action, just as Virgil himself made the descent of Aeneas to the underworld (*Aeneid* VI) the centre of his epic, with an importance which its predecessor in *Odyssey* XI[1] totally lacks; similarly the night raids in earlier epic are not of special importance.

In the detail Zrínyi follows Virgil fairly closely. The object of the raid in Zrínyi is to convey a request for help through to the Emperor, just as Virgil's heroes hope to pass through the enemy lines and inform Aeneas of their danger. The younger of the pair, Juranics, like Euryalus, insists on going in spite of his senior's protest 'You are younger: you deserve to live a longer life' (Zrínyi, IX. 25, cf. *Aen.* IX. 212). They submit their plan to Zrínyi, who at the time is conferring with his second-in-command Deli Vid, as Nisus and Euryalus seek an audience of the Trojan chiefs. Common to both poets are the emotion with which the proposal of the two volunteers is received: the promise of gifts (though not the gift of captives as slaves, which is not in Zrínyi): the drunkenness of the enemy: Zrínyi's raiders kill the high priest

---

[1] This is true even independently of the arguments in favour of the (now generally accepted) view that the Descent of Odysseus to the underworld is a later addition to the *Odyssey*.

Kadilesker, just as Virgil's slay the augur Rhamnes: in both the elder of the two (Radivoj–Nisus) sacrifices first his safety, then his life, for the younger (Juranics–Euryalus), and the details of their capture and death are the same: both episodes end with a similar apostrophe to the heroes by the poet. 'O blessed, O happy, O mighty knights! If my Hungarian verses have any power, your name so worthy of praise shall never die, as long as swift waters flow down' (Zrínyi, IX. 77, cf. *Aen.* IX. 446 ff.). The only major difference is that Zrínyi omits the appearance of the younger hero's mother. Then the ghost of Radivoj appears to Deli Vid in his sleep, wounded and bleeding, and speaks to him ('in Croat', an interesting touch which reminds us, as do many of the heroes' names, that all the nationalities living in Hungary fought the Turk together). 'Be not at all afraid of me, Deli Vid; soon you will be with me, for to you also has God assigned martyrdom, with our leader, and a place in Heaven. So be not forgetful of gallantry, and tremble not before the heathen Turk: I ask for strength for you from God; God be with you—remain a knight' (IX. 93–94). This passage too has its ancestors in earlier epic, notably the appearance of Hector to Aeneas (*Aen.* II. 270 ff.); again Zrínyi has given it a special significance, which the next canto underlines. Well might *Kazinczy say of Zrínyi: 'one of his beauties lies in the fact that he transplants the flowers of the Romans as they did those of the Greeks'.[1]

Zrínyi, then, achieves unity by the scenes in Heaven at the beginning and end of his poem, and by the significance with which he endows the night raid near the middle; the problem of variety is solved by richly diversified episodes which successfully obviate the danger of monotony inherent in the poet's main theme, the siege. Canto III, for instance, well illustrates both Zrínyi's art and the character of the Turks. Mehmet Gujlirgi, the Pasha of Bosnia, is met at Siklós, near Pécs, by Bey Szkender, who warns him of the danger from Szigetvár. But 'Mehmet did not know the Christian, because he had been brought up entirely at court, and believed in the foolish Koran, that one Turk could kill four Christians in battle' (III. 19). So he disregards the advice, feeling quite confident that he can deal with Zrínyi; in any case the weather is too cloudy and rainy for a battle that night. He invites Szkender to spend the evening with him; and Szkender, not pressing his point, accepts. After dinner, as they sit on their velvet cushions, a richly dressed

---

[1] In a letter of 29 August 1824 (Váczy, no. 4384 (vol. 19)).

minstrel boy sings them a song which perfectly expresses Mehmet's mood:

Why should I rail against you, Fortune? when every day you add to my joy; you part not from me, as is your reputation, that you delight only in inconstancy.

In springtime you bless me with the beautiful green forest, with the song of the amorous nightingale, with the manifold variety of the birds of heaven, with the slow plashing of water, with the stirring of the breeze.

You grudge me not the one I love, rather you lend your aid, that she may love me; you never take away my happiness, hourly you heighten my delight.

In summer you give rest and fair quiet, lovely cypress-shade, cool breezes, fine tents stitched with delicate needle, goodly fragrant waters which assuage thirst.

In autumn you bestow bountiful gifts of much fruit, lemons, oranges and fair pomegranates; you leave not an animal in the forest, because you favour me generously with them, and with goodly birds.

But in winter, when all things complain, then my heart delights even more; my soul is not anxious at the mighty storm, because my body is warmed by a fine flaming fire.[1]

[1] Miért panaszkodjam, szerencse, ellened?
Ha bővited mindennap én öröme-
met,
Nem szakasz el tűlem, az mint
vagyon hired,
Hogy állhatatlanságban van minden kedved.

Kikeletkor áldasz az szép zöld er-
dővel,
Szerelmes fülemile éneklésével, 130
Égi madaraknak sok külömbsé-
gével,
Viz lassu zugással, széllengede-
zéssel.

Nem irigyled nékem az én egyese-
met.
Inkább hozzá segétsz, szeressen
engemet;
Soha el nem vészed az én vig ked-
vemet, 135
Neveled óránként gyönyörűsége-
met.

Adsz nyáron nyugovást és szép
csendességet,
Szép ciprus árnyékokat, hűvös sze-
leket,
Gyönge tűvel varrott szép sátor-
ernyőket,
Szomjuság-megoltó jó szagos
vizeket. 140

Ősszel sok gyümölcssel, citrom-
mal, turunccsal
Ajándékozsz bőven, szép poma-
gránáttal;
Erdőn vadat nem hagysz, mert
nékem azokkal
Bőven kedveskedel, és jó madarakkal.

De télen, az mikor minden panasz-
kodik, 145
Akkor az én szűvem inkább gyö-
nyörködik;
Erős fergetegen szűvem nem ag-
gódik,
Mert szép lángos tűznél testem
melegedik.

I enjoy great standing with my Emperor, high is my honour among all men; my great riches can never be exhausted, I have a goodly steed, a sharp blade, a fair love.

But you are tied, Fortune, to my feet, because you would ere now have run away to my enemies had you been free; but you will bring no evil upon me, because you are tied, Fortune, to my feet.[1]

So ends the song, but the next stanza is relevant too.

So sang the boy. But the great *Bán of Sziget (Zrínyi), hearing from peasants of the arrival of Mehmet, prides himself not on the things of the world; he thinks of other matters, and calls together his good knights at once.

He lays an ambush: a battle is fought: and when he 'calls together his knights' in the evening, it is to occupy the Pasha's camp.

The most dramatic episodes, however, occur towards the end of the poem, where they are most needed artistically, as a substitute for the detailed narration of the later stages of the siege, which would not only be monotonous but also might depress instead of inspire. In XI the savage Saracen Demirhám has challenged Deli Vid to single combat under the protection of a safe-conduct. Zrínyi, reluctantly, allows Vid to accept, but 'until the two knights were ready for the combat Zrínyi Miklós stood on the alert, lest the Turk should start some treachery, as was the custom of the heathen enemy' (XI. 55). The combat takes place, and it soon becomes clear that Deli Vid is going to win; but a Turk named Amirassen cries shame on his fellows, with the specious moral argument that it is disgraceful to allow one man to do their fighting for them when they outnumber the enemy by a hundred to one or more, and attacks Deli Vid from behind. Vid kills Amirassen at once, leaps on to the horse of his assailant, and disappears into the Turkish lines, whither we shall shortly follow him. Demirhám is 'amazed' at Amirassen's treachery, 'because (it must be admitted) it was not what he wanted' (XI. 82). We first

---

[1] És vagyon császáromnál nagy tisztességem,
Mindenek között vagyon nagy böcsületem;   150
El nem fogyhat soha az én sok értékem,
Van jó lovam, éles szablyám, szép szerelmem.

De kötve vagy, szerencse, az én lábomhoz,
Mert elfuttál volna eddig gonoszszomhoz,
Ha volnál szabadon; de rám gonoszt nem hozsz,   155
Mert kötve vagy, szerencse, az én lábomhoz. (III. 32–39)

saw him, in the catalogue of the Turkish forces, as 'cruel Demirhám', as some mighty, savage giant: then (VI), as one of the two envoys sent by the Sultan to persuade Zrínyi to surrender, he was impatient of talk (the opposite of his smooth-tongued colleague) and infuriated by Zrínyi's steadfastness. Now this savage shows himself a man of honour—his sense of honour may overspill into personal pride, but his conscience will not let him rest until he has fought Vid in fair combat, and he searches continually for his adversary, whirling his sword like a Fury (XIV. 86) and shouting to Vid that he will find him wherever he has hidden. Vid, after his safe return, had remained within the fort because such were Zrínyi's orders, and, unlike Demirhám, Vid obeys his leader; but now he comes forward with a counter-taunt of treachery. This brings out the noblest side of the Saracen's nature. 'Please, listen to me carefully, Vid. We were both deceived in our minds; neither did you hide, nor did I ever break or dishonour my good faith; it was anger that made me speak of your hiding. . . . Let us delay no longer . . .' (XIV. 90 ff.). So the two heroes go out to their last combat and the poem moves to its greatest climax but one.

Before this climax is reached, however, two whole cantos (XII–XIII) have intervened, together with the raising of the spirits of Hell by the Turkish sorcerer Alderán, and the fire, which occupy the greater part of XIV. The suspense is superbly maintained. XI ends with Zrínyi marching out and fighting invincibly in his grief at the supposed loss of his comrade—Vid is there but cannot reveal himself: XII is concerned with a totally different subject: then the proem of XIII tells us that Zrínyi's hour has come, and a little later we are told that Vid's own days are numbered, though for the moment he deals out death among the Turks, unrecognized and unchecked. Vid's faithful and beautiful Turkish wife Barbara, clad in his armour but wearing a veil like a Turkish woman, has set out to look for him. She encounters a corpulent and comic Saracen who tells her that he is taking the news to Suleiman that Deli Vid is lying in a nearby tent in Turkish uniform. 'When the heathen mentioned Deli Vid, imagine how the lady's face changed' (XIII. 16); so Barbara pursues the Saracen and kills him. However, she is herself pursued by other Turks, surrounded, and questioned; she replies that the Saracen was the slayer of her elder brother, and soon finds sympathizers, though others wish her to be brought

before the local commander. Vid catches sight of her but his emotion does not betray him into giving himself away; he shouts out
that she is his servant. The stratagem fails, however, because a
judge comes up and tells Vid that he will have to prove this in
court. Whereupon the Hungarian attacks and slays the Turks,
seizes his wife, and rides off. The horse

> Karabul, like a bird, made no impress on the ground, but went
> swiftly as a screaming arrow; he could have galloped over the sea, and
> you would not have seen any water on his hoof.[1]

So Karabul disappeared from the sight of his pursuers 'like a mist',
to restore Vid and his wife safely to the welcome of the rejoicing
Zrínyi.

The story of Vid's adventures behind the Turkish lines is itself
divided in two, by the longest digression in the epic, occupying
the whole of XII. It tells of the love of Delimán the Tartar for the
Sultan's daughter Cumilla. Already in I, in the Turkish catalogue,
we learn that

> Cumilla's fair tresses made captive the heart of the youth Delimán,
> and his whole spirit; one glance took away all his strength, so that he
> did not wish to live without her.[2]

'Then he had gone home, but now he returned with a fine army,
pondering how he might win the fair maid. But the poor wretch
was deceived, because in the meantime Bey Rustán had married
Cumilla, as it happened' (I. 73), and Delimán's grief knew no
bounds. 'Guard well against him, vizier Rustán,' continues the
poet (I. 75), 'for he, like a savage wolf, is on the watch to slay you.'
Cumilla is not mentioned again till XII, but we see the two men as
bitter opponents in the council of war in VIII; then at the beginning of XI Delimán meets Rustán, the man he feels least able to
face at that particular moment, when he is smarting with anger and

---

[1] Karabul, mint madár, nem nyom
   nyomot földön,
De mint süvőtő nyil megy ollyan
   sebessen,
Ő futhatott volna által az tengeren,
S nem esmerszett volna, hogy van
   viz az körmén. (XIII. 28)

[2] Cumilla szép haja megkötözé
   szűvét
Ifiu Delimánnak, és minden
   kedvét,
Egy tekéntet vévé el minden
   erejét,
Ugy hogy nála nélkül nem ki-
   vánja éltét. (I. 72)

shame at having been compelled to retreat in a raid on the fort. So
when Rustán taunts him with cowardice the Tartar kills his rival
on the spot.

At the opening of XII Cupid intervenes—the only[1] intervention in
the epic by a deity of classical mythology, and apparently a stock
literary device, yet profoundly true as a portrayal of the power of
love between two people meeting after a long interval. For it is
significant that whereas Delimán is continually before us, Cumilla
has not been mentioned since the brief reference to her in the catalogue, quoted above. The inference is clearly that Delimán, or at
any rate his conscious self, has forgotten her; in fact Cupid says
explicitly (XII. 5) that the wound his arrow had inflicted on Delimán
had completely healed. But now he inflames the two, far apart
though they be, with mutual love, and Delimán,

when he hears the lament of the nightingale, likens his own grief to
the bird's; when his eyes see bright skies, he thinks Cumilla's beauty
the greater.[2]

Cumilla is compared to a wounded hind, as is Virgil's Dido in a
more elaborate simile; but this poet has not only read of Dido and
Aeneas, of Armida and Rinaldo: he has 'struggled with Viola's
cruelty'.

Delimán goes to Belgrade, where Cumilla, encouraged by her
confidante, the old woman Fáti (as is Dido by Anna), writes him a
thinly disguised love-letter, whereupon he visits her without delay;
but now the poet warns us that their love will end in tragedy.
Leaving the lovers 'redoubling kisses around each other's lips'
(XII. 50), we return to the Turkish camp to find it thoroughly
demoralized at its losses, and critical of Suleiman for disregarding
them; the soldiers attribute the present disastrous situation solely
to the absence of Delimán. Suleiman is hurt by these developments, but decides that in the interests of his own dignity it would
be better to accede to the demand that an embassy be sent to
Delimán. A subtle appeal to the Tartar's vanity and honour, combined with the promise that he shall marry Cumilla and that the

---

[1] Apart from three conventional references to the Fates spinning.

[2] Ha az fülemüle sirását hallgatja,   Ha derült egeket az ő szeme látja,
  Annak bujához magáét hasom-   Cumilla szépségét nagyobbnak
  litja;   gondolja. (XII. 11)

Sultan will forget the killing of Rustán, overcomes Delimán's resentment at being summoned, and he resolves to go. He is torn between love and honour, but in the end honour is victorious. He tries to console Cumilla—she must not weep for him; she too will rejoice when he returns in triumph. Cumilla, however, is inconsolable; yet, unlike Dido and Armida, she has no thought of vengeance, and ends her last speech praying that Delimán may be preserved or that she may die. They set out and rest by a spring, from which Delimán fetches Cumilla water to drink; but his goblet is poisoned by drops of the blood of a dragon, from his own sword when he sheathed it after slaying the monster. 'She met the fate she desired' (XII. 108); Delimán, in his uncontrollable grief, killed a multitude of his own men.

None of the Hungarian subordinate commanders is as powerfully individualized as Demirhám or Delimán; but whereas the Turkish warriors fight as individuals (both Demirhám and Delimán, at different times, refuse to obey orders from the Sultan), the men of Sziget are united, by a common bond of loyalty. The leader who is the object of that loyalty, however, is one of the poet's main themes; when he announces at the outset that he sings of 'arms and the knight', this is no mechanical borrowing of the 'arma virumque' of the *Aeneid*, but an important fact about his own epic. But the first of the two leaders whom we see is Suleiman, when the Fury Allecto visits him in his palace in Constantinople. He responds instantly to her call, savagely promising to 'dye his horse in lakes of Christian blood, bury cities and forts in ashes' (I. 48).

The full description of the Sultan, however, is reserved for the impressive moment when his vast host (which the poet has enumerated in a Catalogue) sets out from Constantinople. After describing his steed (an original passage which reveals the poet's own first-hand knowledge of horsemanship), the finery of his dress, the 'terrible dignity' of his glance, Zrínyi proceeds to assess Suleiman's greatness, and emphasizes the importance of what he is about to say. 'I must write the truth, listen now. Sultan Suleiman was our enemy; but except only that in his faith he was a heathen, perhaps there was never such a lord among the Turks. But I can say boldly, without any "perhaps", that there was never on the face of this earth any so gallant and wise among the heathen, any who was victorious in so many battles, in many countries. Gallantry and prudence were united in him; great energy in war was concentrated in him;

had cruelty not corrupted his heart, perhaps he would be the greatest, among Christians too. But when he caused his son Mustafa to be put to death, then above all did he reveal himself; indeed he made his nation hate him. It was on account of the love of Roxa that he did this. Fortune did not play with him as with another; if she wished to terrify him with a blow, with the loss of an army, or with some other injury, he was at all times steadfast in his wisdom. He did not bend like a branch; he stood like a rock amid the foam of the sea, because he examined himself; if Fortune gave him some good, he grew not over-confident, was not puffed up. Such was the man and such the army that came against our country' (II. 44–50).

This portrait is framed by two military actions, the successful defence of the fortress of Palota[1] by the Hungarian Turi, and the opposite of Turi's valour, the ignoble surrender of Gyula by Kerecsényi; these two episodes show that for all the might of the Sultan, the outcome depends on the character of his opponent. They also illustrate the power of the invader, because the two forts are at opposite ends of the country—Palota in the west, beyond the Danube, Gyula (=Alba Iulia, in Rumania) in the east, in Transylvania. The point is further emphasized a little later when we hear (II. 59) that Suleiman is hesitating whether to attack Eger in northern Hungary, or Szigetvár in the south. At this moment, when the Sultan's arm has reached out towards all four corners of the country, we meet his adversary for the first time.

'At that time the renowned Zrínyi was in Szigetvár, having been appointed commander by Maximilian; he was also *Bán of Croatia and the adjoining lands—he is the subject of my story. He had tested the strength of the Turk more than once, and had gallantly destroyed it in every battle. All the Turks knew him well; he was the cause of their greatest ruin. For the final downfall of Turkish camps it was enough to say, Zrínyi is fighting; as clouds roll speedily on before the wind, so did the Turk hasten to flee homewards. God had given Zrínyi such power; his enemies crumbled before him like the sand. God knew him well for His faithful servant, and so blessed him in all his works. Zrínyi one morning, as was his custom always at daybreak, was kneeling before the holy crucifix, and thus his holy lips began to pray: "Holy God of infinite mercy, who helpest me in all my doings, thou art my in-

---

[1] The modern Várpalota.

vincible weapon, my shield, my wall of stone, all my hope.[1] Bow
down thine ear from the high blue heavens, hear my prayer in thy
mercy; pass judgement not in accordance with what I deserve,
but from the infinite mercy of thy heart. . . .[2] My Lord, thou seest
how the teeth of the heathen Turk, the faithless cur, are set on
edge, how he may hurt the Christians; this alone is their purpose,
that they may break us. Permit not, Lord (though we should deserve it), that by thy wrath we be dashed to the ground, that they
laugh at thy holy name, asking proudly of us where thou art.
Show them that thou art a great God, that there is no other God
but thee; he who walks after thee walks not in darkness, but thy
way leads him to eternal joy. . . ." So Zrínyi besought God; He
heard his prayer. Three times was it revealed to Zrínyi, that the
crucifix bent down towards him, saying these words in answer:
"Lo, I have heard thy prayer . . . fear not, for not in vain did I die
for thee. . . . The angels await thee, in readiness: the Cherubim
stand in ordered hosts: they shall set thee at the right hand of my
Father, together with thee they shall rejoice eternally. Soon I shall
take unto myself thy noble soul; so dost thou wish it, so dost thou
know it to be best; but that a crown even brighter may honour thy
head, lo, this is the mercy I give thee. Thou shalt suffer martyrdom
at the hands of the heathen, for thou shalt die bravely for my name.
Zrínyi, listen now to what I say; lo, I will recount thy future.
Suleiman is coming with an army against Hungary, and first he
shall come to thy fortress; he will lie in wait, like a ravening wolf,
to slay thee; he shall lose his power, his might at Szigetvár. But
he shall not see thy ruin, for he shall die by thy gallant right hand:
many thousand Turks must die there: then shall thy soul come
to me. But thy son György shall sustain thy race; he shall awaken
thy shining name, like a phoenix from its ashes he shall arouse his
nation: with such wisdom he shall preserve thy house."' (II. 60 ff.)

Zrínyi's might, then, comes from God; so it is not in battle that
we first see him, but at prayer. This not only points the contrast
with Suleiman, but shows that Zrínyi of Sziget stood in a relationship with God totally different from his fellow countrymen. They
had 'trampled the fair Christian faith underfoot' as God had said
(I. 12): him 'God knew well for His faithful servant' (II. 63).
They were ungrateful (I. 18): he was content with the dominion
God had given him (II. 68). Above all, they were 'stiff-necked and

---

[1] Cf. Psalm XVIII. 2.   [2] Cf. Psalm LXXXVI. 1, 3, 5.

haughty' (I. 12): Zrínyi freely confessed his sins, thereby obtaining God's forgiveness, to prepare himself to fulfil his destiny. For the reader, too, the passage emphasizes that forgiveness has been granted to a man against whom sinister accusations had been made in his lifetime, who had committed his full share of the sins for which God was chastising his country; but now only his heroism remains relevant. Goffredo too is first seen at prayer (*Ger. Lib.* I. 15) but there is nothing in Tasso corresponding to the significance which the passage in Zrínyi derives from its context; nor are we given the words of Goffredo's prayer. Zrínyi the poet has here followed in the footsteps of those contemporaries of the hero of Szigetvár who paraphrased the Psalms in verse,[1] and has combined this Hungarian literary tradition with the opening of *La Gerusalemme Liberata* to meet perfectly the requirements of his artistic purpose.

When we first see Zrínyi of Sziget with his army, he is 'calling his good knights together' at Siklós, and addressing them in an atmosphere of faith, friendship, and mutual confidence—shortly after we had learnt that Suleiman had had his general Arszlán put to death for the failure before Palota. Szkender's warning to Mehmet, which preceded the song of the minstrel boy, is fully confirmed by the events which follow; Zrínyi, whose personal valour matches his alertness and his tactical skill, leads his men to a decisive victory. Yet the climax of the episode is not that victory, but the Hungarian leader's clemency to the Turkish cavalry commander Ibrahim, who, like Altamoro at the end of Tasso's epic (XX. 140), resists to the last, then honourably surrenders to a conqueror whom he himself honours.

The sequel to the victory completes the picture of the Hungarian camp. Zrínyi addresses his men to give thanks for the victory. His external appearance is now described, in a single stanza: 'He rode upright, and stood before the army. On his helmet a fine ostrich-feather lashes the angry breeze: iron covers his breast and gives him strength: in his hand is a great spear' (IV. 14). Then follows the burial of the dead, with the leader's funeral oration— a regular feature of epic, but here enriched by the poet's own experience as a soldier: 'they hearten the wounded with fair words of valour, and bind up their wounds' (IV. 20). After a very brief meeting between Zrínyi and his son, the Hungarians celebrate

[1] See p. xv.

their victory in a feast, in which Zrínyi's generosity towards Ibrahim comes out even more finely in the words of consolation which he addresses to his despondent prisoner, whom he eventually agrees to release in exchange for a Hungarian. Then we pass to the opposing camp.

Unlike his adversary, Suleiman has not been present at the scene of the fighting; when he hears of the battle of Siklós it is from Rumour, the same monster who spread the news of the love of Dido and Aeneas (*Aeneid* IV. 173 ff.), who 'flew more swiftly than wind and bird, than whom none is more wicked' (IV. 52) as the poet briefly describes the creature. Rumour not only proclaims 'with a thousand trumpets' (IV. 53) the defeat and death of Mehmet, but announces 'falsely, as is her wont' (IV. 54) that all the Turkish forts have fallen, all the Turkish forces are slain. The Sultan's first reaction is to disbelieve the news himself, and to keep it from his viziers; when this becomes impossible he calls a council and announces his intention of leaving 'innocent Eger' (IV. 63) in peace and punishing Zrínyi; the viziers are to concentrate immediately all the Turkish forces. The sacrificial omens prove unfavourable, but Suleiman remains confident that 'Mahomet cares for us greatly' (IV. 80).

Whatever the Sultan's ability to resist Rumour, we soon see her power over his troops. In a passage possibly suggested by an incident in the Roman campaign in Germany described by Tacitus (*Annals* I. 66), two wild horses break loose in one of the tents in the Turkish camp about midnight and trample many of the soldiers to death. Someone shouts through the darkness 'If Zrínyi could be here now, by my faith he would throw us all into confusion; God grant that Zrínyi be not here!' One Turk, hearing only the name of Zrínyi, concludes from these words that Zrínyi has indeed come, and runs wildly all over the camp; another shouts 'Zrínyi is upon us, I saw him with my own eyes' and all who hear him flee. A third Turk, meeting an allied contingent, attacks them in the belief that they are the raiders, and captures their leader, supposing in the darkness that his prisoner is Zrínyi himself. Three thousand Turks lose their lives, and the Sultan himself restored order only 'with difficulty, and late' (IV. 103). So ends a canto in which we have become closely acquainted with the two armies and their leaders, as the siege is about to begin. 'On one side Suleiman made great preparations; on the other the *Bán of Croatia attended to the fort' (v. 1). Zrínyi calls his men together, and addresses them in a speech longer than its predecessors (31 stanzas), as befits the solemnity of the occasion. The men 'drew courage from gallant Zrínyi's words', and the oath-taking which follows gives the poet the occasion for a catalogue of the Hungarians (ending with Deli Vid, 'the scourge of the Turks . . . wise, strong, swift, wrathful, as he willed' (v. 59, 62)). The catalogue and the oath-taking, like Zrínyi's speech to his men, mark the opening of a new phase in the story.

When the preparations for the defence of Sziget are complete, one task of vital importance remains for Zrínyi, to provide for the safety of his son. He writes a letter to the King, reporting that all necessary measures have been taken, but also expressing his fear lest God has decreed that Sziget shall not survive the siege; if this is so, he will gladly die. Having therefore commended his son to the royal favour, he ends by bidding the King farewell, and praying for God's blessing on His Majesty. 'Having finished the letter he sealed it and nobly embraced his son György; he spoke these few words of wisdom to him, and the boy listened closely to his father' (v. 76). 'My son, I am seeing you for the last time', Zrínyi begins, and exhorts his son: 'Learn from me the hard way of valour: learn from me toil and loyalty to your country: learn from me to do good: but from others learn fortune and its fruits' (v. 79)—a reminiscence of Virgil (*Aen.* XII. 435–6), but particularly well suited to the present situation. The father then goes on to bid his son serve God, in a passage into which the poet has put all his feeling for the inspiration which he himself has drawn from his forefathers: 'Be not as an unworthy dove born of a hardy eagle, seek your fame from the heathen, with the sword; let it be said, you were a true son of Zrínyi' (v. 83).[1] With these words Zrínyi hands his son the letter, and orders him to deliver it to the King. But György, precisely because he is a 'true son of Zrínyi', will not accept this situation: 'Not thus shall I, the son of the eagle, be a true eagle myself, but an unworthy nestling not fit to live, if I fear so greatly in the face of death. . . . Whatever fortune God has decreed for you, the same should rightly be mine' (v. 87 f.). Zrínyi is deeply moved by the 'great heart' of his son, but must 'extinguish' his 'fire'. 'It is not good to pluck a flower before its time, there is no merit in your desiring death; now, when you could help

---

[1] Zrínyi György (1549–1603), though a lesser figure than his father and his grandson the poet, was a distinguished soldier.

no one by dying, it is your duty to live and serve. . . . Follow me in my great trials, when it is your duty' (v. 94, 96). These words end the canto at the point where its ending most effectively expresses György's reluctant obedience; and naturally the poet does not remind us that Suleiman had put his son to death.

Now arrives a Turkish embassy, consisting of Halul 'whose words flowed as beautifully as if they had been mixed with honey' (VI. 3) and his very different colleague Demirhám. Zrínyi's speech to his men has already forearmed them against Turkish deceit; they will all hear the envoys, for the Hungarians in Sziget are a democracy—'Zrínyi called together all the knights' (VI. 8). Halul uses all the resources of his art: he flatters Zrínyi as the 'fair star of the followers of Jesus' whose fame 'shines as the sun, where the warm dawn rises red, where the dark evening sinks into the sea, where the northern ocean struggles within itself' (VI. 11): warns him of the uselessness of expecting effective Austrian help:[1] and ends with a reminder of the consequences of rejecting the Sultan's 'friendship'.

But the man who devised the ambush at Siklós also knows how to deal with Halul. 'You have expounded in fair words the affection your lord feels for us, and his goodwill. I am surprised; for I have not attempted to win the favour of your Sultan—on the contrary, I have injured him, within the limits of my small ability, wherever it was possible, and with all my strength. . . . If the Sultan desires my friendship, it can be; for he can return what belongs to the Hungarian, and henceforward cease to covet the goods of other Christians; then perhaps I can be his friend. But when you demand Szigetvár in his name, good envoy, you should know what I am about to say: Zrínyi has been through many sufferings with these men—evil, peril, cold, heat. . . . Take my words back to your Sultan; Suleiman shall see what Zrínyi can do' (VI. 39 ff.). On hearing Zrínyi's reply, the Sultan issues orders 'in seething rage' (VI. 53) for an advance force to march out and surround Sziget; he himself will follow them next day. But Zrínyi sends out some cavalry who capture a Turk; the prisoner reveals the Sultan's plan, and the Hungarians win a resounding victory over the Turkish vanguard near the river Almás. Zrínyi is there in person, fighting

---

[1] In three stanzas (VI. 29–31) which were deleted by the Austrian censor and privately circulated by *Kazinczy (cf. his letters of 19 December 1803 (Váczy, no. 635 (vol. 3)) and 14 October 1810 (Váczy, no. 1851 (vol. 8)).

like Hercules or Samson, ready to wade into the river and cut down any Janissaries who attempt to reinforce their comrades from the opposite bank. By nightfall the river is full of bodies; the Turkish advance force has suffered total defeat, and their leader disappears in disgrace from the campaign. Deli Vid has established his reputation as a warrior second only to Zrínyi himself; surrounded, he stood like a 'rock amid the foaming waves' (VI. 103) and slew, among many others, the son of a close friend of Demirhám, the youth Hamviván, and his retainer Kamber, 'than whom mother never bore one more loyal' (VI. 109)—there are good men on the Turkish side too.

Demirhám in his grief rends his garments, 'as if that could be any help to Hamviván' (VII. 3), and persuades Suleiman to come in person to Szigetvár. On his arrival Zrínyi's gunners 'fire a salute to the Turks' (VII. 21), and a good hearty salute it is, too; after two such the Turks 'dared not wait for a third' (VII. 27). But now a far greater blow than this befalls the men of Sziget, in the death of Farkasics.[1] Yet still Zrínyi's 'heart grows braver at the sight of the Turk' (VII. 50 f.) and he launches a fresh attack; while Deli Vid and Demirhám fight their first single combat, 'the other hosts are terrified by strong Zrínyi's hand' (VII. 96).

By now the Sultan is not only 'growing grey' and his heart 'shivering with care and great sorrow' (VIII. 11) but is distraught at the contrast between the confident prophecy of the shade of his father, whose form Allecto had assumed at the opening, and the reality of events; at least to himself he unreservedly admits defeat: 'I, the Sultan, the ruler of the world, have been defeated by Zrínyi' (VIII. 16). He calls a council of war, but characteristically will not attend it himself; he watches it from a hiding-place in accordance with the regular practice of the Sultans, lest the change in him be observed. The council, however, achieves nothing; Delimán and Demirhám both walk out in protest against the prudent policy advocated by the Sultan's son-in-law Rustán, and those who are left can do no more than applaud a speaker who emphasizes that unity is strength. This is Petraf, who has an important success to his credit, the capture of the fort of Gyula.

The decisive turn of fortune, which is symbolized by the night raid and explicitly noted in the proem to X, only accentuates the contrast between the morale of the two leaders. Zrínyi's bravery

[1] See p. 11.

'grows greater when he sees the advance of danger and evil fortune' (x. 6)—it is in this spirit that he has withdrawn into the fort; he inspires his men with 'fair words of confidence' (x. 13), while Suleiman 'dared not go out of his tent' (ix. 99). For the moment, however, Zrínyi does not go out to fight, but holds himself in reserve, till he can attack to the best advantage. Then (x. 74) two Hungarian sentries (like Pandarus and Bitias, *Aen.* ix. 672 ff.) foolishly open the gates with the idea of letting in a limited number of Turks and killing them. This, however, enables Delimán to enter the fort, and he accounts for many Hungarians, while Demirhám 'alone almost destroys the Christian host' (x. 93). Here is an emergency which calls for Zrínyi's personal intervention—an intervention which has been made more telling by its postponement. Events now move to a climax; the Sultan's earlier boasts are confuted, one by one. Zrínyi 'wades in blood like a giant of the waters' (x. 98), retribution for Suleiman's vow to 'dye his horse in lakes of Christian blood' (i. 48): the Sultan had said contemptuously that the Hungarians had no leader (i. 56); now his own forces are 'headless' (xii. 53) and his mutinous troops are accusing him not only of recklessly disregarding losses, but of senility, and demanding that Delimán shall lead them. His enemy, the Zrínyi whose picture the poet leaves in our minds before transporting us away from the scene of the main fighting for the stories of Vid and of Cumilla, is a figure more formidable than ever before.

The proem to xiii tells us that 'Zrínyi's hour is approaching' (xiii. 2), and also Vid's; the phrase brings the end a step nearer than the corresponding passage in x. 3, according to which 'fortune has changed its course' for Sziget. But again it is the Sultan's spirit which sinks further, first into rage, passing 'cruel sentence on his own blood' (xiii. 32), and wondering if Mahomet has deliberately deceived him, then, after more inconclusive discussions, seriously contemplating retreat.

At this point, however, the course of events is decisively altered by the Turkish interception of a Hungarian carrier-pigeon with a message from the men of Sziget to the King, revealing their desperate situation. Again this episode is based on a passage of Tasso (xviii. 49); again it has a definite function in Zrínyi's epic. Without compromising the picture of the Sultan's despair, of his moral defeat, it enables the poet to tell of the progress which the Turks have made. He does not wish to stress this, but rather to bring out the unfailing courage and aggressive spirit of the Hungarians; and he must provide variety. But he prayed at the opening of the poem for the power to write of events 'as they were'; so now the message of the men of Sziget to the King tells us that they are 'near to death'; only five hundred men survive, and their last hour must come in two days—then they will end their lives outside the fort. '25,000 Turkish curs lie here, who came against us in ten assaults, so greatly did they fear us. We shall write no more' ends the message, 'but may God keep Your Majesty in good health and fortune' (XIII. 90–96). At this Suleiman takes heart, gives orders for a great effort, and has incendiary shells distributed.

'Now my compass is bringing me into harbour', says the poet (XIV. 3) as the end approaches. Suleiman accepts Alderán's offer to summon the spirits of Hell, but Hazret Ali warns the sorcerer that a 'God greater than Mahomet' is now with the Hungarians,[1] and that 'the three Fates have cruelly spun the thread of life for Suleiman . . . now you will see how they break it; in vain have the Furies come forth' (XIV. 65). The Hungarians are compelled by the flames to retreat to the inner fort, but Zrínyi attacks again. Vid and Demirhám fight their last fight; then Canto xv opens with the words 'The *Bán saw that his last hour was approaching; he assembled his whole army . . . and thus addressed them: "Knights, you see how you stand, as I stand; not only do Turks and Tartars work us evil, but fire also afflicts us, and steel, and all the elements. In every way God is testing us as a smith tests a work of gold in the fire; and seeing our loyalty, He has caused a fair crown to be prepared for us in Heaven. No more is He wroth with us; He has received the penalty for our sins, and has fulfilled His true laws; now He prepares in Heaven the reward of loyalty, and thither will lead us. So let us not shrink from going forth to a death by which we shall ascend to eternal joy"'' (xv. 1–5). This is as near as the poet comes to suggesting that the knights of Sziget are the redeemers who atone, in a theological sense, for the sins of their countrymen; for the rest he simply portrays them as free from the wickedness, above all the disunity, which has brought the divine wrath on their country. Zrínyi ends his speech: 'Since we cannot remain here, on account of the fire, as soon as God grants that we see the dawn, let us march out of the fort, and show that as we were in our lives, so are we now.' 'Thus spoke great Zrínyi', the poet continues

---

[1] See pp. 9–10.

(xv. 9), 'and the whole body of knights were joyfully ready to obey his words . . . their valiant eyes flash with bravery like diamonds.' So the final preparations are made; the men discard all their heavy armour, Zrínyi burns all the valuables, puts on his finest clothes, which he wore on ceremonial occasions, and marches out to have his words instantly confirmed by divine action.

It is artistically inevitable that even a poet who has prayed to be able to write of events 'as they were' should follow those Italian and Croatian chronicles according to which Zrínyi slew the Sultan with his own hand. After killing Delimán, Zrínyi pursues some terrified Turks to the distant hill where Suleiman, trembling like his soldiers, was watching the battle; the Hungarian cuts his way through the 'many thousands' of guards and kills the Sultan, who dies 'cursing the soul which had sustained his body so haughtily in life' (xv. 99). Suleiman was advanced in years, but this feat of arms in no way compromises Zrínyi's martial prowess; that is the point of the slaying of Delimán, the warrior indispensable to the Turks, and of the 'many thousands' of guards. Moreover, the Hungarian hero was himself fifty-eight years of age, and in his opening prayer had said that 'soon old age will overtake me, soon there will not be the strength in my body to break thine enemies' (II. 76).

When Zrínyi looks back, he sees that his knights have fallen, and is struck down, as they have been, by bullets—not by the sword, for no Turk dared approach Zrínyi in this hour. Immediately he falls the angels descend to take the souls of the knights of Sziget to Heaven; 'the whole choir of angels began fair music, and permitted me to end my words'. So ends the poem, with a prayer that God may accept the son of Zrínyi with favour.

Zrínyi the poet composed his epic with the Turk twenty-five miles away. 'As I write these verses, I am aroused by the wrathful drum and trumpet of Mars. Lo, the Turk at Kanizsa is bringing smoking embers into my country; I must extinguish them' (IX. 3). It was natural that in such a situation he should be more concerned about what he wanted to say than about how to say it; moreover he himself tells us (in the preface which he wrote when he published his poems) that he never corrected his work, because he had no time. While it is clear that infinite pains have gone into the construction of the epic, in the relating of the parts to the whole, there are clear signs of haste in the composition.[1] The generation

---

[1] A few stanzas and lines remained unfinished; we also find an occasional line

immediately after Zrínyi, however, put second things first and considered elegance and polish to be of prime importance. They were also far removed from the spirit of heroic epic; we can hardly imagine that Virgil or Zrínyi would be the favourite reading of, for instance, those typical products of the reign of Maria Theresa whom we meet in *Rosenkavalier*.[1] Only towards the end of the eighteenth century, when Zrínyi's poetry had become a great rarity, was his greatness discovered, with a corresponding fall in the stock of those who, in *Arany's words, 'watered down classical milk', whose fluency was their sole merit. The leading figure in the restoration of Zrínyi to his rightful place was *Kazinczy, whose taste was firmly founded on those classical ideals which he shared with Zrínyi.

Paradoxically, however, the transformation of the language which *Kazinczy himself initiated[2] sometimes sets up a barrier between Zrínyi and the modern reader. In the seventeenth century Hungarian possessed only a small vocabulary—a fact of which Zrínyi himself complains; it had no standard literary language, and Zrínyi's language—the dialect of the south-western region where he lived, mixed with Turkish and Croatian words, and with some Latinisms—is very different from the literary Hungarian of later ages. But these facts are insignificant beside what *Arany has called Zrínyi's 'stern sublimity'.

The 'sternness' is largely the result of economy; *The Siege of Sziget* is relatively short (6,272 lines against the *Aeneid*'s 9,896 and Tasso's 15,336), and the poet does not indulge in the pleasures of elaboration. How concise, for example, is the song of the Turkish minstrel boy, with its strict allocation of a single stanza for the joys of each season, except only for the one additional stanza which describes the delights of sensual love in spring! So with the descriptions of scenery; before the battles of Siklós and the river Almás we are given only the minimum of information we require

with more or fewer syllables than the correct number of twelve (1 line in 72 in the original manuscript of the poem; about half of these were corrected before publication). These are simply slips; but it is otherwise with the absence of the caesura after six syllables in 20 per cent. of Zrinyi's lines, though later poets regarded this caesura as obligatory.

[1] The change is discernible as early as 1664, the year of Zrínyi's death, when *Gyöngyösi produced his poem *The Venus of Murány united to Mars* (*A Márssal társalkodó murányi Vénus*) on which see p. xviii. This work is written in the same metre as *The Siege of Sziget*, but in lines whose impeccably correct caesuras produce a cumulative monotony which shows how right Zrínyi had been to compose differently. [2] See p. xxi.

to follow the action; e.g. 'The Pasha had taken up his position by a great mill, where the Almás, full of weeds, flows slowly murmuring; across the water is Ali Kurt with half the force' (VI. 60). The descriptions of dress are sometimes more elaborate, as with the Sultan, and with the rich garments of the Turkish minstrel boy; but the dress is part of the character, and its description a means, not an end. So the contrast between the appearance of Zrínyi as he addresses his men after Siklós, and the finery in which he arrays himself to march out for the last sortie, is directly relevant to the drama. The Hungarian leader's speeches to his men, on the other hand, may seem repetitive; but the very repetitions reflect his unswerving spirit. This poet is interested above all in human beings.

Not that Zrínyi eschews epic ornament; he makes frequent use of simile, for instance. But his similes observe an austerely high standard of relevance, as is perhaps particularly clear from his direct borrowings. Virgil's Dido 'wanders raving over the whole city, like a hind which a shepherd, hunting with his weapons, has taken unawares and hit from afar with an arrow in the woods of Crete, unwittingly leaving in her the flying steel; she ranges over the Dictaean woods and glades, and the deadly shaft clings to her side' (*Aen.* iv. 69–73): Zrínyi's Cumilla 'rushes hither and thither in the forest, like a hind which a huntsman has wounded in the breast with an arrow' (XII. 22). When the poet allows himself more elaboration, it is because of the importance of the context. Zrínyi's speech to his men when the siege begins is flanked by two similes, both derived from the picture of a mountain gale. 'Zrínyi stands intrepid amid great cares, like the great towering rocks of the lofty Tátra, on which the mighty winds struggle in vain, and spend their strength to no purpose in the siege' (V. 2); then after the speech, in one of the most highly polished passages in the whole epic: 'As when the North wind bursts forth from the Tátra mountains and penetrates that great pine-forest, it raises a great roar, is not checked, grows not weary; before it the tender branch bows and the hard is broken: so great was the sound that rang out among them, for the blood of wrath seethes in every man' (V. 37–38). These similes heighten our sense of the occasion, not least because both are taken from the same scene, although there is no exact parallelism —the wind in the first simile corresponds to the Turks, in the second to the spirit of the Hungarians.

Zrínyi's similes are drawn mostly from Nature, as in the common epic tradition—from storms and winds, and (most often) from wild animals—lions, boars, wolves, bears. A single example must suffice: 'When the smell of honey comes to the nose of a bear, he climbs down a beech-tree after it; he vents his anger on the tree with tooth and claw, and in vain tears away the bark, down to the roots; so both these heroes (Demirhám and the Hungarian Radován) walked round each other, eagerly desiring to deal fatal injury. Demirhám was as angry as a flood which snow has swollen; the others would not yield, so long as he lived' (x. 41–42). Similes derived from animals come naturally to a poet who was as intimately acquainted with wild life at first hand as with his predecessors in epic; but there are also less predictable similes, such as those derived from the main subject-matter of the poem; these renounce the variety which is the main purpose of the simile, but they can be splendidly dramatic, as when Zrínyi prays 'Take unto thyself my soul, which scarce can wait for thee, like a besieged fortress expecting help' (II. 77). Again, there are some remarkable similes taken from folk-lore, like the picture of Zrínyi wading in blood 'like a giant of the waters' (x. 98).

The characters possess no regular fixed epithets, though the poet is not unaware of the power of the epithet. The nearest approach to a fixed epithet is 'jó', 'good', which is applied often, though by no means invariably, to Zrínyi; but when the supreme moment has come, and the poet requires a monosyllabic epithet for his hero, he substitutes 'nagy', 'great', for 'good'.[1] Nothing could be more striking than the replacement, in this context, of one of the commonest adjectives in the language by another, especially as the effect is made in a single passage, and as the other references to Zrínyi by name in the canto (over twenty in number) have no epithet at all.

The Siege of Sziget almost marks the end of Zrínyi's career as a poet; from now on, as *Kölcsey put it, he subordinated the poet in himself to the hero. But the epic was itself the fruit of his military experience as well as of his reading; and the two sources of inspiration cannot be separated, still less do the parallels with Virgil and Tasso imply any lack of spontaneity on Zrínyi's

---

[1] xv. 9 (see p. 28). The poet has used the epithet 'great' of his hero in some earlier passages, but when referring to him by his office of *Bán (e.g. 'the great *Bán of Sziget', III. 40) not by his name.

part—heroic epic is naturally the favourite reading of the hero who is also a man of letters. That is why the battle-scenes and debates, the types of episode closest to the poet's personal experience, are precisely those where his reading of Virgil and Tasso is most in evidence. The distinction between 'authentic' and 'literary' epic has ceased to exist; literature is a part of life. The towers of Csáktornya were not built of ivory.

3

About the time he began his epic, in October 1645, Zrínyi was appointed *Főispán of Zala County, and shortly before the poem was completed, in January 1646, he was created a general by the King. However, there were no major military operations against the Turks for the time being, though the raids from Kanizsa continued; in a letter of 11 August 1646 Zrínyi writes that 'The Turk is continually visiting us'. By April 1648, however, the discipline and vigilance of the Turkish forces had slackened to such an extent that Zrínyi could write: 'We see manifest God's mercy in withdrawing all His goodwill from the Turk.' Zrínyi hoped that it would soon be possible for Europe to unite against the heathen, though first the Thirty Years War must be ended; however, he had sufficient faith in the future to plan the reform of the Hungarian Army. He had all the standard military treatises in his library—Vegetius and the ancients, Machiavelli and the moderns—and now began to write on military subjects himself.

His first essay in this field was the *Short Treatise on Camp Organization* (*Tábori kis tracta*), a brief account of the organization of a camp for an army of 25,000 men. It was never finished, and is probably a fragment of a projected treatise on a much larger scale. It is a practical work, not primarily a contribution to literature, though the task of advocating original and controversial proposals on an important subject inspires Zrínyi to produce in places a foretaste of the power characteristic of his later prose works. Not that the *Treatise* is concerned wholly with administrative and technical detail; Zrínyi also deals with more general topics, and the soldier now explicitly enunciates principles which the epic poet had implied; for instance, he emphasizes the paramount importance of order, 'the soul of every enterprise', leadership, and loyalty to the leader.

On 27 December 1647 Zrínyi was nominated *Bán of Croatia

an office which his great-grandfather, his grandfather and his father had all held; but he refused to take up his post till the long overdue pay claims of the soldiers in the border fortresses had been settled. When finally he entered upon office, on 14 January 1649, he found widespread chaos, misery, and lawlessness. He acted quickly, but some of those most responsible for the condition of the country, notably Alexander Mikulić, a magnate who organized brigandage on a large scale, apparently enjoyed the protection of the Court and had still not been brought to book by June 1658. In addition, there were continual encroachments on estates in Croatia (including Zrínyi's own) by Serbs and Wallachians serving on the Military Frontier; but here too reform was obstructed from Vienna. Then about 1650 the Court launched a new and determined attack, including the use of force, on the Zrínyi cattle-trade with Italy. Zrínyi arranged for his convoys to be escorted by his soldiers, and by Venetian warships; Vienna replied by threatening to send an Austrian garrison into Csáktornya. In November 1650 Zrínyi went to Vienna to protest in person that the revenue from the cattle-trade was essential for financing the necessary defensive measures against the Turks, and threatened to resign his office. This reminded the Austrians that it was in their own interest not to goad him too far, and they called off their campaign, though for a time the attack was switched to Zrínyi's brother Péter, whose share of the family estates included the ports through which the cattle-trade passed. There was some talk of arresting Péter, and of trying him for *lèse-majesté*. Lastly, the death of Zrínyi's wife in September 1650 brought conflict as well as sorrow, because her father attempted to recover the estates which had constituted her dowry, and in the following year organized an armed attack on the most important of these. Zrínyi dealt effectively with the raiders, but in the interests of order and national unity voluntarily renounced his claim to the greater part of the estates.

These difficulties, however, did not entail any slackening of Zrínyi's preparations for the struggle against the Turk, which were continued energetically throughout this period. At the same time the renewal in 1648 of the peace between Austria and Turkey for a further twenty-two years damped the hopes which Zrínyi had placed in the Peace of Westphalia, and the raids by the Turks in Kanizsa did not cease in spite of the Porte's pact with Austria.

Early in 1651 Zrínyi launched a brilliantly successful attack which penetrated deeply into Turkish-occupied Bosnia, and the malaria which he contracted in this campaign did not prevent him from leaving his sick-bed to play his part in repelling a Turkish counter-attack in August.

In September 1651, by a curious parallel to the episode of the carrier-pigeon in *The Siege of Sziget*, Zrínyi intercepted a message from the Grand Vizier to Kanizsa rebuking the commanders of the fort for their rashness, and threatening them with execution. The letter also confirmed Zrínyi's own assessment of Turkish military weakness, and stressed that the situation was critical; the Poles had defeated the Tartars and now threatened the Crimea: the Venetians had destroyed the Turkish fleet in July: the Persians in the east were adopting a threatening attitude, and hostilities had already broken out. Zrínyi was already sufficiently well informed to realize that the Turkish menace might be ended once for all if these hostile Powers united to seize their opportunity.

It was at this moment that Zrínyi decided to publish his poems. The book was entitled *The Siren of the Adriatic Sea* (*Adriai tengernek Syrénája*), as Marino had called himself the 'Siren of the Tyrrhenian Sea'. It contains on the title-page a picture of a knight in full armour sailing a ship; seductive mermaids are swimming alongside the vessel, but the knight ignores them. The idea is reminiscent of the proem to Canto XIV of *The Siege of Sziget*, in which the poet compares himself to a mariner approaching port, though this passage contains no reference to temptation. The *Siren* begins with a dedication 'to the Hungarian nobility' and with a disarming preface addressed to the reader. After explaining that he had written his epic in a single winter, for his own pleasure, Zrínyi continues: 'I can truthfully say that I never corrected my work, because I had not the time; it is the firstborn offspring of my mind. And if I did correct it, it would still not be perfect.' A few changes were made in the epic; one passage (the proem to Canto XIV) was shortened and partly rewritten, and in two other places stanzas were deleted.[1] On the other hand, Zrínyi added single stanzas at the ends of XIV and XV, to make a worthier conclusion to the two most important cantos. He also made a number of

---

[1] One stanza was deleted from the Turkish Catalogue at the end of Canto I, and three near the beginning of II, describing the Hungarian Turi's preparations for the defence of the fort of Palota.

minor changes, and corrected nearly half the lines with the
wrong number of syllables; but the defective stanzas and lines
remained, and nothing was added at the end of the short Canto
II, though the poet had made a note that the passage was defective. Now too he 'had not the time'.

In addition to the epic, *The Siren of the Adriatic Sea* contains
Zrínyi's earlier poems and some more recent compositions. The
two poems on the death of his wife, the *Lament of Orpheus* and
Orpheus with Pluto, are among his least successful works, and
lean as heavily on mythological allusion and artificial conceit as the
least inspired parts of his early poems. *Orpheus with Pluto* breaks
off in the middle of a stanza, and the *Lament*, though it does not
do that, ends very abruptly, and may well be incomplete. The poet
noted in the margin 'istud opus sine studio feci, nec dignum apparet'
(I wrote this work without enthusiasm, and it seems unworthy),
and it is hard to disagree. Then follow some short poems, 'epigrams'
(in the Greek rather than the English sense of the word) on Attila
and his brother Buda, whom he slew, and on some of the heroes
of *The Siege of Sziget*: a poem entitled *On the Cross* (*Feszületre*)
which appears to be a draft version of Zrínyi's prayer in Canto II
of the epic, to which a proem has been added: and finally a noteworthy *Peroration*, in which the poet stakes his claim to immortality: 'Now have I brought to completion my renowned work,
which neither jealous Time nor fire can destroy, which neither
the wrath of Heaven nor steel can damage, which the great enemy
Envy cannot injure. . . . But I seek my fame not only with my pen,
but with my terrible blade in battle.'

It soon became clear, however, that Vienna was not interested in
the opportunity for concerted action against the Turks, and had no
desire to strengthen Hungary by weakening them; Zrínyi was
forbidden to launch any attacks. Denied the chance of serving his
country by his 'terrible blade', he applied himself intensively to
the study of history, and embodied the results of his researches in
his second major work, in prose, *The Gallant General* (*Vitéz
hadnagy*).

The Gallant General expounds the science of war in a collection
of miscellaneous observations—a literary form which enjoyed
great popularity in the seventeenth century, as the number of
sources used by Zrínyi testifies. The work consists of three parts,
all based on foreign models, with two short prefaces to the reader.

The first part consists of six *Discourses* based on an Italian translation by Mutio Ziccatta (Venice, 1639) of *Le Ministre d'État, avec le véritable usage de la politique* by Jean de Silhon, who was Richelieu's secretary, and later became a *conseiller d'État*. The titles of Zrínyi's *Discourses* are:

1. That the science of war is greatly assisted by study.
2. The necessity of diligence, perseverance, and vigilance in a soldier.
3. For the art of war it is not possible to prescribe rules as it is for other matters. Wise strategy consists above all in the general's ability to adapt his plans as time and opportunity dictate. The Italians say: *Diversificare.*
4. The commander must always bear in mind the object of his intentions and direct his every action to achieving that object.
5. One must know how to defeat the enemy and how to make use of victory: one must know how to choose a suitable time for a campaign: now is the time to make war on the Turks and win back what we have lost.
6. The soldier is nothing without good fortune: on the nature of fortune.

The second part consists of *Aphorisms*, 128 passages of Tacitus, all but three with comment, for which Zrínyi used, among other sources, the Italian translation by Girolamo Canini d'Anghiari (Venice, 1620) of the *Spanish Tacitus Illustrated with Aphorisms* by Don Baltasar Álamos de Barrientos, and the *Discorsi sopra Cornelio Tacito* (Venice, 1635) by Virgilio Malvezzi.

The third and last part, which was never completed, is a collection of fifty-two reflections on military subjects entitled *Centuriae*, for which Zrínyi's principal foreign source was *Il novissimo passatempo politico, istorico, et economico* (*The Latest Pastime—Politics, History, Economics*) by Eugenio Raimondi (Venice, 1639). The title of *The Gallant General* seems to have been suggested by Maiolino Bisaccioni's *Sensi civili sopra il perfetto capitano* (*General[1] Observations on the Perfect Commander*) (Venice, 1642), a work from which Zrínyi also obtained some of his material. In addition, the influence of Machiavelli's writings is continually in evidence, both on Zrínyi directly and on his sources.

Zrínyi describes the *Centuriae* in his preface as a mixture of 'what I have seen, heard, and read', and it is the most original of the three parts of his work. The *Discourses* adhere most closely to their model, but even here Zrínyi is no mere translator. Apart from

---

[1] Literally 'civilian', i.e. non-specialist.

the changes necessary to adapt a political as a military treatise, Zrínyi's individuality constantly shows through in the vigour of the style, and in positive alterations to the substance, such as his omission of the anti-Protestant matter which he found in de Silhon.

The Gallant General is a work of literature as well as a military treatise, partly by virtue of its style—'I have taken pains to write in good Hungarian', says Zrínyi in his preface—partly because of the breadth of the author's conception of his subject. Of all his works it is the one on which he spent most time,[1] though again it was never finished. Zrínyi disclaimed any didactic intention, saying that he had written the work to learn, not to teach. Moreover, as he says at the end of his second preface, 'merely to know these things is a small merit, but to act is a great one, and to turn one's knowledge to the service of one's country an even greater'.

In addition, *The Gallant General* lets in a flood of light on *The Siege of Sziget*, by making explicitly many points which the action of the epic illustrated. The study of the past is always relevant to the future, because nothing could happen in the future which would not be paralleled by some event in the past (*Aph.* 23). Thus much of what Zrínyi now says of his own day was equally true of the time of his great-grandfather. No nation is more contemptuous of discipline than the Hungarian, and no nation stands in greater need of discipline (*Cent.* 9); unity, too, is of the first importance (*Aph.* 2). To take a particular example of the parallelism between the two works, Canto III of the epic, the battle of Siklós, contains many themes which recur in *The Gallant General*. Over-confidence (*Aph.* 19, 31, &c.) like that of Mehmet is always dangerous, but never more so than when it leads to a relaxation of vigilance (*Aph.* 4) against an enemy commander with a great reputation (*Aph.* 1, 49) who knows the terrain (*Aph.* 13) and has an efficient intelligence service (*Aph.* 5); Zrínyi learnt in advance of Mehmet's arrival at Siklós. When the battle came, the well-disciplined (*Aph.* 48) forces whom their general had warned against greed for booty (III. 61; *Aph.* 15), while at the same time encouraging them by his eloquence (*Aph.* 28), were inevitably victorious over an enemy corrupted by luxury (*Aph.* 55), symbolized in the epic

---

[1] *Aph.* 66 speaks of the execution of Charles I as having taken place 'last year'; but *Disc.* v, with its reference to the loss of the opportunity of defeating Turkey by an alliance of all her enemies, can scarcely have been written before 1652. It seems probable that almost the whole of *The Gallant General* was written between 1650 and 1652.

by the song of the Turkish minstrel boy. Luxury, in fact, is one of the soldier's worst enemies; and the general, in his personal appearance (*Aph.* 63), must distinguish between those adornments, such as plumes in the helmet, which make the wearer appear formidable (and which Zrínyi of Sziget wears in the epic), and those which create an impression of effete luxury, such as the cloth of gold which Suleiman wore.

As in the epic and in the *Treatise on Camp Organization*, leadership is of prime importance. The general resembles a clock, the many parts of which must all be in perfect order if the whole is to function (*Cent.* 6); he is the 'soul of the army' (*Aph.* 105). His men must obey him gladly; 'it is difficult to catch a hare when the hounds have to be driven after it with a stick' (*Aph.* 73). At the same time 'An army, country or prince, whose hopes are all placed in one man cannot last for long' (*Aph.* 78). Again the men of Sziget have illustrated the ideal; Deli Vid obeys Zrínyi's orders, but in his adventures behind the Turkish lines he shows that he lacks nothing in individual bravery and initiative. To obtain the best results from his men the general must be eloquent, though true eloquence 'does not consist solely in words'; he must reinforce his words by his example in battle—in this passage (*Aph.* 28) Zrínyi refers explicitly to his great-grandfather—and also by his gratitude to his men after a victory (*Aph.* 21), just as in the epic Zrínyi of Sziget thanks his knights after the battle of Siklós. There is, however, room for differences of temperament, and in *Aph.* 97 Zrínyi admits that his own nature is impetuous rather than patient; Zrínyi of Sziget too had always acted on the principle that attack is the best form of defence. The general must, however, be too intelligent to attack recklessly or ineffectively; 'it is a poor slap in the face which is met by two' (*Aph.* 82). He must possess 'vis', might, but also 'consilium' (*Aph.* 18), the intelligence which alone raises man above the animals, the quality in which consists the superiority of Zrínyi of Sziget over savages like Delimán and Demirhám.

But, as the title of *Discourse* VI has it, 'the soldier is nothing without good fortune'. This dictum goes back to classical antiquity,[1] and became something of a commonplace in the Renaissance, but it exercised Zrínyi's mind deeply and ceaselessly. His own motto, which appeared on the title-page of *The Siren of the Adriatic Sea*,

[1] Cf., e.g. Cicero *De Imp. Cn. Pomp.* 28.

was 'sors bona, nihil aliud' (good fortune, nothing else *sc.* is what
I desire); and besides devoting the longest of the *Discourses* to
the subject, he frequently refers to it, both in the epic and in *The
Gallant General.*

Zrínyi in his epic conceives fortune as a gift of God,[1] separate
from merit, and not necessarily its reward. In the description of
Heaven in the last canto (XV. 19) Fortune appears as a servant of
God: 'Fortune and Nature stand humbly below Him, ready to
serve Him', 'Fortune' being a deliberate change (suggested,
apparently, by the *Anticlaudianus*)[2] from 'Virtue' in the corresponding passage of Marino's *Gerusalemme Distrutta (Jerusalem
Destroyed)* (VII. 7). Here Fortune is clearly personified; and though
the absence of gender in Hungarian makes it impossible, in many
passages, to decide questions of personification, Zrínyi elsewhere
(*Aph.* 22) expresses his agreement with those who think of Fortune
as a specifically *female* creature.

For Zrínyi, as for Boethius and Dante (*Inf.* VII. 88), Fortune is
above all changeable, as the epic emphasizes in the lament of
Zrínyi of Sziget over the dead Farkasics (quoted on p. 11), and in
the proems to Cantos IV and X. 'Happy is he who grows not over-
confident in time of prosperity, but awaits the turn of Fortune with
a ready heart' (IV. 5). This is what Mehmet fails to see; he believes
that Fortune is 'tied' to his feet, as the minstrel boy puts it. But
he who understands Fortune, as Zrínyi of Sziget does, is proof
against her changes; 'Fortune is wont to sport with a brave heart,
but the brave do not yield to her' (X. 5); Zrínyi's heart grows still
braver when Fortune turns against him, and the change of
Fortune in no way affects the glory in Heaven which is the ultimate
destiny of the knights of Sziget. So *The Gallant General* says
(without explicit reference to Zrínyi of Sziget) 'gold is known in
the fire [cf. *Siege of Sziget*, XV. 3], the helmsman in a storm, the
soldier when in danger; then let him show that he is playing with
Fortune and not that vagrant lady with him' (*Aph.* 22). 'With me
too does Fortune often play', says the poet (IV. 11), and the simile
(X. 5) 'as a helmsman knows how to wrestle with the foaming
waves, so must a brave heart struggle with Fortune' suggests that
the picture on the title-page of *The Siren of the Adriatic Sea*, of
the knight steering his ship through the waves, represents Zrínyi

---

[1] Zrínyi's treatment of Fortune in the epic shows the influence of Boethius,
De Consolatione.   [2] Cf. p. 9.

the poet himself, in his struggles with Fortune. This is, in fact, a standard image of Fortune in the Renaissance; but it clearly possessed a special, personal significance for Zrínyi.

In the preface to *The Gallant General* Fortune is mentioned as an instrument of God's purpose, just as she was His servant in the epic; but now we are concerned with the historian's observation of events on earth, not with the poet's vision of Heaven. Success cannot be made certain by any human qualities: 'A man has hardly begun a fine scheme, when immediately Death appears there, compelling him to break off his proud plans, and lo! in vain has he toiled, in vain has he embarked on his enterprise. So the motto which is often on my lips, "Sors bona, nihil aliud", applies here too. But who gives this Fortune, I will show in several places; you will see in the last aphorism of the third part,[1] that it is God who directs our condition. Whom He desires to exalt, He blesses with Fortune; He withdraws her gifts from him whom He wishes to strike down, although the man try with all his might to retain Fortune, and profess, with reference to himself, that "quisque suae fortunae faber" (every man is the architect of his own fortune).' In the light of this passage, from the first preface to *The Gallant General*, it is natural for Zrínyi to say, at the end of the *Aphorisms*: 'I desire fortune from God and nothing else. Sors bona, nihil aliud.'

But there is no question of any passive fatalism; on the contrary, in the words of *Discourse* II, 'without these qualities (diligence, perseverance, and vigilance) a general may be wise, but he can never be fortunate. On the other hand, there is no difficulty so great that he cannot overcome it with these assets, no opposition which he cannot coerce. By these qualities, Fortune is compelled not to run away from us; our good counsels are strengthened still further, and our bad corrected; in a word, it is thereby made possible for us to carry our resolutions into effect.' Here Zrínyi is saying that his three virtues are indispensable to military success, and that with them there are no limits to the success which the general *can* achieve; but he is not saying that success is thereby *ensured*, except in the phrase 'Fortune is compelled not to run away from us', which is inconsistent with its context.

The fullest discussion of the subject, however, is to be found in *Discourse* VI, the longest of the *Discourses*, which is wholly devoted

[1] i.e. *Cent.* 52.

to it. This essay gives a vivid impression of the difficulty which Zrínyi found in his theme; after apparently reaching the end, he takes up his pen again with the words 'But we must explain this more fully, for it is the most difficult matter with which I have concerned myself in my life, and from it I have devised a motto for myself.'

The conclusion which Zrínyi reaches at the end of the first half of *Discourse* VI is precisely that which he denies in the preface to *The Gallant General*, that each man is the architect of his own fortune. The contexts, however, show that there is no real contradiction; in the *Discourse* the point Zrínyi is making is that a man cannot make his opportunities, but must use them when they come his way, as a helmsman makes use of the winds; it is by the use he makes of them that he becomes the 'architect of his own fortune'. But it is not true that human ability can decide the whole issue—it was this meaning of 'every man is the architect of his own fortune' which Zrínyi refuted in his preface, and *Discourse* VI begins by stressing that the outcome of any enterprise is controlled by a Power above us. Hannibal and Cicero left nothing undone which they should have done, yet Scipio was victorious and Milo condemned. Andrea Doria had to look on helplessly while the Genoese fleet was destroyed. Moreover, the wicked often prosper; but this is because God does not always choose to work miracles. If He did, if piety and innocence were invariably victorious, He would be doing violence to wisdom, which is His own creation. The mightiest powers do not, however, necessarily last the longest; good and evil deeds receive their reward in this world. But when God selects someone to remedy the sins of the world or the misery of some country, He gives him the necessary powers of mind and body, and the opportunity to accomplish his task. This is Fortune; and it is for the man to use his opportunity. So each man becomes the architect of his own fortune. Zrínyi thus uses the word 'fortune' to mean both the initial ability and opportunity given by God, and the ultimate result.

'External events may be favourable, even indispensable, to a man's fortune; but the form and constitution of the fortune are forged above all in the man himself.' So, at the opening of the second section of his *Discourse*, Zrínyi sums up the results so far reached; the conclusion of the whole essay, however, re-emphasizes the importance of the element outside our control. Zrínyi quotes

Giuseppe Ricci's *De Bellis Germanicis* (*On the German Wars*) (Venice, 1648): 'Wars are brought to glorious conclusions not only by courage and spirit; you are doomed without fortune.' A general, continues Zrínyi, should leave little to Fortune, but for that little, her assistance is as essential as if he had left everything to her. 'So,' ends the Discourse, 'may God but send us good fortune; we need desire nothing more; our understanding, intellect, gallantry, and fame are contained therein.' Zrínyi's prayers for good fortune have acquired a peculiar urgency from his conviction that Fortune has already intervened in his favour by providing a unique opportunity to defeat the Turks. It is for man to use her gifts to the best advantage; and she may not give him much time (*Aph.* 22).

4

In 1653 a peasant revolt broke out on the estates of Count Erdődy in Croatia. This was not only a blow to Zrínyi's ideal of a united country, but (as he explained to the King in a letter of 7 December 1653) a danger from the point of view of national defence, because these peasants supplied the Army with some of its best troops and moreover lived on the border with Turkish-occupied territory. Zrínyi worked hard to achieve the peaceful solution which the national interest urgently demanded; Erdődy, however, adopted an attitude intransigent and equivocal by turns, while at the same time attempting, unsuccessfully, to suppress the rebellion by force. Zrínyi had seen from the beginning that the root cause of the trouble lay in Erdődy's inhumanity to his peasants, and steadfastly resisted pressure to send troops against the rebels; finally, however, on 27 April 1659 we find him reporting to the King on a successful expedition which has 'pacified' the peasants and caused the Turkish forces to disperse, and adding that there will be no more revolts unless the lords give the peasants cause to rebel. Possibly the sight of Zrínyi's soldiers mobilized against the Turks sobered the peasants too; at any rate, they now disappear from history, after six years.

About the same time as the Croat peasant rising assumed serious proportions, in the autumn of 1653, the all-important office of *Nádor (Palatine) fell vacant. Zrínyi had written in the first preface to *The Gallant General* that every man should serve his country to the best of his ability, not choosing for himself any easier alternative; now, as he explained at length in a memorandum of November 1653 to the Prince of Transylvania, Rákóczi György II, he saw it as his duty to stand as *Nádor. The 'easier alternative' was there, and might well have attracted a lesser man—to stay in the Muraköz, where he was universally loved and respected, especially when he could plausibly argue that without him his home region would be like a 'ship without its helmsman'. His prospects of election seemed good; he had precedent on his side—on five previous occasions a *Bán of Croatia had been elected *Nádor—as well as his personal prestige and popularity. His enemies at Court, however, succeeded in preventing his candidature, and secured the election of their own nominee; but in the meantime the death in 1654 of the heir to the throne, had created an entirely new situation, the more so as the King himself was ailing. A letter of Zrínyi to Prince Rákóczi György II, written early in 1655, contains a veiled (and encoded) suggestion that Zrínyi hoped to pave the way for the succession of the Prince, who himself entertained ambitions in this direction, and was supported by other opponents of the Habsburgs. Zrínyi's ideal of an independent, united Hungary, free from religious persecution and class oppression, could be realized only if the right man was King, and his mind was naturally preoccupied with his conception of the ideal monarch. His thoughts on this subject found literary expression in the winter of 1656–7, when he wrote for his 'own amusement', in a fortnight, the *Reflections on the Life of King *Mátyás* (*Mátyás király életéről való elmélkedések*), his next major work. About the same time, on 6 December 1656, the Prince allied himself with Charles X of Sweden, and a month later, without obtaining the approval of the Transylvanian Diet, led an army into Poland, whose throne he hoped to secure as a preliminary to attacking Austria.

For a Hungarian reflecting on the ideal ruler, *Mátyás was the natural, indeed the inevitable subject. Soldier and statesman, connoisseur and patron of the arts, a brilliant Renaissance figure who ruled his country at the height of her power, and died beloved by all classes, *Mátyás had no possible rival in the imagination of his people; he was the symbol of a far-off Golden Age in Hungarian history.

Nor did the subject lack significance for Austria, against which country *Mátyás had led three campaigns, occupying Vienna itself in 1485. In addition, the Habsburgs regarded *Mátyás's father, *Hunyadi János, and his family as usurpers, and considered themselves the rightful kings of Hungary, being descended from the house of *Árpád, the founder of the kingdom, through the female line. It was a Habsburg king, László V, who in 1457 (only a few months, as it happened, before his own death) had imprisoned the sons of *Hunyadi János, *László, and *Mátyás, and treacherously executed *László.

When *Mátyás did ascend the throne in January 1458, his situation, says Zrínyi, was more difficult than that of the baby Hercules in his cradle, when two snakes came to devour him; for Mátyás had to face three enemies, two Emperors, the Holy Roman and the Turkish, also Giskra, who had commanded the Czech forces financed by Vienna to ensure the Habsburg succession. But 'German and Hungarian can never be one', as Zrínyi concludes from his detailed comparative character-studies of the generous, convivial extrovert *Mátyás and the austere, withdrawn, melancholic Emperor Frederick. Even so, he finds it difficult to understand why *Mátyás should have chosen to attack Austria (in 1477) rather than the Turks who had injured his country so terribly; though in connexion with *Mátyás's campaign in Bosnia in 1479 Zrínyi does not omit to note that Frederick sent in an army to ravage western Hungary while the King was away fighting the Turks. However, in a brief reference to the situation of his own day, Zrínyi expresses the opinion that the gulf between Austrian and Hungarian could be bridged if evil counsellors (among whom were to be found Hungarians as well as Austrians) did not poison the King's mind against the Hungarians; but that, he says, is as impossible as to prevent the winds from stirring up the sea.

The title of Zrínyi's work, *Reflections*, shows that it is not a systematic biography; its literary antecedents are rather to be found in works of the type which goes back, ultimately, to Xenophon's *Education of Cyrus*, such as Machiavelli's life of Castruccio and, in particular, Pierre Mathieu's study of Louis XI, which Zrínyi had read in an Italian translation that appeared at Venice in 1637. Zrínyi does not, in fact, attempt to give any complete account of *Mátyás's achievement, 'which it would be useless to compress into a short essay'; in particular, his services to the arts are not mentioned.

This study of a soldier-statesman is the natural successor to *The*

Gallant General, written when Zrínyi's own thoughts were turning towards questions of statesmanship. From a literary point of view, it is a significant step towards the creation of an artistic unity in prose, though it is still constructed in sections; a description of an episode in *Mátyás's life is followed by comment, just like the passages of Tacitus in the *Aphorisms* of *The Gallant General.* And the approach to the subject is the same in both; just as the earlier work discusses the qualities required in a general, so the study of *Mátyás is primarily concerned with the different aspects of the king's character which different episodes in his life exhibit. There is no attempt to discuss events in strict chronological order.

The new work contains both references to and reminiscences of its predecessor. As *Mátyás was mentioned several times in *The Gallant General,* notably in *Cent.* 9 as a leader whose like no longer exists, who could 'do with the Hungarians what he wished', so in the *Reflections* Zrínyi refers to his observations in the earlier work on the decline of discipline in his own day. And in the summary of *Mátyás's achievement at the very end of the *Reflections* there occurs a reminiscence of *Discourse* II: 'His fortune was everywhere great, because his diligence was inexhaustible, because his perseverance was indefatigable, because his courage was invincible, because his vigilance was infallible.'

Zrínyi makes no secret of his admiration for his subject; *Mátyás eclipses all Hungary's later kings as the rising sun obscures the stars. At the very beginning of his essay Zrínyi expresses the inspiration which he has found in his theme, and attributes the lack of great historians in his own day to the fact that there are no kings like *Mátyás. At the same time, he makes no attempt to gloss over *Mátyás's failings. After praising the skill with which the King used his military, financial, and diplomatic resources at the beginning of his reign to deal with the Turks, Frederick, and Giskra, Zrínyi goes on to criticize *Mátyás's ingratitude in imprisoning his uncle Szilágyi, who had done so much to bring him to the throne. At the same time, says Zrínyi, Szilágyi should have known better than to treat *Mátyás as he might any other boy: 'the lion can never be so much of a cub that his claws do not show: and kings are never so young as to be willing to obey orders.' Again, in connexion with the attack on Austria, Zrínyi criticizes *Mátyás for listening to the counsels of overbold advisers who 'never say "No" but always "At 'em!"'" (like Demirhám and Delimán in Canto VIII of the epic). Throughout his reign, too, *Mátyás was both extravagant and aggressive, two faults which, as Zrínyi points out, brought suffering on his people. When he attacked the Czechs in 1468, the Turks profited by his absence to invade Hungary and carry off 'many thousands of souls'. Moreover, the Czech king was *Mátyás's benefactor, and his father-in-law. The attack, launched on the basis of a flimsy claim to the Czech throne, at the instigation of the Pope and the Emperor, in the name of religion, deeply offended Zrínyi; he outspokenly criticized, on specifically Christian grounds, not only *Mátyás's aggression against the Czech Hussites, but also the persecution of Protestants by the Catholic Church of his own day.

The style of the *Reflections* covers a very wide range. At times it is extremely terse, showing that Zrínyi's reading of Tacitus has developed his own taste for aphorism: '*Mátyás had many admirers but few followers'—and with concise accounts of events as headings to the reflections proper, e.g. 'After this the army attacked the Czech King and his country: the Pope of Rome and the Roman Emperor instigated the King to this: it was done under the pretext of religion.' At the same time, in the opening sentence of the *Reflections*, Zrínyi speaks of the lives and deeds of great kings as 'inspiring eloquence'; so other passages recall *Pázmány, rising to a rhetoric resonant with accumulations of parallel clauses, and making liberal use of apostrophe; yet the stylistic transitions are subtly managed, and sudden, jarring contrasts avoided. Most important of all, the wide variety of gifts and potentialities as a prose writer which Zrínyi here displays is sustained and unified by the vigour and vitality which fire the whole of his essay.

5

In the opening paragraph of the *Reflections on King *Mátyás* Zrínyi asks himself whether Nature is now working to produce another king like *Mátyás, and concludes 'at least in our times, this is too much to hope for'. It was indeed. Rákóczi György's Polish campaign resulted in total disaster, and in placing high hopes in him Zrínyi had made perhaps the most serious mistake of his career.

At the same time he suffered personal blows in the successive deaths of two of his children (by his second wife, Maria Sophia Löbl, whom he married in 1652); first his elder daughter died in

August 1658, and in the following spring he lost his only son Izsák.[1] This tragedy reopened the vein of his poetic inspiration, which had been virtually dormant since 1651; he wrote an *Elegy* on the death of his son. He did not, however, publish it, and it remained unknown till 1894, when it was found among his papers. It is in three sections, of which the second is written in a contrasting metre. The following quotation gives the last stanza of the second section and the whole of the third:

Such was the will of the Lord; what can man do? He may not dispute with God. We can only feel shame at our misdeeds, we must endure all things; for every good, for the crosses which we bear, for misfortune, we must bless God.

Lo, now does the old year regain its youth; the hard season of winter has turned to spring, the earth is renewed, the water is refreshed, the forest is cheered, the air on high is full of lovely birds.

The fair nightingale seems to be lamenting its ancient grief in its plaint; but no, rather it is rejoicing, giving thanks to God, looking upwards, praying.

Ah! my spring envious Fortune has destroyed, nay has turned to winter, has delivered my bright eyes to rain, has covered my heart with ice and grief.

My lovely little bird, my little nightingale, ah! suddenly indeed has he flown away; in him was all my hope, but he rose and departed from me like a thin shadow.[2]

---

[1] A second son, Ádám, was born in 1662, and killed in battle against the Turks in 1691.

[2] Igy akarta Isten,   35
Az ember mit tegyen?
Vele nem pörölhetni.
Az mi dolgunk nem más,
Csak mint pironkodás,
Mindent el kell szenvedni;   40
Mind jóért, körösztért,
És bal szöröncséjért
Az Istent köll áldani.

Im mast ifiadik megvénült esztendő,
Tavaszra fordula téli kemény üdő, 45
Ujul föld, frissül viz, vigadik az erdő,
Teli szép madarakkal magas levegő.

Az szép fülemile sirással ugy tetszik,
Régi bánatjáért hogy panaszolkodik,

De nem, hanem még inkább ű viga-
    dozik,   50
Hálát Istennek ad, néz fel, imádkozik.

Ah az én tavaszomat irigy elrontá
Szerencse, sőt még inkább télre
    forditá;
Derült szemeimet essőnek bocsátá,
Jéggel én szűvemet s búval bebu-
    ritá.   55

Gyönyörű madárkám, kicsin füle-
    milém,
Ah igen hirtelen elrőpűle tűlem,
Az énnékem vala minden reménsé-
    gem,
De mint könnyű árnyék elkele
    előlem.

Thus had I seen my future, that after a long time he would redeem me, that he would follow, yes, surpass, my verses and my efforts to help our poor country.

And that with trumpet more resonant he would proclaim Hungarian valour, and sing of the might of a strong arm; and that thereafter he would deserve that men should sing of his own deeds.

Ah! envious Death with terrible scythe has mown down the sweet nightingale in my heart, Izsák, who was as a fair flower standing so lovely, to be the beauty of gardens.[1]

The imagery is bold, because it is spontaneous, and the patriotic touch is not only relevant to the time when the poem was written, but strengthens the total effect by the contrast which it provides with the comparisons of little Izsák to a nightingale and a flower. Here is the personal grief of the poet who had created the farewell scene between Zrínyi of Sziget and his son in Canto V of the epic.

The ruin of Rákóczi György gave the Turk his opportunity to strengthen his position in Transylvania, which Zrínyi's local successes, however impressive, could not save; the Austrians had no intention of intervening, and when, in June 1660, Rákóczi György died (of wounds received in battle), Vienna believed that not only the pretext, but the reason for the Turkish attacks had ceased to exist. So Zrínyi, who had begun a siege of Kanizsa on his own initiative, was forbidden to complete the operation (which a chance fire had made a relatively simple matter), even while the Turks were besieging Nagyvárad[2] in the east; Nagyvárad fell on 27 August. Now, under the impact of this fourfold blow—the death of the Prince, the Turkish devastation of Transylvania, the order to abandon the siege of Kanizsa, and the fall of Nagyvárad, he wrote his last major work in Hungarian, the essay entitled

---

[1] Igy számlálom vala az én jövendő-
met,   60
Hogy sok üdő mulván ez megvált
engemet,
Hogy követi, meg is haladja verse-
met,
És szegény hazánkért igyekezetemet.

S zengőbb trombitával magyar vitéz-
séget,
Fogja énekleni erős kar erejét.   65

És hogy ű is osztán érdemeljen illyet,
Kinek énekelhessék cselekedetét.

Ah, szép fülemilét az irigy halál
Lecsapá kebelemben szörnyü ka-
szával,
Izsákot, mely vala mint egy szép
virágszál,   70
Kertek szépségére mely oly gyönyö-
rűn áll.

(*Elegia* stanzas 7–14.)

[2] Now Oradea in Rumania.

Hands off Hungary! An Antidote to the Turkish Opium (*Ne bántsd a magyart! Az török áfium ellen való orvosság*). The title is taken from a story in Herodotus (i. 85). When King Cyrus of Persia had captured the Lydian capital of Sardis, a Persian soldier was about to kill the Lydian King Croesus, when Croesus' son, who had been dumb from birth, shouted 'Slay not the King!' Just as Croesus' son shouted 'Hands off the King!', so now I, says Zrínyi, seeing a terrible dragon with the crown of Hungary in its grip, am shouting 'Hands off Hungary!', although I am no professional orator, and almost dumb. But I remember the Lord's warning to Ezekiel (Ezekiel iii. 17–18) when He made him a watchman to Israel.

The opening, and other quotations and illustrations, were borrowed by Zrínyi from O. G. de Busbecq's *Exclamatio, sive de acie contra Turcam instituenda consilium*[1] (*Exclamation, or a Plan of Campaign against the Turk*). Zrínyi also follows Busbecq's basic plan to emphasize the urgency of the situation and the necessity of resistance, then to suggest practical proposals. But Zrínyi writes with a force which far surpasses his predecessor, a force which no purely literary debt, only an awareness of immediate and mortal danger, could impart.

The dragon is the Turk who has captured Nagyvárad, carried off many thousands of Hungarians into slavery, ravaged Transylvania, and is trampling on our nation as a savage boar tramples down a fair vine. As a wild animal is ready to die in defence of its lair and its cubs, says Zrínyi, we must go forth to defend our country, and die if need be. To suppose that 'what has fallen, has fallen' is 'vanity of vanities'; but the notion that success will sate the Turk's appetite is refuted by the history of Transylvania. Nor is innocence any protection.

It may be objected that while all this is true, by ourselves we have not the strength necessary for our defence. But why should not the present emergency bring out in us the same qualities that the invasion of Xerxes brought out in the Greeks? 'We must overcome our fortune.' The situation has indeed deteriorated since 1651, when Fortune had assembled an invincible combination of Powers to lay low the Turk. That opportunity, as *Discourse* v had pointed out, had been let slip, and now when Zrínyi systematically

---

[1] Published in one volume with his *Itinera Constantinopolitanum et Amasinum* (Antwerp, 1581).

surveys possible sources of foreign aid, he finds virtually nothing. The Poles are our neighbours, but are weakened by war, threatened by Russia and Sweden, and in any case are under an obligation to Turkey for Tartar help in the recent war against Rákóczi György; they just want peace. The Austrians and Germans are also our neighbours, but (though we must make an honourable exception in favour of our lord the King) they would fear a strong Hungary, and any help they did send us would come 'on a crab's back'—the same phrase used of Austrian aid by Halul, the smoothtongued Turkish envoy in the epic (VI. 31) when trying to persuade Zrínyi of Sziget to surrender. Third come the Italians: they are far away, and divided into many small states, though they would certainly help us if they saw that we ourselves were putting up a determined resistance. Spain is too far away, and involved in Portugal: France is a gallant nation, but only when fighting for herself; the French are 'intolerable when victorious, worthless in adversity': Russia I disregard—not only is the country remote, but the people are uncivilized, worthless as soldiers, and ruled by tyranny. Finally England—'almost another world'—brings the catalogue to a bleak close. In any case, foreign help is no substitute for self-help; 'you don't lick a calf that isn't yours'.

At this point, says Zrínyi, someone may ask me: what do you wish to deduce from all this talk? What do you recommend? It is easy for anybody to declaim, to preach, but the patient needs a remedy. 'I will reply briefly to that, and will redouble my proclamation! Arms, arms, arms are wanted, and good gallant resolve!' We may have declined disastrously since the glorious days of the *Hunyadis, we may have become dissolute, disunited; yet, in spite of everything, we are still 'the most capable, strong, swift, and, given the will, the most gallant nation'.

First and foremost, Hungary must have a standing army, 12,000 strong, adequately maintained; every man must be properly armed, equipped, clothed in good strong cloth, fed, and paid. The right men must be selected and trained. For his discussion of this latter subject Zrínyi does not use his own words, but quotes at length from various passages of Vegetius.[1] This appeal to ancient authority, however, in no way hinders the exposition: a passage like 'Ergo qui desiderat pacem, praeparet bellum, qui victoriam cupit, milites imbuat diligenter, qui secundos optat eventus,

---

[1] Also in Busbecq.

dimicet arte, non casu' (Veg. III pref.) (Therefore let him who desires peace prepare for war, let him who wishes for victory train his soldiers with diligence, let him who hopes for success fight by skill and not by chance) could not be bettered as a summary of Zrínyi's own views.

Our country has plenty of men who would make fine soldiers if properly selected and trained, Zrínyi continues, but at present we have no good officers, so we need temporary help from foreigners with the training. The best source for this help would be Scotland; the Scots have the requisite virtues of gallantry, loyalty, and endurance, and their soldiers are willing to serve abroad. To those who find this proposal inconsistent with my earlier observations on foreign aid, I reply that the Hungarian Army must certainly consist of Hungarians, but a long period of peace has made our nation unaccustomed to discipline; to rectify this situation we need to have our army trained, temporarily, by foreign soldiers; Carthage, France, Portugal, and Russia all furnish precedents.

This standing army should be stationed in one camp; but this does not mean that the border forts should be disbanded. If these are well disciplined and trained, they should be able to resist minor Turkish attacks; any large-scale enemy troop concentrations must be reported by an efficient intelligence service, and met with a force of the size required; for major attacks the help of the main army must be sought.

The proposals I have made are for a peace-time army only; in the event of war we should need to arm not only 12,000 men, but the whole nation. Other peoples who are further away from the Turks may dress in 'purple, velvet and damask'; we must put on armour. To those who say that we are certain to be overwhelmed by sheer weight of numbers, I reply that when we have laid the foundations of our military strength, we can easily build on them. Besides, if we ourselves act energetically, others will be moved to help us. Let all who trust in God and love their country join with me in singing the song of Deborah: 'My heart is toward the governors of Israel, that offered themselves willingly among the people. Bless ye the Lord.' 'Volenti nil difficile', ends Zrínyi; where there's a will, there's a way.

The *Turkish Opium* is the only one of Zrínyi's works in Hungarian prose which is truly a unity. Each section follows logically from its predecessor; starting with the urgency of meeting the present perils, we consider possible allies abroad; having eliminated them and reached the conclusion that Hungary must rely on her own strength, we go on to define in what that strength is to consist, then to describe how it is to be used. We then find that this solves our earlier problem; for, as Zrínyi has already said briefly when considering Italy as a possible source of aid, our own efforts will inspire others to exert themselves on our behalf. So the foreign help which was earlier discounted, because then we were thinking of it as a substitute for self-help, will be forthcoming, and we shall be enabled to overcome the desperate situation described at the opening of the work. The shape of the *Turkish Opium* reinforces the point made by its substance.

A quotation from Demosthenes near the beginning of the work gives an indication of its nature; this is Zrínyi's Philippic, most of it written as if for delivery, and the rhetoric reaches a power unknown in his work hitherto, far surpassing anything in Busbecq, anticipated only in one or two passages of the *Reflections on the Life of King *Mátyás*. There, however, Zrínyi was 'reflecting' to himself; now he is addressing the nation. The style varies accordingly —stirring, sonorous periods rouse the emotions, concise and precise analyses of military problems convince the intellect; possible objections are anticipated and answered. And the ideals are those for which Zrínyi had always worked, and which Hungary had never needed more.

6

Meanwhile, in Transylvania, Barcsay, the Prince whom the Turks had installed after the death of Rákóczi György, had been deposed and executed early in 1661 by Kemény János, one of Rákóczi's generals who had recently returned from Tartar captivity in the Crimea. Soon, however, the Turks began to make menacing preparations to eject Kemény. The Prince appealed to Vienna for help, and the Austrians sent a small force of mercenaries in the summer of 1661, under the Imperial Commander-in-Chief, Count Raimond Montecuccoli. During this period Zrínyi was making his own preparations independently; early in 1661 he had ten cannon made in Vienna, and harassed continually the Turkish attempts to reinforce Kanizsa. He reconnoitred the banks of the Mura facing Kanizsa and began to build a new fortress on the left bank of the river, on Turkish-controlled territory, in an admirable position to prevent Turkish raids and pave the way for a future attack.

This was the most aggressive step any Hungarian had taken against the Turks for a very long time, and its necessity was recognized by many, even by some of Zrínyi's enemies in Vienna. The Court's true feelings, however, and also the spirit in which Montecuccoli had been sent to Transylvania, were revealed when the Turkish counter-preparations frightened the Government into sending Zrínyi a peremptory order to desist from the construction of his fort. Zrínyi sent his engineer Wassenhof to Vienna to explain the position, but this brought merely a repetition of the previous order; whereupon, on 5 July 1661, Zrínyi wrote a memorandum to the Hofkriegsrat (War Council) setting forth the whole situation, and making an appeal which was by no means easy for the Council to reject without abandoning the pretence of being willing to help, not least because of the determination with which Zrínyi expressed his readiness to defend the Christian cause to the end, if necessary alone. The Court was reduced to an embarrassed silence, and the commanders on the spot were instructed to help Zrínyi if the Turks attacked him.

The work of construction proceeded so quickly that the Sultan had the Pasha of Kanizsa replaced and executed, and the Porte also impressed upon Reninger, the Austrian Ambassador, the harm that the building of the fort was doing to Turco–Austrian relations. Urgent dispatches from Reninger eventually decided Vienna to comply with the Porte's wishes; already Zrínyi was being slandered at Court as a disloyal adventurer who was building the fort in pursuit of his private interests and ambitions.

While Zrínyi was engaged on the work of construction, Montecuccoli's troops on the way to Transylvania were inflicting appalling cruelties on the inhabitants of the districts through which they passed, and in the end they did not achieve their object. Montecuccoli withdrew without engaging the enemy, and Kemény was defeated and killed by the Turks near Segesvár[1] in January 1662. At the same time Vienna launched a persecution of Protestants so savage that the Hungarian counties instructed their deputies in the Diet of 1662 to refuse to discuss any other subjects until the evacuation of the Austrian troops and the suspension of the persecutions had been successfully negotiated. Perhaps no

[1] Now Sighişoară in Rumania.

greater tribute was ever paid to Zrínyi than by the fact that it was to him, a Catholic, that the Protestants turned to act as their spokesman at the Diet. He made a stand which won him fame abroad, and in a book published in London in 1664 in his praise he is described as the 'Protestant Generalissimo of the Auxiliaries in Hungary'.[1]

During 1662, when the atrocities perpetrated by Montecuccoli's troops had become widely known, that general published a self-justificatory statement which aroused widespread indignation, and brought a reply from Zrínyi, devastating equally in the cogency of its content and in the sharp edge of its style. This work is not only Zrínyi's masterpiece in Latin, but the effortless range of his quotations, extending to many classical Latin authors and modern books, is a most remarkable testimony to his wide reading and retentive memory—for he wrote the work while attending the Diet in Pozsony,[2] away from his library. He ends with a quotation from the contest of Ajax and Odysseus in Ovid—a favourite passage of his which he clearly knew almost by heart—'denique quid verbis opus est? spectemur agendo' (*Metam.* XIII. 120) (What need is there then of words? Let us be tested by action).

Montecuccoli was the very antithesis of all the principles of war advocated in *The Gallant General*—inert and dilatory, whereas for Zrínyi (*Aph.* 9) there was perhaps nothing more essential than speed: a dogmatist who applied immutable principles to all situations, whereas for Zrínyi *diversificare* (*Disc.* III) was of prime importance: egoistical and conceited. His appearance on the scene was among the most formidable obstacles Zrínyi ever had to face, because he not only did no good, but also positive harm, by wrecking the organization of national resistance.

Moreover, the religious persecutions were so greatly intensified that by 1664 the Protestants in the north were seriously contemplating surrender to the Turks. Zrínyi, who had always, as his epic shows, appreciated the importance of religious unity in the struggle with the Turk, must have regarded this as a disaster; but his position was very delicate, for he could scarcely afford to antagonize the Hungarian Catholics at a time when his relations with the Court were as bad as they had ever been on account of

---

[1] See pp. 59, 60.
[2] Now Bratislava in Czechoslovakia.

his construction of his new fort and his disagreement with Monte-cuccoli.

The desire of Vienna to keep the peace in the east at Hungary's expense was further increased by the emergence of the problem of the Spanish succession. Early in 1663 it was certain that the Turks were preparing a large-scale attack, and Zrínyi attempted again to warn the Court of the danger and advise on the best means of defence; but not only were his suggestions rejected, he was for-bidden to strengthen his defences, and five regiments were trans-ferred from the east to Spain. With astounding folly the Court continued to negotiate with the Turks, even to the extent of offer-ing to hand over Zrínyi's new fort; the Turks played for time and strengthened their attacking force. The only defensive measure undertaken, and that as a result of a personal visit by Zrínyi to Vienna in May 1663, was the dispatch of 6,000 men to defend the Styrian border against a Turkish invasion of Austria proper.

With regard to his new fort, Zrínyi's situation was becoming increasingly similar to that of his great-grandfather at Szigetvár; he himself drew the parallel in a letter to an Italian friend on 30 April 1663. He had collected a considerable force, some 20,000 men, to defend it; and his determination was in no way affected by the knowledge that there was no possibility of receiving foreign aid. When the Pasha of Kanizsa sent Zrínyi a warning that if the incursions from his new fort did not cease the full might of the Turkish armies would be brought against him, the poet both replied and acted in the spirit of Zrínyi of Sziget.

But the Turks did not attack Zrínyi; instead, they turned north-wards, defeated a poorly organized Hungarian force which had been sent against them, and invested Érsekújvár.[1] Montecuccoli prudently withdrew to the Austrian border, leaving Érsekújvár to its fate. But it was another matter when a Turkish force 100,000 strong began to move up from Belgrade; the general terror spread even to Vienna, and in July Zrínyi was permitted to attack 'pru-dently'. Having also repelled a Turkish force of some 6,000 men which attempted in August to take his new fortress by surprise, Zrínyi was appointed 'totius nationis Hungariae dux' (commander of the whole nation of Hungary), a command independent of Montecuccoli, with military authority equivalent to that of a *nádor. The Court had totally changed its attitude now.

[1] Now Nové Zámky in Czechoslovakia.

Zrínyi could not have assumed command at a more unfavourable moment; Érsekújvár had already fallen, and he disposed of fewer than 15,000 men. Fear of Montecuccoli's depredations had made the counties reluctant to send their forces to fight away from home, and Montecuccoli himself refused to co-operate with Zrínyi on the ground that the country had been so laid waste that it would be impossible to provision a force consisting of their joint strength. Nevertheless, by a series of well-timed raids (in which, true to the precepts of *The Gallant General* [*Aph.* 13], he made full use of his knowledge of the terrain), Zrínyi completely broke the Turkish offensive on the Danube and compelled the enemy to withdraw in the early autumn. During October and November he reorganized his army into an effective fighting force. Military discipline was strictly enforced; at the same time there was to be absolute freedom and equality in religion—Protestant troops would have Protestant chaplains. This army repelled a strong attack by a numerically superior Turkish force at the end of November.

However, probably because of personal jealousies, Zrínyi was relieved of his command as early as December, and with him went his imaginative plan of launching a winter offensive up the Drave to prevent the Turks from crossing the Danube. No doubt Machiavelli and all the text books frowned on winter campaigns, but Zrínyi had observed the Turkish dislike and inaptitude for winter fighting; already at Siklós, in Canto III of *The Siege of Sziget*, we find the Turks certain that the wet weather will prevent any enemy activity, and the *Turkish Opium* too had referred to the possibility of successes in winter, because of the same Turkish weakness.

Although no longer 'commander of the whole nation of Hungary', Zrínyi had recently won some striking successes and could not be ignored completely, so the Court tried to please everybody and divided the army into three forces. One, under Souches, was to operate in the north: a second (the largest) was placed under Montecuccoli's command to carry out his plan of attacking along the Danube, with Buda as the ultimate objective: while a third, under Zrínyi, was to attack up the Drave. Zrínyi had in all about 20,000 men at his disposal.

His views on the desirability of a winter campaign were fully confirmed by events; the bridge over the Drave at Eszék,[1] for

[1] Now Osijek in Yugoslavia.

over a century a key point in Turkish communications in Hungary, was destroyed early in 1664, and a succession of forts in southern Hungary (not far from Szigetvár) captured. Here was a most convincing practical demonstration of the principles of *The Gallant General*—of speed (*Aph.* 9), of how to win victories without bloodshed (*Aph.* 30). But the seeds of future trouble were sown too, in the form of discord between Zrínyi and Count Hohenlohe, the commander of the Rhenish confederate troops fighting with him: Zrínyi refused to allow Hohenlohe to give priority to the capture of the citadel of Pécs (the town having fallen) in order to acquire booty (*Aph.* 15)—strategic considerations must come first, and the operation would have cost many dead and wounded. We also hear of Zrínyi intervening in person to protect Turks when German soldiers under his command attacked them in spite of the safe-conduct which they had been given after the surrender of a fortress. There were to be no Amirassens[1] in Zrínyi's army.

But victories have to be followed up as well as won (*Disc.* v, *Aph.* 66). At this stage Zrínyi was optimistic and, with every appearance of enjoying the royal favour, he proceeded to the siege of Kanizsa, paying his troops out of his own pocket till help should come. However, Montecuccoli was smarting under the loss of prestige he had suffered, and objected to the diversion of troops away from his Danube front: Hohenlohe was angered by Zrínyi's refusal to allow the Rhenish troops to loot Pécs. Nor were these Zrínyi's only influential enemies; but, under pressure from both within the empire and without (notably Venice and the Vatican) the Court had no alternative but to allow the siege of Kanizsa to proceed, though the appointment of Hohenlohe and Count Strozzi as joint commanders with Zrínyi boded no good for the future. Various delays gave the Turks time to prepare their defences and rebuild the vital bridge at Eszék, and finally Hohenlohe and Strozzi, misrepresenting the relative strength of the two sides, outvoted Zrínyi and called off the siege in June 1664; he had no option but to follow them. But there was worse to come, when, as a result of the Grand Vizier's sending his main force to the relief of Kanizsa, Montecuccoli was sent to the southern front. Zrínyi had in fact innocently urged this step himself, never suspecting that his colleagues would persist in their refusal to co-operate and in making his position impossible, still less that while he was absent at

[1] See p. 15.

Csáktornya Montecuccoli would allow the Turks to take the new fort which Zrínyi had built, without offering any resistance. Finally in August 1664, a few days after Montecuccoli had won his sole victory, at Szentgotthárd[1] on the Austro–Hungarian border, the Peace of Vasvár was signed, and the policy of Vienna brought to its logical conclusion. To sign any peace at this particular moment was, in a sense, to play into the hands of the Turks; but the signing of one which confirmed them in all their recent acquisitions, even agreeing to pay them an indemnity, naturally brought to a head the growing and widespread feeling of indignation with Austrian policy. Almost unanimously the Hungarians, who had been excluded from the peace negotiations, declared that they would refuse to recognize the treaty. Abroad, feeling ran highest in France, where not only was Zrínyi admired and respected, but Louis XIV's Spanish and German plans required that Austria should be kept occupied in the east. In March 1664 Louis had presented Zrínyi (to his great surprise) with a gift of 10,000 thalers, and France interpreted the Peace of Vasvár as a hostile act by Austria; French troops had fought at Szentgotthárd. In the autumn informal discussions were opened in secret between the Zrínyi brothers and the newly appointed French Ambassador to Vienna, Gremonville, with a view, ultimately, to forming an alliance with France and liberating Hungary with French assistance. At the same time the Austrians were giving much thought to the Turkish question, and the Hungarian leaders were invited to a meeting to be held in Vienna on 25 November 1664; but on 18 November Zrínyi was killed by a wild boar when hunting.

He was mourned almost throughout Europe; many poets expressed their grief at his death, and a volume entitled *Honor Posthumus* was published in London in 1665. Some idea of his reputation abroad can be formed from Jacobus Tollius's sixth *Epistula Itineraria* (first published in 1671, but describing a visit to Csáktornya in 1660)[2] and from a book published in London in 1664 (before Zrínyi's death), *The Conduct and Character of Count Nicholas Serini, Protestant Generalissimo of the Auxiliaries in Hungary, the most Prudent and Resolved Champion of Christendom.* Of these two, Tollius's account is of particular interest as the record of a personal meeting with Zrínyi at his seat. The Dutch scholar was profoundly impressed, not only by the strength of

---

[1] Now St. Gotthard in Austria.   [2] See p. 3.

Csáktornya as a fortress, but by the sight of the arts housed so generously in surroundings so wild—by the 'outstanding' library, the museum with its collection of ancient coins, the gardens. When preparing his *Letters* for publication, Tollius paid special tribute to Zrínyi's generous hospitality and to his linguistic gifts: Zrínyi spoke Hungarian, Croat, various Slavonic dialects, German, Latin, Italian, and Turkish all like a native. The one black spot is Zrínyi's treatment of his Turkish prisoners, in which respect Tollius's account makes it clear that he was not in advance of his time. The most remarkable tribute from a visitor to Csáktornya, however, and in a sense the most remarkable of all, is that contained in the account by the Turk Evlia Çelebi of his visit as an envoy in 1660. Zrínyi clearly treated the Turkish embassy with outstanding courtesy and hospitality, and the very exaggerations in Evlia Çelebi's narrative (besides being often delightful in themselves) are a most impressive tribute to the respect in which the Turks held their enemy.

The Conduct and Character of Count Nicholas Serini is the first and longest section (111 pages out of 168) of a book by one 'O.C.' on the three 'scourges of the Turk', the other two being George Castriotis, the Albanian hero, and Tamberlain. It was printed early in 1664; a corrigendum inserted after the printing was completed refers to a victory of Zrínyi's in February of that year. Though somewhat confused in its arrangement and not always accurate in its chronology, the work shows considerable knowledge of its subject, and quotes in translation part of Zrínyi's dispatch to the King reporting a major victory on the banks of the river Mura in November 1663. It is not, however, an attempt at a systematic biography, but rather a panegyric on Zrínyi, as general and as man. The author draws a good deal on his imagination, yet much of what he says about his hero is based on fact: 'There is not a Nook, Corner, Pass, Bridge or Avenue of Hungary, Croatia, Silesia, Austria or Stiria etc. but he hath observed'; 'never was any General more loving to his soldiers, never any more beloved by them.' 'He alloweth his followers equity, but not indulgence: freedom but not licentiousness' with the result that 'no perishing families curse him, no ravished Virgins meditate revenge on him, no children starved for the bread he took out of their mouth.' 'This' then 'is he who put the Grand Seignior to a cold sweat, and the Prime Vizier to the fit of an ague'; but of his writings, not a word.

At home he rapidly became a legendary figure. Various rumours circulated about his death—that he had been killed not by one boar, but by twelve; or by a bullet. All felt instinctively that an epoch had come to an end; certainly the situation deteriorated sharply in the following years. Though Gremonville cautiously avoided committing his sovereign, the contacts with the French led to a somewhat ill-defined and clumsy conspiracy, which was detected. Zrínyi's brother Péter, who had succeeded him as *Bán of Croatia, ended his life, along with others, on an Austrian scaffold in 1671; a fearful wave of persecution followed, both religious and political, and in 1673 Vienna suspended the Hungarian constitution. This provoked a rebellion in the north, led by *Thököly Imre, whose successes decided the Emperor Leopold in 1681 to restore the constitution and remedy many of Hungary's grievances. But by now it was too late; *Thököly's victories had fatally encouraged the Turks, and in 1683 the Sultan launched a major invasion which reached Vienna. The invaders were, however, later repelled, and this time their defeat was final. Buda was recaptured in 1686, and the Turkish occupation of Hungary was over, having lasted some 150 years—a period which Zrínyi could have shortened by at least thirty.

He was largely denied the opportunity of winning fame with his 'terrible blade', but he has won it by his pen, and he remains an outstanding example of the man of letters who was also a man of action, the type represented in English literature by such figures as Sir Walter Raleigh and Sir Philip Sidney. Perhaps his importance lies most of all not in his pen or in his sword alone, but in the completeness of the union between them.

II

MIKES (1690–1761)* LETTERS FROM TURKEY

I

AUSTRIAN rule in Hungary proved to be in many respects scarcely less brutal and oppressive than that of the Turks, and Hungarian discontent grew steadily in the last quarter of the seventeenth century. Active resistance, however, remained sporadic and disorganized; only in 1701 did it find a natural rallying-point, when Prince Rákóczi Ferenc II escaped from an Austrian prison, in which he had been held for a year as the result of the interception of a letter of his to Louis XIV.

The grandson of Rákóczi György II,[1] Ferenc II was also related to the Zrínyis; his mother was the daughter of the poet's brother, Péter. In addition, his stepfather was the rebel leader *Thököly. By temperament, however, he was the very opposite of the head of a national rising, and only gradually came to accept his position; but eventually his pity for the sufferings of his people forbade him to hold back any longer, and in 1703 he formally raised the standard of rebellion against the Austrians; four years later the Hungarian Diet proclaimed the dethronement of the Habsburgs and elected Rákóczi Prince of Hungary. The Prince succeeded in destroying the class hatred which he had inherited, and achieved an unprecedented national unity; but his ultimate failure was made virtually certain by Marlborough's victory at Blenheim in 1704. When Louis XIV withdrew his previously generous financial support, and Rákóczi failed to find other allies, his fate was sealed. In February 1711, two months before the rebellion was ended by the Treaty of Szatmár,[2] he left Hungary

---

[1] On Rákóczi György II see pp. 44 ff. Rákóczi Ferenc II is by far the most important member of the family, and 'Rákóczi' by itself always refers to him; it was his troops who marched into battle to the strains of the *Rákóczi March*, the melody which Berlioz made famous when he introduced it into *La Damnation de Faust*.

[2] Now Satu Mare in Rumania.

for ever, accompanied by a group of faithful followers. The exiles went first to Poland, then (after a fruitless voyage to Britain)[1] to France, where they arrived in January 1713. Frenchmen admired Rákóczi for his personal qualities; as the Marquis Desalleurs, Louis XIV's envoy to the Hungarian leader, had written in 1705: 'C'est un Prince vertueux, laborieux, affable, généreux, bienfaisant; il est très exact dans la practique de la religion; on ne peut rien ajouter à sa valeur.' But though he received Rákóczi as his guest, Louis XIV had no intention of starting a new war against the Habsburgs; the Treaty of Rastatt was signed in March 1714, and with the death of Louis XIV in 1715, the Prince's prospects became even less hopeful.

In 1717 Rákóczi finally accepted the invitation, several times renewed, of the Sultan Ahmed III to go to Turkey, where one of his principal lieutenants, Bercsényi, had arrived some time before from Poland. The Turks hoped to use the Hungarian exiles as a bargaining counter in their negotiations with the Habsburgs, and Rákóczi was received with the honour due to a Prince. The Hungarians arrived in Gallipoli on 10 October 1717; on that day also a member of Rákóczi's suite, Mikes Kelemen, wrote the following letter (no. 1 of the collection now known as the *Letters from Turkey* (*Törökországi levelek*)) to an aunt of his in Constantinople, to whom all the letters in the collection are addressed.

Gallipoli, 10 October 1717

My dear Aunt,

Thanks be to God, we arrived here safely today, having set out from France on 15 September. Our Prince, thank God, would be in good health, if only the gout were willing to take its leave of him; but let us hope that the Turkish air here will drive it away.

My dear aunt, how good it is to walk on the earth. You see, even St. Peter was afraid, when his legs sank in the water;[2] how should we sinners not be afraid, when our ship turned over from one side to the other, in waves as great as the mighty mountains of Transylvania. Sometimes we sailed on their peaks, sometimes we fell into valleys so deep that we were waiting only for those mountains of water to descend on us; yet they were humane enough not to give us more to drink than was proper. It is

---

[1] On the way to France, in November 1712, a select group of four went to Britain. The voyage itself was almost disastrous—the ship was nearly sunk in a storm; then the Queen refused to receive Rákóczi, in deference to representations by the Austrian Ambassador. However, the Prince was warmly welcomed by the citizens of Hull.   [2] Cf. Matt. XIV. 30.

sufficient that we are here, in good health; for you can fall ill on the sea too, not only on land, where, if your carriage shakes you, you grow tired, and have a better appetite for food; but on board ship the continuous shaking and tossing makes the head dizzy, churns up the stomach, and makes you like a drunken man who cannot hold his wine. My poor tummy could not escape this distress for the first two days or so, but after that I felt I must eat like a wolf.

Our Prince had not yet disembarked, when a Tartar Khan, who is here in exile, sent him some presents, among other things a fine horse with its saddle. Here they have given the Prince good lodging, though we are housed like dogs; still I like being here better than on board ship.

My dear aunt, it's already two years since I heard from you, or rather, it would be, if the year were only one month long. I hope, my dear aunt, that from now on, since we are breathing one air, I shall get your nice letters more often. But since we are several hundred miles nearer each other, I suppose you must love me all the more; for myself, however fond of you I am, I can't write any more; for I feel as if the house were going round, as if I were still on board ship.

Mikes Kelemen was born in August 1690, the month of *Thököly's short-lived seizure of the throne of Transylvania, at Zágon,[1] a village in the land of the *Székelys, in south-eastern Transylvania. His father had been cruelly put to death by the Austrians when Kelemen was still scarcely more than a baby; his mother remarried shortly afterwards, her second husband being a Transylvanian nobleman named Boér Ferenc, a Catholic, who converted his stepson. After completing his education at the Jesuit school in Kolozsvár,[2] Mikes was recommended in 1707 by his uncle to Rákóczi, and entered the service of the Prince as a page. It was the very year in which Rákóczi became Prince of Hungary.

When the defeat of the Rákóczi rebellion was certain, peace came without a fight to a finish, and the terms of the Treaty of Szatmár were not harsh; it was followed by an amnesty, under which Mikes could safely have returned home, as did his step-father. But instead he chose to follow his Prince into exile, and accompanied him on all his travels, being in fact one of the four who went to Britain. At this time Mikes certainly hoped to return home, with the Prince; the Turks, however, were not prepared to support any attempt to win back Hungary by military action, and Mikes's early letters contain more than one sad reference to the

---

[1] Zágon is situated twenty-eight kilometres south-east of Sepsiszentgyörgy (now Sfântul Gheorghe in Rumania.)   [2] Now Cluj in Rumania.

Porte's willingness to make peace after a single defeat (they had recently suffered a reverse at Belgrade); but, as Mikes says so often, 'we must commit ourselves to God's will'.

During this period the Hungarian exiles moved about a good deal, and life was not very comfortable for Mikes: 'My house consists of four stone walls; it has a window of wooden boards, where the wind can enter from all directions; if I block it up with paper, the mice and rats get through the paper for their dinner. My furniture consists of a small wooden chair, my bed is made on the floor, and my house is heated by a little coal in an earthenware dish. But do not suppose, after all this, that I am the one most deserving of pity; ten of us have no wooden chair, no bed such as I have, nor even wooden boards in their windows. Flurries of snow can come in on to the beds—but can you call it a bed, a coarse blanket spread on the ground? Well, it's in palaces like these that we're living, but hope being very necessary to man, and as necessary as food, as we are in bad houses now, so we hope that we shall yet move into good ones. Shall we ever live to see that? But we have lived to see the arrival of the Spanish Ambassador', and Mikes passes to a more pleasant subject, by a typically sudden transition. (Letter 10, Adrianople, 15 March 1718.) But life was hard, and not only because of physical discomforts. Although the Turks liked the Hungarian exiles and were kind to them, the language difficulty, and still more the hosts' contempt for Christianity, were formidable barriers to real friendship. Besides, Mikes could not help feeling homesick, though he always summons his belief in God's goodness to fight his nostalgia. 'So, my dear aunt, let us not resist, but definitely turn our backs on Transylvania, that beloved fairyland, and adore God's wonderful decrees concerning us. . . . You see God's goodness; if He conceals Transylvania from our view with one hand, He feeds us with the other.' (Letter 14, Adrianople, 6 June 1718.) There were also compensations in the form of valuable friendships, notably with the French Ambassador at the Porte, the Marquis de Bonnac and his wife, who entertained Mikes, giving him that company and social life which were indispensable to his nature. Mme de Bonnac, a cultivated and well-read lady, was delighted by his voracious interest in literature, and regularly lent him books; he was thus enabled to acquaint himself with much that he had previously missed, through lack of contact with the literary circles of the Court, when actually living in France.

The year 1718 brought a blow. On 21 July the Peace of Passarowitz was signed between Turkey and Austria, and Mikes now faced the possibility of an indefinite period in exile. 'If I must stay here, it's good-bye to the wedding-dance.' (Letter 16, Adrianople, 15 August 1718.) The 'wedding-dance' could mean either a dance by the wedding-guests with the bride or one by the bridegroom himself with the bride; Mikes makes no reference to himself at this point, but when the Peace was signed he was nearly twenty-eight and still unmarried. Again, in a later letter (Letter 39, Rodostó, 18 November 1720), 'our way to Transylvania has been blocked by twenty-four stone walls', an allusion to the twenty-four years for which the Peace was to be valid. The Peace of Passarowitz was followed twelve days later (2 August 1718) by the Quadruple Alliance between England, France, Holland, and Austria, in which the parties agreed to exclude from their territory any subject of any of the four Powers whom that Power had declared to be a rebel. This applied to Rákóczi whom the Austrians had formally branded as a traitor in 1715, and consequently created difficulties of protocol for Bonnac in his relations with the Hungarians.

Although the Turks had made peace, they rejected Austrian demands for the extradition of Rákóczi and his suite, demands which were made with some insistence: 'The Austrian Ambassador is thinking above all how he can hurt us; but we're not hurting him one little bit.' (Letter 32, Yeniköy, 10 October 1719.) The Ambassador took particular exception to the presence of Bercsényi and his wife in Pera, the district of Constantinople where he himself lived (Letter 28, Yeniköy, 16 July 1719), and where, incidentally, Mikes's aunt also lived (Letter 21, Yeniköy, 16 December 1718). Finally the Porte complied with the Ambassador's request that at least the Hungarians should be moved further away from the capital, and decided to settle them all permanently at Rodostó (Tekirdag) on the Sea of Marmora.[1] Letters 36 of 24 April 1720 and 37 of 28 May 1720 describe respectively the journey to Rodostó and the place itself.

'I will begin with our departure from Yeniköy on the 16th. The galley was ready, waiting for the Prince; he was greatly honoured by the Sultan's sending a galley for him. This galley was one of

---

[1] Letters for which no place of origin is given in the reference are addressed from Rodostó.

the largest; it had 26 pairs of oars, with three or four men on each oar; 220 slaves in all rowed the galley. In addition, there were a hundred armed marines, so that in all there were 400 of us on board.' They arrived at Rodostó at 11 a.m. on 21 April 1720, and the Prince was accorded a ceremonial reception. After recording these events Mikes proceeds to describe what he observed during the voyage.

'My dear aunt, he is a lord indeed, who voyages in a galley. The great rule, even in the smallest matters, is absolute silence. With two hundred men rowing the boat, you may indeed believe that it is well rowed; they pull all together, and put the fifty-two oars in the water all together. The oars are at least thirty feet long. It is a fine and enjoyable sight, but when you think that those poor slaves are nearly all Christians, and that they must stay there as long as they live, your heart goes out to them. Moreover, rowing the galleys is very heavy work, which no one who has not seen it can imagine. You would think that all the slaves' arms would be wrenched right off, so hard does the oar jerk them.

'It is true that they give them their food, but their clothes are just rags. Ours, however, were clothed in shirts to work, because the Prince was there; and although for this reason they did not treat them badly, at other times the slaves must work shirtless, and endure a beating for the smallest offence, as the poor wretches said themselves. To give an order, a whistle is blown—the slaves know what that means, and instantly buckle to. Their benches are set in order one after the other on both sides, as in a church, with a gangway in the middle, where the officers walk ceaselessly up and down, looking to see if any are not rowing well, or are talking with one another. They must each stay in his place, to which they are chained, and as soon as they cease rowing, they must sit down, and must sleep on the spot. They may never stand up, except when they are rowing, and then you hear a very sad clatter—for you can hear only the clattering of the many chains.

'All this may make you say that these poor slaves must surely sigh for their freedom; nevertheless there are some who have grown accustomed to their wretched life. I spoke to two Hungarian slaves who have been in the galleys for twenty years, and asked them if there were not some way of securing their freedom. Their only reply was: "Why should we go to Hungary now? Our wives and children are perhaps already dead—and how should we make a living there? Here we are fed, and by now we have got used to this misery." I certainly did not expect this reply from them, and in their place I should think differently. All nationalities were represented on our galley: Hungarians, Germans, Frenchmen, Poles, Russians. There were not so many nationalities in Noah's ark, except for the animals.'

There was much to be thankful for in Rodostó: 'We must be grateful to God for bringing us here, for we are housed far more spaciously than in that miserable Yeniköy.' Mikes, with one servant, had the whole house of a rich Armenian, with a small garden, and he could say, at the beginning of the next letter (37, 28 May 1720), 'Now here we are, with a real hearth and home, and I like Rodostó, without being able to forget Zágon. But seriously, my dear aunt, we are in a very pleasant place here.' He goes on to describe Rodostó at length. It is a fine, large town, in a beautiful situation on the coast, surrounded by arable land 'like a well-cultivated garden', and with vineyards 'enough for a county anywhere else' and vegetable gardens as well as ploughed fields. The methods of cultivation are in many ways different from those he knew at home; vine-poles, for example, are not used, and the branches of the vines are bent down and shade the ground, thus keeping it moist—a necessary protection for the trees in so dry a climate. Different methods of growing vegetables, too, are used. Cotton is grown on a very large scale, Turkey being so much warmer and flatter than Transylvania. The crop is gathered in May and October; the work is done by women, being in fact the only work which women do out of doors.

The town, too, is fine, with a splendidly spacious market-place. The houses, however, do not look attractive, because they have no windows facing the street; the Turks do not want their wives to be able to look out. 'What a fine thing is jealousy!' There are four nationalities living in the town, Turks, Jews, Greeks and Armenians; the Hungarians live in the Armenian quarter, only a step from the fields. The arrival of the exiles made a considerable difference to the life of the place; it caused a slight rise in prices, but by way of compensation it made the town much quieter and more orderly. Previously, women and girls had been afraid to walk in the streets even during the day-time, and if they did so at night they were certain to be abducted. 'Imagine in what condition they returned.' There were even murders. Now, however, the Hungarians are quite numerous, and their guard of thirty Janissaries could teach any criminal a lesson; so now anybody can safely be out till late in the evening.

After describing Rodostó and its environs, Mikes proceeds to give an account of the daily life of the Hungarian community. Rákóczi, himself a deeply religious man, enjoined an almost monastic strictness: 'no monastery has a more rigorous rule than the Prince's household.' Rákóczi himself rises at 6 for Mass, the servants having been called (by the beating of a drum) half-an-hour earlier: Mass is celebrated again at 8: at 2.30 the Prince goes to the chapel alone for half-an-hour: Vespers are at 5 p.m. For the rest, the Prince's chief occupations are hunting and writing.

Socially, the Hungarians have to be largely self-contained. Mikes would clearly have liked to mix with the other communities, if there were any response forthcoming; 'you can't go for walks or wander in the fields all the time; but friendship with the people here is impossible. No foreigner can visit anyone in his home; the Armenians, especially, are more afraid for their wives than the Turks. I have not yet seen my neighbour's wife; I have to pass by the gate ten times a day, and if she happens to be there, she runs away from me as if I were the devil, and shuts the gate. . . . There are Turkish lords, but paying a visit to a Turk is a boring business; for one thing, I don't know Turkish; then if you call on him, first it's "sit down", then he gives you a pipe of tobacco and a cup of coffee, says a few words—after which he'd stay silent till ten, if you waited.' Not that this exclusiveness was an expression of resentment against the new arrivals; Greek, Armenian, Turk, and Jew had always lived strictly apart. In spite of this difficulty, however, Mikes was able to satisfy his curiosity about the customs of other nations. Letter 42 (20 November 1721), for instance, contains a good deal of information about Armenian marriage customs: 'An Armenian does not eat with his wife for a week or two after the wedding (I do not know why) although they sleep together. Weddings take place at a definite time of year, particularly in this month, when the new wine has fermented, and the sausages have been made.' He goes on to quote a poem he has written on the life in Rodostó. As he says, he has 'never been on Mount Parnassus', and this composition, though without the slightest pretensions to any poetic quality, tells us a good deal about Armenian weddings.

'Do not look for gaiety at a Greek or Armenian wedding. They scrape the fiddle, and it grates on your ears. It has only two strings,

and makes a nasty noise; it could never play more than one tune.
The Armenian bride is married with pomp at night, by the light
of many candles; she takes the oath with the bridegroom in church,
right joyfully. The next day she is taken through the streets, from
house to house; they cover her head, because they do not want
her to see. She might easily fall on her nose if she were not assisted, but she is guided on both sides; old women help her. She
stands right proudly at the entrance to each house; there a kerchief
is placed round her neck, sufficient for a gift. From there they
take her on, and halt her at another house. The bridegroom goes
on ahead of her, in all his finery, including his sword. When they
have done all the streets and collected enough presents, they take
the bride to the house of the bridegroom, and begin the festivities.'

The news from abroad was discouraging. 'When the Emperor,
the French, the Spaniards, and the English have made an alliance
with one another,[1] who should dare to raise his hand against them?
And from whom can the poor Hungarians in exile hope for comfort?
I see nowhere except France; but it can also fairly be said that the
French are treating our Prince with ingratitude. Even now he is
applying to be admitted into France; but the Duke of Orleans, far
from granting permission for this, or even replying to the Prince's
letters, will not have his name mentioned in his hearing, because,
as Orleans says, of the alliance with the Emperor. Such is friendship and kinship with princes. When we were in France, this duke
always showed his great friendship to the Prince, and in addition
they are related, because the Duke's mother and our Prince's wife
are of the same family.'[2] (Letter 39, 18 November 1720.) Then on
18 February 1722 Rákóczi's wife died in Paris at the age of forty-
three. 'The Prince truly mourns her from the bottom of his heart,
but he has also been released from a great sorrow, because the condition of the Princess always compelled sorrow. True, they lived together very little, but the bond remained.' (Letter 43, 16 April 1722.)

In November 1723 Mikes's mother wrote to him, making a last
appeal to him to return home; she had been interceding on his
behalf for three years, and had now successfully paved the way
for his return. 'I am not surprised when I hear others say that a man

---

[1] The Treaty of The Hague (1720).

[2] Rákóczi's wife was Charlotte Amelia of Hesse-Rheinfels; Orleans's mother
was the Princess Palatine, her second cousin. Both were descended from the
Landgrave Maurice of Hesse-Kassel.

can forget his country; perhaps I could forget mine, if I had not received a letter the other day from my mother, saying that she will secure pardon for me if I wish to go back; and since the Prince is mortal, what might not happen to me in a foreign country after his death?[1] All this may come to pass, and I certainly see nothing but uncertainty in my destiny; but both here and elsewhere, we must simply commit ourselves to God's will.' (Letter 51, 19 December 1723.) In the event he made no move; his loyalty to the Prince came first, a fact the more remarkable because his mother's appeal reached him at a time when it was particularly likely to succeed. Apart from the perpetual problem of boredom, there had been an outbreak of plague in the summer of 1722; sometimes as many as 150 people were buried in a single day. The Hungarians moved out of Rodostó and lived under canvas at Büyük Ali, three miles away; but they did not escape, and there were several deaths among the Prince's staff. In February 1723 the exiles suffered further loss, when Rákóczi's envoy to the Porte, Horvát Ferenc, died: 'Even at the age of sixty-nine his manner was so fresh, and he was always good-humoured; none of us was more gay. What a fine thing is a good nature! That he forgot his own country need cause no surprise; a man who spends forty-three years in a foreign land is bound to forget where he belongs.' (Letter 47, 15 April 1723.) About the same time the wife of Bercsényi, the Prince's second-in-command, fell into a decline: 'So far her favourite subject of conversation has been her return home, but now she realizes that she will see Heaven before Hungary. Certainly the former is better than the latter, but what harm would it do to go to Heaven from Hungary?' (Letter 47.) She died a few days later.

'Will he marry again? There is no unmarried lady here except Zsuzsi and two widows; as regards Zsuzsi, another might be thinking of her, but the richer is the more powerful. That is enough for now; there is no point in writing a long letter about something sad.' (Letter 48, 26 April 1723.)

Zsuzsi was the daughter of Bercsényi's secretary, Kőszeghy Pál, who was also a poet, and wrote a trilogy in verse (of which one part only survives) about his master's exploits. When Kőszeghy died, in 1703, Zsuzsi was only two or three years old, and Bercsényi brought her up; she accompanied him into exile at Rodostó.

---

[1] Rákóczi was born on 27 March 1676, and was thus fourteen years older than Mikes.

'Little Zsuzsi has been given a very meagre share of beauty, but
she is a good sort, upright, and kindness itself.' (Letter 24, Yeniköy,
24 January 1719.) When Bercsényi lost two or three of his servants
and his priest in the plague, he and his household moved into the
house where Mikes was living 'as if he would be braver among us;
but I don't mind, because little Zsuzsi will be nearer. At this you
will say "Oh! How can you think of such a thing in time of plague?"
My dear aunt, while we live, we carry Nature around with us; we
must love our rib, whether we wish to or not.' (Letter 43, 16
April 1722.) Then (Letter 49, 22 August 1723) Mikes wrote:
'I see from your last letter that you are a true prophet . . . . Others
are now almost certain, but I am quite certain, because I had to
learn the secret, that any moment now Zsuzsi will be Bercsényi's
wife.' The wedding took place quietly in October. 'She certainly
deserves the title of Countess, and we may marvel at what God
has ordained for her, in what ways He takes under His Providence
orphans in a foreign land. . . . I know someone, as you do, who is
in need of marriage as greatly as Bercsényi is, but "non habet
pecuniam" (he has no money). Not only does a fiesta cost money,
the bridal dance does too.' (Letter 50, 15 October 1723.)

Mikes was anything but a confirmed bachelor; although in one
of his earliest letters (4, Adrianople, 7 November 1717) he foresees that his aunt will tease him for talking about marriage and will
say he is 'like a blind man speaking about light', he often returns
to the subject. He begins his first letter of 1725: 'In the New
Year let's be gay, and if we can, let's get married.' (Letter 59, 16
January 1725.) But to whom? Greek and Spanish girls have hopelessly expensive tastes, French ones care only for cards and singing; 'Give me a Transylvanian wife, for I know no country where
the women more richly deserve the name of "wife" than in our
fairyland.' (Letter 59.) In spite of his restraint and humour it is
abundantly clear that Zsuzsi's marriage to Bercsényi was a cruel
blow. After an interval in the letters he tells his aunt: 'The
reason [i.e. for my not having written sooner] is that for a whole
month our Prince has been ill and has been unable to stand on
his feet, because of the gout. To this you could reply that my
fingers were not suffering from the gout, and I might have written;
my answer is that both my heart and my mind have been laid low
by the gout. I should not even have seen the newly married wife,
had I not been obliged to go there with the Prince; nevertheless I

must confess that the obligation gave pleasure to the gouty heart, and when I was there a few angry reproaches for not having been to see them for so long, cured me.' (Letter 51, 19 December 1723.) Mikes's friendship with Bercsényi and his wife was in no way impaired; when Bercsényi fell ill in the autumn of 1725, Mikes was a regular visitor to his bedside, and no one could question the sincerity of the visitor's grief ('your heart goes out to him') at the sufferings of Bercsényi from the combination of a terrible disease and surgery without anaesthetics: 'It is like watching the martyrs of old under torture. I certainly cannot describe to you the horror of having to see such a sight; so what must be the agony of the patient himself?' (Letter 66, 29 October 1725.) On 6 November Bercsényi's 'exile ended', and he 'received the reward of his many sufferings, and not he, but those whom he has left behind orphaned here in a foreign land, call for pity. But the great immortal Master will care for them. Our Prince was with him throughout, and showed his friendship to the end.' (Letter 67, 6 November 1725.)

What would Zsuzsi do now? 'I know someone who would wish to make Zsuzsi discard her weeds, but she is unwilling. I do not know the reason, though I do know that they loved each other when she was only a girl. Is it because she does not want to relinquish the title of Countess, or because he has not much gold glittering in his box? It is enough that she has no inclination, though the love is there. Since we are Christians, let us say that what God has not decreed for someone, he shall not possess.' (Letter 68, 12 November 1725.) The love was there, sure enough: 'What put it into your head to ask me who the Templars were, and why they were suppressed? I'd rather laugh with Zsuzsi for half-an-hour than spend ten hours writing about that!' (Letter 71, 13 March 1726.) 'I often go to see the widow Zsuzsi, who is preparing to go to Poland. . . . If she does not stay here, the friendship will not be broken. . . . It is nothing new, if I say that marriage depends on God.' (Letter 73, 24 May 1726.) She left for Poland the same summer, and the sight of her packing was almost too much, even for Mikes. (There has been another outbreak of plague) 'but what is the point of talking about disease, let us talk about something else. What I have to say is no joyful thing, for the little widow Zsuzsi is just making her preparations, and every one of her belongings I see her pack into her trunk is like so many knives driven into my heart. . . . I try often enough to persuade her to stay.

I think that perhaps her heart advises her to do so; but I cannot win her mind, because her eyes are used to seeing full coffers, and her husband's purse was much stouter than mine is. She may caress me, but she has an eye to the future—she fears for the thousand gold pieces she was left, and is afraid of getting through them too soon. She knows that I can do nothing about this, and sees that all my fortune, all my assets are built on ice. So she seeks advice, not from her heart, but from her mind; how can I argue against that? It is certain that the intelligence gives us better advice than our hearts; for the heart only sighs over the present, but the intelligence thinks about the future. . . . Why should I wish anyone to bear my misfortunes as well as their own?' (Letter 75, 28 July 1726.) Soon afterwards Mikes fell ill with malaria, but he cured himself, as he tells his aunt, with 'a precious Transylvanian remedy. Everybody laughed at it, especially the Prince, when I told him. This precious remedy is cabbage soup—if that does you good, why go chasing after costly remedies from India? But now I am afraid of a worse ague, which will be severer than the first one, and which a whole barrel of cabbage soup cannot cure; in three or four days Zsuzsi sets out for Poland. God knows whether I shall ever see her again or not. It's a fine thing not to die of grief— otherwise they'd have to bury me in four days' time.' (Letter 76, 17 September 1726.) Nor did he ever see her again; she lived the rest of her life in Poland, and died there in 1750. Mikes heard the news of her death, but he did not mention it in his letters to his aunt. 'People often say that the best remedy for what cannot be remedied is to forget. It is difficult; but time helps a little, then wisdom gives us the strength to endure'—as he had said in letter 77 (4 December 1726).

2

There were, however, arrivals in Rodostó as well as departures. Most of these were French, but in June 1727 'I cannot delay the news any longer, because I should be sorry if you learnt it from another, my dear aunt, that the Prince's second son, having slipped out of Vienna and gone to France, arrived here from France the day before yesterday. You can judge with what joy such a father as our Prince welcomed his son of twenty-six, whom he had never seen before.[1] Only a father can appreciate the love a

[1] When Rákóczi György, the Prince's second son, was born, his father was in prison.

father feels for his son; however, I did observe that the son did not greet the father with that heartfelt joy with which the father received the son. . . . We may say of our Prince's son that he is a fine young man, intelligent and sensible, but only by nature; for knowledge has not adorned those qualities, nor has a good education embellished them . . . . An unpolished diamond is almost like quartz. Our young Prince has had no education; they have tried to prevent him from learning anything, and have succeeded. I am surprised that he can write, however badly. His father observes all these things, and feels them bitterly; but what can he do? Now the reed is beginning to thicken, and bends less easily. His elder brother is still walking about Vienna; much good is spoken of him —some day we shall see. One hears a lot about this son too. As far as I have observed the young Prince's nature, he is quiet and not irascible. . . . I do not know if he will grow accustomed to our monastic life; here he is starved of his natural pastimes. I know his father tries to keep him happy, and sends him off to hunt, in fact goes with him.' (Letter 82, 17 June 1727.)

Mikes's suspicions that the young Rákóczi would find the life at Rodostó boring were well founded; he himself, too, knew what boredom meant. 'We have grown tired of living here, and are not accustomed to going to Mass every day, abstaining from meat on fast days, and just running through the pages of a book from morning till night. We go hunting, it is true, but only to avoid being at home; we look for some quarry for half an hour; the rest is boredom.' (Letter 83, 19 July 1727.) Above all, he missed the charm of female company; the women in Rodostó were kept in purdah. 'In the end we shall have customs like those of the Greek monks on Mount Athos.' (Letter 83.) No wonder the young Prince suffered; indeed the boredom began to affect his health— though Mikes remarked that 'I see nothing else wrong with him'. (Letter 84, 20 August 1727.) His father took him to the nearby mud-baths and medicinal springs; Mikes accompanied them. He had been there before; the place clearly enjoyed a great reputation, and the Hungarians had visited it very soon after arriving at Rodostó.

'Not far from here, there is a place with a lot of puddles, about thirty yards square. About this time of year, those who are suffering from any illness bathe in the mud there. They come in carts, with their wives and children, from a distance of forty or fifty miles. You can see twenty or thirty carts round the mud; there is a multitude of men, women, and children lying in it, just like swine. . . . I don't know where the inhabitants got the idea, but they consider the mud very beneficial, though I have never observed that it did anybody any good. I myself went into that filthy mud, along with the others, not out of necessity, but in order to be able to say that I had lain in the mud. In summer this mud is also a favourite playground for the buffaloes. The Greek priests, in order to earn a few coppers, say that the mud must first be consecrated; otherwise it would do no good. But a mud-bath is still not enough; for in accordance with tradition and the command of Hippocrates, when you come out of the filthy mud, you have to go to the waters, and drink as much as possible for three days, if you want to be purged as clear as crystal. So we, wishing to follow the old-established custom of the people, went there and found at least two hundred men, women and children. But since the Greek priests lose no opportunity of making a few coppers, the water too must be consecrated; otherwise it would do no good. It flows out of the rocks, but even so is not pure; then the crowd of people disturb it, and drink the muddy water. We began drinking the day after our arrival; there was a large cauldron full of water over a fire, for the water must be drunk hot. Many of us drank; but, my dear aunt, what water! . . . We thought at first that it was like the mineral water we have at home, but when we tasted it, we couldn't swallow a drop; it was just pure salt water, and had a nasty taste into the bargain. All the same we had drunk on an average between eight and nine litres each by the third day.' (Letter 38, 23 August 1720.)

So when he went with the Prince and his son:

'We gave our young Prince a good drink. But you must drink these waters not by the glass, but by the goblet; so much that anyone who can fill his stomach with thirty litres by the third day has no further need of the remedies of Hippocrates. True, our young Prince did not drink as much as this, but the cure for his trouble is the monk's dance.[1] There is no better remedy than this; it is good for both body and soul, and there is no finer dance. Some historians say that the bridal dance is more gay; you know better than I do.' (Letter 84, 20 August 1727.)

But no remedy did any good, and György went back to France after a stay of only nine months. 'Our poor Prince, who is very

[1] i.e. patience.

fond of his children, parted from him with difficulty. But we know what is to be learnt in this country; nowhere does one become so bored as here. You can make no acquaintances, call on nobody, and if you have no occupation you enjoy, you turn all the time in an eddy of boredom. A gift of God is needed for everyone to spend his time as our Prince does; till lunch he reads and writes, and to see him after lunch, you would take him for a craftsman— he drills, carves or works at the lathe. His magnificent beard is often so full of shavings that he laughs at himself; he perspires as if he had to earn his bread by his labour. Everybody admires him, and he laughs at those who complain of boredom.' (Letter 88, 24 March 1728.)

References to boredom are pathetically frequent in the letters of this period. Mikes writes with that humorous bitterness which is the expression of a temperament the reverse of embittered, but he feels the need of a change of scenery. Wishing he were back on the shores of the Bosphorus, he writes: 'How I loved watching the huge great ships passing in front of my window, and all the beautiful little boats! Here I see nothing but the horrifying dark Armenian women.' (Letter 80, 7 May 1727.) And the rigorous regularity of Rákóczi's mode of life is irksome at times: 'I know no cloister where the rule is observed as it is with us. Certainly any of our number who becomes a monk would have no need to serve a year's novitiate, for here everything is done by the hour and the minute. I have a little dog; he knows the rule as well as I do. When the drum beats and I go to Mass, he doesn't so much as look at me; but as soon as it sounds for lunch, he jumps up at once and comes to me.' (Letter 80.) At other times, however, Mikes discusses exile seriously: 'To complain about the long duration of exile is useless and not good, because we do not thereby shorten it, but make it still harder and longer. Suffering is far more grievous when combined with restlessness, and suffering with complaints is prolonged by God, because when we complain we are, as it were, kicking against His will. If we could persuade ourselves that exile was given us by God for our good, we could endure it easily. Nor is it otherwise; for in all things God considers only our good.' (Letter 87, 19 February 1728.)

One of the worst effects of boredom is that it engenders discord and mutual suspicion. 'How many of our number have we buried, yet accursed envy survives through it all; only discord is in good health, and grows no older. Perhaps these things will also bury us, if God does not, of His goodness, take them from us. Exiles should surely live better than their brothers at home; but so far I have experienced only the reverse. Indeed, the more our numbers are reduced, the more do envy and discord multiply. . . . True, our devout Prince always tries to expel them from our midst, but so far he has not succeeded. . . . Since our arrival here, I have thought that the sole cause of this lies in the fact that exiles do not have to pay for anything, and soon grow tired of exile. They have few occupations, and become bored; if they live together, they grow tired of themselves, and of seeing nothing but one another's features all the time; finally from boredom springs the bestial bastard progeny of which we have spoken above.' (Letter 96, 24 December 1731.)

Life in Rodostó might be boring, but dramatic events were taking place in the outside world, and Mikes followed them closely. In 1730 the Sultan Ahmed III was deposed in a rebellion led by two Janissaries, the Albanian Patrona, and Musli Pasha. Mikes begins his letter on this subject (Letter 91, 5 October 1730) in a mood of breathless excitement, and proceeds to give a detailed account of the rebellion; then letter 92 (27 November 1730)—like its predecessor, one of the longest of all Mikes's letters—describes how the 'players' in the 'comedy' were 'paid', in other words how Patrona overreached himself, then walked into a trap set by the new Sultan, Mahmud I, to be killed along with his followers. In Europe, too, Mikes correctly remarked that the death of King Augustus would mean a war over the Polish succession (Letter 98, 4 March 1733), and the letters continue to record the course of events, until Mikes's whole attention was claimed by the onset of the Prince's final illness.

Mikes knew his master well enough to be able to detect that something was wrong, even when the Prince was still able to conceal his condition, and resist; he watched with close and anxious attention, for loyalty to his Prince had been his sole reason for following him into exile. As he had earlier said: 'I have spent my whole life in exile, and left my country for ever at the age of sixteen! It is certain that the quest of freedom was not in my mind at the time, and if my exile has lasted till now, the truth is that this has been due to my blind affection for my Prince.' (Letter 85, 8 November 1727.) His feelings are clear from a trivial yet revealing episode related in letter 111 (25 March 1735). Rákóczi was visibly shivering, and 'he asked me if I did not feel cold. I replied that the weather was pretty warm, and that I did not. He replied that he felt very cold. At this I was immediately terrified, but reflected afterwards that as spring advanced his health would change.' But it did not, and Rákóczi died shortly afterwards.

'8 April 1735. What we feared is now upon us. God has made orphans of us, and today has taken from our midst our dear lord and father, some time after three o'clock in the morning. Today being Good Friday, we must mourn the death of both our heavenly and our earthly father. God has postponed the death of our Prince till today, to sanctify the sacrifice of his death with the merits of Him who died for us on this day. Such was his life and such his death, that I believe the words "Today thou shalt be with me in Paradise" were spoken to him.

'Let us shed copious tears, for truly has the mist of grief descended on us. But let us weep not for our good father, because God has taken him after so much suffering into the heavenly abode where He gives him drink from the glass of bliss and joy, but let us weep for ourselves, that we have been made utter orphans. It is impossible to describe what great weeping and grief there is among us today, even among the humblest of us. Judge, if you can, in what condition I am writing this letter.' (Letter 112.) Then follows an account of the last days of the Prince. The Hungarians felt like a 'flock without a shepherd' (Letter 113, 16 April 1735), and instead of diminishing, their grief increased with the passage of time (Letter 114, 17 May 1735). Small wonder that Rákóczi had said in his memoirs: 'I cannot find words to express the marks of affection, loyalty, constancy and devotion which I have received.'

3

So far there have been surprisingly few references in the letters to Mikes's own duties. It is clear, however, that his functions were purely domestic and administrative. He was a steward, in charge of the domestic arrangements, the purchases, the servants. He appears to play no part in negotiations with the Turks, and does not hear immediately of major decisions, like the choice of Rodostó as the permanent home of the Hungarians (Letter 34, Yeniköy, 25 March 1720). In addition, Mikes's perpetual thirst for company and friendships contrasts strongly with the Prince's contemplative nature and liking for solitude. Yet the bond between them was very close; and it was only strengthened by their temporary misunderstandings, as on the occasion when Rákóczi queried an item in the accounts, and Mikes—momentarily and untypically— 'flared up' at the Prince's apparent lack of confidence in him, to repent later and to recall the episode sorrowfully after the death of the Prince (Letter 121, 15 August 1736).

Mikes's importance now greatly increased. He and his colleague Sibrik, the Prince's majordomo, were responsible for the funeral arrangements, for opening and reading the will,[1] and for the distribution of the allowance placed at their disposal by the Porte, which had sent an official, Ibrahim, to investigate their needs. Ibrahim suggested, and all the Hungarians agreed, that the Prince's elder son József should be sent for from Italy. The late Prince, too, had been eagerly hoping that József would come, but instead the young Rákóczi had been reported to be on his way to Rome. 'I think he should have come here first; but the love of a parent is deeper and more constant than the love of a son.' (Letter 107, 12 October 1734.)

Meanwhile Mikes's load of responsibility, and of sorrow, was further increased by the death of Sibrik—'our good father Sibrik' (Letter 117, 8 October 1735), whom he had plainly found a wholly sympathetic colleague. Sibrik had been in failing health for some time: 'I have cause to fear that the management of the whole household will fall to me, for Sibrik's illness grows more serious every day. And the thought of the predicament into which I shall have fallen by the time the young Prince arrives costs me hours of sorrow.' (Letter 115, 18 July 1735.) Mikes had, apparently, been largely in charge of the funeral arrangements, and had made a journey to Constantinople to bury the Prince in secret beside his mother, Zrínyi Ilona, the poet's niece.

After some months a letter arrived from József, giving full authority in the administration of the estate to Bonneval, the French soldier who, after fighting by the side of Prince Eugene against the Turks, in 1729 changed sides, went to Turkey, and adopted the religion of Islam. He had been a supporter of Rákóczi's; but Mikes was understandably saddened, and is undoubtedly

---

[1] The Prince left Mikes and Sibrik 5,000 florins each, but the money was in France and 'God knows when we shall obtain it' (Letter 113, 16 April 1735). He also left Mikes a watch and a ring (Letter 118, 15 November 1735).

right when he says that the late Prince too would have been saddened to see his son preferring 'to entrust his affairs and his estate to a foreigner rather than to those who have served his father from their childhood. But I can excuse him, because he does not know his father's servants, whereas Bonneval he did know, in Vienna, when he was a general, before he repudiated the faith.' (Letter 119, 18 January 1736.) Pending the arrival of the young Prince, Mikes had all the responsibility without the authority, for Bonneval was not on the spot; and there were severe financial difficulties to contend with. 'It is a month since we sent for him. Till he comes no one will be paid, though all will receive their board as before. This can be managed on the daily allowance of 10 thalers, but no one can expect more.' (Letter 116, 15 September 1735.) This was a drastic reduction: 'our poor Prince had 60 thalers per day; he could pay well, and did pay well' (Letter 116). Inevitably, there was trouble: 'A superior cannot flatter himself that he can win the affection of his subordinates gratis, if they can expect nothing from him, as mine cannot from me. But we must always make it our sole aim, that our subordinates shall love us rather than fear us.' (Letter 117, 8 October 1735.) Malicious tongues began to stir up feeling against Mikes for not distributing the late Prince's property, and to accuse him of keeping it back for himself. 'Let them speak, so long as I keep straight.' (Letter 120, 15 May 1736.) Still József did not arrive: 'The Prince writes in all his letters that he is coming, but he is not here yet. However, we are growing more and more needy, troubles and complaints are growing more and more bitter, and since they do not know whom to blame, they direct their complaints against me, as they see me all the time: I wouldn't mind, if only it did them any good.' (Letter 121, 15 August 1736.)

Finally, in December, József arrived, alone, though the exiles in Rodostó had expected both the brothers. To Mikes the young Prince was an unknown quantity; he looked angry on arrival, but the main thing was that he had come. 'I must rejoice, because I have been rescued from my troubles. There was no more than 10 thalers left for the expenses of the whole household. But He who gave us teeth will give us food.' (Letter 122, 6 December 1736.)

But the Hungarians soon found that 'the apple has fallen a long way from its tree' (Letter 123, 2 January 1737)—the Hungarian equivalent of 'like father, like son' being 'the apple does not fall far from its tree'. Mikes's initial impressions of the young Rákóczi were unfavourable, but he waited till March before writing on his new master at length. 'We expected this young Prince to be our comfort, but he has come to be our sorrow. The fine rule which his father had prescribed among us, which for so many years, till his death, he tried so hard to observe, and to make us observe, was upset by the son in a couple of days; . . . the mist of utter disorder has descended on our house.' (Letter 124, 8 March 1737.) Whatever may be thought about the rigours of the late Prince's 'monastic rule' (and Mikes himself had found them irksome at times), there can be no doubt as to the results of its sudden abolition. 'Order has been followed by utter disorder, wisdom by folly, goodwill by anger and estrangement; so much so that the thirty years of our exile have seemed less grievous than these last three months.' (Letter 124.) But one great load was taken off Mikes's mind, one cause of 'anger and estrangement' ended, when József instituted discreet inquiries into Mikes's stewardship, and 'found nothing against my honour. He admitted this to me himself.' (Letter 124.) About the same time there was an earthquake: 'Even the earth beneath us cannot rest.' (Letter 124.) Nor did matters improve, as is clear from letter 125 (20 July 1737), which also includes a penetrating and at the same time fairminded assessment of the Prince. 'I am amazed that we are standing on our feet and not on our heads. It is certain that God gave us many fine talents in this Prince. He endowed him with a splendid brain, and if he had been trained and educated as is desirable, his achievements would have merited praise. But his nature should have been bridled and disciplined in his early youth; instead he was left free in all things, and his nature became disorderly, changeable and inconstant—that is why he is so irascible and variable. He was never taught, nor was he induced by nature, to try to make himself loved rather than feared. He was not brought up amid plenty, but only without any constraint; yet he does not know the meaning of thrift, or how to keep what one has, or how to give, or what is love of one's country, because he has never been able to keep in touch with his country.'

Meanwhile war had broken out between Turkey and Russia, and in 1737 Austria broke the Peace of Passarowitz and entered the war as Russia's ally. Previously, the Turks had taken the greatest care not to do anything which might offend Austria; when Rákóczi

József, soon after his arrival in Turkey, paid a visit to Constantinople, the Porte had peremptorily ordered him to return to Rodostó at once. Now, however, the reason for such caution had ceased to exist, so he was summoned to Constantinople, and told that the Porte was now in the fullest sense the enemy of the Emperor, and proposed to use the Hungarian exiles to terrify him. 'If the poor Prince were alive now, what would he think? What would he do? I often heard him say that he did not desire war between the Porte and the Austrians, because he had a horror of fighting by the side of the Turks, and would rather die here than see Transylvania ravaged on his account.' (Letter 126, 13 September 1737.)

When József went to Constantinople he took with him a small party, of which Mikes was a member, and the Hungarians were royally received. There were no immediate developments, but soon after arriving in Constantinople Mikes had a most interesting experience—he saw an elephant for the first time in his life. He devotes the second, and longer, of the two paragraphs of the letter reporting his arrival in Constantinople (Letter 127, Constantinople, 16 September 1737) to a description of the 'great animal' of which he had heard so much from his childhood onwards. 'This great animal has a hide like a mouse's. His head is as it is shown in pictures; his ears are like a lady's fan. Two massive teeth grow out of his mouth, one on each side; they are as thick as my arm, but long, and cannot be used for picking up food—but it is certain that Nature has given them to him to use, and certain also that a turner with his lathe can produce many fine and precious works of art with them. But what I marvelled at most of all in this animal was his nose; though I cannot call it a nose, because there comes out of the end of his nose an appendage such as a turkey has. But this animal's is more than a yard long, and as thick as my arm. It bends like a whip, and its end is like a pig's snout. Two holes go all the way up it, as it were two hose-pipes. The animal draws in the water through this nose, when he drinks, and sprays himself with it when he washes; he feeds himself with it, and it corresponds to our hands. He picks up a copper or a bundle of straw with it, or fans himself all over, since he cannot use his tail for this purpose. Anyone he strikes with it is well and truly struck. In a word, you cannot imagine how useful it is to him, until you have seen. His legs are of uniform thickness, like columns, and are as thick as a man's thigh. The height of the one I saw was about eight feet, but it was only a baby. God is wonderful in His works. That's enough about that great animal.'

The pomp and generosity with which the exiles were now received were all too familiar, from Mikes's memories of the welcome accorded the old Prince when he first landed in Turkey; this was where Mikes had come in. 'We have begun the comedy; they imagine that the greater the honour they accord us, the greater will be the terror they strike into the Austrians. This is the second time I have seen such a comedy in this country. We'll see what our exit is like.' (Letter 128, Constantinople, 11 October 1737.)

On 3 December the reception reached its climax; the Prince was received in audience by the Sultan. 'Now, my dear aunt, I must write only of pomp. Today we have been through a great ceremony, which I will describe even if it is boring.

'Yesterday the Porte notified the Prince that he would have an audience of the Sultan today, so this morning at early dawn the Prince, with his whole court, went on board ship, to disembark at the Gate of Constantinople, where the Chauz Pasha (Commander of the Guard) was awaiting us, with many guards and horses. The Prince mounted the Sultan's steed; we also mounted our horses, and reached the Sultan's second gate at eight o'clock. When the Prince dismounted, he was made to sit for a short time in the gateway; this was simply to demonstrate that anybody, whoever he is, must wait at the gate of the Sultan. After a short while the Chauz Pasha announced that it was now possible to enter. Going through the second gate, we found ourselves in a courtyard almost exactly like the first one. In this courtyard, however, there were, on the right-hand side, a company of Janissaries, about a thousand strong; about five hundred dishes of food had been placed on the ground, some distance from one another. When we had reached the centre of the courtyard, there was a shout; whereupon the Janissaries, with a great roar, rushed on the dishes, as if on an enemy, each trying to seize a dish first. In a moment, there was not a single dish left on the ground. The custom is that the Sultan shall entertain the Janissaries in this way on pay-day; he interprets it as a very bad sign when the Janissaries are not disposed to run for the food. On the left-hand side, by the path, there were twelve steeds in line, each held on silver chains by two men. All these steeds were richly caparisoned, especially the last four, all of which had a harness studded with rubies; on their heads they wore plumes, and tassels worked with pearls. I have never seen finer or more splendidly decked horses than these. The Prince, preceded by two Chauz Pashas, went into the council-chamber. The Deputy Grand Vizier and the other high dignitaries rose, greeted him, and seated him in the usual place. The council-chamber is a large, square, vaulted palace. The Deputy Grand Vizier was seated in the Vizier's place in the middle by the wall, with the other officials on each side of him. Over the head of the Vizier is a small window, from which the Sultan can see and hear everything, but cannot be seen himself. . . .[1] In a short time two Chauz Pashas came for the Prince and led him in, having placed a ceremonial cloak of marten fur on his shoulders. As soon as he came before the Sultan, the Prince greeted him, and the Sultan replied: "Your father was loyal to me for a long time; I think you will follow his example." The Prince then left the presence of the Sultan (we were all wearing ceremonial cloaks too), and outside the second gate mounted the Sultan's steed, which had been given him as a present; we also mounted our horses and set out for our lodging. The Chauz Pasha preceded the Prince, and accompanied him to his lodging, and that was the end of the comedy, and of this letter.' (Letter 129, Constantinople, 3 December 1737.)

In his next letter (Constantinople, 16 December 1737), Mikes reports the deposition of a Vizier, a frequently recurring theme in the correspondence. Often Mikes reflects on the fickleness of fortune exemplified by a fall from so great a height of power and wealth, but eventually 'If we embarked on a sermon about the changeability and inconstancy of life and fortune every time a Vizier is deposed, there would be no end to it.' (Letter 170, 15 September 1747.)

The Hungarians now called on the new Vizier 'with great watery pomp—it was raining heavily' (Letter 131, Constantinople, 25 January 1738.) 'The Vizier gave the Prince a seat beside him, and after a short time had coffee brought; a cloak of marten fur was placed on the Prince, and we too were given cloaks. Then the Vizier and the Prince rose, and the Vizier handed the Prince the document in which he recognized him as Prince of Transylvania; the Prince handed the Vizier the text of the alliance with

[1] Like Suleiman in the *Siege of Sziget* (VIII. 21); cf. p. 26.

the Porte. They bade each other farewell—and we got our cloaks wet in the heavy rain.' (Letter 131.) The 'comedy' being finished, the Hungarians left Constantinople, and after a three weeks' journey through mud and snow reached Cernavoda in Rumania. The journey was relieved by the inhabitants of the 'good Bulgarian villages' where 'it was possible to find food, and plenty of wine. There is also a sufficiency of ham, which is a very rare delicacy in Turkey. But you must first make the sign of the cross before the Bulgarian woman, and then she will give you ham; otherwise she will not. The reason is that if she gave a Turk ham, and the others saw her, she would suffer for it. Cernavoda is in a horrible position, but it is a large village, and there are some fine houses in it. The inhabitants are half Rumanians, half Bulgarians, with only a few Turks. But there are rich merchants here; they trade most of all in Transylvania. The houses are all alike. I'd write more if I had any more to write.' (133, Cernavoda, 19 February 1738.)

At this stage, the Turks seemed both determined and optimistic that Transylvania would be won back; the Prince received a letter from the Vizier promising a force of 30,000 or 40,000 men ('but in this matter I am a Thomas', says Mikes (Letter 134, Cernavoda, 5 March 1738) and instructing the Prince to go to Vidin in Bulgaria. 'God knows what for. They are treating us like children, and mean to use us as scarecrows; the Porte thinks that as soon as we reach Vidin, the whole of Hungary and Transylvania will mount its horses and come over to us. Perhaps it might be so, if the old Prince were alive, but God forbid that anyone should come over to us now—and may He preserve you.' (Letter 134). There was also local diplomatic activity; Mikes was sent by the Prince to pay a courtesy call on the voievode, Constantine.

The ten days' journey to Vidin 'was not dull, because we went through very beautiful country, almost the whole way along the banks of the Danube. True, it was something of a desert, because the villages have been abandoned in the course of the fighting. This beautiful country is inhabited entirely by Serbs, who do not work very hard. The head-dress of the women is very ugly.' (Letter 135, Vidin, 7 April 1738.) The Prince was ceremonially received by the Governor, Hadsi Mohammed, who was about to set off with at least 50,000 men to attack Orsova[1] (Letter 136, Vidin, 11 April 1738).

[1] In Rumania.

'The centre (of Vidin) is not attractive; the suburbs are ugly, bare and muddy. But in the outskirts of the town there are fine squares. Here, however, we see sad sights every day—slaves being led from street to street, men, girls, women with children. She is a happy woman who is bought together with her child, for it often happens that mother and child are sold to different buyers; in an hour they part, never to meet again. What usually happened was that a Turk, wanting to sell a poor German, took him from street to street, shouting "Ten thalers, six thalers, five thalers"; but there were no offers. (The Turks were poor, and had not a copper for themselves, let alone enough to keep a slave.) Then the Turk, enraged that nobody wanted to buy the slave, took him into a coffee-house and sold him for a cup of coffee.' (Letter 136.)

On 5 July the Vizier arrived at Vidin from Niš[1] with 80,000 combatant troops and 'guns drawn by sixty buffaloes' to reinforce Hadsi Mohammed in the attack on Orsova. He invited the Prince to join him in his camp, at Kladovo,[2] 'a miserable Serbian village. The famous stone bridge of the Emperor Trajan was here, and a section of it still survives.'[3] (Letter 138, Kladovo, 11 July 1738.) Orsova fell on 15 August, and now 'they shout "Allah" there, and not "Wer da?"' (Who goes there?) (Letter 139, Kladovo, 26 August 1738.) The Turks, however, were still reluctant to invade Hungary; on 25 August the Vizier instructed József to make preparations to move against Temesvár[4] with a Turkish force of 30,000 men; but on the following day he was informed that the Hungarians would instead be going to Vidin. Mikes's reaction to this change of plan was thankfulness that 'God has saved our dear country from being pillaged.' (Letter 139.)

'Now we can say for certain that the comedy is over, that we have been honourably taken off the programme at the theatre, and that the Vizier has dispensed with our services without any ceremony.' This opening to letter 140 (Vidin, 1 September 1738) was prompted by a complete change in the Porte's attitude to the Prince; the Vizier had repeatedly snubbed him and invented transparent pretexts for not seeing him. Moreover, the Prince's health, which had never been good since his arrival in Turkey, had taken a decisive turn for the worse, and was further aggravated by

[1] In Yugoslavia.   [2] In Yugoslavia.
[3] This bridge is more commonly associated with Turnu Severin, opposite Kladovo on the Rumanian bank of the river. It is near the 'Iron Gate'.
[4] Now Timişoară in Rumania.

his fits of anger; by October he had become very ill, and was continually in a fever. He appeared to have no confidence in the followers of his father; in fact he allowed no one to come near him except 'a vagrant doctor, a cook, an Italian deserter (a musketeer), and two women. That is his court—people whom a few days earlier he did not know.' (Letter 143, Cernavoda, 7 November 1738.) On 10 November he died at Cernavoda aged thirty-eight. Mikes writes about him in a way which is critical yet charitable: 'The defects of this Prince lay not in his nature but in his upbringing. He had a fine mind and a good heart, but he had never been warned against anger. His outbursts passed off immediately, but occurred frequently. Nor had anybody ever advised him to seek to win the affection of others. In a word, if his father had been able to bring him up, his nature would have been quite different.' (Letter 144, Cernavoda, 10 November 1738.) Again: 'That he had no affection for his own nation need cause no surprise, for he had been brought up in a place where our nation is hated. But he had a particular dislike of us, whom his father loved. It is enough to say that the poor man's whole life and work in this country were just like a fire of straw.' (Letter 147, Cernavoda, 4 June 1739.) Much of what Mikes says about Rákóczi József is reminiscent of his earlier observations on the younger brother, György, especially as regards the defects in their character and education. The personalities of his sons were part of the old Prince's tragedy.

So the Hungarian exiles were once again without a head: but 'soon we shall not need a head. The other day we buried one more of our number; there is room under the shade of a plum-tree for those who remain now.' (Letter 145, Cernavoda, 15 December 1738.) Mikes was clearly pondering deeply on his exile at this time, and continues the same letter: 'The will of our Creator be done. He has held us up as an example before our whole nation, and happy are those who will learn from us, who will remain united with their country, who will not leave their nation and their inheritance for a cause as insubstantial as smoke. May God grant that nobody follow our example, and that the story of our long exile be heard with horror.

'But, my dear aunt, were we the first exiles? Certainly not. Did we learn from others? No. Will others learn from us? No. Why not? Because at all times particular reasons have led, are leading and will lead men into the situation in which we are now. He alone will be more fortunate whom the Lord takes as it were a captive into His own domain. I never had any reason for leaving my country other than my great affection for the old Prince; though before my heavenly Father there were also other reasons for my leaving. I must adore His decrees.'

József had requested in his will that he should be buried by the side of his father, but this wish was overruled by the Porte, and he was buried in a Greek Orthodox church at Cernavoda. Turkish officials arrived to take the control of the Rákóczi estate out of the hands of Mikes, to whom József had (surprisingly enough) entrusted it; they made an inventory of all the Prince's property, and sequestrated it. 'Such is the world!' (Letter 145.)

4

After the death of the Prince the party of Hungarians was broken up into small groups, to each of which was assigned a separate destination, so that they might be at hand in case of risings against the Austrians in different parts of Transylvania. Mikes was sent to Iaşi, by way of Bucharest. 'If I cannot see Transylvania I shall see her cloaks, for we shall be going past those snow-covered peaks. If I cannot drink beer in Zágon,[1] I will drink from the waters of the river Buzău,[2] and will greet them in your name too. ... Before I finish this letter, and put away my writing-things, I cannot resist telling you a little comic anecdote—I have written material for sadness in plenty.' (Letter 146, Cernavoda, 1 June 1739.) The earlier letters were full of anecdotes, but this is the first one Mikes has told his aunt since the death of the old Prince. It tells of how some thirsty Austrian musketeers obtained wine by pretending to bury a body at the gate of the house of a Greek priest, who gave them five pails full of wine to induce them to go away. 'Judge of the priest's amazement when he saw that the body stood up and was the first to drink the wine.' (Letter 146.)

'Our journey was a delight, and a bride might have been delighted to accompany us, for all the way from Bucharest to Iaşi she could

---

[1] Mikes' birthplace (see p. 64, n. 1.).

[2] This river rises in the Transylvanian Alps near Zágon and flows through the town of Buzău into the Danube. Earlier (Letter 142, Ruschuk, 14 October 1738), on a Danube trip with Rákóczi József, Mikes had contemplated, with similar emotions, the river Olt where it flows into the Danube at Nikopoli in Bulgaria.

have walked over all the many kinds of lovely flowers—everywhere the fields were carpeted with flowers, so that we rode over nothing but carnations and tulips. . . . If only our fleeting delight had not been mixed with the jitters; for we had reason to fear that some vagrant ruffians would come upon us. We'd have shown them our papers, with the Sultan's seal, but that would have had no effect, I know; and they'd have served us up to Lobkowitz[1] for lunch, even if they had to take us by force.' (Letter 149, Iași, 21 June 1739.) But Mikes did see the Transylvanian Alps—'I would gladly have gone to Zágon, but the Lord hid from me the roads leading there; the whole earth is His.' (Letter 149.)

Mikes had company on the journey, for his fellow exile Zay travelled with him as far as Iași. There, however, they parted, for Zay had been ordered by the Porte to go on to Khotin,[2] and Mikes found himself alone in an unattractive and unfriendly town; the boyars are 'like bears. I do not know whether it is in their nature, or whether they just do not dare to converse with strangers; but they are very savage. I have been with a few, whose coat of arms is an eagle with two heads—they claim to be of the family of the Canta-cuzeni. Perhaps my landlord too is of that family—I have looked at his coat of arms—although he is a tailor. That anyone here should call on a stranger, or invite him to lunch, as is the custom among men, is not a thing you need expect from these bears.' (Letter 150, Iași, 22 July 1739.) The voievode received Mikes officially, but showed little interest in him, and his feeling that he was the 'only inhabitant of the town' (Letter 150) was relieved only by the kindness and hospitality of the Archbishop, and by an Italian priest with whom he had his meals. The town itself 'is on a hill, but in quite a beautiful position. The inhabitants have to go a long way to fetch water. Five or six dilapidated monasteries enable one to call it a town; judging from the houses, one would regard it as no more than a village.' It had great possibilities as a commercial centre, being in this respect greatly superior to Bucharest. The surrounding country was exceptionally fertile, and 'where can you see finer cattle than here? Where can you eat tastier beef? And the wine is worthy to be served at any table. . . . But the inhabi-tants are like wild animals; they leave the wonderfully lovely and good earth uncultivated and live in the forests.' (Letter 150.)

[1] Christian Georg Lobkowitz, the Austrian governor of Transylvania.
[2] In the Soviet Union (Bessarabia).

Besides, 'every day you hear all kinds of bad news; the Russians are approaching Khotin; everybody is terrified and preparing to leave. May God take care of me! He knows why He brought me here.' (Letter 150.) Nor was there much likelihood of resistance to the invader; the voievode's army, on a generous estimate, was perhaps 1,500 strong. Soon the news that the Russians had crossed the Dniester caused panic in the town. 'Since I started this letter, my landlady has called me away three times, saying that the Cossacks are already in the town. I give her plenty of reassurances, but I too would rather not be here. From morning till night there is nothing but reports of the Cossacks. The only Litany you hear is "From the Cossacks, good Lord, deliver us". I am ceaselessly sending messages to the Deputy Viziers asking to be moved from here, and they are ceaselessly assuring me that they will take care of me. But I am ceaselessly in a state of unrest, as I have never been before. The hardest thing is that there is nobody here with whom I can speak a word. If only I could read or write—but it is impossible; there is a ceaseless din in front of our gate. I cannot set out on my own—it is impossible, until the voievode himself gives the word. It is misery to be here among these terrified people. There is no better course than to commend myself into God's hands.' (Letter 151, Iași, 23 August 1739.) Soon the danger drew even nearer, when the Cossacks occupied Khotin; the inhabitants of Iași, on hearing the news, moved their belongings into the churches. Finally, in early September, Mikes's representations to the voievode, and a personal interview, secured the necessary permission to depart, and he left Iași on 4 September, to his infinite relief. There was still danger, not now from Cossacks but from straggling groups of defeated Turks, but he reached Bucharest safely, where he had the delight of meeting one of the other Hungarians, Pápay, who was ill but overjoyed to see him; on the other hand, rumours about the Cossacks (who had taken Iași) were rife in Bucharest also. 'It's as if they were looking only for me' (Letter 154, Bucharest, 23 October 1739). And at one point they would have found him in bed, for he was completely immobilized for two days by a fever. 'You can judge, my dear aunt, what a state I was in, for on the very day when I was in bed and could not move a muscle, my servant told me that . . . the Cossacks were said to be not far away. . . . I was only waiting for them to enter my house, for I knew that they are such savages that they would not even present their visiting-cards.' (Letter 154.) However, after some blood-letting he recovered.

Then the rumours abated, and Mikes spent the winter in Bucharest. It was exceptionally severe, from the middle of October onwards. Conditions were the same throughout Europe, and people travelled in carts over the ice from Denmark to Sweden—an almost unprecedented occurrence. Only the arrival of a letter from his aunt saved Mikes from freezing, and 'if I don't freeze this year, I shall henceforward be unfreezable' (Letter 155, Bucharest, 15 March 1740.) 'Water, mill and miller' were all frozen; there was a terrible shortage of bread, and people snatched it out of one another's hands in the street. Fuel was equally scarce. Prices soared. The social problem was as hopeless as ever: 'there is a boyar here whom I have known since my childhood, but he shows not the least sign of friendship towards me.' (Letter 155.)

When peace was restored,[1] the Porte sent the Hungarians back to Rodostó, where they arrived on 21 June: 'you may ask what we did all the time on the journey. I don't know myself—all I know is that we slept a lot.' However, the journey was enlivened by the Bulgarian girls who danced and sang for the travellers in the villages, though the singing sounded like 'a locksmith's file on iron'; and the girls themselves were picturesque figures, decked in the copper coins which they used as jewellery. In addition, when you enter a Bulgarian village, an old woman comes up to meet you, with a riddle, and sprinkles you with grains of corn: 'you have to give her something, because she is under no obligation to sprinkle her corn over you for nothing.' (Letter 157, Rodostó, 22 June 1740.)

So 'God brought us back in safety to our old, gloomy home.' (Letter 157.) The party was now sadly reduced in numbers; of those who had originally followed the old Prince into exile, only four survived. Some of the most important figures in Europe, too, died about the same time: Pope Clement XII, the King of Prussia, the Queen Mother of Spain, the Tsarina, and above all Charles VI, so that the Habsburgs were now extinct in the male line. 'All these events may cause great changes in Europe' comments Mikes (Letter 160, 27 December 1740); in fact the struggle for the Austrian Succession was already impending. For the exiles, however, the old boredom returned. 'Having nothing to talk about, we just talk

[1] The war was ended by the Peace of Belgrade, signed in September 1739.

about the weather.' (Letter 161, 15 March 1741.) 'You ask, my dear aunt, what we do, and how we spend the time. In reply to the former question I say that our main occupation is eating and drinking; to the latter I reply that we sleep and walk on the beach. Is that not sufficient occupation for an exile? But we are waiting for someone to take us home, as in Jerusalem the sick by the pool of Shiloh waited for the angel to trouble the waters, and cast them in. But those waters were troubled by an angel, not by a man. Let us commit ourselves to the Angel of Wisdom. . . . I must wish for the good of my country and not only my own.' (Letter 164, 21 August 1741.) In addition Mikes had taken up gardening, and planted some vines. They produced two bunches of grapes, and 'I rejoice in them as much as if I owned the hill of Tokaj'[1] (Letter 161).

When the cause of Maria Theresa triumphed, the Hungarian exiles requested permission to return home. This was refused, and Mikes comments on the refusal with wry humour: 'We must be grateful to the Queen for excluding us from our country, where many things conspire to wear away one's life. Here we have no trouble with bailiffs or auditors; there are no lawsuits to give us a headache. No billeting-officer afflicts us. We have no worries over the acquisition or loss of estate. We do not envy another's lot, his honours, his advancement or his country seat. I imagine that others do not envy our lot either. We hear no landlady's grumblings or laments that she is without this or that. We do not have to rack our brains to think what estate we can leave our children, how to bring them up, what office or marriage we can obtain for them.' (Letter 165, 15 September 1741.)

For most of the time Mikes is as keen a correspondent as ever, awaits his aunt's letters as eagerly as ever, follows current affairs with undiminished interest: he still appreciates Rodostó ('How beautiful it is to live in a country town like ours—you can go out into the fields when you wish' (Letter 181, 16 September 1750)). At the same time there are signs of decreasing vitality. There is a gap in the correspondence from October 1743 till August 1746, for which no explanation is given; as Mikes himself says, 'Before we used to write to each other oftener; . . . perhaps we are growing

[1] In north-eastern Hungary. The adjective formed from the place-name 'Tokaj' is 'tokaji' (written without a capital); it is used substantivally in the sense of 'Tokaj wine'.

old?' (Letter 185, 20 May 1752). When his aunt asks for information on the Turkish court Mikes simply gives her, spread over six
years, a translation (made from Briot's French version, Paris,
1670) of extracts from Sir Paul Rycaut's *Present State of the Otto-
man Empire*. Morever, events are reported briefly, even abruptly,
often without comment; but the terseness of these later letters has
a character of its own, though wholly unlike Mikes's earlier
expansiveness; an example is the account of the recently deceased
Sultan Mahmud: 'It can be said that he was a great emperor:
also that he was fortunate in war: it can be said too that he had no
desire to commit acts of aggression, but wished to rule in peace.
Some attempts were made to stir up strife against him; but he
forestalled them, quelled them, and beheaded the ringleaders to
prevent a repetition. The people loved him greatly, both Christians
and Turks; he for his part was well disposed towards the Christians.
He ruled his empire peacefully; he was not cruel—he changed his
Viziers often, but not one did he put to death. It can be said of him
that he was a great emperor, though small in stature.' (Letter 194,
14 December 1754.)

In October 1758 the death of Zay left Mikes the sole survivor
of the Hungarian exiles, and the Porte created him a 'general'
(başbuğ). He now brought his correspondence with his aunt to
a close. 'When I wrote my first letter to my aunt, I was twenty-
seven; this one I am writing in my sixty-ninth year. Deducting
seventeen years from this, I have spent the remainder in fruitless
exile. I ought not to have said "fruitless", because there is nothing
fruitless in God's ordinances, for He orders all things to His own
glory. Therefore we must be careful so to use them, and then every
ordinance of His affecting us will be for our salvation. Then let
us desire nothing other than God's will. Let us ask for a life
sanctified, a good death, and salvation. And then we cease from
asking, and from sin, from exile, and from unfulfilled wishes.
Amen.' (Letter 207, 20 December 1758.)

He lived for three years more, before falling a victim to plague
in 1761; but his last years were brightened by the granting of
official permission to correspond with his relatives in Transylvania. He would not return home; as he explained to his half-
brother, 'the long years of exile, the life in a foreign land, I will
not say have become second nature to me, but I have grown accustomed to them'. It was too late to start a new life now; and

perhaps Mikes had already said his last word on the subject of his exile, in his final letter to his aunt.

5

As a record of Mikes's life in Turkey, the letters leave certain gaps; only a few of his fellow exiles are mentioned, for example, and of his literary activity apart from the letters[1] he tells his aunt nothing. Instead he writes of contemporary events, relates anecdotes, and above all expresses the faith which helped him to endure his exile. Second only to this faith comes his love for his country: 'I like Rodostó without being able to forget Zágon', he had said on arriving at his new home (Letter 37), and he never 'forgot Zágon' from the moment when he compared the great waves on the voyage to Gallipoli to the mountains of Transylvania. His description of Rodostó contains many comparisons with his homeland, although he had left home many years before; moreover, his love of his country prompts discourses on a wide variety of topics. For instance, one of the first things he noticed at Rodostó was the rich cotton crop, and in letters 60 and 61 (22 April and 23 May 1725) he returns to this subject from the point of view of the homeland. Cotton would not grow in Transylvania, he says, though it would in Hungary; 'but, my dear aunt, since cotton would not grow in our homeland, you could do the country another service, by which your name would deserve to be inscribed in letters of gold in the history of Transylvania. . . . I should laugh if you were the first to establish the silkworm there', and Mikes embarks on a long

---

[1] Mikes translated many religious and educational works by French authors, or from French versions. Of Charles Gobinet's *Instruction de la jeunesse* he did two translations, one as early as 1724, the second in 1744. (These were done from different editions of the original; the first is in dialogue form, the second a continuous exposition.) He also translated F. A. Pouget's *Institutiones catholicae in modum catecheseos* (1744): Benedict van Haeften's *Regia Via Crucis* (1747), which he sent to his relatives at home in 1759: Étienne François Vernage's *Pensées chrétiennes* (1747): Nicolas le Tourneux's *Histoire de la vie de Jésus-Christ* (1748): Nicolas de Mélicque's *Le caractère des vrais chrétiens* (1749): Claude Fleury's *Les mœurs des Israélites* and *Les mœurs des chrétiens* (1750): Antoine de Courtin's *Traité de la paresse* (1751): Augustin Calmet's *Histoire sainte de l'Ancien et du Nouveau Testament et des Juifs* (1754): and a commentary on the Gospels and Epistles by an unknown author, in 1741. He also produced, in 1745, an adaptation rather than a translation of some of the stories in Mme de Gomez's *Les journées amusantes*, a work on which he drew also for many of the anecdotes, and for other material, in his letters to his aunt. None of these versions (except the last) has been published, and none is mentioned in the letters.

discourse on silk and the silkworm (partly taken from Mme de Gomez), giving information both practical and historical, including the story of the importing of the first silkworms into Europe by Justinian. Mikes's dream was in fact destined to be realized, though not by his aunt, and (almost certainly) not till some years after his death.

Mikes's concern for his homeland shows itself very strikingly in his remarks on education. In letter 62 (11 June 1725) he observes that 'a country's happiness depends on the good education of its young people'—and proceeds to list the defects of the educational system in his own country. A boy never leaves his native village till he is ten or eleven, and by then evil communications have had plenty of time to corrupt good manners; he may attend some college from the age of twelve or thirteen till he is twenty-four or -five, but he learns nothing of many important subjects. Of physics the young noble knows no more than the miller or the blacksmith, of economics he is totally ignorant; he does not know which countries border on his homeland, or the course of the rivers that flow through it. All he acquires is some Latin and a smattering of Aristotle, and when he comes home he is ashamed to show even what little know-ledge he possesses; his only interests are in riding a fine steed, wearing a magnificent cloak, in hunting, drinking, and 'paying court to Venus'. He soon forgets the learning he has acquired, and 'if he did not have to write to his bailiff, perhaps he would forget reading and writing too'. Mikes also stresses the importance of the education of women: 'Is it not the case, my dear aunt, that a well brought up, well educated, intelligent girl, when she marries, will be able to bring up her son well, educate him and teach him, thus fitting him for the service of his country? Therefore, it is to the advantage of a country to give girls a good upbringing and educa-tion.' Mikes has in fact already urged that girls should be given a proper education, in letter 27 (Yeniköy, 18 June 1719), where he points out that a well educated wife will be a good correspondent for her husband when he is away: 'the husband would not wish to write to his wife merely about onions and tithe-wine, but he would also put down on paper the thoughts arising from other things they share, and from his love, if his wife could read and write; otherwise he will write to her as he would to a stranger. . . . To this some shamefully short-sighted mothers reply that it is not good for a girl to be able to write, for then she can write to her lovers. Ah! what clever talk is this! As if the writing was the cause of the evil, and not the evil the cause of the writing!'

A most conspicuous feature of the letters is the frequency of historical digressions, and of anecdotes. The historical digressions are sometimes on a considerable scale; replying to a query of his aunt's about the Templars, Mikes relates their history (Letter 71, 13 March 1726) in a way which earns her 'gratitude and praise'. He also likes to reflect on current events, with reference to the past; for instance, in letter 84 (20 August 1727), replying to a letter of his aunt's containing the news that the Queen of France has given birth to twin daughters, he laments the misfortune of so many ladies of royal birth in being sent to a convent; some queens have been great rulers. 'Let us look at England; her queens have always ruled well. Elizabeth was a very great queen. She would have been even greater, had she not dimmed the lustre of her reign in two respects: first, if she had not had her aunt (the wife of her younger brother)[1] put to death when she was so innocent; her greatest fault was her beauty, and the Queen hated her for it. This Elizabeth also gave perhaps ten princes her word that she would marry them, but . . . she died a maid. The joke is that she even sent a message to the Pope that she would marry him if he proposed to her. The other point is that she did great harm when she made herself the head of the Church.'

The anecdotes in the letters generally arise out of their context; the news that England and France are at war (Letter 199, 30 April 1756) prompts one of the rare anecdotes in the later letters, the story of the 'archduke of the ungrateful' which Mikes happened to be reading,[2] the Englishman who sold as a slave on Barbados the savage girl who had saved him from being killed by her tribe. By contrast, a story which really pleases him he will relate just because it 'occurs to' him. An example is the tale of Charlemagne's daughter Emma and her lover Eginhart, whom she carried through the snow so that no footprints should be visible; he tells this story twice (Letter 103, 15 March 1734 and Letter 200, 17 January 1757), the first time because it 'occurred to' him just when he was going to seal up his letter, the second time to make the point that no Sultan

---

[1] Mikes appears to think that Mary Queen of Scots was actually married to Edward VI.

[2] In a French translation of *The Spectator* (no. 11). This is the story of Inkle and Yarico.

would have behaved as magnanimously as Charlemagne did on this occasion. A typical Sultan is Mahomet II in the story of Irene, which incidentally inspired one of the landmarks in Hungarian drama, the tragedy *Irene* by *Kisfaludy Károly[1] (1820).

'After the capture of Constantinople a very beautiful maiden was taken to a Pasha, who handed her over to the Sultan on account of her beauty. The Sultan fell in love with her, and for three whole days spent all his time with her; nobody could approach him, and he issued no orders. The Vizier and the other Pashas took exception to this, and the Vizier was deputed to go to the Sultan and inform him that the whole army were at a loss what course of action to follow. The Vizier reported this to the Sultan, who commanded him to summon the Pashas into his presence. The Pashas assembled before him; the Sultan had the girl, whose name was Irene, most ceautifully dressed. The Pashas began to admire her beauty, and the Sultan asked them if it was not worth while to spend three days with so beautiful a maiden. They all shouted their agreement that it was. Then the Sultan said to them "Then why did you all grow angry, and why did you suppose that I had forgotten my duty? But I will show you at once that even if I love my pleasures, I can renounce them, and am worthy to be your commander." At this, incensed against the Pashas, he drew his sword and beheaded the poor girl . . . then immediately he had the councillors beheaded too. . . . Inability to take Constantinople would have been less shameful than this act of the Sultan.' (Letter 63, 7 September 1725.)

Mikes's liking for stories of affection and devotion, and his revulsion from their opposites, are absolutely clear. To take one further example, when he hears that the Spaniards have taken so many forts in Italy 'that they may be leaving nothing for next year', it 'occurs to' him to tell the story of the siege by Conrad III[2] of the castle of Weibertreu (as it came to be known) at Weinsberg in 1140. 'Since the surrender of the fort was delayed, he was wroth with all the inhabitants, and sent them a message that he would spare only the women, but would slaughter all the men. So on the following day every woman or girl had to leave the fort—but he allowed them to take whatever they could carry on their backs.

[1] See p. xxiii.

[2] Mikes, writing from memory, makes the besieging emperor Charles V and does not recall the name of the fort.

The next day, the Emperor, with his whole camp, was dumb-
founded at the sight of the women leaving the fort, all carrying a
man on their backs—the women carrying their husbands, the
girls their fathers. . . . The Emperor spared the whole town.'
(Letter 108, 14 December 1734.)

The letters give a vivid picture of Mikes himself; what of the
aunt to whom he confided his inmost thoughts? Her letters are a
constant source of delight to him; he waits impatiently for them,
and complains when they are too short. 'I have no cause for complaint, because your letters are coming to hand; but some are so
short that I reach the end when I have scarcely begun to read them.
I receive some letters which I could wish consisted of only two
words, because they are boring; but yours have so good a flavour
that I could almost eat the paper.' (Letter 75, 28 July 1726.) Her
letters make him laugh when he is happy (Letter 56, 15 September
1724), and when the Prince dies, 'if it were possible to find comfort,
I could find it in your letters' (Letter 116, 15 September 1735).
The correspondence is a source of no less delight to her; nor is
this surprising, as the content of her letters seems very similar to
that of his. She shares his interest in current affairs, in religion, in
history, in Turkish life and customs; her letters, like his, contain
anecdotes.

Of herself, however, Mikes's aunt appears to write relatively
little. We gather that she is a Transylvanian (Letter 32, Yeniköy,
10 October 1719), though apparently not a *Székely (Letter 162,
15 May 1741). It is clear from the last paragraph of letter 1 (p. 64),
that she had already been living some time in Turkey when
Rákóczi and his followers arrived there. It appears to be impossible for her to 'keep your promise, and spend three or four months
of the winter here with the Hungarian ladies' (Letter 32), though
she seems to be coming over for frequent short visits in this period.
But after a time we hear no more of these visits, and she does not
seem to be closely in touch with Rákóczi's suite in general, though
we gather that she had been friendly with Bercsényi's wife,[1] and
when the latter died, Mikes wrote 'I know you will be at the funeral'
(Letter 48, 26 April 1723). The aunt also became a friend of

---

[1] She also asked Mikes why Bercsényi's wife had a black nose, although her
face was white. The answer was that she had had her face gilded to conceal
pock-marks; then, later, she had wanted the gold removed, which had proved
a difficult operation, and left black stains on her nose (Letter 22, Yeniköy, 28
December 1718).

Zsuzsi's, and on the day of Zsuzsi's marriage to Bercsényi, Mikes writes: 'I know that the lady who today has become Bercsényi's wife will be writing to you, and that she can write about more secret matters than I can.' (Letter 50, 15 October 1723.) For a time, too, the Bercsényis had lived in Pera, the same part of Constantinople as Mikes's aunt; but she cannot have known them well at that time (although she had met them), because it is Mikes who tells her when the Bercsényis are moved out of Pera after representations by the Austrian Ambassador. True, he says 'perhaps you know this perfectly well', but he seems not to be quite sure (Letter 28, Yeniköy, 16 July 1719), though he implies in the same letter that his aunt and the Bercsényis saw a good deal of one another. But he often tells her of events in the capital where she is living; at first he is surprised, indeed embarrassed, that she should be asking him about the procedure when the Sultan receives an ambassador in audience (Letter 29, Yeniköy, 9 August 1719), but thirty years later he answers without comment a request for information about the Sultan's court (Letter 172, 20 May 1748). The aunt was not, however, in Constantinople throughout the period covered by the correspondence; during the Patrona rebellion she was in Paphlagonia (Letter 91, 5 October 1730), and about the same time Mikes reveals that she is living no longer in Pera (Letter 93, 25 March 1731), but in Adrianople (Letter 94, 15 April 1731). When Mikes goes to Constantinople with the coffin of the Prince, the possibility of meeting his aunt is not mentioned (Letter 115, 18 July 1735), nor does it arise when he goes there with Rákóczi József (Letter 127, Constantinople, 16 September 1737). In fact, it is not clear where she is living at this time; Mikes writes five letters from Constantinople (Letters 127–31, 16 September 1737–25 January 1738) followed by one from Adrianople (Letter 132, 5 February 1738), all without any reference to the possibility of a meeting. Besides, it is remarkable how little we learn about the aunt in other respects too; one letter (only one) mentions her son and daughter (Letter 62, 11 June 1725), where Mikes praises her concern for their education.

Who was she? In the book into which Mikes copied his letters to her, he headed them 'The Letters of M. K. to Countess P. E. in Constantinople'. But all attempts to trace her led nowhere. It is now just over a century since *Toldy, the pioneer historian of Hungarian literature, put forward the view that she was not a real person at all; and this solution seems to be placed beyond doubt (and it is now beyond controversy) by the last letter, quoted on p. 94. 'When I wrote my first letter to my aunt, I was twenty-seven; this one I am writing in my sixty-ninth year.' This clearly implies that the first letter of our collection is also the first letter Mikes wrote to his aunt; that first letter itself, (quoted on pp. 63 f.), however, implies equally clearly that they have been corresponding for some time. Again, the prayer and 'Amen' which conclude the last letter are, like the reference to the first letter, manifestly written as a farewell to the whole series; but real correspondences are not ended thus unilaterally.

Mikes copied his letters to his aunt into a book, which was preserved after his death at Rodostó, where there was still a Hungarian colony; it seems to have come into the possession of one Horváth István, a former galley-slave whom Rákóczi had ransomed. In 1786 Horváth, now in extreme old age, handed it over to another Hungarian, who brought it to Vienna, and gave it to the editor of a Hungarian periodical there. The news of its arrival was made public in this periodical, but the first edition of the letters did not appear till 1794.[1]

In 1878 an examination of the watermarks of the pages of the manuscript showed them to be divisible into three groups, and suggested that all the letters in each group were written, or rather that the fair copy was written, at about the same time. Letters 1–122, covering the period 1717–36, were copied in 1737 or 1738: letters 123–57, covering the period from the arrival of Rákóczi József in Rodostó (1737) till Mikes's final return (1740) were copied about 1740 (and headed 'Letters relating to the arrival of Prince Rákóczi József in this country'): the last group, covering the period 1740–58, were copied about 1758. But the letters were not necessarily composed and copied at the same time; and whether or not we regard the watermarks as conclusive evidence for the date of copying, most of the autobiographical passages in the letters must have been written very soon after the events described—the vividness and detail of the narrative put this virtually beyond doubt. Possibly Mikes kept a diary of his doings from day to day, and when composing his letters in their final form, made selections from this diary, at the same time adding other material—the digressions,

---

[1] This first edition was not complete, as the Austrian censorship required the omission of one letter (203); it was not restored till *Toldy's edition of 1861.

the anecdotes, and also some at least of the passages on current affairs, for these contain several anachronisms. For example, in letter 171, dated 15 April 1748, Mikes reports the Treaty of Aix-la-Chapelle, which ended the War of the Austrian Succession; in fact, however, the Treaty was not signed till 18 October 1748, preliminary agreement having been reached by the end of May. For each letter, then, there are four dates: first, the date on the text of the letter: second, the date of composition of the autobiographical matter, most often identical, in all probability, with the date on the letter: third, the date of composition of the letter in its final form, for which there is very often no definite evidence: finally, the date of copying into the book, for which we have the evidence of the watermarks.

But however exactly the work was written, there is no doubt of the achievement. Literary appreciation was slow to come; at first the letters were regarded rather as an historical source. Later, poets invested the last surviving follower of Rákóczi with an aura of heroic and patriotic glory, creating an imaginary Mikes who sometimes bore little relation to the real Mikes revealed in his *Letters from Turkey*. Nor should we forget the aunt to whom he wrote them; she may have been only a shadow, yet in a sense she overshadows all the other characters whom we meet in the letters. It is her benign inspiration which has made Mikes's exile the reverse of 'fruitless', in a way he cannot have foreseen. He stands out, in an age otherwise barren of literary achievement, as a writer who made Hungarian prose speak with a natural ease and a spontaneous fluency previously unknown, who created a style perfectly suited to express the character of the man.

III

VÖRÖSMARTY (1800–1855) * FROM CLASSIC TO ROMANTIC

I

To win fame by a Virgilian epic is a paradoxical opening to the career of a Romantic poet; and perhaps still more surprising is the fact that the fame which Vörösmarty won when his epic appeared in 1825 was above all a tribute to the man who had fulfilled the literary hopes of a nation. For the Hungarian classicism was not a fortress of established tradition to be assailed, but rather a foundation upon which he hoped to build a lasting literary revival and so save his culture from the extinction with which foreign pressures threatened it. So, in his appeal for subscribers to his epic, Vörösmarty could say that he 'considered this metre (hexameters) the most suitable, because it is commonly used for telling of heroic deeds by those languages which permit of scansion by quantity, and with us it is so well naturalized that it needs no commendation from me'.

Hungary already had her Horaces who with their lyre 'roused the seed of *Árpád from its slumbers';[1] but for decades she had awaited the advent of a poet who should sing how *Árpád and his Magyars settled in Hungary in A.D. 896, as Virgil had told of the founding of a kingdom in Italy by Aeneas and his Trojans. The Hungarian Virgil would be honoured no less highly than was Virgil himself as the Roman Homer. This was the honour attained by Vörösmarty with his epic, in ten cantos, *The Flight of Zalán* (*Zalán futása*), Zalán being the Bulgarian leader of the resistance to the Magyars.

Both the *Aeneid*[2] and the *Iliad*[3] had been translated into Hungarian hexameters; several poets had begun epics on *Árpád, though none had progressed beyond the earliest stages. However, the

---

[1] Vitkovics *To Virág Benedek* (*Virág Benedekhez*) (1805).
[2] By the Jesuit priest Baróti Szabó Dávid on whom see p. xix. His translation of the *Aeneid* was published in 1810–13.   [3] By Vályi Nagy Ferenc (1821).

Unitarian minister Aranyosrákosi Székely Sándor, in 1823, had produced a hexameter epic in three cantos on a similar subject, the settlement of the *Székely people in Transylvania. The young Vörösmarty had kept well abreast of these literary developments, and on the bookshelves of his father, a poor (though noble) farm-bailiff, had early found Virgil and Horace in the original. By the time he began his epic he had written a considerable quantity of poetry, much of it in the classical metres,[1] and burnt a good deal more because it was 'dry'; but very little of his work had been published, and several of his poems were rejected by editors, sometimes for unexpected reasons. In 1823, for example, *Kisfaludy Károly (whose own works show relatively little classical influence) returned a Virgilian pastoral poem submitted by Vörösmarty for publication in the almanac *Aurora*, asking 'Could you not work some Graecisms into this otherwise beautiful and sweetly composed idyll? The title, *The Shepherd and the Herdsman* (*A juhász és bojtár*), extraordinary though this may seem, will deter many readers. I myself have experienced this prejudice, especially among the fair sex.'

But however favourable the times might be for a Hungarian classical poet, the outlook for his country in 1823 was grim. The Diet had not been in session since 1812, when the Emperor Francis had dissolved it for refusing to agree to his financial demands; Hungary was under absolutist government by rescript, to which the counties were putting up a resolute passive resistance. The atmosphere of Vörösmarty's epic is accordingly as different from that of Virgil's as Hungary's history from Rome's, though both poems are inspired by patriotism.

Ancient glory of ours, where tarriest thou in the mists of night? Centuries have gone down on thee, and thou walkest alone, with dying light buried deep beneath them. Over thee float dense clouds and the unwreathed form of gloomy oblivion. Where is one who, giving his bold lips to the song of war, shall arouse with his words the clarion call of the dark depths, and after the tardy centuries shall worthily bring before our eyes the leader *Árpád of the leopard-skin, and the power of his people, destroyers of armies?[2]

[1] Including, for instance, a Horatian ode on Szigetvár (1822).

[2] Régi dicsőségünk, hol késel az éji   Fénnyel jársz egyedül. Rajtad sürü
  homályban?   fellegek és a
  Századok ültenek el, s te alattok   Bús feledékenység koszorútlan alakja
  mélyen enyésző   lebegnek.

This, then, is an epic of war and conquest: 'flag-decked pikes and sword-blades cleave the air before my soul', sings the poet (I. 27–28). At the same time, he finds the battle-scenes uncongenial, indeed painful to compose: 'O while my lips tremble as they sing of the slaughter, hide away, ye fair shining stars, in the heavens, that dark midnight may descend on my brooding soul' (v. 281–3). Moreover his Virgilian sense of the tragedy of war easily overspills into a sympathy for the defeated which comes near to frustrating the main purpose of the epic. True, the enemy leaders whom we see in the Catalogue in Canto II are mostly monsters or villains—'terrible Viddin . . . like a ravening tiger' (31–32), the bastard Csorna who 'cares nought for God or man' (51), Philo of Ossa 'than whom there is none more cunning in the East' (98)—but Zalán himself enlists our sympathy at the outset: 'Princely Zalán sadly surveys the broad plain of Alpár. Now his castle is gloomy and silent as an estate of yellow Death, and in its decline has changed the pomp of the past for humble mourning. Proudly it stood before; powerful over the foe, offering good cheer to a neighbour who approached with goodwill, ceaselessly it rang with the noise of unbridled merriment. Now the sound of plaint and wail breaks its deep silence; and in the emptied halls stumble with feeble step terrified women, soulless men, and knights who have come from the deadly battle, mutilated by their wounds' (I. 35–45). Nor is the effect produced by this passage counteracted by the peremptory tone of the ultimatum which Zalán sends to *Árpád, to 'clear out of my land, even today' (I. 79); we soon find the enemy leader described as 'Zalán persecuted by Fate' (I. 102), and in the last line of the whole epic, as he flees to Belgrade after final defeat, 'wrapped in grief, he looked only from afar on his own'. Indeed, the title of the epic itself reveals Vörösmarty's unconscious sympathy for the beaten foe; others who tackled this theme proposed to entitle their work '*Árpád' or an 'Árpádiad'.

However, the enemy leaders are at least differentiated; the Hungarians, on the other hand, tend to be monotonously idealized warriors. When we first see *Árpád (I. 157), only his external appearance, his mighty form, is described; though invested with

Hol vagyon, aki merész ajakát hadi
dalnak eresztvén,   5
A riadó vak mélységet fölverje sza-
vával,

S késő százak után, méltán láttassa
vezérlő
Párducos Árpádot s hadrontó népe
hatalmát?   (*Zalán*, I. 1–8)

all the virtues of the perfect soldier and leader, he remains a some-what shadowy figure. He tells his men, as he sings to them in camp, that he wishes to be remembered after his death simply as the 'princely leader of the armies fighting for the homeland' (VI. 361); and for the reader he is just this, and no more. He commands the devotion of his men, but not the inspiration of the poet. He is pious, but the god to whom he prays and sacrifices is a purely synthetic creation by Vörösmarty (based on the deity in Székely's poem), an imaginative attempt to reproduce the religion of the early Magyars, of which virtually nothing is known.

There are two principal deities in *The Flight of Zalán*, Hadúr, literally 'Lord of Hosts', and Ármány, in whom Vörösmarty por-trayed the Zoroastrian Ahriman. Hadúr is essentially a sun-god (e.g. VII. 1); on one occasion his rays miraculously revive a dying hero (X. 153 ff.): Dawn is his servant (VI. 588). At the same time he is anthropomorphized to the extent of fighting with a sword (VIII. 497) and reaching out with his hand to tear up a mountain peak with which to smite the evil power in their decisive duel (VIII. 562). Ármány, attended by Curse, Fear, and the centaur (VIII. 539) Tumult, is a huge 'man-eating' winged dragon (VIII. 510), armed with a spear—a real monster of folk-lore. Partly, though only partly, because they are not introduced at the outset, these deities do not make *Árpád appear as the instrument of any higher power or cause, except in so far as his final victory is pre-ceded by the combat between Hadúr and Ármány, in which the latter is slain, and his 'evil soul' flies back to Hell (VIII. 578). There is certainly a very difficult problem for the poet here, as Christian and classical deities would be equally inappropriate to the subject, and no obvious alternative solution suggests itself; but this attempt to reproduce the beliefs of the heroes scarcely gives the epic a convincing religious background.

Moreover, both the god and the leader of the Hungarians are only part-time participants in the action; this is particularly true of *Árpád, of whom we see nothing for long periods. Much of the poem is in fact taken up by episodes which are irrelevant as well as independent. Not that *Zalán* lacks any of the regular in-gredients of classical epic: battles, catalogues of heroes, debates, are all here; but we completely miss that sense of structure by which Zrínyi (at the same age and writing in far greater haste) brings the course of events gradually but surely to its appointed end. The *Iliad* has been described as a 'drama with retardations'; in *Zalán* we have the retardations, the episodes, but no drama.

For the most important of these episodes Vörösmarty transports us into fairyland. He does this almost apologetically: 'Great-hearted leaders, let me leave the battlefield for a little while . . . let me weave a tender garland for faithful love. Perhaps she is not unworthy of song, who receives in her bosom the hero when he returns tired from the terrible combats' (I. 378 ff.). So the poet introduces the story of the maiden Hajna and her love for the hero Ete, which runs right through the epic. When we first see Hajna, she is 'scouring heaven and earth with her eyes' in search of her lover, and as she bathes in the river Bodrog, the child of Dawn, a Fairy of the South, approaches on his steed and is captivated by her beauty; but she rejects his love and will not follow him. Her brother finds her, and takes her home, where Ete joins them (I). Soon, however, Ete must go forth again into battle, for he has offered himself, when Ármány demanded a victim (II); he is wounded, but Hadúr saves his life (III). Then the native peasants rise against the Magyars, and Hajna's father is obliged to flee, with his household; on the journey they are pursued and Hajna is lost (V). Hadúr, however, sends a guardian spirit, attended by fairies, to protect her and lull her to sleep. The Fairy of the South now reappears, drives away the guardian spirit, and awakens Hajna by his embrace; but again she rejects his love, and this time his life is forfeit to Hadúr. After the Fairy's death his magic steed, Tomboli, gives utterance and tells Hajna that his master had instructed him to carry her whithersoever she wished (VI); so she is finally reunited to her lover (IX).

*Kazinczy[1] may have found the fairies a poor substitute for classical mythology; but in this fairyland a new poetic diction was born.

Flow slowly, Bodrog, in the silent bosom of thy sandy bed, glide softly through the woods, warm western breeze, disturb not the maiden as she thinks of the noble young hero, and leaves all else forgotten far away.[2]

---

[1] Letter of 16 March 1827 (Váczy No. 4751 (Vol. 20)).

[2] Folyj lassan, Bodrog, föveny ágyad   Meg ne zavard a lányt, mikor a deli
    csendes ölében,   hősfire gondol,
    Halkva suhanj el az erdőkön, langy   És minden mást messze felejt.
    nyugati szellő,   400   (I. 399–402)

As Hajna bathes in the river,

The sun had now reached its setting, and wrapping its pure horizon and the Western regions in a faint hue of flame, surrendered water and earth to the cool mist of eventide. Then on a dun steed, by the cold light of the stars, came the fair child of Dawn, a Fairy of the South, like a flying cloud, gliding in the clear air. His radiant golden hair sparkled, and was drawn back behind him, with the leopard-skin over his shoulder, on the wings of the gentle breezes; on his left side his sword clattered in its golden scabbard, and in his hand he held his lovely pipe, which gleamed with pearls.[1]

This and similar passages are among the earliest literary fruits of the reform of the language, and are of historic importance; nevertheless they do not provide variety within the epic, but rather transport us outside it. There are other departures too from epic convention; not the least important of these is the poet's reference to himself in the proem. 'Having hung with the carefree eyes of a child on the fleeting beauty of the maiden, and changing to plaints the songs of my joy, that was lost to her, I filled heaven and earth with useless pleas. But now that the storm-tossed days of my youth are past, I feel in me the power—and have faith in my power—to sing of *Árpád (I. 14 ff.). In November 1817 Vörösmarty became tutor to three sons of a wealthy landowner in south Hungary, Perczel Sándor, in order to keep himself at Pest University, which he had entered the same autumn; his father had died in July of that year, and as the eldest son he had become the breadwinner of a large family. It is in a poem[2] dating from the spring of 1822 that he first mentions a 'vainly yearning love'; he had fallen deeply in love with Perczel Etelka, the sister of his pupils. His love was not avowed, not reciprocated; in any case

---

[1] Alkonyodásra jutott már a nap, s
    tiszta határát
  És a nyugvó tájt bágyadt lángszínbe
    borítván,
  Általadott vizet és földet hüvös esti
    homálynak.   440
  Ekkor barna deres paripán, hűs
    csillagi fénynél
  A Hajnal szép gyermeke jött, egy
    délszaki tündér,

Mint repülő felleg, szállván a híg
  levegőben.
Tündöklött pedig ékes arany haja,
  s a kacagánnyal
Lenge szelek szárnyán maradozva
  utána huzódék,   445
Balja felől aranyos hüvelyében csat-
  toga kardja;
És vala gyöngyökkel ragyogó szép
  sípja kezében.   (I. 438–47)

[2] The Alcaic poem *To my friend Teslér* (*Teslér barátomhoz*). Teslér was the friend who first introduced Shakespeare to Vörösmarty.

there were insurmountable social barriers, for Vörösmarty's family, though technically 'noble', was humble and poor. It was Etelka who inspired the portrait of Hajna, as the poet tells us himself:

Valley of the South, ancient homeland of the secret of my heart, there too the lovely eyes of a maiden blaze, with like fire. She spares me not, but slays me, even afterwards, with her shining radiance. Whither have I thus strayed? . . . I return, Hajna, to thee.[1]

And the tragedy of the Fairy is Vörösmarty's own tragedy. 'Maiden, weep not,' the Fairy's last speech begins, 'let not your laments disturb the end of my existence. Maiden, weep not, my love no more moves me to grief' (VI 568–9). It was this tragedy, more than anything else, which brought out the poet in Vörösmarty. At the same time it is clear that Vörösmarty, though a great hexameter poet, was not primarily an epic poet; and once the appearance of *Zalán* had served its purpose as a status-symbol for the national literature, it was soon forgotten; indeed even at the outset it found few readers. Politically, it could not have appeared at a more opportune moment; its publication coincided almost exactly with the Emperor's decision to repent and convoke the Diet. It was widely, though not unanimously, acclaimed; the Hungarian Virgil had come. On the other hand, of the eighty-eight subscriptions about one-third came from personal friends of the poet: *Kazinczy, though as the translator of 'Ossian' he was pleased by the Ossianic opening, found the poem as a whole hastily composed and deficient in the classicism on which he had based the revival of Hungarian literature.[2] For his juniors, now a majority, epic itself was an outdated form. The link between literature and life, so conspicuous in Zrínyi, had snapped; not only was Vörösmarty himself a civilian, but warfare had changed—generals now won their victories not by displaying in single combat the virtues of the tawny lion, but by watching troop movements through a telescope or by sticking pins into maps. By 1838 we find the poet himself remarking that *Zalán* was known only by name, and that everybody praised it rather than read it. Nevertheless he had found

[1] Délnek völgye, szivem titkának régi
hazája,
Dél völgyében is ily tüzes a lány
szép szeme. Rajtam

Nem könyörűl; de megöl ragyogó
sugarával utóbb is.
Vagy hova vesztem el így? . . . Meg-
térek, Hajna, tehozzád.
(IX. 37–40)

[2] Letter of 16 March 1827 (Váczy No. 4751 (Vol. 20)).

the Virgilian hexameter a most congenial medium, and continued till 1832 to use it for long narrative poems, though not for another epic. He did in fact plan one, but never completed it.

The successors to *Zalán* meet the main criticisms to which the epic is open; first of all, though the poet's imagination still takes him to fairyland, as in *The Valley of the Fairies* (*Tündérvölgy*) (1826)[1] and the unfinished but remarkable *Island of the South* (*A Délsziget*) (1826), fairyland and history are kept apart, in separate works. Secondly, the historical poems bring us progressively nearer the present: *Cserhalom*[2] (1825) relates an episode of the Cumanian attack on Hungary in 1068, *Eger* (1827) describes the heroic and successful resistance of the defenders of that town, commanded by Dobó István, to the Turkish besiegers in 1552. The background to the poems becomes correspondingly less nebulous; in particular the siege of Eger is well documented, and was sung by *Tinódi, the greatest of the sixteenth-century bards, only a year after the event, in 1553.

Cserhalom, in a single canto (745 lines), tells the story of Etelke, a Hungarian maiden whom the Cumanian chieftain Árboc has taken prisoner. She is of outstanding beauty; as another Cumanian puts it,

Fair is the swan, when from the skies of her homeland afar she quietly comes to settle on the waters of a foreign lake. There, lightly poised, she cleaves the waves, as moon and stars descend to her with silver rays to sport. Happy art thou, Árboc son of Böngér, lovelier is thy maiden than the swan, and no darker is her breast than its plumage.[3]

Árboc guards his treasure in his tent, and not only is 'slow to bring her into the general rejoicing' (78) with which the Cumanians are celebrating their victories, but rejects a demand from the King, Ozul, to hand her over to him. Etelke, for her part, while

---

[1] The only poem of the group not in hexameters; it is written in the stanza used by Zrínyi in his epic.

[2] A hill near the Transylvanian village of Kerlés (now Chiraleş in Rumania), the scene of a Hungarian victory over the Cumanians.

[3] Szép a hattyu, midőn távol hon- Hold és csillag ezüst sugarakkal
jának egéből   játszani hozzá.   95
Csendesen érkezvén idegen tó hab-   Oh Böngér fia, boldog vagy, szebb
jain űl le.   a te leánykád,
Ott az özönt könnyű lebegése hasítja,   S nem feketébb, mint a hattyúnak
s leszállnak   tollai, keble.   (92–97)

expressing affection for Árboc, warns him of the might of the Hungarians, and asks to be restored to her father. Árboc refuses, in a speech which for all its tenderness, for all the beauty of the description of the island in the East to which he declares he will take her, has menacing overtones; but now the Hungarians attack. Among the attackers is Etelke's aged father, who has roused his countrymen to battle; they win a decisive victory, in which Ozul is killed by the Hungarian hero, Prince László.[1] Árboc flees with Etelke, but is overtaken and slain by László, to share the fate of his king. The maiden now kneels before her rescuer and begs to be allowed to bury Árboc, who 'was not cruel; he fell at my feet with the fair speech of love' (687–8). The request is granted, then László takes Etelke back to her father.

Cserhalom solves the problem raised by the prominence of the sub-plot in *Zalán*; the roles of history and episode are reversed—the story of Etelke is the main theme, to which the historical battle supplies the background. The result is wholly successful; the characters live as *Árpád never could. In *Eger*, on the other hand, the poet makes the siege itself his main subject, and now succeeds, primarily because enough is known about the action for his purpose. The poem extends to three lengthy cantos, 2,760 lines in all; yet the episodes, without losing any of their vividness, remain episodes.

The siege itself is splendid material, more varied than the siege of Szigetvár, which it rivals in heroism, though different in the outcome. The debate in the Hungarian Diet, to which Dobó's lieutenant Mecskei appeals for help: the heroism of the defenders in the siege, and the vital part played by the women and other noncombatants whom Dobó had providently brought into the fortress: the ingenuity of Bornemisza Gergely, the Archimedes of the Hungarians, in inventing incendiary devices ('wreaths of flame', II. 559) with which to attack the besiegers—the same Bornemisza whose plea for unity had been the decisive speech in the Diet: the two Turkish embassies, especially the second, in which Dobó compels the envoy to eat the paper on which his message is written—then before he has finished the Hungarians show mercy, and give him a drink: the treachery and punishment of the Hungarian, Hegedűs: the night raid by the three Nagy brothers, with the same tragic outcome as the raids of Nisus and Euryalus,

[1] The future king (reigned 1077–95) and saint (canonized 1192).

Radivoj and Juranics: the final abandonment of the siege by the
Turks—all this is true drama, and Vörösmarty knows it. The
proem itself is dramatically conceived, and written in the present
tense, as if by a contemporary of the events to be described. The
poet brings out, too, the basic difference between the two sides,
no less vividly than Zrínyi, though without the same religious
emphasis;[1] the Turks are ruled throughout by terror and cruelty,
the Hungarians (except for the traitor Hegedűs) are as closely
united as the men of Sziget. Dobó himself, though not quite a
Zrínyi of Sziget, is a fine leader of men, from the opening reference
to his 'eagle's eyrie' (I. 14) onwards; and he appears not only as
leader but as father, for his daughters, Dalár and Ída, are in Eger
too, nursing the wounded. It is the tragic love of Ída for the Turk
Omár which forms the subject of the principal episode.

We first see Omár as a Turkish envoy, on the earlier of the two
embassies; there he is silent, 'seemingly pondering other things'
(I. 75), and the sight of Ída moves him to tears. Only later does the
poet reveal that he is a renegade Hungarian who once loved Ída,
but believing his love to be unrequited, deserted in despair to the
Turks—and now bitterly regrets his desertion. He will not fight
against the country of his birth, and when battle is joined he flees
towards the Hungarian lines. For this the savage Turk Arszlán
stabs and all but kills him; the Hungarians approach and are
moved by his pleas for mercy, in their own language. They take
him back on their shields to Eger, where he comes under the care
of Ída herself, and pours out his sorrow at having yielded to the
whisperings of 'pain and the devil of jealousy' (II. 366); he reaffirms
his love, to which Ída responds by kissing him, before going to
seek assistance; but when she returns he is 'wounded no more'
(II. 469), and she does not long survive her lover. This tragedy of
human frailty is not free from that sentiment which the twentieth
century views so differently from the nineteenth; yet it has true
pathos, and provides exactly the right contrast to the successful
heroism which forms the main subject of the poem. In addition, a
contrast to the story of Ída is provided by the brighter—and
lighter—tale of the love of a Turkish maiden for her Hungarian
captor.

---

[1] In the battle by the church (II. 721 ff.) the poet contrasts the din of war
with the 'gentle voice' of the bell, and the Turks are sometimes described as
'pagans'; but such references are incidental.

Between *Cserhalom* and *Eger*, Vörösmarty wrote *The Valley of the Fairies*, which develops the inspiration of the Ete–Hajna episode in *Zalán* just as the historical narrative poems continue the main theme of the epic. It begins as a knightly romance, and Vörösmarty discards the hexameter in favour of the four-line Alexandrine stanza (the metre used by Zrínyi for his epic) in which was written the sixteenth-century romance *Argirus* by Gergai Albert, an adaptation of an Italian 'bella istoria'.[1] Vörösmarty also evokes the atmosphere of the Argirus-romance by introducing archaisms into his language. The hero of *The Valley of the Fairies*, Csaba, fights for the fair maiden Jeve with his rival Döngöre; during the combat Döngöre deliberately casts his spear at Jeve and deals her a mortal wound. As she is dying, the 'shining child of the Sun' descends, and, having covered her with the raiment of a fairy, transports her 'beyond the sun to a star lovely with groves' (stanza 49); so when Csaba slays Döngöre, his victory has lost all its meaning, and he throws away his sword, disconsolate. But at the behest of Jeve's father he goes forth to fight the fairy who has captured his beloved, and after successfully repelling bears and snakes he reaches the Valley of the Fairies. Now the waters swell to a flood, and dragons swoop down from the heavens, bringing a storm; but calm is restored, and now arises 'a fair maiden of the sea, in pure foam' (120). It is Jeve, who recognizes Csaba, and they embrace; but the hero, though certain that this maiden can help him, does not realize who she is; and the harsh insistence with which he tries to extract from her an answer to his question where he can find his beloved, causes her to shrink back in fear. Csaba now must fight dragons, fairies, finally the child of the Sun himself, before he can restore Jeve to her father. Only when she has returned does she wake from the magic sleep in which the child of the Sun had wrapped her, to be at last reunited to her lover.

Here Vörösmarty gives free rein to the 'flame of his imagination' (stanza 1), to achieve just such a romance as the Ete–Hajna story in *Zalán* might have become had it been an independent work and not part of an epic. The poet himself soon came to take a cynical view of *The Valley of the Fairies*, and *Bajza was right to describe it as 'a work of eternally great value, written for an eternally small public'; but the theme was perfectly suited to Vörösmarty's genius.

[1] See p. xv.

In the same year as he wrote *The Valley of the Fairies* (1826), Vörösmarty returned to the hexameter for *The Island of the South* (*A Délsziget*); but the material of this poem is as far removed from epic as could be imagined; it is, in fact, 'a new theme of which I write, one great, pleasing, terrible, a small child and a barren island in the South' (3–4). In the first line the poet, like a priest at an ancient mystery-rite, bids the uninitiated keep at a distance, and there is a mystical element in the poem. It appears to be an allegory of the childhood of the human race, together with the Fall, somewhat resembling a Platonic myth; but as it was never finished,[1] its precise meaning must remain uncertain, though the opening plainly suggests that man's power over his environment is due to a gift from God rather than to his own ingenuity. At the beginning of the poem, when the boy in his 'lost boat' has been driven by the sea on to a 'blessed island', the voice of a star brings him 'news from God, good news . . . let the treasure of Nature be opened unto you' (I. 62–63); and in a short time a heather-bush gives utterance and provides the boy with 'a pipe embracing many voices' (I. 133), by which he gains power over the winds and the beasts. Later a girl emerges; the boy saves her from the 'son of Death' and they live together, 'their hearts untroubled by the siege of love' (I. 593–4).

At the opening of Canto II a voice from Heaven gives them names.[2] Soon they kiss for the first time, whereupon the island splits open and parts them. The boy Hadadúr cries out against the cruelty of Heaven, and a storm carries him away into a desert; the girl Szűdeli, who shed tears but did not curse, is borne along by a gentle breeze; groves and brooks spring up in her path, and fairies build her a palace. Meanwhile Hadadúr, forsaken and famished, barely restrains himself from killing a child in his despair; but then he is fed by three ravens, who let fall into his lap the meat over which they are fighting, and his faith in God is restored. The poem breaks off just after the opening of a new episode, with the appearance of armour and a steed for Hadadúr.

The Island of the South promised to be one of Vörösmarty's masterpieces; but even the existing fragment is far more than

---

[1] One canto (611 lines) and part of another (306 lines) were completed.

[2] Hadadúr and Szűdeli. The boy Hadadúr, we have already been told (I. 24), is 'the child of lightning-souled Attila', which indicates a connexion with the Hun-legend.

merely tantalizing. Here is part of the description of the emergence of the girl:

There the form of a young maiden floated gently forward. When the gaily coloured little bird, escaping from the black cleft in the rock, had rowed on free wing to Heaven, its first song of joy gave birth to this sweet maid, in the pure heights of ether; breezes reared her, rocking her on grasses and a carpet of scarlet flowers. The stars of evening descended to cover her tender limbs, and the virgin dew gave her milk to drink; her soul was light, a pure ray of light eternal.[1] [The bird had been captured by the boy so that he might have it to sing for him until his pipe had absorbed its song.]

The Island of the South was followed by *Eger*; then Vörösmarty came to accept the fact that only heroes could write heroic poetry. As he said in his poem *Zrínyi* (1828), 'As the eagle is conceived on high amid storms, and is hatched out in grim rocks near the home of the lightning: so you brought into the world, amid the flashes of battle, the thoughts your mind conceived as you fought; that is why the murderous struggle seethes . . . in your song.' (58 ff.) Thus none of Vörösmarty's three remaining hexameter poems is truly heroic. The first, the single-canto *Széplak* (1828)[2] describes how a knight of King *Mátyás, away from home fighting Czech marauders, allows his already jealous mind to be poisoned by rumours of his beautiful wife's infidelity; so when he returns to find her reading what in fact is a wholly innocent letter, he kills her on the spot, to be then tortured to death by remorse when he has read the letter and so learnt the truth. The story is movingly told, especially in the portrayal of the wife, and of the youth to whom she offers innocent hospitality; but it is rather a subject for a ballad than for 482 hexameters.

Széplak was followed in 1830 by *Rom*, an allegorical poem in which the deity Rom (=Ruin) vows to fulfil three wishes for the

---

[1]   Ott egy kis lánynak alakja
Lenge szelíden elő. Mikor a vak
    sziklatorokból
Megmenekedve szabad szárnyakkal
    evez vala égnek   380
A kis tarka madár, első öröméneke
    szülte
Akkor ez édes lányt, a légnek tiszta
    fölében;

És szellők nevelék füveken ringatva
    s virágok
Bíborain. Gyengéd tagait betakarni
    leszállt a
Csillagos esthajnal, s szűz harmat
    tejjel itatta;   385
Lelke pedig fény volt, az örök fény
    tiszta sugára.
    (1. 378–86)

[2] Literally 'Fair Abode'; it is the name of the knight's seat.

first pilgrim who visits his desolate palace. An unhappy youth comes, and chooses first the solitude of the pastoral life, then 'he asked for land inhabited by men, in place of the barren loneliness' (121), and becomes a rich, happy landowner. Then he yearns for family life: 'his heart seeks . . . a heart to beat for him' (198), and this wish too is granted in the form of a happy marriage, blessed with a son. Now the man whom Rom has favoured sets forth to see 'towns and villages' and finds a people ruined by 'battle and quarrels' (304 ff.) and enslaved; he longs to collect an army and free them, a longing which not even his domestic happiness can overcome. But his three wishes have already been exhausted; Rom denies the fourth, and all the dream of happiness is destroyed. The subject of the poem is the insatiability (not the vanity) of human wishes, and, still more important, the inseparability of individual happiness from national unity and liberty.

The last of Vörösmarty's longer hexameter poems, and a work more substantial than its immediate predecessors, is *The Two Neighbouring Castles* (*A két szomszédvár*) (1832), in four short cantos.[1] The warrior Sámson Tihamér returns from the Hungarian victory over King Ottokar (in 1278) to find his home deserted— his family has been extirpated in a single night by Káldor, the lord of the neighbouring castle. Tihamér resolves on vengeance, and expressly requests the King not to punish Káldor by due process of law but to let him, the sole survivor of the Sámson family, challenge each member of the enemy house in turn to combat. The King, reluctantly, agrees. First Tihamér kills Káldor's champion warrior; then two of Káldor's three sons, independently of each other, set out at night on an attempt to murder the challenger in his own castle, but 'blinded by vengeance' (II. 371) kill each other in error.

Tihamér now proceeds to slay Káldor's servants, one after the other, till Káldor instructs his youngest son, Simon, to shoot down the foe with an arrow from a secret passage, while he, the father, is fighting him. Simon, 'a tall, pale young man' (II. 37) and not a warrior by temperament, refuses thus to allow 'dishonour to add to the weight of mourning' (III. 37), but volunteers to fight Tihamér in honourable combat, and carries out this intention in defiance of his father's threat to 'tear him in pieces' (III. 49–50), with the inevitable result that he too is slain by the avenger. The

---

[1] 1,360 lines in all. (The ten cantos of *Zalán* contain a total of 6,685 lines.)

final combat, with Káldor himself, follows, the longest and most evenly balanced of all; then, having killed his last adversary, Tihamér puts on Káldor's armour (which was in fact booty from his own family) and goes to the castle of his enemies. There Káldor's daughter Enikő, now the sole surviving member of her house, whom the dying Simon had begged Tihamér to spare, is waiting in an agony of suspense. Enikő brings a glass of water to him whom she supposes to be her father; whereupon Tihamér 'as if he had not already beheld pain sufficient for his heart, lifted up the helmet on his head. At this sight fair Enikő . . . fell swooning, and the blood seemed to have departed for ever from her lovely cheeks. Tihamér, in terror, rushed up to her as she fell, and in his arms that knew not softness, the maiden, white, rested like a flower cut down by the scythe' (IV. 245–55). Tihamér buries her, and now, 'like a house consumed by fire, stood at the end of his dreadful deeds' (IV. 277); haunted by the ever-returning vision of the maiden he fled, leaving the castles to crumble, while 'the winds made their howling song resound far over the bare plain' (IV. 322, the last line of the poem), and the reader reflects on the bitter irony of the title.

The older critics were appalled by the ferocity of this poem; *Berzsenyi expressed in his review the hope that Vörösmarty would in future 'select for his Muse finer, that is more human and more natural subjects, and not consider such cannibals as the heroes of the two neighbouring castles worthy of his lyre', though he also found the narrative to be 'of a high degree of artistic perfection'. Such criticisms are not without force; but perhaps an even greater danger is that the continual slaughter will not revolt the reader but bludgeon him into indifference, especially if he feels that the poet has no higher aim than to horrify. This is partly due to the monotony of the succession of combats, which the episode of Káldor's two elder sons scarcely varies, but even more to the poet's failure to give his story a universal significance. Both the main adversaries are simply monsters; true tragedy is to be found only in the fate of the beautiful and innocent maiden Enikő, whom her father had so long and so carefully shielded from all knowledge of the feud. Moreover, the length of the poem, although it is short by epic standards, tends to blunt the edge of a story which would have been better treated in a ballad, or possibly in a drama. Whether or not it is reasonable to detect a certain impatience with his medium in the unmistakable signs of hasty composition which *The Two Neighbouring Castles* betrays, it is clear that the instinct which now guided Vörösmarty to abandon the hexameter was sound. Not only had epic now become part of the past, but the extended hexameter poem was an unsuitable medium for the subjects suggested by Vörösmarty's Romantic inspiration.

2

By 1832 the fame which *Zalán* had won was fully consolidated. In 1826 Vörösmarty had taken the brave decision to devote himself wholly to literature; he resigned his tutorship with the Perczel family in August of that year, and moved to Buda. Now followed a period of extreme financial difficulty; moreover, in the autumn of 1827 a visit to his mother, whom he found in great poverty and poor health, decided him that he must, for her sake, pursue the legal career for which he had qualified three years earlier. At the last moment, however, the situation was saved when he was offered, and accepted, the editorship of one of the principal literary periodicals of the time.[1] Now his position progressively improved; in 1830 he became an ordinary member of the Academy, and in 1832 he sold his collected works to a publisher; they appeared in the following year.

Much of Vörösmarty's early work,[2] in addition to his longer hexameter poems, is written in the classical metres; their suitability to Hungarian had been one of his first literary discoveries, in which he had found delight as a boy of fifteen. Much again treats of the regular themes of Horace's odes, patriotic poems in Alcaics, of the type which *Berzsenyi and others had acclimatized in Hungary, being particularly prominent. At the same time Vörösmarty used classical metres[3] for a personal lyric whose subjectivity may seem incongruous so long as we think only of Horace, and forget Sappho and Alcaeus and Catullus in lyric, or Propertius in elegy. Vörösmarty's classical period in fact coincided with the period of deepest subjective and Romantic feeling in his life, when he sings of himself as he only rarely does in later years.

[1] The monthly *Tudományos Gyűjtemény* (*Anthology of Learning*), which lasted from 1817 to 1841. It had also a literary subsidiary, the *Koszorú* (*Garland*).

[2] Actually the *Works* which appeared in 1833 contains little written before 1825, though Vörösmarty had been writing poetry since 1816, when he entered the Piarist Gymnasium in Pest.

[3] Cf. p. 108, n. 2.

This was due primarily to his love for Perczel Etelka, which from 1822 was the dominant factor in his emotional life. It plays its part in the longer poems—not only in the story of the Fairy in *Zalán*, but also in the fact that the exoticism and interest in the remote history of his people which these poems exhibit were prompted by the need to escape from the unbearable emptiness of life.[1] He portrays his own state of mind in a lyric entitled *The Burial of the Heart* (*A szív temetése*) (1826), which begins as follows:

Much have you endured already; there remains but this, my heart, bear but this, then I will praise you. I will say: you are a stone; not a stone: a heap of iron, and a rock of diamond harder than iron. Already you know what gives pain; learn to know also that which kills the soul, know and endure it, as befits a man.[2]

The development of Vörösmarty as a poet in the following years is to a large extent the story of his emancipation from the despair of the letter to Zádor quoted in note 1 below, and from this grim determination to deaden his emotions.

When Vörösmarty moved to Buda in August 1826 he found a flourishing literary life in the city. True, the censor was still there, and Vörösmarty's *Grief of Mikes* (*Mikes búja*) (1826) had to be published under the title *Lament of an Old Servant over the Grave of Pompey*, as no reference to the *Rákóczi rebellion would be tolerated. But the whole atmosphere had been transformed by the Diet of 1825, especially by *Széchenyi's epoch-making offer of a year's revenue from his estates towards the foundation of a Hungarian Academy of Sciences. The nostalgia for a glorious past which could never return—the mood of *Zalán*—now seemed no less outdated than classical epic itself. In addition, and perhaps most important of all, continuous personal contacts replaced

---

[1] This seems a fair inference from Vörösmarty's letter of 27 August 1825 to the lawyer Zádor, almost the only friend before whom he discarded his habitual mask of reserve and unburdened his innermost feelings. In this letter he expresses his longing to be able to accompany an old schoolfriend, Maróthy, who had set out on an expedition to Russia to explore the original home of the Magyars: 'then I could go to the Caucasus, that it might bury me; here even the earth will hurt my dead body. I do not believe that my pain can cease.'

[2] Sokat türél már; még csak ezt, kebel,
Csak ezt viseld el, aztán megdicsérlek,
Azt mondom: kő vagy; nem kő: vashalom,

S vasnál keményebb gyémánt szikla vagy.
Hiszen te ösmered már, ami fáj, 5
Ösmerd meg azt is, ami lelket öl,
Ösmerd s viseld el, mint kell férfinak.

correspondence as the medium for the exchange of ideas. *Kazinczy had guided the revival of Hungarian literature through its earliest stages from his remote estate at Széphalom in the north; but the central figure of the twenties, *Kisfaludy Károly, who made his almanac *Aurora* the focus of a new literary life, lived in Pest. This same *Kisfaludy who in 1823 exhorted Vörösmarty to 'work some Graecisms' into his idyll had already begun to direct literary taste along very different lines. His successes made writers the friends of their public just as the establishment of literary life in the city brought them closer to one another. Besides, *Kisfaludy and the 'Aurora-circle' now felt strong enough to discard foreign influences which had served their purpose—not only Graecisms, but also the sickly and artificially induced melancholy of the lyricism which had come to Hungary from Germany in the last quarter of the eighteenth century, and which was now replaced by personal lyric springing from the poet's own deepest feelings.

Moreover, Hungarian poets now found a new source of inspiration in the folk-song of their own land; from 1817 onwards, the folk-song exercised an ever-increasing influence on literature.[1] In 1826, the same year as Vörösmarty moved to Buda, there appeared *Kölcsey's essay *National Traditions* (*Nemzeti hagyományok*), and Vörösmarty produced much poetry inspired by folk-song in the period 1828–33; in the 1833 edition of his works *Popular Poems* (*Népi költemé-nyek*) appear as a separate category. Not a literary theorist, he found the *Kölcsey and the *Kisfaludy conception of the 'popular poem', the more highly developed derivative and the simple imitation, equally congenial. To take an example of the former type, the lover's lament in *The Veil* (*A gyászkendő*) (1828) could not be mistaken for a folk-song—the deer-simile, familiar from Virgil, Zrínyi, and *Zalán*, alone shows the literary origin of the poem—but equally unmistakable is the source of the poet's inspiration:[2]

Why did you wait no longer for me, my fair beloved, my rose-tree! Ah me, ah me! Why did you wait no longer for me?

You might have waited: here I am, I faint like a wounded deer; ah me, ah me! Now will I follow you to the grave.

---

[1] See p. xxiv.

[2]
Mért nem vártál még reám,		Vártál volna: itt vagyok,
Szép szeretőm, rózsafám!		Mint lőtt szarvas, bágyadok;
Hej baj, hej baj!	15	Hej baj, hej baj!
Mért nem vártál még reám?		Most utánad elhalok.	20

Flower not, rose-tree! Veil, hang there! Ah me, woe is me! Never will
I rise again.

A contrast in every way is provided by the hero of *Student
Gábor* (*Gábor diák*) (1830) who unexpectedly finds himself compelled by family responsibilities to lift his nose from his book:

> Student Gábor, deep in thought, was sitting on a bench, with a huge
> book in front of him; he wouldn't look up for all the world, only a fly
> settled on him. Now he does look up, and there he sees a sprightly girl. 'Oh
> how red your cheeks are, little girl, let me pluck a rose or two from them.'
>
> . . .
>
> Student Gábor, deep in thought, was sitting on a bench, with a huge
> book in front of him; he wouldn't look up for all the world, only it's the
> rosy day of Whitsuntide. But here comes the girl, rocking a baby in her
> arms: 'Why, I'd never have thought it!' 'Now all the world couldn't
> make mock of me.'
>
> 'How he smiles, the little bastard!' 'He's just like his father.' 'What
> shall we do, what shall we do, my darling?' 'I know, I'll jump into the
> Danube.' 'Jump, indeed! Come to the priest.' So spoke Gábor to the
> girl, and shut his book, very sadly: 'Never, never, another Whitsuntide
> like this!'[1]

In prose, similarly, the first of Vörösmarty's few short stories,
The Moonlit Night (*A holdvilágos éj*) (1829) is reminiscent of the
folk-tale, though with more than a touch of parody. Three starving
Slovak students, after regaling one another with stories of the
freakish deaths of their ancestors, laugh themselves into uncon-
sciousness. A cock (who is in fact a lost soul) appears, and after

Ne virágozz, rózsafa!
Fátyolkendő, függj rajta!
  Hej baj, nagy baj!
Nem kelek én föl soha.
    (stanzas 4–6 (end))

[1] Gábor diák mélyen elmerűlve
Űl a lócán, egy nagy könyv előtte;
A világért fel sem pillantana,
Ha egy filégy reá nem szállana;
De már erre csak felpillánt,   5
S im meglát egy fürge leányt.
'Ejnye, húgom, beh piros az orcád,
Hadd szakasszak róla egy pár rózsát.'

  . . .

Gábor diák mélyen elmerűlve
Űl a lócán, egy nagy könyv előtte;

A világért fel nem pillantana,   35
Pedig itt van piros pünkösd napja.
De elébe jön a leány,
S egy csecsemőt ringat karján:
'Ej, ej már ezt mégsem hittem volna!'
'Most a világ engem sem csufolna.' 40

'S hogy mosolyog istenadta fattya!'
'Épen olyan, mint az édes atyja.'
'Mit csináljunk, mit tegyünk galam-
    bom?'
'Én tudom, hogy a Dunába ugrom.'
'Semmi ugrás! jer a paphoz.' 45
Így szól Gábor a leányhoz,
S nagy szomorún a könyvet becsapja:
'Soha, soha, ilyen pünkösd napja!'
    (stanzas 1, 5–6 (end))

voluntarily preparing himself for the table, imperiously bids the students eat him, which they do. But when, later, he reappears, he sternly rebukes them for their inhuman treatment of him; though he then proceeds to relent so far as to produce a table laid for a banquet, and three beautiful maidens to be their wives. Then he crows loudly—and they wake up.

*Kölcsey's remarks in *National Traditions* about the Hungarians' neglect of their cultural past applied as much to literature as to folk-song. The key figure in remedying this defect, the pioneer historian of Hungarian literature, was *Toldy, whose *Handbuch der ungrischen Poesie* (1828) opened a new period in the appreciation of Hungarian poetry both at home and abroad; in the same year he published first editions of some old Hungarian literary texts, which inspired Vörösmarty to splendid ballads—a medium which would have been ideal for the story of *Széplak* or *The Two Neighbouring Castles*.

Nor was his horizon limited to his own country. As early as 1814 Vuk Karadžić had published an anthology of Serbian popular poetry, followed by a large collection which appeared between 1823 and 1833. Karadžić's work attracted considerable attention in Hungary; *Toldy, for instance, wrote an essay on *The Folk-Poetry of the Serbs* in 1827; but it was Vörösmarty who gave the 'Serb manner', with its characteristic trochaic rhythm and its repetitions of words in consecutive lines, a definite place in Hungarian poetry.

In 1831 came one of Vörösmarty's finest masterpieces, when the fairyland of the longer poems combined with the world of folk-song and with Hungary's literary past to inspire the drama *Csongor and Tünde*. Vörösmarty's 'hexameter period' was followed by a 'drama period' in which his large-scale works were all plays. But his career as a dramatist had begun far earlier, and he had been writing plays throughout the years we have been considering.

3

As early as 1820 Vörösmarty's friend Teslér had introduced Shakespeare to him, and the impulse to imitate what he read asserted itself as quickly as with the Latin poets he had taken from his father's bookshelves. He began with historical dramas, the first being *Salamon* (1821–2) in which evil counsellors wreck an agreement on the succession between King Salamon (reigned

1063–74) and his cousins Géza and László. The ensuing dispute leads to the deposition of Salamon. Vörösmarty then projected a trilogy on the conflicts between King Zsigmond (reigned 1387–1437) and the nobles. After extensive revision, necessitated partly by the censorship, the plan was finally compressed into two plays, *Zsigmond* (1823–4) and *The Exiles* (*A bújdosók*) (1830). Of these, the latter, describing the rebellion and treacherous execution of Kont István,[1] is by far the more important. The immediacy of its main theme, the oppressive rule of a foreign king,[2] combines with the tenderness of the scenes with Kont and his family to produce some memorable passages; in particular, Hungarian blank verse here spoke with a new poetry, and *Arany, to refute the view that Hungarian iambics are unsuitable for delivery, chose as his example Kont's speech as he hands over his sword to the King's emissary:

> Sword, thou who didst guard Kont's honour, could'st thou feel the grief of this parting, even thy grim metal would melt, and thou would'st flow in tears of steel from my hand.[3]

At the same time, the plot-structure and characterization of all these plays show their author's lack of experience, and even *The Exiles*, the best of them, is in the last resort poetry but not drama, just as *Zalán* is poetry but not epic.

Vörösmarty's other youthful plays (apart from works which remained incomplete) consist first of two prose comedies, of which the earlier is the one-act *Y War* (*Ypsilon háború*) (1821, revised 1824), a dramatization of a recent philological dispute as to whether certain words should be spelt with Y or J. The letters appear as characters—an idea more entertaining in its conception than rewarding in its execution. The second of these comedies is *The Melancholy Student* (*Az elbúsult diák*) (1824), in which a young law student, having hopelessly mishandled his first case, departs in despair into the country and pretends to be a wizard, but is eventually united to the notary's beautiful daughter whom he had previously captivated. This work, consisting of three short sections, is

---

[1] Placed by Vörösmarty's sources in 1395, by others in 1388.

[2] Zsigmond, Margrave of Brandenburg, was a son of the Emperor Charles IV.

[3] O kard, mely őrzéd Kont becsü-
  letét,   480
  Ha érzenéd e búcsúbánatot,

  Megolvadozna zordon érced is,
  S acél könyekkel folynál el kezemből.
  (*The Exiles*, Act IV. 1. 480 ff.)

really a series of humorous sketches (and as such is vivid and amusing), though it can scarcely be considered as a single play. Written when Vörösmarty himself was reading for his legal examination, it was probably an occasional piece for the entertainment of his friends. These works were followed in 1827 by the one-act tragedy in verse, in the style of Ossian, *Hábador*, set in the dawn of Hungarian history. A knight, having slain his brutal rival for the hand of his beloved, is himself killed accidentally by an arrow from her bow, and the maiden dies of grief over the body of her lover.

In 1831, however, appeared a play which eclipsed not only its predecessors but also its successors, the one work by which Vörösmarty the dramatist lives today: *Csongor and Tünde* (*Csongor és Tünde*). Based on the same Argirus-romance on which Vörösmarty had also drawn for *The Valley of the Fairies*,[1] the play shows how the young hero Csongor, as he relates in the opening lines:

> I have travelled in every country, every distant land, and the one who lives in my dreams, the glorious heavenly beauty, I have found nowhere on earth.[2]

He finds, loses, and regains what he is seeking, and is finally united to his beloved, the fairy Tünde, in spite of all that the powers of evil, particularly the witch Mirigy, can do to thwart him. Here was a subject congenial indeed to Vörösmarty's lyrical inspiration, which is seen at it most exquisite in such passages as the song of the spirits as they fly down to earth for their sport:

> Ever we play, and the hours pass, in the air is our home, beneath the stars. And when the star comes forth, smiling, at eventide, the fields of heaven sparkle after it. After the star follows our little band, we pass, playing as we go, through the gates of Heaven. Who calls us down, who calls us down, who calls us to earth? The heavens sparkle, gleaming; lovely is the earth.[3]

---

[1] See p. 113.

[2] Minden országot bejártam,
Minden messze tartományt,
S aki álmaimban él,
A dicsőt, az égi szépet
Semmi földön nem találtam.   5

[3] Játszadozunk,
S az óra halad,
Légi lakunk
Van csillag alatt.   525

S a csillag, ha este mosolyogva kijő,
Tündöklik utána az égi mező.
Csillag után
Jár kis seregünk,
Menny kapuján   530
Át játszva megyünk.
Ki hí le, ki hí le, a földre ki hí?
A menny ragyog, ékes; a föld gyönyörű.   (v. 522 ff.)

But lyrical beauty will not of itself make a drama. Not that Mirigy's initial hostility to Csongor, which is the mainspring of the action, lacks plausibility; malevolence is characteristic of her kind, and it is quite natural that when he sees and recognizes her at the opening of the play, he should think of her as an old enemy, the 'wicked, malicious beldame' (I. 17). She, in her turn, vows not to depart until the 'horns' of his pride have come into her clutches (I. 158-9). The fact that the particular causes of her hostility lie outside the play is unimportant.

The first act is comprehensible as a simple lyrical fairy-tale; but not the second. The power which Mirigy has established over Tünde by cutting off a lock of her hair compels her to leave Csongor; his only guide in his search for his beloved is an enigmatic clue, let drop by her fairy attendant, Ilma, that 'the middle of three roads which meet on a plain will lead to the goal' (I. 448). So we find him at the beginning of Act II, vainly attempting to identify the 'middle' of the three roads. Along come three travellers, a Merchant, a Prince, and a Philosopher, whose values are quite different from Csongor's. 'Fairyland is here, in my pocket' says the Merchant (II. 44): 'Fairyland is where I am: come, be my knight!' answers the Prince (II. 80-81): the Philosopher replies to Csongor's inquiry with contemptuous pity:

World of poets, lovely fairyland! What a pity that it is a dream, for children! Wake up, or, if it is better to dream on, go dream away your dream; for reality is a false hope—
Csongor. Destroy me not; this one wish gives me life.[1]

So when they have gone on their way, Csongor sums them up:[2]

And is this all for which man lives? Dark, empty, boundless breast, O terrible must be thy loneliness! So my travellers will not set me on the path. One embraces base dust as an idol, the second would lay the world in ruins, just that he might be its master. And this third is the most horrible of all: like Death he walks on living feet and bears a bleak

---

[1] Költők világa, szép tündérvilág,
Mi kár, hogy álom, gyermeknek való!
Ébredj föl, vagy, ha még álmodni
   jobb,
[2] See footnote 1 on p. 126.

Menj, álmodd vissza, amit álmodál,
Mert a valóság csalt remény —
   Csongor.   Ne ronts el,
Ez egy kívánság éltet.   (II. 157 ff.)

grave in place of a warm heart. O Love, light a star for me, and be my guide to reach Fairyland.[1]

Just then Csongor hears a cry, from a fourth and very different character. It is Balga, who has just fallen from the branch of a tree, striking instantly a note of comic relief.[2] Balga calls himself the 'tailor of the barren earth' (II. 189), who 'clothes it with ears of corn '(II. 193); it is this immortal embodiment of the endearing qualities of the peasant whom Csongor chooses as his companion, and he will give the drama the same contrasting robustness which the mechanicals impart to *A Midsummer Night's Dream*. Balga's vision of life may be earthbound—on his path are 'pubs before and behind' (III. 77): Csongor's initial reason for accepting him may be that 'Fortune favours the foolish' (II. 208): but unlike the three travellers, Balga's heart is in the right place. And our eyes too have been opened by what Csongor saw at the cross-roads; this is not only a fairy-tale but a picture of human existence.

Balga too has been parted from his beloved, who immediately after their betrothal grew wings and left him; but Csongor can help him, for he knows that the lost sweetheart has been transformed into none other than Tünde's fairy attendant Ilma. So Csongor and Balga proceed on their journey together, two contrasting types as perfectly suited to each other as Don Quixote and Sancho Panza; following the footprints of their loved ones: dogged by goblins, who devour Mirigy's daughter yet are allied to the witch in their hatred of Csongor: bewitched by Mirigy and her magic well: tempted by visions of sensual love: overcome, first Balga by fatigue (which the goblins are quick to exploit), then Csongor by sleep: while Tünde and Ilma come to the land of Night, where the Queen condemns them to perpetual banishment from Fairyland to the transient earth—'earthly love has drawn thy heart' (V. 131).

---

[1] S ez minden, amiért az ember él?
Setét, üres, határtalan kebel,
Oh, a te magányod rémítő lehet! 170
S így utazóim útra nem vezetnek.
Egyik, mint bálványt, hitvány port
ölel,
A másik rommá tenné a világot,
Csak hogy fölötte ő lehessen úr.

S ez a legszörnyebb mindenek
között: 175
Mint a halál jár élő lábakon
És puszta sírt hord hő kebel helyett.
Oh, szerelem, gyújts utamra csil-
lagot,
S te légy vezérem Tündérhon felé.
(II. 168 ff.)

[2] 'Fallen off a branch' is the literal meaning of the Hungarian equivalent of 'down-and-out'—a point explicitly made by Csongor. The adjective 'balga' means 'foolish, stupid'.

Csongor and Balga, pursuing respectively visions of a beautiful maiden and of roast pigeon with wine, now find themselves back at the three cross-roads, in despair. Csongor sees that he has 'companions in misery' (v. 223)—the Merchant, now on crutches through gout and reduced to beggary: the Prince, overthrown (yet still retaining a certain tragic grandeur): the Philosopher, a madman discoursing on 'invitality' (v 363)[1] and immortality. Their fate shows that Csongor's view of them was right.

Both Mirigy and Csongor are taken prisoner by the goblins; but the hero, as he lies in bonds under a tree, hears music and dreams of his love, and Tünde induces his captors to release him. Both pairs of lovers are finally united, first Balga to Ilma, whom Tünde tells to 'Rule your husband with power, and as a punishment fatten him as long as he can move and eat' (v. 890)—Balga's reply to this dread command is to kiss Tünde's 'littlest little toe'. At last Tünde removes her veil and reveals herself to Csongor; in the words of the last line of the song which ends the play, 'only love is awake'.

Csongor and Tünde had to remain unique, and Vörösmarty let it be so. However, he continued to write plays, though all his later dramatic works are comparatively uninspired, and today are scarcely remembered. The explanation of the poet's puzzling persistence with the drama (moreover *Csongor and Tünde* itself was coldly received) lies not in his failure to understand the nature of his genius, but rather in the literary situation and atmosphere of his time, in which writing was itself a patriotic duty, to establish a secure Hungarian literary tradition.[2] No doubt quantity often came before quality; but palates become fastidious only at a distance from the danger of starvation, and the survival of Hungarian literature could by no means be taken for granted.

In 1821, while Vörösmarty was absorbed in his Shakespeare, the dramatist *Katona produced an essay on *Why the dramatic art cannot gain ground in Hungary*. He gives six reasons: first, the lack of a permanent theatre and the social prejudice against itinerant actors: second, national pride, which is 'a signpost showing the writer that the way to fame is to write not a well-constructed

---

[1] The Hungarian word formed from 'to live' as 'immortality' is formed from 'to die' commonly means 'inability to live' in the sense of 'shiftlessness', 'helplessness'.

[2] Cf. the quotation on pp. xxiii f. from Eötvös's funeral oration on the historian Szalay.

play, but a patriotic drama replete with vainglory' (so quality was not forgotten, by some at least): third, the need of more printing: fourth, the censorship (*Csongor and Tünde* was in fact banned by the Pest censor, possibly because of the downfall of the Prince or the nihilism of the Philosopher, but it was then passed by the censor at Székesfehérvár, who was less strict, and besides was a friend of Vörösmarty's): fifth, the lack of constructive criticism: sixth, the lack of material rewards for the writer. Most of *Katona's points apply to all forms of literature; but drama was in a specially difficult position. Not till 1837 was a permanent Hungarian theatre founded in Pest,[1] though in 1833 the Academy had set up a Drama Committee (of which Vörösmarty was one of the most active members). Performances were rare, and the drama reached the public more often by way of the printed word. It is the lack of theatrical experience which is the root cause of the slow pace, excessive length, and lifeless characterization of much of Vörösmarty's dramatic work.

The immediate successor to *Csongor and Tünde* was the comparatively unimportant *Treasure-Seekers* (*Kincskeresők*) (1833), in which we see a miser seeking for hidden treasure, and brutally forcing a rich suitor on his daughter, who loves a poorer man. The rich suitor, however, is leading a double life, being also the chief of a gang of brigands; he entices the lovers into a cave, and in the duel which follows, the poor young man kills not only the brigand chief but also his beloved who has thrown herself between the combatants. He commits suicide, so that the miser is left alone to curse the world.

Vörösmarty calls the play a 'tragedy', but the subject is entirely lacking in tragic sublimity, and it is significant that the closest parallels to the plot are comedies—Plautus' *Aulularia* and Molière's *L'Avare*—that is, apart from the German Romantic dramas of the day which were Vörösmarty's immediate models. Moreover, there are few traces of Vörösmarty the poet, and the characterization is not only nebulous but inconsistent; the miser whom his daughter, in the second line of the play, describes as 'hardhearted' is just not the same man as the father who shortly afterwards reveals to his daughter—somewhat late in the day from her

---

[1] At Kolozsvár (Cluj), however, a permanent theatre had opened as early as 1821, and several Transylvanian magnates proved enlightened patrons of the drama.

point of view—that the rich suitor is his landlord, from whose clutches he hopes to extricate them both when the treasure is discovered.

In the same year as *Treasure-Seekers* appeared (1833), Vörösmarty won an Academy award with an ambitious five-act tragedy, *Blood-Wedding (Vérnász)*. At the opening of this play the powerful lord Telegdi falls in love with a girl named Lenke who has given him a drink at the hermit's cell where he was passing, and he resolves at once to marry her. He reflects on his past—how sixteen years earlier, when he was away at the wars, rumours had reached him of his wife's unfaithfulness with her rejected suitor, Tanár. On returning home Telegdi, in a fit of rage, had punished his wife by having the two children exposed, believing their father to be Tanár. The wife had died broken-hearted, and now Telegdi, haunted by the past, wishes to remarry:

A fair lady took from me my salvation; from the hand of a fair lady I ask for it back.[1]

The Treaty of Nikolsburg (1621) between Prince *Bethlen Gábor of Transylvania and the King of Hungary has just been signed, but the violent, quick-tempered young soldier Kolta will have none of it, and resolves to fight on. A rejected suitor of Lenke's enlists his support for an attack on Telegdi's castle, and in this raid, which takes place immediately after the wedding of Telegdi and Lenke, Kolta is taken prisoner. Lenke, however, has already been removed to safety by the hermit who had brought her up (and who had also tried unsuccessfully to stop the wedding). The hermit had terrified the old servant of Telegdi's who was guarding Lenke, by producing a token, and the servant had let Lenke go. As the hermit soon afterwards told Lenke, she is Telegdi's own daughter, and the token was the same which the children wore when they were exposed.

Kolta now secures his release by undertaking to find Lenke for Telegdi, and eventually the two young people meet and recognize each other, by the token, as brother and sister. But it is the hermit who appears at Telegdi's castle, in their place, to reveal himself as Tanár, Telegdi's former rival. Telegdi immediately strikes Tanár

---

[1] Szép hölgy vivé el tőlem üdvömet,
Szép hölgy kezéből kérem vissza azt.
(I. 590 f.)

down, but before dying the hermit reveals not only that the exposed children were Telegdi's, but also that they are none other than Kolta and Lenke. And Telegdi, one of whose men had reported seeing Kolta and Lenke embracing, had given orders for Kolta's murder, which it proves too late to revoke. Lenke becomes a nun; Telegdi, utterly broken, is drawn on by the ghost of Tanár over a precipice.

Blood-Wedding at first sight suggests a Victor Hugo trying to improve on the story of Oedipus, and the plot is open to the criticism that nothing is less horrific than horror made an end in itself; at the same time, there is nothing like the obsessive emphasis on the incest which mars the latter part of Sophocles' drama. A varied sequence of events also mitigates the horror, though at the price of extending the play to an excessive length. Not that this is the only reason why it is so long; it lacks conciseness throughout, and the events preceding the opening of the action are related on three separate occasions, revealing the inexperienced dramatist's anxiety lest the audience fail to grasp the plot. Telegdi's soliloquy and dialogue with his old servant, however, the first of these expositions, emphasizes dramatically that his past is ever-present.

Telegdi's tragedy is that the wrath of a moment has impelled him to deeds which cannot be undone; yet, though he feels 'the weight of sin that cannot be repented' (I. 313), and embarks on his second marriage with a real concern for his young wife's happiness, he remains the haughty lord; in particular, the hideously gleeful cruelty with which he contemplates his captive, Kolta, costs him the sympathy we extend to a tragic hero whose only flaw is a hot temper. Nevertheless, the tragic atmosphere is excellently maintained. The dramatic irony: the recurrence of Telegdi's temperament in Kolta: the servants' racy chatter (in prose) as they prepare the house for the wedding, light relief yet ominous—these and many other features of the play are of the essence of tragedy.

Blood-Wedding was followed in 1835 by an even longer comedy, *The Secrets of the Veil* (*A fátyol titkai*). Vilma, the daughter of a rich landlord, on a visit to Pest with her maid Lidi, overhears three men discussing how they will make their encounter eternally memorable, since they have met 'on this blasted heath, like the witches in *Macbeth*'. The trio finally agree to win the hand of a lady, and marry, in four weeks, without falling in love. Vilma and Lidi, profoundly shocked by what they have heard, plan to make the trio fall in love with them. Just then they catch sight of another man, not a member of the trio, one Hangai, who has gone to sleep on the grass. Vilma likes the look of him, but is shocked again when she sees the book on the dangers of love which he has been reading; so she removes it and substitutes *Himfy*, the famous collection of love-lyrics by *Kisfaludy Sándor. Hangai wakes, and in an amusing parody of the scene in *A Midsummer Night's Dream* where Titania wakes to find beside her Bottom with his ass's head,

What soft screams arouse me from my slumbers?[1]

he catches sight of the ladies, reads the substituted book, and the misogynist in him is already staring defeat in the face.

Vilma is attracted by him too, and decides to test him by talking about 'Vilma' as if she were someone else, a friend of hers, and tell him how cruel 'Vilma' is; so the next time the two meet, Vilma is veiled. Hangai declares to Vilma veiled his love for the lady he knows as Vilma, and Vilma veiled, though jealous of her 'friend', undertakes to try to soften her heart for him. However, the next time they meet, Hangai has transferred his affections from the cruel Vilma of his imagination to the sweet-natured veiled lady, so much so that Vilma begins to lose her nerve. The situation is, however, restored (though some contemporary critics remained shocked at her coquetry) when she receives Hangai at her home and gradually prepares him for the final revelation that she and the veiled lady are one and the same.

Concurrently with the drama of Vilma and Hangai, the farcical story of the discomfiture of the trio is unfolded in prose which contrasts excellently with the verse of the Hangai scenes. The ladies avenge themselves by arranging for separate letters addressed to Vilma's elder brother to fall into the hands of each member of the trio, for them to deliver to him. Lidi, Vilma's maid, will meanwhile give each member of the trio the impression that she is working for him against the others, and instruct one to appear before Vilma's brother as a backwoods nobleman, one as a fashionable man-about-town, and the third as a poor scholar—the three types Vilma's brother cannot endure. In the event, all three find themselves calling on Vilma's brother at the same time. Just as they are planning revenge a new letter is planted on them, supposedly from

[1] Mely lágy sikoltás ébreszt álmaimból?

Vilma to her lover, giving plans for an elopement. The trio decide to come to the rendezvous themselves; but there they find not Vilma but her unattractive aunt Katica, and flee in terror. However, all ends happily, for the trio are reconciled to Vilma as she is united to Hangai, and tear up their agreement to marry without love.

Here is abundance of comedy of all kinds—delightful caricature of the stock Hungarian types, topical allusions, parody (notably of Shakespeare), as well as the humour of the main plots; but Vörösmarty has composed the individual episodes without regard for the scale and cumulative effect of the whole, and has created a maze of complications in which he himself does not always appear quite sure of the way. The play has all the virtues—except the vital virtue of economy.

In August 1837 the opening of the Hungarian Theatre of Pest marked the beginning of a new epoch in the history of the drama in Hungary. Vörösmarty wrote a 'prelude' for the occasion in dramatic form, entitled *The Awakening of *Árpád (Árpád ébredése)*, in which *Árpád returns to earth to see the nation he has founded, and finds it 'broken by inertia' (137). He observes a cross-section of Hungarian society coming to the new theatre, and drives away the evil spirits, Scorn, Slander, Starvation, and others, which are persecuting the symbolic figure of the Actress. This piece is closely related to the occasion for which it was written, an occasion intimately linked to national aspirations, the more so in view of Vienna's repressive policy at the time, of which the arrest of *Kossuth three months earlier was only a single example. At the same time, in spite of the introduction of *Árpád, the emphasis is entirely on the arts of peace; the primitive warlike virtues of an earlier age are expressly renounced. The choice of Vörösmarty to write the 'prelude' was a well-deserved tribute to his work for the Hungarian theatre, work for which he now received new inspiration. In the periodical *Athenaeum*, which he launched in the same year, 1837, in collaboration with his friends *Bajza and *Toldy, he wrote dramatic criticisms of the first importance. He worked tirelessly to raise both the social standing of the actor (as *The Awakening of *Árpád* shows) and the standards of his acting—the actor must know his lines, and when he knows them, must not gabble or mumble, rant or 'quack' them. Vörösmarty was also a pioneer of the appreciation of Shakespeare in Hungary, and his translation of *Julius Caesar* (first published in 1840, first performed in 1842) set new standards and inspired his fellow poets to translate other plays; his own version of *Lear* was completed early in 1854.

At the same time, 'original drama is the soul of the national theatre', as he wrote; and in 1838 he produced a new tragedy, *Marót *Bán*, which marks a real advance on *Blood-Wedding*. It is more concise, being only three-quarters as long as its predecessor; and while the plot is no less horrible than that of *Blood-Wedding*, the horror appears less gratuitous because the setting, and some at any rate of the events, are real to a spectator with historical imagination.

Marót *Bán is set in the Turkish attacks on Hungary at the end of the fifteenth century. Like so many Romantic dramas it is a study of revenge. The Turkish Bey Haszán has lost his father and three brothers in a single battle, all killed by Marót, who has also captured Haszán's sister and given her to a servant of his. Haszán, for his part, had earlier taken Marót's younger brother prisoner; more recently, by feigning willingness to negotiate a ransom for the brother, he had also secured the person of Marót himself; so he is in a position to avenge himself. He has trained Marót's brother, Bod, 'as the instrument of his vengeance' (I. 438), to ensnare Hungarian ladies for his harem, and now requires him to secure Marót's wife Ida; when both Bod and Ida are safely in his hands, he will reveal Bod's identity to Marót, and then execute the *Bán. At the same time Haszán suspects that Bod is in love with Ida, and this suspicion suggests to the Turk a plan by which he may give himself the additional pleasure of causing Marót to kill his own brother. He sets Marót free for ten days to collect a sum of money to ransom himself; Marót, he foresees, may well surprise Bod and Ida and kill his wife's lover, unaware who that lover is.

Haszán's suspicion about Bod and Ida proves well founded, and Marót himself overhears their mutual declarations of love. Overhearing also a messenger bringing Bod the news of his death, Marót decides to stage his own 'funeral'. He surprises Bod and Ida at the 'tomb' and now reveals himself, as his men seize and bind Bod; but just then Haszán appears with a force to attack Marót's castle, and Marót surrenders.

Now Marót becomes a prey to conflicting emotions. At first his one desire is to take vengeance in person on the guilty pair;

for this reason he refuses to hand Bod over to Haszán. Haszán, satisfied that Marót will kill Bod, yields this point, but insists on the surrender of Ida—only thus can his desire for vengeance be gratified. Ida falls at her husband's feet and begs for forgiveness; Marót at first rejects her pleas, then relents, only to surrender her after all when Haszán appeals to his sense of honour, as a Hungarian, to abide by his pledged word.

Haszán had sent his servant to Marót with the gift of a sword which would prove Bod to be Marót's brother, intending it to reach Marót after Bod's execution. But the messenger arrives before the sentence has been carried out, and there follows a tremendous scene between the two brothers. Marót is willing to forgive Bod if he joins in the fight against the Turk, and Bod sets off immediately. He kills two Turks; rushes into Haszán's tent, then, finding that he cannot rescue Ida, slays her too (off-stage), and is struck down by Haszán from behind. By now, however, the Hungarians have won a decisive victory; Marót puts Haszán to death, and, left alone in the world, vows to continue the fight against the Turk.

This grim drama lacks even the little light relief which the servants provide in *Blood-Wedding*. All the main characters are unsympathetic; our admiration for the proud dignity of Marót when we first see him as a captive is gravely compromised by his lust for vengeance when he discovers his wife's infidelity (though he never approaches the diabolical cruelty and cunning of Haszán), and in the circumstances his sense of honour, on which Haszán successfully plays, is no virtue but (at best) a weakness. We may sympathize initially with Bod; but our sympathy is inevitably compromised by the deceit with which he simulates the deepest and most intimate emotions as he plies his trade, and his words as he leaves to fight the Turks express the most savage thirst for vengeance:

Creator! Give the Turk lives a hundredfold, that I may be able to extinguish them all, one by one.

Yet, as in so many of Victor Hugo's characters, there is good in them both; and the scene in which they confront each other as brothers is perhaps the most powerful in all Vörösmarty's plays.

Vörösmarty's next tragedy, *The Victim* (*Az áldozat*) (1840), takes us back to the original settlement of Hungary by the Magyars.

The father of the fair maid Zenő had refused to join the emigrants, or to marry his daughter to any of their number; so her lover, the hero Szabolcs, son of one of the seven leaders of the Magyars, stayed behind to be with her. But Zenő eloped with Zaránd, one of the emigrants; so Szabolcs set off in quest of her to Hungary, where we find him at the opening of the play.

Meanwhile, however, Zaránd has tired of Zenő, and discarded her with the utmost brutality and cynicism in favour of Csilár, Szabolcs's own sister. But nothing can kill Zenő's love for Zaránd or her faith that he will return to her; when she meets Szabolcs, who forgives and comforts her, while also making clear his intention to avenge himself on Zaránd, her thoughts are for Zaránd— she will win back his love by revealing Szabolcs's plans for vengeance. Zaránd, however, has caught sight of Zenő and a man together, and insists (as he did not with Csilár in the same situation) that she tell him who the man was. When she refuses he decides to offer her as a human sacrifice to the god Hadúr. In the very moment when Zaránd's knife is raised over Zenő, Szabolcs intervenes, in time to save her life (though not her reason), and slays Zaránd in a duel which Zenő still tries to avert, for she loves Zaránd to the end. The play ends with Szabolcs (somewhat artificially) justifying his action to the followers of Zaránd, and placating their hostility by his eloquence.

The Victim is scarcely shorter than *Marót *Bán*, but its action can be summarized more briefly, because there is less action to summarize; the memorable moments of the play are lyrical rather than dramatic. There is scarcely the dramatic material for five acts; and although the dramatist has the right to expect us not to ask questions outside the play, it is doubtful whether this right can be extended to cover Szabolcs's failure to intervene decisively at once—a failure the more surprising in so high-ranking a prince. Vörösmarty's main interest, however, is in Zaránd and Zenő; not in Szabolcs, nor in Csilár, who plays no positive part in the action, being simply the bride before her wedding in a state of bliss (including ignorance). Zenő's tragedy, the main theme of the play, in its essence belongs less to the ninth century than to the nineteenth, or even the twentieth; modern too in its flavour is some of the detail, like the priest who disapproves of the sacrifice but dare not offend the powerful Zaránd by refusing to serve as an accessory to it.

The Victim is unhistorical drama; its successor, also set in the past, is undramatic history. The lack of dramatic qualities is, however, partly due to the fact that it is the first play of another projected historical trilogy, on the *Hunyadi family; and into this first play, *Czillei and the *Hunyadis (Czillei és a Hunyadiak)* (1844) Vörösmarty put his picture of the period as a whole. A vast and varied pageant passes before us, but the drama is obscured (and practical difficulties created) by the number of scenes not directly connected with the main plot, and by the profusion of characters, who can scarcely be accommodated even in this longest of all Vörösmarty's dramas.

In 1456, while the Commander-in-Chief and former Regent, *Hunyadi János, is fighting the Turkish besiegers of Belgrade, an alliance is formed against him and his sons by the powerful lords who are his enemies. We see these in the first act, two being especially prominent; first, the *Nádor (Palatine) Gara, whose daughter is engaged to *Hunyadi's elder son *László. Gara calls himself the 'friend of all men', yet even now he is planning to gain the upper hand over his present allies. Secondly there is the uncle of the young King László V, the sensual intriguer Czillei, who is also thinking in terms of supreme power for himself. The only bond which unites Gara and Czillei is their hatred of *Hunyadi, and (the direct result of that hatred) their hope for Turkish victories.

Just as the hypocritical Czillei is drinking the health of *Hunyadi János, the news arrives that the Commander-in-Chief has died before Belgrade. Now the plotter sets to work in earnest. He sends a letter to his father-in-law Brankovics, with a plan for murdering *Hunyadi's two sons: he calls a Diet, at which he himself is nominated Regent by the King, while another enemy of the *Hunyadis, Újlaki, is appointed Commander-in-Chief. At the Diet Czillei makes another hypocritical speech, offering the *Hunyadi boys not only friendship but paternal affection; at the same time *Hunyadi László's impassioned defence of his father's anti-Turkish policy (in reply to a proposal by the new Commander-in-Chief to surrender the border forts) increases Czillei's determination to eliminate him.

But Czillei's all-important letter to Brankovics had been entrusted to Henrik, whose beloved Ágnes had been taken by Czillei to be the concubine of the King; Czillei wished to corrupt the King's moral fibre in order to smooth his own path to power. Henrik shows the letter to *Hunyadi László, who confronts

Czillei with it, demanding the resignation of the Regent on pain of a complete exposure. Czillei tries to fight his way out, but is killed by the young *Hunyadi; the King, after reading the letter, decides that Czillei's punishment was deserved. In the closing words of the play, however, another of the conspirators against the *Hunyadis declares that 'blood demands blood'; and in the sequel *Hunyadi László will be treacherously seized and executed.

In *Czillei and the *Hunyadis* the translator of *Julius Caesar* has returned to Shakespeare from the Romantic drama, and here too is a conspiracy; but there is no Brutus, no Antony, and the villainy of the sensual coward Czillei has no trace of tragic grandeur —still less could he say, with his literary ancestor Richard III, 'O coward conscience, how dost thou afflict me!' The episodes, though lively and varied, suffer by their very number—as in *The Secrets of the Veil*, Vörösmarty could not bring himself to leave anything out—but some are delightful in themselves, notably the glimpses of *Hunyadi László's younger brother, the scholarly fifteen-year-old *Mátyás, the future architect of the Hungarian Renaissance. Finally, one wonders how the trilogy might have formed a satisfactory artistic whole, whether the problem of 'blood demands blood' could have been finally solved, as Aeschylus, for instance, solves it at the end of the *Oresteia*. History suggests that it was possible, by taking the story as far as *Mátyás's accession and consolidation of his power; but such indications as there are suggest that Vörösmarty planned to go no further than the death of the reigning King, László V.[1] It is perhaps significant, not only that this trilogy was never finished (the second part, *Hunyadi László*, exists only in drafts and fragments), but also that Vörösmarty wrote no more plays.

4

Just as Vörösmarty produced both the last classical epic of importance in Hungarian literature and some of the first examples of the ballads which succeeded epic as the regular medium for narrative poetry, so also he both wrote some of the last Horatian odes and founded the ode as a modern literary form.

The climax of Vörösmarty's achievement as a narrative poet, and a favourite of his own, is *Fair Ilonka* (*Szép Ilonka*), written in the early autumn of 1833. It is the story of King *Mátyás and

[1] He died in 1458.

two people who come to Buda to join the crowd which hails the victorious King's triumphant return from the siege and occupation of Vienna in 1485.

Fair Ilonka[1]

I

The huntsman lies long and thoughtfully in wait for his keen arrow to find a fleet quarry; ever higher, ever brighter, the swift sun points to noon. He waits in vain; his quarry is resting by the source of a cool spring amid the hills of Vértes.[2]

The huntsman stays for long in his hiding-place, waits till twilight gives a token of fortune; tensely he waits till the sun goes down, and lo! the fortune for which he waited has appeared. Ah, but not a wild beast; a light little butterfly, and a fair slender maiden, darting as in flight.

'Gay butterfly, lovely golden butterfly! Surprise me, alight on me, little bird; or lead me to where you will settle, where the sun sinks to rest.' She speaks, and runs, escaping, light and playful as a deer in flight.

'By God!' said the huntsman, starting up: 'a right royal quarry!' And at once, forgetting all else, ardently he sets off in the steps of the maiden. He for the maiden, the maiden for the butterfly—they contend for fairy delights.

'Got you!' says the girl, with joy, as she captures the flying insect; 'Got you!' says the huntsman, stretching out his right hand to the maiden with delight; from her trembling hand the little butterfly escapes; she is held captive, by the radiance of a noble eye.

[1]   *Szép Ilonka*

I

A vadász ül hosszu méla lesben,
Vár felajzott nyílra gyors vadat,
S mind fölebb és mindig fényesebben
A serény nap dél felé mutat.
Hasztalan vár; Vértes belsejében   5
Nyugszik a vad hűs forrás tövében.

A vadász még lesben ül sokáig,
Alkonyattól vár szerencsejelt:
Vár feszülten a nap áldoztáig,
S ím a várt szerencse megjelent: 10
Ah de nem vad, könnyü kis pillangó
S szép sugár lány, röpteként csapongó.

'Tarka lepke, szép arany pillangó!
Lepj meg engem, szállj rám kis madár;
Vagy vezess el, merre vagy szállandó   15

Ahol a nap nyúgodóba jár.'
Szól s iramlik, s mint az őz futása,
Könnyü s játszi a lány illanása.

'Istenemre!' szóla felszökelve
A vadász: 'ez már királyi vad!'   20
És legottan, minden mást feledve,
Hévvel a lány nyomdokán halad.
Ő a lányért, lány a pillangóért,
Versenyeznek tündér kedvtelésért.

'Megvagy!' így szól a leány örömmel,
Elfogván a szállongó lepét;   26
'Megvagy!' így szól a vadász, gyönyör-rel
A leányra nyújtva jobb kezét;
S rezzent kézből kis pillangó elszáll;
A leány rab szép szem sugaránál.   30

[2]   A range of hills west of Budapest.

II

Stands the house of grey-haired Peterdi still? Lives the son of former battles still? The house still stands, though the farm is decayed, and the aged man himself has sat down, his glass filled. Around him are the slender maiden and the guest: in the flame of his eyes burns alluring magic.

For Hunyadi,[1] for glory fallen, the cups now sparkle; for the great names of the grey-haired leader and the country the tears of the aged hero have been shed; now his tears, once his blood flowed freely, in the siege of Belgrade.

'Fair young ray of my fallen leader's sun', now says the aged man 'long live the King!' Blood rushes to the huntsman's cheeks; his cup remains untouched. 'Why leave your cup untouched? Take it up, my young friend, and follow your father.

For twice could I be your father, and if I have drunk, it is to no base men that I have lifted my glass. He whom I have named is a man from head to foot; he brings no shame on blood so heroic!' And deeply moved, with dignity in his eyes, the youth rises, a full glass in his hand:

'Then long live the seed of the heroic leader, may he live as long as he lives for the country! But may his life be cut off in the moment when first he rises in revolt against her; better no king, than one faithless; an evil king, a feeble king is a burden on the people.'[2]

II

Áll-e még az ősz Peterdi háza?
Él-e még a régi harc fia?
Áll a ház még, bár fogy gazdasága
S telt pohárnál űl az ősz maga.
A sugár lány körben és a vendég: 35
Lángszemében csábító varázs ég.

S Hunyadiért, a kidőlt dicsőért,
A kupák már felvillantanak,
Ősz vezére s a hon nagy nevéért
A vén bajnok könnyei hulltanak;   40
Most könyűi, vére hajdanában
Bőven omlott Nándor ostromában.

'Húnyt vezérem ifju szép sugára'
Szól az ősz most 'éljen a király!'
A vadásznak vér tolúl arcára   45
S még kupája illetetlen áll.
'Illetetlen mért hagyod kupádat?
Fogd fel gyermek, és kövesd apádat.

Mert apád én kétszer is lehetnék,
És ha ittam, az nincs cenkekért;   50
Talpig ember, akit én említék,
Nem gyaláz meg ő oly hősi vért!'
S illetődve s méltóság szemében,
Kél az ifju, tölt pohár kezében:

'Éljen hát a hős vezér magzatja,   55
Addig éljen, míg a honnak él!
De szakadjon élte pillanatja,
Melyben attól elpártolni kél;
Egy király se inkább, mint hitetlen:
Nyűg a népen a rossz s tehetetlen.'   60

---

[1] i.e. *Hunyadi János.

[2] Lines 57–60 ('But may . . . the people') were deleted by the censor, and the poem first appeared (in *Aurora*) without them.

Ever louder, ever warmer grew the merry talk in which the swift hour passed. The maiden gazed at the ardent stranger, faithfully and yet more faithfully. 'Who can he be, where is his homeland?' thought she, but her lips did not speak the words.

'You too, fair flower of the forest, this glass salutes and honours! May God one day bring you up to Buda; the huntsman will await you, with your grey-haired father; up in lofty Buda you will find me dwelling, at the court of *Mátyás.'

So speaks the huntsman and says farewell, the blare of the horn summons him: he must go. No word, no assurance can make him stay with his hosts. 'Remember to return to us, good huntsman, should we not visit you.'

Fair Ilonka spoke modestly, standing on the last step of the small porch; the youth kisses her forehead and sets out in the moonlit night. The house is quiet, ah but not at rest; the power of love has stirred it.

III

Peterdi and his lovely grandchild have set off to visit Buda; at every step the wonderment of the old man grows, he is amazed at all the new things he sees. The maiden secretly awaits a happy meeting, when the sweet hour comes.

Buda is thronged, rejoices anew; the people await the return of the victorious King, who has revenged himself on his evil neighbour, in his wrath which laid siege to Vienna. Many loyal eyes look towards him with longing; but the face of fair Ilonka is not gladdened.

S mind zajosban, mindig hevesebben
Víg beszéd közt a gyors óra ment.
A leányka híven és hivebben
Bámulá a lelkes idegent.
'Vajh ki ő, és merre van hazája?'   65
Gondolá, de nem mondotta szája.

'Téged is, te erdők szép virága,
Üdvözölve tisztel e pohár!
Hozzon Isten egykor fel Budába,
Ősz apáddal a vadász elvár;   70
Fenn lakozva a magas Budában
Leltek engem Mátyás udvarában.'

Szól s bucsúzik a vadász, rivalva
Inti őt a kürthang: menni kell.
Semmi szóra, semmi bíztatásra   75
Nem maradhat vendéglőivel.
'Emlékezzél visszatérni hozzánk,
Jó vadász, ha meg nem látogatnánk.'

Mond szerényen szép Ilonka, állván
A kis csarnok végső lépcsején,   80
S homlokán az ifju megcsókolván,
Útnak indul a hold éjjelén.
S csendes a ház, ah de nincs nyugalma:
Fölveré azt szerelem hatalma.

III

Föl Peterdi s bájos unokája   85
Látogatni mentenek Budát;
Minden lépten nő az agg csodája,
Mert sok újat meglepetve lát.
A leányka titkon édes óra
Jövetén vár szép találkozóra.   90

S van tolongás s új öröm Budában:
Győzelemből várják a királyt,
Aki Bécset vívó haragában
Vérboszút a rossz szomszédon állt.
Vágyva néz sok hű szem ellenébe: 95
Nem vidul még szép Ilonka képe.

'Where is he, that gracious stranger? What turn has fortune taken in his life? Is he at home, or has he perhaps gone to distant parts, to range over the cool retreats of the deer?' she asks, with secretly anxious thought; now her cheeks burn, now their colour dies away.

And there gallop forward, with countenances on which the storm of war has settled, Újlaki and the Garas,[1] now reconciled. And the King comes, the heroic elders surrounding him, aware of his majesty. Greyhaired Peterdi recognises his guest—it is the King: 'A blessing on his life!'

'Glory to his name, a blessing on his life!' loudly proclaim all loyal lips; a hundred times hill, valley and the enclosed walls re-echo to his name. Pale as a snow-white statue stands fair Ilonka, speechless, numb.

'Shall we indeed go to the huntsman at the court of *Mátyás, dear child? It is better for us in the wilds of the Vértes; our little home there will give us peace.' The grandfather spoke with understanding grief, and the sad pair went on their way, their steps stricken with care.

If you have seen a fair flower in bloom droop through inner sickness—so did fair Ilonka, fearing the light, droop beneath her secret sorrow. Her companions were feelings aflame, painful memories, dead hopes.

Her life, brief yet an agony, passed away, fair Ilonka languished to the grave; her languishing was the fall of lilies: her face, the face of innocence and grief. The King comes and stands in the deserted house; they rest in their eternal home.

'Hol van ő, a nyájas ösmeretlen?
Mily szerencse fordúlt életén?
Honn-e, vagy tán messze költözötten
Jár az őzek hűvös rejtekén?'   100
Kérdi titkon aggó gondolattal,
S arca majd ég, majd szinében elhal.

S felrobognak hadvész-ülte képpel
Újlaki s a megbékült Garák.
S a király jő, fölség érzetével   105
Környékezvén őt a hős apák.
Ősz Peterdi ösmer vendégére,
A király az: 'Áldás életére!'

'Fény nevére, áldás életére!'
Fenn kiáltja minden hű ajak;   110
Százszorozva vissza zeng nevére
A hegy és völgy és a zárt falak.
Haloványan hófehér szobornál
Szép Ilonka némán és merőn áll.

'A vadászhoz Mátyás udvarában,   115
Szép leánykám, elmenjünk-e hát?
Jobb nekünk a Vértes vadonában,
Kis tanyánk ott nyúgodalmat ád.'
Szól az ősz jól sejtő fájdalommal,
S a bús pár megy gond-sujtotta
        nyommal.   120

És ha láttál szépen nőtt virágot
Elhajolni belső baj miatt:
Úgy hajolt el, félvén a világot,
Szép Ilonka titkos bú alatt.
Társasága lángzó érzemények,   125
Kínos emlék, és kihalt remények.

A rövid, de gyötrő élet elfolyt,
Szép Ilonka hervadt sír felé;
Hervadása liliomhullás volt:
Ártatlanság képe s bánaté.   130
A király jön s áll a puszta házban:
Ők nyugosznak örökös hazában.

[1] Former enemies of the *Hunyadi family (cf. on the play *Czillei and the *Hunyadis*, p. 136 f.).

It may be characteristic of the taste of the time that the first words of this poem which occurred to Vörösmarty were the third and fourth lines of the last stanza (129–30, 'her languishing . . . and grief.'); but no reaction against sentimentality can obscure the skill, especially in the epithets, with which the scene is set, or the delicacy with which the identity of the huntsman is first suggested (20, 'a right royal quarry') then gradually revealed, or the sympathy with which the characters are portrayed—notably old Peterdi, in relation to both the King and Ilonka—or the conciseness of the narrative; this is a story which not long previously Vörösmarty might well have tried to turn into an epic.[1]

A little over two years later, in 1836, against a background of renewed terror, Vörösmarty wrote the ode which won him universal honour as the foremost poet of the nation; it has taken its place beside *Kölcsey's Hymn (Himnusz), as Hungary's second National Anthem.

A Call[2]

To your homeland, Hungarian, be unshakeably faithful; it is your cradle and then your grave, it nourishes you and then covers you.

In the whole wide world there is no place for you other than this; whether the hand of Fate bless or smite you, here you must live, here you must die.

This is the land where so often the blood of your fathers flowed; to this land have a thousand years linked every holy name.

[1] As indeed a less gifted writer two generations later did try.

[2]   *Szózat*

Hazádnak rendületlenűl
Légy híve, oh magyar;
Bölcsőd az s majdan sírod is,
Mely ápol s eltakar.

A nagy világon e kivűl   5
Nincsen számodra hely;
Áldjon vagy verjen sors keze:
Itt élned, halnod kell.

Ez a föld, melyen annyiszor
Apáid vére folyt;   10
Ez, melyhez minden szent nevet
Egy ezredév csatolt.

Itt küzdtenek honért a hős
Árpádnak hadai;
Itt törtek össze rabigát   15
Hunyadnak karjai.

Szabadság! itten hordozák
Véres zászlóidat,
S elhulltanak legjobbjaink
A hosszu harc alatt.   20

És annyi balszerencse közt,
Oly sok viszály után,
Megfogyva bár, de törve nem,
Él nemzet e hazán.

Here the armies of the hero *Árpád fought for a homeland; here the arm of Hunyadi[1] smashed the yoke of slavery.

Liberty! here were carried your bloodstained banners, and the best of us fell in the long struggle.[2]

And amid so many misfortunes, after so much strife, diminished but not broken, a nation dwells in this homeland.

Homeland of all peoples, wide world! bravely it calls to you: 'The sufferings of a thousand years demand life or death!'

It cannot be that so many breasts have poured out their blood in vain, and so many loyal hearts have broken in grief for the fatherland.

It cannot be that mind, might and a will so sacred should languish uselessly beneath the weight of a curse.

Still must come, still will come a better age, for which fervent prayer yearns, on the lips of hundreds of thousands.

Or there will come, if there must come, a noble death; over the burial a bleeding country will stand.

And the grave into which a nation has sunk will be surrounded by the peoples, and tears of mourning will stand in the eyes of millions.

Be unshakeably faithful to your homeland, Hungarian; it gives you life, and when you have fallen, covers you with its mound.

In the whole wide world there is no place for you other than this; whether the hand of Fate bless or smite you, here you must live, here you must die.

S népek hazája, nagy világ!
Hozzád bátran kiált:
'Egy ezredévi szenvedés
Kér éltet vagy halált!'

Az nem lehet, hogy annyi szív
Hiába onta vért,
S keservben annyi hű kebel
Szakadt meg a honért.

Az nem lehet, hogy ész, erő,
És oly szent akarat
Hiába sorvadozzanak
Egy átoksúly alatt.

Még jőni kell, még jőni fog
Egy jobb kor, mely után
Buzgó imádság epedez
Százezrek ajakán.

25 Vagy jőni fog, ha jőni kell,
A nagyszerű halál,
Hol a temetkezés fölött
Egy ország vérben áll.

30 S a sírt, hol nemzet sűlyed el, 45
Népek veszik körül,
S az ember millióinak
Szemében gyászköny űl.

35 Légy híve rendületlenűl
Hazádnak, oh magyar: 50
Ez éltetőd, s ha elbukál,
Hantjával ez takar.

40 A nagy világon e kivűl
Nincsen számodra hely;
Áldjon vagy verjen sors keze: 55
Itt élned, halnod kell.

[1] The reference is to the victories of *Hunyadi János over the Turks.
[2] The reference is to the rebellion of *Rákóczi, the mention of whose name was forbidden.

This poem expresses a new spirit; different from that of *Kölcsey's *Hymn* of 1823—'O God, bless the Hungarian . . . this people has atoned for the past and the future' (Isten, áldd meg a magyart . . . Megbünhödte már e nép / A multat s jövendőt)[1]— strikingly different from the sense of the hopeless inferiority of the present to the past which *Berzsenyi acquired from Horace his model, and which pervades *Zalán* and so many other poems of the time; in the *Szózat* speaks one who faces the future.

The Virgilian epic and Horatian ode had thus been replaced by modern successors; but the classical elegiac couplet retained its vitality, both for the short epigram or epitaph and for longer poems like Vörösmarty's noble elegy on the death of the actress Mme Hubenay in 1844 at the age of twenty-six, or the poem he wrote for the *Gutenberg-album* produced in 1840 to commemorate the four-hundredth anniversary of the invention of printing:

For the Gutenberg-album[2]

When Night tires and the priests of false dreams desist, and the sunlight bursting forth produces no more a counterfeit of knowledge;

When the sword falls from the brute hand of Force and no dagger debases the holy era of peace;

When from beasts and devils the rich blackmailers of the people and the wretched peasants advance to humanity;

When light spreads from West to East and a heart that knows sacrifice ennobles the mind;

When the peoples of the earth, in council together, shout together in voices that lay siege to Heaven,

---

[1] These lines, the first line and last two lines of the first stanza, are repeated in the last stanza, with the substitution of 'szánd' (pity) for 'áldd' (bless).

[2]   *A Gutenberg-albumba*

Majd ha kifárad az éj s hazug álmok
    papjai szűnnek
S a kitörő napfény nem terem
    áltudományt;
Majd ha kihull a kard az erőszak durva
    kezéből
S a szent béke korát nem cudarítja
    gyilok;
Majd ha baromból s ördögből a nép-
    zsaroló dús   5

S a nyomorú pórnép emberiségre
    javúl;
Majd ha világosság terjed ki keletre
    nyugatról
És áldozni tudó szív nemesíti az
    észt;
Majd ha tanácsot tart a föld népsége
    magával
És eget ostromló hangokon össze-
    kiált,   10

And out of the din one word thunders forth clearly: 'Truth!'[1] and Heaven at last sends down this long-awaited envoy:

Only that will be a worthy triumph for you; then will the world give you a monument worthy of your name.

It could be plausibly argued that the day when Gutenberg shall be worthily commemorated is here placed at an indefinite point in the future; but the poem is not the work of a pessimist, and in fact the 1839–40 Diet marked a reversal of the previous policy of terror. For example, *Kossuth was released from prison in 1840. But when the Hungarian looked beyond his own frontiers to Poland, he found a very different picture. The Polish fight for freedom had been followed with close sympathy in Hungary in 1830 no less than in 1939; one of the Perczels, a former pupil of Vörösmarty's, had been arrested for an illegal attempt to take a small force to fight alongside the Poles, and the poet himself, who had already commemorated their tragedy in an earlier poem, *The Homeless One* (*A hontalan*) (1835), now made it the subject of one of his greatest odes, *The Living Statue* (*Az élő szobor*), written probably in 1839 or 1840. Here is the second of the two alternatives set out in the *Szózat*.

The Living Statue[2]

I am a statue, but my every limb aches; the seething pain of blood rages in my veins; a dull throbbing runs through my numb muscles; my nerves struggle, immobile.

Before my eyes pass visions of the days when the people were consumed by their struggles: they sacrificed their blood for holy, eternal justice: and visions of the hordes of the North, that slew for pay.

And I see the shades of my children, who fell in the last battle, and the

S a zajból egy szó válik ki dörögve: 'igazság!'
S e rég várt követét végre leküldi az ég;

Az lesz csak méltó diadal számodra, nevedhez 13
Méltó emlékjelt akkoron ád a világ.

[1] The Hungarian word 'igazság' means both 'truth' and 'justice'.

[2] *Az élő szobor*

Szobor vagyok, de fáj minden tagom;
Eremben a vér forró kínja dúl;
Tompán sajognak dermedt izmaim;
Idegzetem küzd mozdúlhatlanúl.
Szemeim előtt képek vonúlnak el 5
A népemésztő harcok napiból:

Véráldozók a szent, örök jogért;
S bérért ölők éjszak csordáiból.

És látom gyermekimnek árnyait,
A vég csatában elhullottakét, 10

name of my savage persecutor written in blood on the walls of Warsaw and the burning villages.

And I hear the din of battles lost, the sinister whispers of traitors, and alas! I cannot hurl down on their heads the terrible curses of the deceived.

And I cannot weep, though in my eyes tears well up a hundred times like a hot shower: when they reach the grim world outside, they stiffen into cold, hard pearls of ice.

In my brain one crazed thought pursues another, like a storm: the holy patriot fire, ready for sacrifice, and base perfidy following close behind.

And every scourge of misfortune, which has befallen my people after so much bloodshed; great glory in the morning of the struggle; penury, death, shame in its twilight.

And in my heart—O unspeakable suffering!—the ardour of sacred vengeance seethes in revolt; it is a blazing house, falling in flames on its own master, whom no hands of neighbours snatch away to safety.

And my heavy breast, where pain dwells eternally, is filled with sighs; but there stands on it, as a barrier bewitched, the marble cover of the suffering heart.

I cannot speak; my groans are dumb cries; speech and prayer die away on my lips. The hawks of thought and feeling only breed within, on my tormenting flames.

Varsó falán s az égő falvakon
Vad üldözőmnek vérrel írt nevét.

És hallom a vesztett csaták zaját,
Az árulók bal suttogásait,
S fejökre hajh le nem zúdíthatom   15
A megcsalottak szörnyü átkait.

S nem sírhatok, bár hő zápor gyanánt
Szememben a könny százszor meg-
    ered:
Midőn kiér a zord világ elé,
Hideg, kemény jéggyöngyökké
    mered.   20

Agyamban egyik őrült gondolat
A másikat viharként kergeti:
Szent honfitűz, mely áldozatra kész,
S rút hitszegés, mely nyomban
    követi:

S a bal szerencse minden ostora,   25
Mely népem érte annyi vér után;
Magas dicsőség a harc reggelén;
Inség, halál, gyalázat alkonyán.

S szívemben—oh mondhatlan szen-
    vedés!
Lázongva forr a szent boszú heve;   30
Gyúlt ház az, mely ön gazdájára ég,
Kit nem ragad ki szomszédok keze.

S holott örökké él a fájdalom,
Nehéz mellem sohajjal van tele;
De rajta áll megbűvölt gát gyanánt   35
A szenvedő szív márvány fedele.

Nem szólhatok; nyögésem néma jaj;
Szó és fohász kihalnak ajkimon.
A gondolat s az érzés ölyvei
Csak benn tenyésznek gyötrő lángi-
    mon.   40

My sword hangs raised, athirst for the battle, but my straining arms do not move; my feet stand benumbed, and I cannot flee from my great torments.

Melt, ye petrified limbs, burst forth from my ravaged breast, O sigh! be as an earthquake at night, heavy and wild with grief and wrath.

And thou, suppressed word, leave thy prison, break through the heart of the generation of the indifferent, that every cowardly ear on the globe of the earth may ring with thy thunder.

Brief, but great, are the words I wish to speak: 'Man, world, nature, nations! If there is justice on earth, mercy in Heaven, look on me and my torments!'

This period saw also the production of other large-scale patriotic odes. In *To Liszt* (*Liszt Ferenchez*) (1840) the 'renowned musician of the world' who at the same time remains a 'faithful kinsman' wherever he may travel, is exhorted to 'make a song resound for us' (his countrymen) in a poem of sustained nobility whose rhetoric is yet perhaps in the last resort conventional. *To the Lady of Rank* (*Az úri hölgyhöz*) (1841) reminds the heartlessly cosmopolitan lady of fashion, in tones of anger scarcely controlled, that 'the speechless mouths of the little ones beg you to give them a homeland. Withdraw not that gift—a blessing or a curse waits on your reply' (85–87). If invective has a place of honour in literature, this is a fine example, though the conception of the poet's position in society which it implies now seems totally strange to us.[1] Not that Vörösmarty could fairly be accused of a deficient sense of chivalry, in relation to the social structure of his day, because the 'arrogant Goneril' whom he pillories (a type not an individual) belongs to the stronger class—more than adequate compensation for being of the weaker sex. Last of this group of poems, and perhaps the most interesting, comes the *Song of Fót* (*Fóti dal*), written for a party to

Emelten függ a harcra szomju kard,	S te elnyomott szó, hagyd el börtönöd,
De nem mozdúlnak a feszűlt karok;	Törj át a fásult nemzedék szivén, 50
Dermedten állnak lépő lábaim,	Hogy megcsendűljön minden gyáva fül
S nagy kínjaimtól el nem futhatok.	Mennydörgésedtől a föld kerekén.
Oldódjatok, ti megkövűlt tagok, 45	Kevés, de nagy, mit szólni akarok:
Szakadj fel dúlt keblemből, oh sohaj!	'Ember, világ, természet, nemzetek!
Légy mint a földrendítő éji vész,	Ha van jog földön, égben irgalom, 55
Bútól, haragtól terhes és szilaj.	Reám és kínaimra nézzetek!'

[1] Rumanian poetry provides a parallel from more recent times in Octavian Goga's *Letter to the Comtesse de Noailles, Princess Brîncoveanu* (1913).

celebrate the vintage, given by the novelist *Fáy at his vineyard in the village of Fót, on the north-eastern outskirts of Budapest in October 1842. The inconsequent opening—

A pearl in wine rises upwards; so it should. No one can deprive it of this right. Let everything that is a pearl burst forth and rise to heaven; let the clod remain on the base earth.

The body is revived and nourished by a feast, but what gives it its soul is the wine.[1]

—and the abrupt transitions produce an improvisatory effect exactly right for a convivial occasion, and Vörösmarty avoids excessive solemnity by postponing the introduction of his patriotic theme till one-third of the way through the poem, and by his skill in combining the serious and the festive elements in his song:

Let every wish of ours be a holy prayer, and let our manly hearts be the temple of our holy prayers. And let us drain this glass for the country; a glass of wine for the country won't do any harm.[2]

The 'wish' is that

May loyal concord keep her sons united, to conquer the dread shadows of night; powerful abroad, at home flourishing and free, may she stand secure beneath justice inviolable.[3]

In the fundamental confidence, combined with an awareness of the sacrifices which may be required, with which the poet contemplates the future, the *Song of Fót* resembles the *Szózat* (which it closely rivalled in popularity), however different the two poems may be in other respects.

[1] Fölfelé megy borban a gyöngy;
　　Jól teszi.
　　Tőle senki e jogát el
　　Nem veszi.
　　Törjön is mind ég felé az　　5
　　Ami gyöngy;
　　Hadd maradjon gyáva földön
　　A göröngy.

　　Testet éleszt és táplál a
　　Lakoma,　　10
　　De ami a lelket adja,
　　Az bora.

[2] Légyen minden óhajtásunk　　105
　　Szent ima,

S férfi keblünk szent imáink
　　Temploma.
És ürítsük a hazáért
　　E pohárt:　　110
Egy pohár bor a hazáért
　　Meg nem árt.

[3] Hű egyesség tartsa össze
　　Fiait,
Hogy leküzdje éjszak rémes
　　Árnyait:
Künn hatalmas, benn virágzó　　125
　　És szabad,
Bizton álljon sérthetetlen
　　Jog alatt.

In addition to his activity as writer and critic, Vörösmarty was a key figure in the work of the Academy. He played an important part in the standardizing of Hungarian orthography and grammar: was joint editor of a grammar, which appeared in 1834 and again, in expanded form, in 1846: collaborated in a dictionary of Hungarian dialects (1838), in a Hungarian–German pocket dictionary (which appeared in 1838 and 1843), and in the preliminary work for a *Complete Dictionary of the Hungarian Language*.

Perczel Etelka had married in 1833 and, with the assistance of a busy life, the wound in Vörösmarty had gradually healed. Yet his work was not the whole of his life, as is clear from a remarkable poem of 1839, inspired by some new emotional experience which also revived memories of the past:

Late Desire[1]

Beyond my youth, beyond my burning desires, in whose path grief cruelly opened up; beyond the hopes, over which the finger of disappointment coldly wove a shroud the colour of night; beyond the life of the heart, I was peacefully enjoying the gifts of Fate and the mind, the fine day of autumn. But when I caught sight of you, my fair sunlight, I wished anew for my vanished days; I wished for all that the dreams of its fancy believed: the sweet sorrow, which gave me so much delight; joy drowned in pain, which tortured me so often. Vainly, uselessly! Youth and hope are lost for ever on the sea of years; to hope is so hard in the twilight of life, and the mind forbids love after hopes have vanished.

But 'the mind forbade' in vain; in 1841 Vörösmarty met Csajághy Laura, the younger sister of the wife of his friend *Bajza,

---

[1]   *Késő vágy*

Túl ifjuságomon,
Túl égő vágyimon,
Melyeknek mostohán
Keserv nyilt nyomdokán;
Túl a reményeken,   5
Melyekre hidegen
Éjszínű szemfedőt
Csalódás ujja szőtt;
Túl a szív életén
Nyugodtan éldelém   10
Mit sors s az ész adott,
Az őszi szép napot.
De hogy megláttalak,
Szép napvilágomat,
Kivántam újolag   15

Már eltünt koromat;
Kivántam mind, amit
Ábrándos álma hitt:
Az édes bánatot,
Mely annyi kéjt adott,   20
A kínba fúlt gyönyört,
Mely annyiszor gyötört.
Hiába, hasztalan!
Ifjuság és remény
Örökre veszve van   25
Az évek tengerén:
Remélni oly nehéz
A kornak alkonyán,
S szeretni tilt az ész
Letünt remény után.   30

and in 1842—the same year in which his *New Works*[1] (*Ujabb munkái*) received the highest Academy award—he wrote:

Thirst[2]

I am thirsty, but it is not for wine that I thirst, and no water can slake my thirst. . . . For flame am I athirst, for flame, for fire, for your soul, that plays in the fire of your eyes; I thirst for the dawn on your fair cheeks, and for the honey of the smile on your lips.

Another poem of 1842 bears the title *I am angry with you* (*Haragszom rád*)—'I am angry with you, because my peace is gone'—and early in 1843 came the *Reverie*.

Reverie[3]

For your love I would ravage my mind and its every thought, and the sweet lands of my imagination; I would tear my soul to shreds for your love.

For your love I would be a tree on a mountain-top, I would don its green foliage, I would endure the wrath of lightning and storm and I would die each winter for your love.

For your love I would be the stone on which a peak presses, there would I burn with subterranean flame, with undying pain, mutely suffering, for your love.

For your love I would ask for my torn soul back from God, I would adorn it with virtue more glorious, and offer it joyfully to you for your love!

---

[1] This edition, in four volumes, contained Vörösmarty's poems and plays of the period 1832–40 (omitting *Blood-Wedding* and *Marót *Bán* but including the translation of *Julius Caesar*.)

[2]   *A Szomju*

Szomjas vagyok; de nem bort szom-
     jazom,
És szomjamat vízzel nem olthatom.
                    *

Én lángot szomjazom, lángot, tüzet, 5
Szemed tüzében játszó lelkedet;
Szomjúzom a hajnalt szép arcodon,
És a mosolynak mézét ajkidon.

[3]   *Ábránd*

Szerelmedért
Feldúlnám eszemet
És annak minden gondolatját,
S képzelmim édes tartományát;
Eltépném lelkemet   5
Szerelmedért.

Szerelmedért
Fa lennék bérc fején,
Felölteném zöld lombozatját,
Eltűrném villám s vész haragját   10
S meghalnék minden év telén
Szerelmedért.

Szerelmedért
Lennék bérc-nyoma kő,
Ott égnék földalatti lánggal,   15
Kihalhatatlan fájdalommal,
És némán szenvedő,
Szerelmedért.

Szerelmedért
Eltépett lelkemet   20
Istentől újra visszakérném,
Dicsőbb erénnyel ékesítném,
S örömmel nyújtanám neked
Szerelmedért!

It was a long time before Laura became aware that she was the object of such feelings as these on the part of the foremost poet of the day, and still longer before she finally overcame her bewilderment and her doubts whether she and a man some twenty-five years her senior could find happiness together—doubts which indeed were shared by their friends. By the time of their engagement the gay and sparkling girl had become the 'pensive one' to whom this poem (early 1843) was addressed:

To the Pensive One[1]

(To Laura)

Where is the light of your fair eyes lost? What seek they in the doubtful distance? Perhaps the dark flower of times past, on which the tear of disappointment quivers? Perhaps in the moonlit veil of the future the terror of awful shapes approaches you, and you cannot trust in the prophecies of your fate, because you once sought it by a false way?... Bring back, oh bring back the light of your fair eyes; let it return like a bird which has flown away but comes back when it has found its own green branch, though the leaves of the whole forest tempt it. Remain in our midst with your young eyes, restore the brightness on the face of your friend: if you have been his daylight, take not fair noon away, give not in its place grief and tears.

On 9 May 1843 Vörösmarty and Laura were married. The poet remained uncertain of his ability to make his young wife happy, and there were material worries too, especially when a family came (their first child was born in April 1844); fame did not mean money. The resulting emotional stress was aggravated by renewed anxious questionings about the fortunes of the country. The *Szózat* had been based on the straight alternative of the survival or destruction of the nation as a whole; but this proved an oversimplification. The nation was not a single whole, and the unity

---

[1]   *A merengőhöz (Laurának)*

Hová merült el szép szemed világa?
Mi az, mit kétes távolban keres?
Talán a múlt idők setét virága,
Min a csalódás könnye rengedez?
Tán a jövőnek holdas fátyolában   5
Ijesztő képek réme jár feléd,
S nem bízhatol sorsodnak jóslatában,
Mert egyszer azt csalúton kereséd?
· · ·

Hozd, oh hozd vissza szép szemed
    világát;
Úgy térjen az meg, mint elszállt madár,
Mely visszajő, ha meglelé zöld ágát,
Egész erdő viránya csalja bár.
Maradj közöttünk ifju szemeiddel, 45
Barátod arcán hozd fel a derűt:
Ha napja lettél, szép delét ne vedd el,
Ne adj helyette bánatot, könyűt.
    (1–8, 41–48 (end))

proclaimed as the ideal in the *Song of Fót* was shattered not only by the widening of the breach between *Széchenyi and *Kossuth[1] (whose positions Vörösmarty tried to reconcile) but more fundamentally by the realization that the nation was divided into two hostile camps by social barriers. This point had already been adumbrated in the essentially optimistic Gutenberg-poem; but soon Vörösmarty found himself contemplating not the vision of a bright future, but rather the distance separating that future from the present. As a result, he virtually abandoned the ode—of the two examples dating from 1843–4, the earlier *Love of Country (Honszeretet)* (1843) is as conspicuously lacking in sublimity as the later *Hymn (Hymnus)* (1844) in spontaneity. The most important poem of this period is of quite a different type. In the reflective *Thoughts in a Library (Gondolatok a könyvtárban)* (1844) the poet, taking the contrast between the paper of a book and the rags from which it was made (and their possible origin) as symbolical of the gulf between the ideal and the real, faces a final pessimism:

A book has been made from the garments of a people enslaved and of cowards, and now freedom and the heroic age relate their great history in it. Loyalty, friendship tell their tale on a page made from the clothes of base, treacherous perjurers. Hideous falsehood everywhere! The deathly picture of the pale leaf condemns the written letters.

Rags of countries! your name is a library. But where is the book which leads to the goal? Where is the happiness of the majority?—Has the world advanced because of books?[2]

'Yet we must strive' (80):

What is our task in the world? to struggle, and give nourishment to the desires of our souls.[3]

But the gloom deepened; the old inertia remained—the Hungarian of the satirical allegory *Fate and the Hungarian (A sors és a*

[1] See p. 172.

[2] Könyv lett a rabnép s gyávák köntöséből
S most a szabadság és a hősi kor
Beszéli benne nagy történetét.   35
Hűség, barátság aljas hitszegők
Gúnyáiból készült lapon regél.
Irtózatos hazudság mindenütt!
Az írt betűket a sápadt levél
Halotti képe kárhoztatja el.   40
Országok rongya! könyvtár a neved,

De hát hol a könyv, mely célhoz vezet?
Hol a nagyobb rész boldogsága?—
Ment-e
A könyvek által a világ elébb?

[3] Mi dolgunk a világon? küzdeni,
És tápot adni lelki vágyainknak.
(107–8)

magyar ember) (1846) is a 'rusty knight' whose active days belong
to the distant past, and who now spends his time lost in a cloud of
pipe-smoke. In addition, elections of county officials were marked
by exceptional violence—the country whose representative body
'goes to vote at the sound of the drum' and is 'tyrant and servant
in one, not even at peace with itself'[1] had 'broached its own blood-
vessels'.[2] Then in 1846 Poland again provided a terrible example
of what could happen, with the peasant revolt in Galicia. So the
last stanza of *Mankind* (*Az emberek*) (1846) contrasts strongly with
the close of *Thoughts in a Library*:

> Man pains the earth; after so many years of war and peace the fratri-
> cidal curse flourishes on his brow; and when we might believe that he is
> learning, he treacherously plots a greater crime. The race of mankind is
> a crop sprung from dragon's teeth: there is no hope! there is no hope![3]

The gloom deepened, but it was not unrelieved. Vörösmarty's
view of life includes also the sympathy of the poor woman in
The Poor Woman's Book (*A szegény asszony könyve*) (1847)[4] who
tore her prayer-book in two to lend one half to her neighbour:

> A poor woman, God sees her, without a friend on earth, aged, poor
> and helpless, she sits by herself in her quiet home. She mourns not;
> long ago she mourned, when her good husband died; but her dress
> mourns still: her heart fears bright colours. She is not busy—how could
> she be? And for her meagre lunch she needs no servant. At lunch she
> has no guest, only the memory of times past.[5]

Again, in a popular vein, Vörösmarty relates, for instance, the
final happiness which rewarded Mák Bandi's inability to tear

---

[1] *Houses of Parliament* (*Országháza*) (1846), 8–9, 12–13.
[2] *Fate and the Hungarian* (*A sors és a magyar ember*) (1846), 133–4.

[3] Az ember fáj a földnek; oly sok   S midőn azt hinnők, hogy tanúl,
Harc- s békeév után   50   Nagyobb bűnt forral álnokúl.
A testvérgyűlölési átok   Az emberfaj sárkányfog-vetemény: 55
Virágzik homlokán;   Nincsen remény! nincsen remény!

[4] *The Poor Woman's Book* is a portrait of Vörösmarty's mother (who had
died, at the age of sixty-four, in 1834), but with characteristic reticence the poet
gives no indication of this fact, which we know only from his biographer *Gyulai.

[5] Egy szegény nő, Isten látja,   De ruhája mégis gyászol:
Nincs a földön egy barátja,   Szíve fél a tarkaságtól.
Agg, szegény és gyámolatlan,   Dolga nincs, hogy volna dolga?
Ül magán a csendes lakban.   Kis ebédhez nem kell szolga,   10
Gyásza nincsen, gyásza rég volt,   5   S az ebédnél nincs vendége,
Még midőn jó férje megholt;   Csak a múlt idők emléke.

himself away from his home village where his beloved had temporarily rejected him for another (*Mák Bandi*) (1842), and the loyalty of the soldier's sweetheart who was still waiting for him at the end of his eight years' service (*The Soldier*) (*A katona*) (1844). There is also the humour of the delightful portrait of the boy Petike consoled in his amorous melancholy by his mother (*Petike*) (1841) and the carefree cheerfulness of *The Slovak Student's Song* (*A tót deák dala*) (1843):

> If I get depressed because I've no money, or never had any, my trousers, my boots are nothing but patches and still my shoe pinches: I just gaze at you and I get better at once, huge world, glorious world![1]

The Slovak Student's view of life appears also in Vörösmarty's own correspondence.

In 1847, the despair of *Mankind* was belied by the turn of events, in particular by the unification of the opposition. So in the strikingly terse *What's the Matter* (*Mi baj?*) (1847)—remarkable also for its treatment of a patriotic theme in unadorned language—the poet's many criticisms of his unpractical nation are finally dismissed: 'But all this doesn't matter, if you have a soul.' (61–62.)

5

Though an advocate of 'agitation' (forrongás), Vörösmarty had always ruled out revolution as a method of achieving the nation's aims; but this did not mean that he stood aloof from the events of 1848–9. He later[2] described himself as 'an onlooker rather than a leader'; but though less than a leader, he was certainly more than an onlooker. He was Vice-President of the 'Opposition Circle' (Ellenzéki Kör); Chairman of the Recruiting Committee of the National Guard: he served on a committee of inquiry into the Press, and on the Commission for the Maintenance of Public Order (Közcsendi Bizottmány): he drafted the national proclamation issued on 31 March 1848: in June he was elected a Deputy. He threw in his lot with *Kossuth and the radicals, though within their ranks his influence was always exercised on the side of moderation.

---

[1] Ha kedvem elborúl,   Csak rajtad bámulok,
 Mert pénzem nincs, vagy nem is volt,   S tüstént kigyógyulok,
 Nadrágom, csizmám csupa folt,   Roppant világ,
 S kapcám mégis szorúl: 5   Dicső világ!

[2] In a letter of November 1849 to his wife.

In August 1848, for instance, he supported *Kossuth's compromise proposals on the organization of a National Army[1]—that units already in existence should remain for the time being within the organization of the Austrian Army, and continue to use German as the language of command.

In January 1849 Vörösmarty followed the *Kossuth Government to Debrecen—where he and his wife looked after Petőfi's family when the younger poet had joined the army—then in June he returned with the revolutionaries to Buda, where *Kossuth appointed him a judge. In July, however, the situation worsened again, and the Government moved to Szeged; Vörösmarty went with them but left his family behind in Pest, where his younger daughter died, at the age of eight months. Early in August, as the Austrian and Russian net closed in on Hungary, he had to flee from Szeged, and for some time lived the life of a fugitive in north-eastern Hungary. Finally, in December, after the defeat of his country, he returned to the capital, broken in health and spirits, and prematurely aged. Early in 1850 the military court before which he appeared found itself able to clear him (the collective death sentence passed on all deputies of *Kossuth's Parliament having been revoked) and he was a free man. But in the new absolutism Hungarian literature no longer provided a livelihood, and he moved into the country, first near his birthplace, then to his birthplace itself, to cultivate a small plot of land on which generous friends helped to establish him.

During the whole of this period he wrote very little. The numbed silence of defeat (combined with the destruction of some politically compromising poems) requires no explanation; but in 1848, too, though he produced numerous articles, he wrote only three poems, none of particular significance—a short poem of eight lines acclaiming the newly won freedom of the Press, *Free Press* (*Szabad sajtó*), a *Battle-Song* (*Harci dal*) with a refrain closely modelled in both content and rhythm on that of the *Marseillaise*, and a short epigram (a single elegiac couplet) administering a paternally benevolent rebuke to Petőfi, whose ardent single-mindedness had been revolted by the compromises of the practical politicians on the army question. Vörösmarty's patriotic poems had referred to the future, a natural consequence of the role of the poet as prophet: the *Szózat*, which had won him a

[1] To fight the Serbs, who had invaded southern Hungary in July.

unique standing, had spoken of a decisive day in the future: now that future was in the present. Perhaps his pen was paralysed by suspense; at any rate his reticence reasserted itself, and in April 1848 the death of his three-year-old younger son was commemorated in verse by Petőfi and others, not by the bereaved father himself.

In 1849 he wrote only two poems, both after the catastrophe of defeat and surrender. The first was a contribution to the album of a hostess, while he was in hiding: 'Dark thoughts cloud my mind. . . . My wish is: may the world perish. . . . With a damned soul I cry uselessly into the great Infinite: that for which I lived is ravaged. From such a man, noble lady, what can you request for your album? Give me rather faith, a sign, a ray of hope, that my nation still lives.' The second poem of 1849 is a furious *Curse* (*Átok*) of *Görgey for treacherously (as Vörösmarty considered) surrendering to the enemy.

Vörösmarty's next poem, the *Prelude* (*Előszó*)[1] of 1850, describes how once

Green branches flourished on the peaks of the earth. Man lived in his work, ant-like: the hand struggled, the spirit moved, careful reason burned, the heart hoped.[2]

Then

The storm broke. Its blood-freezing hand, playing at ball with the heads of men, threw them into the sky, while its feet trampled on human hearts. Its breath caused life to wither, the world of the spirit was put to sleep, and across the face of the darkened heavens the flashes painted, in savage light, the wrath of hostile gods.[3]

Finally the 'winter and quiet and snow and death' (34) give place to a mocking counterfeit of spring, a picture terrifying enough in all conscience; yet the use of allegory marks the first faltering steps

---

[1] The precise significance of the title (which was added after most of the poem had been composed) and the meaning of the first line 'When I wrote this, the skies were clear' are obscure.

[2] Zöld ág virított a föld ormain.   Emberfejekkel labdázott az égre, 20
  Munkában élt az ember mint a   Emberszivekben dúltak lábai.
    hangya: Lélekzetétől meghervadt az élet,
  Küzdött a kéz, a szellem működött,   A szellemek világa kialudt,
  Lángolt a gondos ész, a szív remélt. 5   S az elsötétült égnek arcain
                                         Vad fénnyel a villámok rajzolák le 25
[3] A vész kitört. Vérfagylaló keze   Az ellenséges istenek haragját.

towards some degree of detachment. Hungarian literary life gradually began to revive; in 1854 Vörösmarty completed his translation of *Lear*, in which the utterances of the King on the heath are so close to the spirit of the *Prelude*. His health and strength, however, were now failing; he was beset by incessant financial and practical difficulties, as he struggled pathetically to start a new life as a small farmer; but he maintained to the end that what had happened was not the death of the nation, of which the *Szózat* had spoken. He died on 19 November 1855; but a year earlier he had roused himself once more to write *The Old Gipsy* (*A vén cigány*), in which the poet, addressing a gipsy fiddler who is a double of himself, points the way beyond the storm of the *Prelude*:

The Old Gipsy[1]

Play, gipsy, you have drunk your wages, sit not idly, uselessly; what good is care, with bread and water? Fill that cheerless cup with wine. This life on earth has been ever the same, now freezing, now burning with flame. Play, who knows how long you will yet be able to play, when your worn bow will be a stick; heart and glass are filled with grief, with wine, play, gipsy, and care not for care!

Let your blood seethe like the waters of a whirlpool, let the marrow in your brain quake, let your eye blaze like the flame of a comet, your strings resound wilder than the storm, hard as hail, the generation of men is gone.—Play, who knows how long you will yet be able to play, when your worn bow will be a stick; heart and glass are filled with grief, with wine, play, gipsy, and care not for care!

Learn a song from the ringing thunderstorm as it moans, howls, wails, weeps and roars; it tears up trees and shatters ships, chokes life, kills man and beast; there is war now in the wide world, the grave of

[1]   *A vén cigány*

Húzd rá cigány, megittad az árát,
Ne lógasd a lábadat hiába;
Mit ér a gond kenyéren és vízen,
Tölts hozzá bort a rideg kupába.
Mindig így volt e világi élet,   5
Egyszer fázott, másszor lánggal égett;
Húzd, ki tudja meddig húzhatod,
Mikor lesz a nyűtt vonóbul bot;
Szív és pohár tele búval, borral,
Húzd rá cigány, ne gondolj a
        gonddal!   10

Véred forrjon mint az örvény árja,
Rendüljön meg a velő agyadban,

Szemed égjen mint az üstökös láng,
Húrod zengjen vésznél szilajabban,
És keményen mint a jég verése,   15
Oda lett az emberek vetése —
Húzd, ki tudja meddig húzhatod,
Mikor lesz a nyűtt vonóbul bot;
Szív és pohár tele búval, borral,
Húzd rá cigány, ne gondolj a gonddal!   20

Tanulj dalt a zengő zivatartól,
Mint nyög, ordít, jajgat, sír és bömböl;
Fákat tép ki és hajókat tördel,
Életet fojt, vadat és embert öl;
Háború van most a nagy világban,   25
Isten sírja reszket a szent honban.

God in the Holy Land trembles. Play, who knows how long you will yet be able to play, when your worn bow will be a stick; heart and glass are filled with grief, with wine, play, gipsy, and care not for care!

Whose was this stifled sigh, what is it that cries, weeps in this wild onset, who is hammering on the vault of Heaven, what is it that sobs like a mill in Hell? A falling angel, broken heart, maddened soul, beaten armies or rash hopes? Play, who knows how long you will yet be able to play, when your worn bow will be a stick; heart and glass are filled with grief, with wine, play, gipsy, and care not for care!

It is as if we heard anew over the plains the wild grief of the rebel, the blow of the murderous brother's cudgel, the funeral speech of the first bereaved, the flapping of the vulture's wing, the undying torment of Prometheus. Play, who knows how long you will yet be able to play, when your worn bow will be a stick; heart and glass are filled with grief, with wine, play, gipsy, and care not for care!

Let the blind star, this unhappy earth, roll on in its bitter juice, and let it be purged in the fire of the storm from the wrath of so much crime and filth, of so many fancies; and let Noah's ark come, enclosing in itself a new world. Play, who knows how long you will yet be able to play, when your worn bow will be a stick; heart and glass are filled with grief, with wine, play, gipsy, and care not for care!

Play—but no; leave your strings in peace, once again there will be a festive day on earth; when the wrath of the storm tires, and strife

Húzd, ki tudja meddig húzhatod,	Húzd, ki tudja meddig húzhatod,
Mikor lesz a nyűtt vonóbul bot;	Mikor lesz a nyűtt vonóbul bot;
Szív és pohár tele búval, borral,	Szív és pohár tele búval, borral,
Húzd rá cigány, ne gondolj a gond-	Húzd rá cigány, ne gondolj a gond-
dal! 30	dal! 50
Kié volt ez elfojtott sohajtás,	A vak csillag, ez a nyomoru föld
Mi üvölt, sír e vad rohanatban,	Hadd forogjon keserű levében,
Ki dörömböl az ég boltozatján,	S annyi bűn, szenny s ábrándok dü-
Mi zokog mint malom a pokolban?	hétől
Hulló angyal, tört szív, őrült lélek, 35	Tisztuljon meg a vihar hevében,
Vert hadak vagy vakmerő remények?	És hadd jöjjön el Noé bárkája, 55
Húzd, ki tudja meddig húzhatod,	Mely egy új világot zár magába.
Mikor lesz a nyűtt vonóbul bot;	Húzd, ki tudja meddig húzhatod,
Szív és pohár tele búval, borral,	Mikor lesz a nyűtt vonóbul bot;
Húzd rá cigány, ne gondolj a gond-	Szív és pohár tele búval, borral,
dal! 40	Húzd rá cigány, ne gondolj a gond-
Mintha újra hallanók a pusztán	dal! 60
A lázadt ember vad keserveit,	Húzd, de még se, — hagyj békét a
Gyilkos testvér botja zuhanását,	húrnak,
S az első árvák sírbeszédeit,	Lesz még egyszer ünnep a világon;
A keselynek szárnya csattogását, 45	Majd ha elfárad a vész haragja,
Prometheusz halhatatlan kínját.	S a viszály elvérzik a csatákon,

bleeds to death in battle, then play with new ardour, and let the gods delight in your playing. Then take up once again the bow, and let your stern brow be gladdened. Let your heart be filled with the wine of joy; play, and care not for the cares of the world.

Akkor húzd meg újra lelkesedve,	65	Szűd teljék meg az öröm borával,
Isteneknek teljék benne kedve.		Húzd, s ne gondolj a világ gond-
Akkor vedd fel újra a vonót,		jával. 70
És derűljön zordon homlokod.		

IV

EÖTVÖS[1] (1813–1871) * NOVELIST AND STATESMAN

I

A MAN's achievement often contrasts with his family background; but seldom more strikingly than that of Baron Eötvös József. Perhaps the first Hungarian novelist whom we honour as a master rather than as a pioneer, he was born into an exclusively German-speaking home; outstanding among Hungary's liberal reformers, he was the son and grandson of pillars of Austrian rule who were not only conservatives but also brutes. Both his grandfather, Baron Eötvös Ignác senior (1763–1838) and his father, also christened Ignác (1786–1851), held a succession of high offices and made the name of Eötvös odious to Hungarians, the latter particularly by his ruthless suppression of the unrest in northern Hungary which followed the cholera epidemic of 1831. His favourite words to a rebel brought before him, 'Amice carissime, cras pendebis' (My dearest friend, tomorrow you shall hang), found their way into dictionaries of quotations.

These antecedents were, however, counterbalanced by Eötvös's mother, from whom he inherited a deep human sympathy, and by his tutor Pruzsinszky József, who inspired in him a determination not only to learn Hungarian, but to clear the family name of its associations with foreign oppression. Pruzsinszky had himself suffered for liberty, having served nearly three years' imprisonment for misprision of treason in connexion with the *Martinovics conspiracy of 1795, and seems a surprising choice as tutor to the son of Baron Eötvös Ignác. According to one account, the father's object was to turn his son against liberal ideas by setting Pruzsinszky before him as a dreadful example. If there is any truth in this story, the plan misfired badly.

---

[1] The initial 'E' is not pronounced: see p. ix.

The young Eötvös early acquired a love of literature, of German from his mother and her friends, of Latin from Pruzsinszky. He did brilliantly at school; then at Pest University, which he entered in the autumn of 1826 to read philosophy and law, he distinguished himself in every subject—except Hungarian language and literature; there was still too much leeway to make up. But the seed planted by Pruzsinszky bore fruit, as was inevitable, in the enthusiastic atmosphere of the years following the Diet of 1825, and Eötvös soon began to contribute to the national literature; in September 1835 he was elected a corresponding member of the Academy for his services in this field.

His first works were all dramas; after all, he had been a keen theatre-goer from the age of seven. His first original play,[1] *The Apotheosis of the Critic (A kritikus apotheosisa)* (1831), is a short dramatic allegory attacking *Bajza, who had inveighed against the veteran *Kazinczy for translating some poems written by a Hungarian in German, Pyrker's *Perlen der heiligen Vorzeit (Pearls of the Sacred Past)*. Eötvös saw *Bajza's attack as a piece of coarse and malicious ingratitude towards the man without whom the revival of Hungarian literature could never have been achieved.

The Apotheosis of the Critic was followed by two full-length plays, the comedy *The Couples (A házasulók)* (1833), negligible except for the interest attaching to its author's first attempts at satire, and the tragedy *Revenge (Boszú)* (1834), which marks a considerable advance on its predecessor. Set in Turkey, it aims to horrify, and is exactly what Eötvös himself in later life called 'impossible' drama;[2] but it has some fine passages, especially in the eventual realization by the principal character that 'he who would coerce his fate is buried with the edifices he has built' (v. 204–5).

It was, however, his poetry which first won Eötvös recognition as a writer. This seems strange today, though anthologists still remember his first poem *The Frozen Child (A megfagyott gyermek)* (1833), a sentimental ballad about an orphan who freezes to death beside his mother's grave, and the *Farewell (Búcsú)* to his country, which he wrote on his departure for a tour of Europe in 1836, served as a model to many of his contemporaries. Above all, the ballad *The Castle and the Cottage (A vár és a kunyhó)* (1837), on

---

[1] His first work of all (which remained unpublished) was his translation of Goethe's drama *Götz von Berlichingen* (1830); he also translated Victor Hugo's *Angelo* (1836).   [2] See pp. xxiii f.

the tragic love of a lord's son and a girl of humble birth, has a real power which leaves no doubt of Eötvös's concern with the human aspects of the structure of society.

This concern had early been aroused by first-hand observation; in 1831, the year of his first appearance in print, Eötvös had also begun his public career as an under-notary (aljegyző) in his county, and in the following year his father took him to Pozsony[1] to the Diet. No Diet could have stimulated more effectively the zeal for reform in a young man. Reform was in the air, and Eötvös heard it urged by some of the greatest orators of the day, notably the poet *Kölcsey, and *Deák, the future architect of the 1867 Compromise. He learnt, too, not only the arguments by which reforms are opposed but the methods by which they are obstructed. The effect of this experience on the young man whom *Kölcsey described in his diary as an 'amiable, ardent child' can be imagined. When, having returned from a year's tour of western Europe, he produced his first major essay, the dissertation on prison reform (*Vélemény a fogházjavítás ügyében*) (1838), Eötvös urged at the outset the importance of action: 'the best way to start is to start something.' Yet he was no hothead; reform must be based on definite principles.

Eötvös's essay examines fully both the physical and the moral harm done by the prison conditions of his time. He discusses prison hygiene in detail, for it is an essential aspect of his main thesis that a penitentiary system must ensure that the criminal shall suffer no more than the punishment imposed by his sentence. This thesis naturally leads Eötvös to include moral problems in his survey, though such reforms as had been achieved in Hungary were concerned almost solely with the physical health of the prisoners. He emphasizes particularly the danger that hardened criminals may corrupt their cell-mates, and sees solitary confinement rather as a precaution against this danger than as a method involving psychological perils of its own. Indeed, for short-term prisoners and those awaiting trial he prefers solitary confinement, with individual work (the Philadelphia system) to the Auburn system, by which the prisoners work together (though in silence).

There must, he declares, be proper provision for the rehabilitation of discharged prisoners; otherwise the bonds joining a man to his fellows will be broken, with disastrous results—for the prisoner

[1] Now Bratislava in Czechoslovakia; it was then the capital of Hungary.

is still our fellow man and our fellow citizen—quite apart from the impossibility of certainty that no innocent man is ever imprisoned. Punishment must have a corrective value, and the only true and lasting correctives are work and religion. The whole problem is essentially a human one, and now success is possible, for 'it is the greatness of our age that it loves mankind'.

Eötvös's main source was Bentham; but he read widely, and supplemented his reading by personal observation; thus he tells us that he had been opposed to the classification of prisoners as being either unjust and invidious or pointless, until he saw the system in operation at Geneva, and found that it provided exactly the right kind of incentive.

The country which he explored most fully on his European tour was France. He met Lamartine, Chateaubriand, Guizot, and his idol Victor Hugo, whom he had acclaimed in 1836 in the preface to his translation of *Angelo*, and now championed more fully in an essay of 1837 entitled *Victor Hugo as Dramatist* (*Hugo Victor mint drámai költő*).

This work is not only shorter than the essay on penal reform, but less intelligent, and reckless in its generalizations. Yet it contains the essentials of Eötvös's literary creed; a dramatist's main need, he says, is a 'moral conviction', so that he can promote justice, instruct and improve his audience. But to achieve this aim he must give pleasure; here is a definite warning against dreary didacticism.

In the course of his travels Eötvös covered much of southern France on horseback. He visited the Grande Chartreuse, and it was this visit that inspired the book which made him famous and determined the medium for his life's work as a writer, the novel *The Carthusian* (*A karthausi*). It appeared in 1839–41 as Eötvös's contribution to the *Flood Book* (*Árvízkönyv*) which he himself brought out to help the publisher Heckenast, a devoted servant of Hungarian literature who had suffered in the disastrous Budapest flood of 1838.

The Carthusian embodies the memoirs of a young French count who, after two unhappy love-affairs, decides to enter the monastery. It is introduced by a prologue in which the author tells us how the memoirs came into his hands, and warns us that they are only for the reader 'who is not left cold by the sufferings of a soul created for good and noble deeds, who is interested more by the secret history of a heart than by the cleverly woven plots of novels.' Then follows the 'history' itself.

I was born and brought up, the count relates, near Avignon. From my father I was sundered by the gulf between two generations separated by the French Revolution; my mother I loved deeply, but she died when I was eight—how different everything might have been if she had lived, that we might share each other's sufferings! My father sent me to the Jesuit College at Freiburg, a gloomy establishment—the claims of the heart are ignored in modern education. However, I made one close friend, Armand, a boy of similar temperament to my own, also from Avignon, whose financier father had gone bankrupt and committed suicide when Armand was twelve. We toured Switzerland together, and Armand saved my life in a storm on Mont Blanc, in gratitude for which my father adopted him and sent him to Toulouse University with me.

Soon after coming down from the University, I fell in love with a beautiful young widow named Julia. 'Only he whose soul has been seized as if by madness . . . who knows nothing, wills nothing, but only feels, and at once casts away everything to this one feeling, who neither hopes nor fears—he loves as I loved.' I was supremely happy with Julia, and as I recited Petrarch to her, in the very place where he had composed his poems to Laura, I was only expressing my own feelings. Before leaving for Paris (whither she too was bound independently) I declared my love to her, and the look she gave me left me in no doubt that she loved me too. The revolution of July 1830 was now proclaimed, and Armand, from whom I had drifted apart, reappeared and announced that he too was going to Paris, where a new life was dawning for the nation.

I planned to give Julia a lovely surprise by visiting her at her Paris apartment; but when I called she was out. This filled me with unhappiness and foreboding. I dismissed these feelings as childish; but then suddenly, as I was walking down a narrow street, she emerged from one of the houses, arm-in-arm with a man whom I had seen before in the church at Avignon, shaking off a woman who had turned out to be Julia herself. I determined to find out who this man was.

Shortly afterwards Julia invited me to lunch, which made me infinitely happy, and I was warmly received by her father, an aristocrat of the old school. During the party I noticed a servant delivering a letter to Julia, which caused her face to go white and her hand to tremble; then later, when at last we were alone, she asked me to take to her friend the Marquise de Valmont a letter of vital importance, a letter on which depended not her own fate, but the fate of one dearer to her heart than herself. We embraced, and she wept on my shoulder and called me by my name, Gustave.[1]

On my way back from delivering Julia's letter, I met Armand, who was now disconsolate at the outcome of the revolution, and could see nothing but the gulf between himself, a man of the people, and me, a count, so that I had difficulty in persuading him to accept an invitation for the evening, which Mme de Valmont had extended to us.

The company included the man whom I had seen with Julia. Mme de Valmont told me that he was a M. Dufey, a hero of the revolution; Julia's father returned his greeting with conspicuous frigidity. The old man was wholly sceptical about the revolution; the new nobility had all the vices of the old without any of the virtues, and he himself had no wish to move in a society in which the grandson of his footman shone. He seemed annoyed by the silence with which I received these observations. But when, later, I went to stay on his country estate near Paris, he came to accept me, and on his death-bed blessed Julia and me. She promised, in her father's presence, to be my wife, and later reaffirmed her love for me. The wedding-day was fixed; Armand, for whom I had obtained a post as secretary to Julia's father, was in charge of the arrangements.

One day, however, I happened to see Armand lose 10,000 francs or more at the gaming-table, and my inquiries revealed that a jeweller's bill, for which Julia's father had given Armand the money, had not been paid. Soon after, I overheard Armand negotiating with a money-lender; at that very moment Dufey came up and agreed to act as surety, saying, however, that he had a request to make to Armand. Armand, in his extreme financial embarrassment, was willing to do any favour Dufey cared to ask. Next day, when I went to the jeweller's to pay the bill, I found that it had already been paid.

At my urgent insistence, Mme de Valmont showed me Julia's letter. Julia confessed to her friend that she loved Dufey, that all her struggles against that love had failed. Her father refused absolutely to allow her to marry him, and when she saw how much I

[1] Only at this moment does the reader learn the hero's name.

loved her she had almost become resigned to marrying me. More-over, there had been a temporary breach between her and Dufey, but Armand, whom Dufey had saved financially, had successfully interceded on behalf of his benefactor. Julia's father died soon after, leaving all his money to me except her dowry, and cursing her and prophesying her unhappiness.

Immediately after the death of her father, Julia received a letter from Dufey renouncing his love for her. I was present when this letter arrived, and Julia fell fainting into my arms. At that moment Armand entered the room. My anger at his treachery burst out, whereupon he challenged me to a duel. In the combat I was woun-ded; Julia watched over my bed for three nights, then disappeared. I recovered and went back to my father.

One day as I was contemplating the amphitheatre at Nîmes, in ruins like my heart, a man came up to me. It was Arthur, the son of a rich merchant of Nîmes, whose father had set him to work in the family business, thereby repressing Arthur's artistic impulses. I tried to console him and help him in his unhappiness, and took him to Rome; but he was no real companion to me, being too young to understand my grief, and I was almost happy when the time came for us to part. I returned to Paris, and became very friendly with the sympathetic Mme de Valmont, who also re-minded me of my Julia; unfortunately, however, our friendship became the talk of the town, and the slanderous rumours which were circulating about me made me feel obliged to resign a diplomatic post which I had accepted. Now Arthur visited me unexpectedly, and in my desolation he seemed a dear friend; he had given up art for pleasure, and suggested that I should meet some of his companions.

The two members of Arthur's circle whom I came to know best were the cynical Werner, a retired German business man, and an elderly caricature of youth called Lafard. One day when out walking with them in the Champs-Élysées we met Betty, the most beautiful *grisette* of Paris. I took up a challenge from Lafard (whose advances Betty had resisted) to win her love, and bet 1,000 napoleons and a feast all round that I would succeed in six months without making use of my money, provided only that the wager was kept secret. So I made Betty's acquaintance, pretending to be a poor law-student from Provence. In the weeks that followed, my friend-ship with her became closer, till one beautiful sunset evening she saw that I was unhappy, and confessed her love. This turned my unhappiness to joy, for nothing has greater power to console than the sympathy of a gentle feminine heart; at the same time, my conscience, which had for long troubled me, now became more and more uneasy about the deception I was practising. But when Betty eventually learnt that I was really a count, it was the result of a chance coincidence; she was deeply moved that I could so love her when I was really a rich nobleman, and this made me profoundly happy. To safeguard her from the corrupt society in which I had been living, I took a house in the country.

Henceforward, however, our relationship changed. I became first bored with her, then contemptuous of her vanity, then came almost to detest her as a coquette, when I saw how she tried to be pleasant to Arthur (the only friend I allowed to visit my house), who had fallen in love with her—though I knew that she loved me and not him; she was in fact wholly dependent on me for her happiness. On one of his visits to us, Arthur asked me for a loan, admitting frankly that he had lost his own money gambling; he spoke of suicide as a possible solution, and I was unable to console him. His love for Betty was another cause of his unhappiness, and he went on to taunt me for keeping her 'like a Turk'. Unfortunately Betty overheard this and begged me to let her go back to Paris; her pleas, combined with Arthur's accusations of jealousy, eventually overbore my resistance.

My success was duly celebrated,[1] though the bet itself remained a secret. Lafard had told me that one of the guests, a certain Duke Amalfi, was going to play a splendid joke on his shy mistress, by opening the door of her room suddenly in front of the whole company. The joke was played, and the mistress proved to be— Julia. She froze the party into silence, and Amalfi's attempts to placate her were vain—she would leave the next day. While Werner was beating Arthur at dice in another room, Julia told me how Dufey had deserted her, and when her child by him was on the point of dying of hunger, she agreed perforce to the proposition made to her by an old procuress who was acting on behalf of Amalfi. I offered her my legacy from her father, but she refused— she had already seen more than enough of the unhappiness which wealth can bring. She told me that she was going to Perth, to

---

[1] This scene, the climax of the whole novel, is commonly known as the 'orgy-scene'.

stay with the family of a minister whom she had met in Switzerland. I assured her that I would never forget her.

In his cups, Lafard had betrayed the secret of the bet. I could
only confess the truth to Betty and beg her to forgive me; but the
blow had broken her— 'What does M. le comte care if this heart
rejoices or breaks?' At that moment a shot rang out; I instantly
cried out 'Arthur!' and we rushed into the other room, to find him
lying dead.

In the chaos which now ensued, Betty disappeared. Determined
to marry her and make her happy, I went to her house the next day,
but found only a letter, addressed to me, in which she reaffirmed
that she had loved me and always would love me, and ending 'May
God give me the strength to carry out my resolve!' Three weeks
later the body of a woman, dressed in clothes corresponding to
hers, was found in the Seine. I myself was deterred from suicide
by Julia, and resolved to come to this cloister—which is near
where Betty had been brought up—and expiate my sin before
dying.

(At this point the continuous memoirs end; the novel concludes
with a series of entries from Gustave's diary containing an account
of the following subsequent events.)

While convalescing from a lung complaint, the result of my
wound sustained in the duel with Armand, I met a man who
proved to be Armand himself. He had broken with Dufey and
joined the Foreign Legion, from which he had been invalided
out. He then worked on the estate of a French settler in Algeria
who had befriended him, married his benefactor's daughter, and
returned to France with his wife, two children and his father-in-
law, to live happily as a farmer.

I was continually haunted by dreams of Betty; then my doctor
told me that she had not drowned herself but gone back to her
father. Her health soon began to fail, but before her death my
doctor was able to arrange for me to visit her. She blessed me, and
forgave my friends (whom she considered solely responsible for
the tragedy) and myself. After her funeral I took to my bed, and
have remained there since.

At this point Gustave's narrative ends, and the friend, Vilmos,
to whom he entrusted his papers, records his death. The novel
closes with Vilmos's description of a funeral in Perthshire which
he chanced to witness, the funeral of a mother who had lost her

child. Vilmos went up to the grave and read on the tombstone the name JULIA.

No summary of the plot of this novel can convey any idea of its intensely introspective atmosphere. The action is continually retarded by long reflective passages; but the introspection is not confined to these—it pervades the whole narrative. Gustave knows no state of mind but crushing grief or blissful happiness, and always faithfully records his emotional reactions to events. Like a true Romantic he is continually asserting the claims of the emotions and sees life from an emotional point of view; as he himself says 'My nature wished to seize on the poetical side of everything.' He was made, he tells us, 'to dream, not to act', and early acquired a distaste for politics. He is, in fact, the exact opposite of the vigorous, outward-looking young reformer who created him; Eötvös was certainly of a thoughtful cast of mind—in 1833 he had produced a collection of aphorisms entitled *Inner and Outer World* (*Bel- és külvilág*)[1]—but this is quite a different matter from the unceasing melancholy introspection of Gustave.

At the same time it is impossible to regard *The Carthusian* as inspired by purely literary considerations, by nothing more than a desire to produce a Hungarian counterpart to such works as Benjamin Constant's *Adolphe* or Goethe's *Werther*—in spite of the explicit comparison of Arthur to Werther. Eötvös could never have worked in the spirit of art for art's sake which he had already scouted in his essay on Victor Hugo; a novel by him must be saying something about life.

The novel shows clearly the sufferings which aristocratic pride can inflict, which Julia's father inflicted on her, which Gustave himself inflicted on Betty (although the corrupting influence of Werner and Lafard was only marginally stronger than Gustave's own better nature). But those who overthrew the hereditary aristocracy were no improvement on it; the attack of Julia's father on the new nobility is justified by Dufey's conduct throughout, and underlined by Armand's disillusionment at the results of the revolution. These social aspects are of major importance; but they are not the whole story. At the beginning of the novel, Gustave's father counsels him to be 'calm, cautious and selfish'; at the end, Gustave reaches the conclusion that 'the greater part of my griefs were caused solely by my own selfishness' and gives Vilmos and his

[1] Cf. p. 219.

children this last message: 'let the memory of my life protect your souls against selfishness . . . only for the selfish is there no consolation on this earth.' Here is the point of the whole book; subjective, egocentric Romanticism is a mistaken attitude to life, and carries with it its own penalty.

Eötvös, then, was no artist for art's sake; nevertheless *The Carthusian* was a landmark of major importance in the development of his style. The exhausting length of many of the sentences cannot obscure the skill with which they are constructed, and the descriptions—Mont Blanc, the bustle of Paris, the beauty of a sunset—contain all the poetry missing in Eötvös's verse, as indeed do many of Gustave's reflections. The style of the dialogue, too, is highly artistic; sometimes, indeed, inappropriately so. For example, when Julia, about to marry Gustave, refuses to explain to him a letter which she has received, he weeps, and she, observing his tears, asks him what grieves his heart. '"You ask this?" I said, carried away by my pain "O ask this earth why it is dark, when the sun sets: ask the child why it weeps, when it mourns over its mother's grave: ask the tree why it withers, when cut off from its roots. And what are these things, compared to my grief?"' (ch. 34). In judging such passages, allowance must be made for the taste of the period; Eötvös is certainly not lacking in dramatic sense—the 'orgy-scene' alone proves that. At the same time, there are incredible coincidences, improbable episodes, overdrawn characters; this is a first novel by a man of twenty-five. Nor was it unanimously acclaimed, or generally understood, by contemporary critics; but we do not need to invoke these facts to explain why such a man as Eötvös never wrote such a book again.

2

Eötvös became a member of the Upper House of the Diet in 1839, and soon established himself as a leading figure in politics. In his private life, financial disaster to his family was followed by a marriage which was to prove outstandingly happy. He met Rosty Ágnes, the daughter of a county *alispán, in 1839: they danced together at the celebrations in honour of Liszt's visit to Budapest in the winter of 1839-40: in February 1842 they became engaged and were married the following September, settling at Pozsony in 1843.

In 1840, shortly after the second of the three instalments of *The Carthusian* had appeared, Eötvös published two important political essays, *Poverty in Ireland* (*Szegénység Irlandban*) *Emancipation of the Jews* (*A zsidók emancipatiója*).[1] The two are strikingly similar. Both are animated by the same concern at human suffering, and also by the same ultimate optimism. In both emotional force is matched by intellectual power and methodical argument, above all by a practical approach to the problem. In both Eötvös's exposition begins with the same emphasis on the importance of the past for a right understanding of the present; Ireland's present plight is the direct result of centuries of oppression and suffering: so with the Jews, the persecution to which they have been subjected throughout their history has inevitably left its mark on individuals —for persecution does degrade its victims; but they should be treated with sympathy. And virtue can never be wholly obscured. If we judge a nation by the strength of family life among its people, by the retention of its national identity, by its devotion to religion, Ireland's merits shine out; and the capacity to resist persecution which the Jews have shown in the past is sufficient proof that 'the rock which our blows have failed to break asunder is not going to weaken the structure of our country if incorporated in it', as indeed experience elsewhere has already demonstrated. Repression, on the other hand, can never achieve lasting success; its intensification at length provokes a reaction and concessions become inevitable. The first concessions, however, may produce an avalanche, a revolutionary situation which may bring good in the future but which is temporarily disastrous, for only domestic peace can make a nation happy. Here Ireland is relevant to Hungary: 'It is sometimes good to look beyond our frontiers, for much is to be found there which may perhaps be prophetic for us.'

Both essays open with an appeal to the emotions, but thereafter Eötvös achieves his object of proving his thesis 'by cold arguments and dry statistical facts, although it is difficult to remain calm when it is a question of the oppression of our fellow men'.[2] Particularly impressive is the survey of the history of Ireland, and the reading to which it testifies. In both essays the opponent's case is carefully examined and refuted: the 'arguments' and the 'facts' point the same way as emotional sympathy and the Christian

[1] i.e. an examination of the case for admitting the Jews to full citizen rights.
[2] From the introduction to *Emancipation of the Jews*.

injunction to love one's neighbour; and the solution follows inevitably.

The most widely read mouthpiece of reform in the early 1840's was *Kossuth's paper, *Pesti Hírlap (Pest Journal)*; and to some it certainly seemed to represent the first stirrings of a revolutionary avalanche. In particular *Széchenyi, himself the pioneer of reform, violently attacked *Kossuth in his book *People of the East (A kelet népe)* (1841) as an instigator of class war and hatred of authority, at the same time criticizing certain proposed reforms, including changes in the penal and educational systems, from an extreme conservative standpoint. It was natural for Eötvös to defend *Kossuth against this attack, and he produced, in the same year as *Széchenyi's book appeared, his *'People of the East' and the 'Pest Journal'* (*Kelet Népe és Pesti Hírlap*), in which he pointed out that the *Pest Journal* was not stirring up class war but giving publicity to real abuses, and that *Széchenyi was attacking free speech. But perhaps the most important features of *'People of the East' and the Pest Journal'* are the statement that 'Peace is the first condition of our national development' and Eötvös's desire to reconcile the two antagonists. He begins his essay by stressing that both *Széchenyi and *Kossuth are friends of progress, *Széchenyi being in fact the pioneer of reform in Hungary, and ends with the confident prediction that their reconciliation is inevitable. Certainly Eötvös himself provided an exemplary combination of advocacy of a particular viewpoint with consideration for the unity of the reform-party as a whole.

Already in the essay on penal reform Eötvös had mentioned the major injustices resulting from the differences in prison conditions in different counties, and in a speech in the Diet on 9 May 1844[1] he said bluntly: 'Hungary needs centralization; and in my opinion centralization can be achieved only by an increase of the influence exercised by the legislature on the counties.' To advocate simultaneously independence (within the Monarchy), radical social reform and centralization was to cut right across the common division between conservative pro-Viennese centralism and the radical nationalism which attached great importance to county autonomy; so Eötvös's group of 'centralists', all intellectuals, were dubbed the 'Seven Wise Men of Hungary' and were received with

---

[1] *On Holding Annual Sessions of the Diet* (*Az országgyűlés évenkénti tartásáról*) in which Eötvös argued that the Diet should meet annually.

that peculiar mixture of bewilderment, derision, and respect which 'egg-heads' so often evoke.

But reform was urgent, and it is significant that Eötvös's fullest statement of the centralist case is entitled *Reform* (*Reform*) (1846)[1] and begins with the sentence 'Our country cannot remain in its present condition.'

First and foremost, says Eötvös, Hungary is not a nation, because constitutional rights are enjoyed only by 'nobles', who make up about 5 per cent. of the population; taxation, military service, and all other public burdens are borne entirely by the other 95 per cent. Secondly, even if we disregard the above point, Hungary totally lacks the conditions of progress, a combination of order and freedom, efficient and uniform administration by a Government strong but responsible to a legislative body exercising its rightful functions. Instead, we have a Government not responsible to the legislative body, and a Diet to which fifty-two counties (differing widely in the size of their noble populations) each send two deputies, whom they supervise closely and may recall. The counties also manage their own executive and their own judiciary; thus judges are elected by those whom it will be their duty to try impartially. Moreover, even within the nobility, power is often concentrated in a few leading families, who have ways of producing the desired results at elections. And in all sections of public life conditions and policy differ enormously in different counties.

Nobody with Eötvös's keen sense of the relevance of the past to the present could underrate the strength of his countrymen's feelings about the county system, which had preserved the nation and her constitution through three grim centuries; and Eötvös himself agrees that to abandon it before devising other constitutional guarantees would be disastrous. At the same time, he adds, while a defeated nation, like Hungary after Mohács, will survive only if it is decentralized, a centralized nation is harder to defeat. Besides, the counties' right of petition and power of non-co-operation are effective only against a Government concerned to rule constitutionally, and only against positive breaches of Hungary's laws by the Government, not against sins of omission.

But maintenance of the *status quo* and passive resistance are no solution; a man who locks himself up in a room for fear of being

---

[1] It was first published in Leipzig, to avoid the censorship.

subjected to some compulsion is not free. Past misgovernment must now be forgotten, and confidence established. The focus of this confidence, and the instrument of reform, must be the legislative body. England under the Stuarts did not withdraw into municipal life on the ground that Parliament was too weak; she made Parliament strong. In responsible parliamentary government, with a free legislative body elected by a proper system of representation, lies the key to the future.

The class-distinctions which *Reform* attacks were also the subject of Eötvös's last play, the four-act comedy *Long live Equality!* (*Éljen az egyenlőség!*) (1844). The central figures of the drama are *alispán Hegyfalvy, his second wife, his son, and his daughter. The son, Vilmos, is in love with Ilka, the daughter of Count Ábrányi, but dare not reveal his love; the daughter, Irma, loves Gyula, the son of the lawyer Perlegi. Perlegi is noble and well-to-do, but his father was a cobbler, so Irma, as well as her brother, finds her way to happiness barred by class prejudice.

Hegyfalvy hints to the Count that the marriage of Vilmos and Ilka might well be a happy ending to the fathers' dispute over a piece of land; to this suggestion the Count, inwardly furious, reacts by helping Gyula to marry Irma in secret. However, Vilmos overhears the conversation between the Count and Gyula, and sees in the Count's plan a possible way of solving his own problem.

We do not see Hegyfalvy's wife till Act II, Scene ii; but then she proves to be every bit as fierce and formidable an autocrat as we have been led to expect. She is equally indignant at the slight implied by the Count's opposition to Ilka's marrying Vilmos, and at the notion that 'the son of an upstart pettifogger whose father was a cobbler' should aspire to Irma's hand. Vilmos obtains his stepmother's consent to his plan to marry Ilka secretly, for Mrs. Hegyfalvy is delighted at the prospect of humiliating the Count. At the same time she is suspicious about Irma and Gyula; but Vilmos pooh-poohs her fears on this score, telling her that Irma's letters are a cover for Ilka's letters to him. So Mrs. Hegyfalvy orders her lawyer Gáborszky to intercept no more of Irma's letters, and when he is caught red-handed defying this order dismisses him. But the last letter intercepted by Gáborszky was one from Ilka giving details of the rendezvous for her secret marriage to Vilmos, and the lawyer plans to obtain his revenge by wrecking the whole scheme. Perlegi too is thirsting for vengeance, for Hegyfalvy has refused him Irma's hand for Gyula. He learns from Gáborszky that Ilka is planning to elope with Vilmos, and resolves to go to the rendezvous himself.

In the last act the characters gradually gather, at first unobserved by one another, at the cave which was the lovers' rendezvous. Irma and Gyula appear, married, and Irma begs her father's pardon. He is pained, but preserves his dignity; his wife, on the other hand, explodes with a fury which she curses the language for its inability to express. The Count reveals the part he has played in bringing about the marriage; he himself would have considered Gyula an excellent son-in-law, and are we not living in the enlightened nineteenth century? But these admirable sentiments have been overheard by Ilka, who now approaches with Vilmos. Vilmos had learnt from Irma of Gáborszky's activities, and he and Ilka have succeeded in meeting at a new rendezvous, and marrying. So the Count sees that he has been caught, and tries to make the best of it—as do the others, except Mrs. Hegyfalvy.

This is the only play by Eötvös to have enjoyed any success at all on the stage; and certainly the interest is well maintained with some delightful dramatic irony. Yet partly because of Eötvös's preoccupation with his social theme, which is the main point of the play, partly because of his chronic inability to write effective dramatic dialogue, the characters scarcely come to life, except the Count and Mrs. Hegyfalvy. However, some of them are of special interest because they are reincarnated as living human beings in Eötvös's next work, his masterpiece, the novel *The Village Notary* (*A falu jegyzője*), which appeared in 1845. There we shall meet again the weak *alispán dominated by his second wife, the sneak lawyer, the loving daughter; there the real people whose shadowy ancestors figure in *Long Live Equality!* as the Hegyfalvys, Gáborszky and Irma, appear portrayed with a sureness of touch which can leave no doubt that Eötvös's true literary vocation was the novel and not the play.

3

The Village Notary is a story of life in an imaginary county; so the reader, acquainted with Eötvös as the leading centralist in politics and as a disciple of Victor Hugo in literature, knows what to expect. More particularly, it is the story of two men, Tengelyi, the village notary, who is noble, and Viola who is not. Viola, in fact, is a bandit, and the first event we see (and Tengelyi sees) is the arrest of an old gipsy, Peti, who has been seen talking to someone who might have been Viola. Nyúzó, the Chief Justice (főbíró) of the district, whose name means 'flayer' and who 'stands before us as the consoling thought that the Scythian blood from which our race is sprung has not yet ceased to flow in this country' had issued orders that whatever happened an arrest must be made; so Peti is produced, in the pillory, struck by the gendarmes on the way, and saved from a summary court (statárium) only by the intervention of Réty Ákos, the *alispán's son.

Tengelyi, the village notary, looks older than his fifty years, and presents the appearance of one whom 'time has hardened rather than broken', like an oak. From the beginning of his career he had tirelessly championed the oppressed, and repeatedly suffered for it, till Réty the *alispán, who had earlier proved a false friend, secured him his present post. The notary is a man of inflexible integrity and strong principles, but his family, far from feeling the authority of a despot, is united by close bonds of mutual love and confidence; so he just laughs when his sixteen-year-old daughter Vilma, as she comes out to meet her father on his return home, makes him promise not to be angry at some action she has taken behind his back.

For the moment, however, we leave Tengelyi's house for the wood beyond the garden of Réty's castle, where we meet the *alispán's tall, dark, masculine, imperious wife (his second wife, so Ákos's stepmother), who has a voice to 'make the walls of Jericho tremble and the servants turn pale'. Now, towards dusk on this October day, she is talking with the family lawyer, Macskaházy (macska = cat). Macskaházy's man Czifra had apparently made an unsuccessful attempt to steal some papers belonging to the pastor, Vándory. These papers are now at Tengelyi's house, with the notary's own papers; but they can easily be removed. Réty's wife is scandalized by this suggestion; but, as Macskaházy points out, if he simply tells his man how much it would mean to him to see the papers, and casually proceeds to make other equally irrelevant remarks, is that incitement to robbery? So the conscience of Réty's wife is placated. Unfortunately, however, their conversation is interrupted by Ákos, with his hounds, and by the sound of a man in the undergrowth. Ákos, who enjoys teasing sneaks as much as he does brutes like Nyúzó, leads the terrified Macskaházy off on a chase, but they find no one.

Tengelyi's daughter Vilma, it turns out, has taken the wife and children of the bandit Viola into her home. Her father praises her for this action, but at the same time he is horrified at the possible consequences, for the bandit's devotion to his wife is a byword, and he will certainly visit her: what if he is apprehended in the notary's house? Viola was in fact the man Ákos had heard in the wood, and now we see him for the first time—a man 'richly gifted by nature', and far from glorifying in his life as an outlaw, he describes it in terms of the utmost bitterness, as worse than death. We gather that he has committed murder, though we learn no details. On hearing (from the gipsy Peti) where his wife and children are, Viola does indeed come to Tengelyi's house and succeeds in catching a glimpse of them through the window and escaping, though Nyúzó and his men are there.

The next day, a second conversation in Réty's garden (very different from the first) between Ákos and his sister Etelka reveals that Ákos is deeply in love with Vilma, but feels little hope for the future because of the strength of parental opposition from both families. Fortunately, however, Etelka is a friend of Vilma's, and a welcome visitor to Tengelyi's house, as well as a sympathetic sister, and clearly will do all she can to help Ákos. One day when Etelka was talking with Vilma at the latter's home an obsequious, repellent Jew called, wanting to see Tengelyi and prepared, indeed determined, to wait until the notary returned. Vilma was convinced that he was spying for Nyúzó, and showed him the door; she had in fact to behave with a wholly uncharacteristic brusqueness to get rid of him, though her hostility turned into sympathy when her father returned and described how the company at Réty's castle had beaten up the Jew for fun.

All the main threads of the plot—the scheme of Réty's wife and Macskaházy to steal the papers, Ákos's love for Vilma, Viola's love for his family and gratitude for Vilma's kindness to them, converge at Tengelyi's house on the evening before the election of the county officials. Thanks to Etelka's good offices it has been arranged for Ákos to visit Vilma, but it is a misty autumn evening and he arrives only after agonizing delays. His visit could take place only in the notary's absence, for Tengelyi is uncompromisingly hostile to the whole Réty family (except Etelka), and has forbidden Ákos the house. The notary's wife Erzsébet, however, hopes that Ákos will be her son-in-law, and also that Vilma will be spared the sufferings which she herself had endured as the result of her parents' desire that she should marry Macskaházy. Just as Ákos and Vilma have declared their love to each other a loud crash is heard, followed by a cry and men's footsteps. The Jew has stolen the papers, with Macskaházy's man Czifra standing on guard; but Viola too is there, and has caught the thief, knocked him out, and wrested the papers from him. Ákos rushes to the scene. A shot is heard and he falls to the ground, wounded.

At the election, when Tengelyi comes to vote (and is already threatening to report the fact that proper secrecy is not being observed), his nobility, and hence his right to vote, is challenged by Nyúzó and Macskaházy; indeed, only the intervention of Ákos's friend Kislaky Kálmán saves him from physical violence. He is required to produce his papers, and on arriving home not only discovers that they are missing but hears news which, for him, points to the certain conclusion that Vilma's honour has been compromised by Ákos.

Meanwhile the Jew has put out his story, accusing Viola of the theft of the papers. When Viola's wife, Zsuzsi, hears of this lie, she vigorously denies the possibility of her husband's guilt; then a reference by Mrs. Tengelyi—as unconscious as it was unfortunate —to Viola as a 'bandit' moves Zsuzsi to relate how he became one. He had been a prosperous peasant and their life had been supremely happy; then Nyúzó, who hated Zsuzsi for repelling his advances, and her husband because he was always chosen by the peasants to be their spokesman, required Viola to present himself in person to provide a relay of horses when Zsuzsi was in labour. Viola refused, as he had already fulfilled his obligations; so he was taken by force, and beaten on the way. As he was about to be tied to the whipping-post, all bleeding, he broke loose and, now beside himself, seized an axe which was lying nearby, killed one man and wounded another. He escaped, and has lived the life of an outlaw ever since. Having told her story, Zsuzsi announces her intention of leaving the notary's house and setting off to recover the papers and clear her husband. She departs, blessing her friends for their kindness. At the same time Ákos (still in bed from his wound) sends his friend Kislaky Kálmán to obtain the papers from Viola.

Viola's situation soon becomes critical, for his hide-out is accidentally betrayed to his enemy Czifra, and a race ensues between his friends and his foes to reach him. Zsuzsi and Viola's friends find their way barred by the river in flood, so Nyúzó and his men, with Macskaházy and Czifra, reach Viola first. Their siege of the deserted cottage where Viola is hiding is repelled; but at the last moment Macskaházy saves the situation with an 'angelic' idea for which Nyúzó embraces him—to set the building on fire and shoot down Viola's men as they come out. Viola could have escaped, but will not leave a wounded comrade who had once saved his life; finally he rushes out, blinded by the smoke, with the papers, which Macskaházy snatches from him. He surrenders, exhausted, and is taken away to be tried by a summary court (statárium). Zsuzsi's party arrive shortly afterwards and realize that Viola has been captured, not killed.

The trial of Viola is the longest scene, and one of the most memorable, in the novel.[1] It could have been achieved only by a writer whose literary gifts were equalled by his experience and observation of men in committee and debate. The characters of the judges are nicely differentiated; Nyúzó (who has been reappointed to his office, as Réty was successful in the election) and Macskaházy we already know well; but two others deserve mention for their concern that the case should be tried expeditiously— Baron Sóskuty cannot bear the thought of distressing his hostess by being late for lunch: for Zátonyi, the embodiment of the justice of an earlier age, it is a matter of duty as well as routine to pass the death sentence. But the central figure in the trial is the young lawyer Völgyesy (a hunchback), who was serving the court as notary. He caused a sensation at the outset by reading out the regulations slowly and clearly: he went on to object that the case lay outside the scope of a *statárium*: he queried the evidence of the Jew and Czifra, which agreed in every detail: he challenged Nyúzó's membership of the Bench, as the Chief Justice was a personal enemy of the accused: he encouraged Viola to give evidence, when the prisoner's sole desire was that the inevitable end should come as soon as possible—'here I am, gentlemen, hang me' —whereupon Viola told the whole story of Tengelyi's papers.

---

[1] As Mr. L. Czigány has pointed out, the trial-scene was selected for special praise by English critics when an English translation (by Otto Wenckstern) of the novel appeared in 1850; cf. e.g. *The Times*, 3 April 1850.

A majority, however, voted against minuting this evidence; in fact, Völgyesy was defeated at every turn—as notary he had no vote—till finally he resigned in protest, leaving the court-room shortly afterwards. But resignations have another aspect, besides the impressiveness of the protest; old Kislaky (Kálmán's father), the presiding judge, who 'had never made the acquaintance of the darker side of life' and had been horrified by the proceedings, now found himself alone. Eventually, after prolonged hesitation, he passed the death sentence. All alike, from their different stand-points, reproach him for his weakness, his own conscience most of all; but he is relieved of this last burden by his son, Kálmán, who, with Ákos's servant, the old hussar János, rescues Viola during the night in a thrilling episode (with an excellent slapstick interlude) which provides the ideal contrast to the trial.

Viola, then, is saved, and his friends take him and his family to start a new life in another county, under an assumed name; but Macskaházy still has the papers. Etelka overhears him exulting in his prize, and just as she is discussing with her brother what to do, Réty comes in, to have a serious talk with Ákos about his relationship with Vilma. Réty's opposition to the marriage is moderate; but his wife, who enters imperiously a little later, completely loses her temper, calling Ákos an ungrateful viper and Vilma a harlot, whereupon Ákos turns on his stepmother and shatters her by denouncing her as the accomplice of thieves. Réty, who still knows nothing about the robbery, orders his son to leave home, and Ákos calls on Pastor Vándory, who successfully intercedes with Tengelyi and secures the notary's happy consent to the marriage.

The joy in Tengelyi's home is equalled by the misery at Réty's. Réty's wife first has to tell her husband the whole story; then, when she refuses Macskaházy the promised official commendation (for the papers are not in her hands), the lawyer demands 50,000 florins, backing his demand by a threat of denunciation, and so breaks her resistance. Then, feeling very pleased with himself, he goes to Tengelyi's house—choosing a time when the notary is out —and offers to return the papers in exchange for Vilma's hand. Just as his wife is showing Macskaházy the door for making this proposal, Tengelyi returns, and, infuriated, drives the visitor out of the house, shouting 'This man will yet die by my hand!'

That night Viola visits Macskaházy to demand the papers; the lawyer, terrified, produces them, but at the same time threatens

Viola with a pistol. A struggle ensues; Viola stabs Macskaházy to death and flees with the papers. The servants then appear on the scene, too late to catch or identify Viola, but in time to hear Macskaházy say 'My papers' and 'Tengelyi' before dying. The Jew was found hiding nearby and was arrested, though all had seen Macskaházy shake his head when the Jew had been brought before him.

Having escaped, Viola puts a letter through a window of Tengelyi's house, proposing a nocturnal rendezvous for the return of the papers. After much hesitation the notary decides to keep the appointment; but on the way he hears shouts of 'Murderer!' and hurries home without having met Viola, dropping his stick on the way. This piece of evidence comes out in the course of Nyúzó's investigations into the murder, as does the earlier quarrel between Tengelyi and Macskaházy; Réty, horrified, persists in believing that Tengelyi must be innocent, but he cannot resist Nyúzó's demand for the notary's arrest. At this point Pastor Vándory intervenes, to remind Réty that he is his half-brother, and has made great sacrifices for Réty's career, including the renunciation of his half of their joint inheritance, his right to which is attested by the papers. Vándory insists that Réty must do more to help Tengelyi.

Meanwhile the Jew had contracted typhus in prison, and had not long to live; but before dying he revealed to Vándory, in the presence of witnesses, the whole story of the theft of the papers and the truth about the murder of Macskaházy. Seeing Vándory leave the prison and return later with other men, Réty's wife visits the Jew herself and tries to bludgeon him into retracting his statement; but the dying prisoner recoils from her in horror, whereupon she goes home and poisons herself. The Jew had earlier disclosed, to the pastor alone, that Réty's wife had offered him 2,000 florins to kill Macskaházy; but the statement he made before the witnesses had not implicated her at all.

Still Tengelyi cannot be saved unless Viola comes forward; and the old hussar János, though determined not to hand Viola over to the authorities, volunteers to try to trace him, and ultimately succeeds. Viola had a good house and holding, but was not happy; he had left his native village, he lived in constant fear of detection, and his conscience, the ever-present thought of the murders he had committed, had destroyed his peace of mind. Nor had he any hopes for the future; he had lost his children from illness, and

Zsuzsi's health too was beginning to fail. On hearing János's news, Viola resolves to repay his debt to Tengelyi, and sets out. At the last he is intercepted by gendarmes and fatally wounded (by a gendarme who turns out to be Czifra); but Ákos, who with Vándory was watching the pursuit—from the same hill whence Tengelyi and Vándory had seen Peti's arrest at the opening of the whole novel—reached Viola in time to receive the papers from him. Viola found the strength to reveal himself as the murderer of Macskaházy, and died asking God to forgive his persecutors and talking of Zsuzsi.

Zsuzsi died soon after her husband; Ákos and Vilma, Kálmán and Etelka became happy couples; Réty and old Kislaky resigned their offices; Nyúzó was dismissed after a scandal over improvements to his house; János became manager of Ákos's estate, but was not happy until, after a year, a son was born to Ákos and Vilma; Tengelyi, released from prison, rejoiced in the family happiness around him and in the good works he could now do in the district.

By contrast with its predecessor, *The Village Notary* is packed with incident, excitement—and drama; one can imagine what a splendid opportunity a great actress might find as Réty's wife in her last scene, with the long-postponed suicide, the venomous yet despairing reflections on the past, all so much more dramatic than anything in Eötvös's plays. And apart from the power of individual scenes, the novelist knows exactly when to end an episode and move to its most effective successor. The whole, too, for all its complexity, is a superb unity; there are no detachable sub-plots—the destinies of all the main characters are inseparably linked. Perhaps there is too much overhearing, though the overhearers are always posted in places dramatically probable for them. And this is a world of real people—not only the principal characters, but many others, such as Tengelyi Erzsébet, the kindly soul, the loving wife and mother who has shared all her husband's sufferings yet unconsciously takes for granted the structure of society which has caused them; above all, the old hussar János, with his intense love of children, expounding his philosophically resilient view of life in a racy idiom rich in military metaphor and reminiscence. It is no accident that János plays a leading part in remedying the two major injustices in the novel—the death sentence passed on Viola and the imprisonment of Tengelyi.

The victims of these injustices are differentiated by the obvious fact that whereas Tengelyi is innocent, Viola has committed one murder and goes on to commit another. Yet his virtues shine out from the start. Apart from his love for his wife, for which he is famous, he is absolutely loyal to his friends and trustworthy, with no thought for his personal safety when more important considerations are at stake, and so unlike the romantic outlaw of fiction that he curses the fate that has compelled him to flee from his fellow men. His humanity shows up perhaps most strongly in the contrast between him and the real criminal type, Czifra, who not only despises Viola for 'feeling pity every time a child cries' (ch. 13) but hates him for the justice he enforced when Czifra was a member of his band. At the same time, as his wife says, he is 'passionate and sometimes headstrong' (ch. 16), and it is the subjection of this character to the most cruel provocation which has made him a murderer and an outlaw. 'Not I,' he says (ch. 38) 'but Fate willed that I should become a murderer; but Fate willed also that I should suffer for committing murder.' So his conscience allows him no peace. And to the end he retains the perception to see things as they are—a fact which, perhaps more than anything else, reveals the true quality of the man.

In a just society Viola would have lived the happy, quiet life of a prosperous farmer; Tengelyi, on the other hand, is a born reformer whose social position has made him ineffective. Yet he remains throughout a widely respected figure, though the 'hardening' which we observed at the opening has made his character such that his enemies find particular delight in humiliating him, and his bitterness at the injustices he has endured causes him to harbour unjust suspicions himself. In particular, he lumps all the Réty family together, believing that Réty was a party to the conspiracy to steal the papers, and that Ákos has indeed dishonoured Vilma. At the same time, the notary is always determined to act rightly; after the murder of Macskaházy, even when he is still unaware that suspicion has fallen on him, he probes his conscience with a scrupulousness bordering on the morbid, feeling that he may have been an accessory to the crime, and later goes to prison with complete composure, dignity, and faith in the ultimate victory of the truth.

Like Tengelyi and Viola, the less attractive characters (with the possible exception of Macskaházy) are a mixture of virtues and defects. Even Nyúzó has a redeeming moment when, during the interrogations he conducts after the murder of Macskaházy, he is moved by the sight of Vilma and deals gently with her. Still, it remains true that the principal characters divide naturally into the victims of oppression and its instruments. Not that this justifies those who criticized the novel as an over-simplified conflict between black and white; the instruments of oppression differ so widely in the amount of positive evil, as distinct from weakness, in their natures. Besides, the fundamental division is true to life; every member of a society deeply corrupted by injustice either commits, condones, or suffers evil. And Eötvös endows his groups of characters with the appropriate collective characteristics; 'We poor do not desert one another', says a victim of Nyúzó's cruelty early in the novel, and the whole story confirms her words: the thieves, on the other hand, are not as thick as they look. Such a division, however, fails to bring out the importance of those characters who embody and justify hope in the future, Ákos and Kálmán—a hope symbolized both by the two young men in themselves and by the contrast with their fathers. For the novel is ultimately optimistic. The only survivor among the main malefactors, Nyúzó, is quietly removed from office; and although there are no sensational reforms, the county is undeniably a better place to live in at the end of the novel than it was a year earlier, at the beginning.

The style of *The Village Notary* is as different from that of *The Carthusian* as the Hungarian village from Paris. Romantic effusion has given place to close observation and concentrated irony; there is a point, a revelation of character, in almost every phrase. Only in the last chapters, as Viola's tragedy approaches its end, are we reminded of the emotionalism of the earlier novel; though the deaths of Zsuzsi and her children are not in themselves a gratuitous appeal to the emotions, but must be judged in relation to the mortality rate of Eötvös's day. The concentration of the style, however, often does not affect the length of the sentences; there are many periods no less involved than those in *The Carthusian*, as the Latin and German elements in Eötvös's literary background assert themselves.

As is fitting, the principal source of humour in *The Village Notary* is a lover of England. The younger brother of Réty's election rival Bántornyi, Jakab, or James as he preferred to be called, has modelled himself on England in all things. He is determined that after the pre-election dinner which he proposes to give, toasts must be drunk to the Church, the Army, and the Navy: he is the moving spirit in the foundation of a society to oppose cruelty to animals (while typhus is raging in the prison) and an automatic choice as its president in view of his interest in horse-racing and fox-hunting. Nor is the humour wholly satirical; the *főispán's visit to the Bántornyis is an excellent piece of slapstick (as well as providing exactly the right relief after the attempt of the Jew to reconnoitre Tengelyi's house), and there is a particularly delightful episode when the dean, whose duty it is to welcome the *főispán, puts on by mistake the cloak of the pastor of the neighbouring village, takes from the pocket and reads out the latter's address of welcome to his bishop, which is gloriously inapposite on this occasion. In addition, the pre-election scenes are enlivened by parodies of pompous political speeches which are among the first of a long and splendid line in Hungarian literature.

Eötvös's primary aim, however, was to right wrongs. This aspect of *The Village Notary* provoked a lively controversy, and the novelist was accused of 'violating' art by placing it at the service of politics. He replied[1] that 'a writer . . . who, . . . imagining himself a demigod, sees in the sufferings of his age only a subject for artistic studies . . . we may admire him on his icy pinnacle, we may envy him; but our esteem and affection are merited only by one to whom God has given a heart'. Replies to critics, however, are not the only or even the main type of digression in the novel; the narrative is liberally interspersed with reflections and comments by the author. The lengthier of these regularly occur at the beginnings of chapters, and by delaying the action heighten the suspense; but that is certainly not their purpose—they deal with the subjects on which Eötvös felt most strongly. For instance, at the end of one chapter (35) we learn that the Jew is dying of typhus in prison, and János has just volunteered to search for Viola; but the next chapter opens with an exceptionally long digression on prison conditions and the county public health authorities. Such passages, though often brilliantly written, are artistically irrelevant, and add little or nothing to what the action itself shows us; indeed a purely implicit reminder of the urgency of prison reform, for instance, would have been more effective. Certainly, when

---

[1] In the novel itself (ch. 20); it appeared serially, and the critics did not wait till the whole was complete.

Eötvös revised the novel for a second edition in 1865 several of the digressions were omitted, though not for artistic reasons—his apology for 'arguing too much'[1] is palpably ironical. In the epilogue he had expressed his 'most fervent desire that this novel should become improbable, as soon as may be'; and it is because some passages (such as one on the abandonment of Latin) were no longer relevant that he omitted them; it was as true as ever that 'I wanted not to entertain, but to be of service'. And if we discount the digressions (as is not difficult) and consider the plot by itself, the fact that it is so devised as to expose as many social evils as possible in no way detracts from its dramatic and artistic qualities. Eötvös had said in his essay on Victor Hugo that the writer must give pleasure if he is to be an effective influence; and perhaps the greatest achievement of *The Village Notary* is its success in 'entertaining' as well as 'being of service', in conveying its message through characters who live.

4

Eötvös followed up *The Village Notary* immediately with a historical novel, *Hungary in 1514* (*Magyarország 1514-ben*), which appeared serially during 1847 and was completed in January 1848. The title, with its reference to the Hungarian Peasants' Revolt, shows that Eötvös's theme is again social oppression; and there had been a peasants' rising in Galicia[2] in 1846.

The peasants in Hungary in the early sixteenth century were no worse off than in many other countries; all the same, when Eötvös makes one of his peasant characters, named Gáspár, tell his life-story, he feels it necessary to add a footnote: 'Anyone who may consider that this picture of the condition of the peasants at the time is exaggerated can be referred to any of our historians, or to our statute-book.' Gáspár's daughter had been taken by his lord as his mistress, and would have nothing more to do with her parents; of his sons, two had died fighting in the lord's army, and a third had been shot dead by the lord for inefficiency on a hunting expedition. The parents fled because Gáspár feared lest he be tempted to break the commandment 'Thou shalt not kill'; they were brought back by force, and his wife died of the cruelties inflicted on her during the journey (ch. 13).

[1] In the digression on prison conditions (ch. 36).
[2] The southern part of Poland, also under Austian rule.

Then in 1514 chance brought the Hungarian peasants together. The Primate, Cardinal Bakócz (or Bakács), a man of peasant origin who had acquired immense wealth, had been unsuccessful in his candidature for the Papacy, but was entrusted with the organization of a crusade; he appointed as its leader a *Székely soldier named Dózsa György. The volunteers for the crusaders' army came almost entirely from the non-nobles, and eventually the crusade turned into a revolutionary movement to end the social oppression, and the peasants defied an order to disband under threat of excommunication. They won some considerable, but no decisive, successes; and with the prolongation of the struggle their defeat became inevitable. Dózsa himself was taken prisoner. At first the rebels had emphasized their loyalty to the Crown and affirmed that their quarrel was only with the lords; but later on some of them acclaimed Dózsa as king, against his own will. The lords' leader, Zápolya, the voievode of Transylvania, therefore made the punishment fit the crime by having Dózsa crowned at a coronation ceremony in which throne, sceptre, and crown were all of red-hot iron; and the ferocity of the subsequent reprisals against the peasants was given statutory expression in the laws passed by the Diet after the defeat of the revolt; they were condemned to 'real and perpetual servitude', in which status they remained till 1547. Matters were made still worse by the coincidence that the jurist Werbőczi completed the task with which the King had entrusted him, of codifying the legal rights of the various classes, just in time to bring the results of his work before the 1514 Diet. Thus the purely vindictive legislation passed by that Diet was incorporated in Werbőczi's *Tripartitum*, thereby achieving an authority which lasted till 1848, alongside the jurist's formulation of the privileges of the nobility. Such was the past which shaped the present as portrayed in *The Village Notary*, and which might be repeated in Hungary as in Galicia.

Eötvös prefixed to *Hungary in 1514* a short statement of the principles on which he had written his historical novel. In addition to the artistic and moral tasks which any writer must discharge, he says, the historical novelist must 'popularize history', adhering, however, strictly to historical truth; so Eötvös studied his period with scholarly thoroughness from the original sources, to which he often refers in footnotes. This preface (and the austere title of the novel) may well arouse apprehensions in the reader; but they are immediately allayed by the opening scene which most vividly portrays a nation.

The streets of Buda are crowded with people making for St. George Square (Szent György tér), to see the *Székely knight Dózsa, who is to be ceremonially ennobled by the King for his gallantry in defeating and slaying a Turk in single combat. This is a festive occasion; but it is overshadowed by the memory of past greatness. As an old soldier in the crowd puts it, 'we have no *Mátyás any more'; a generation earlier Dózsa's exploit would have seemed quite ordinary. Even more conspicuous is the fact that this is a country ruled by a high-handed oligarchy; most (though not all) of the peasants we see are visibly cowed by terror. The rulers are also mutually hostile—at one point there is almost an armed clash between Cardinal Bakács's soldiers and the *Nádor's retainers. The King, *Ulászló II, had degenerated into a state of almost total inertia, more particularly since the death of his wife; the power lay in the hands of Bakács, who was the prime mover in arranging the ceremony about to take place, which he hoped would arouse enthusiasm for his crusade.

Many lords had gathered in the palace for the reception in honour of Dózsa; but the central figure himself was ill at ease. He was simply dressed, by contrast with the court dandies; and as a *Székely he hated the class from which came his rulers, the voievodes of Transylvania—the *Székelys had in fact rebelled in 1505, and among Bakács's reasons for wishing to honour Dózsa was the hope of effacing recent bitter memories among his people. The crowd in the streets had applauded the *Székely knight, but in the palace no friendly hand was stretched out to greet him, and soon some of the lords began to tease him. Stung to fury, he burst out with a bitter attack on the cruelties committed against his people, and only the kindly tact of the Treasurer, Telegdi, a man whom all respected, restored the situation.

We now move into fiction as Telegdi receives in his Italianate palace his guests the Ártándis, father and son. They have been delayed on their journey to Buda; they stopped to help the richest merchant of Pest, Szaleresi and his daughter Klári, who had been attacked on their small country estate by robbers—the crusaders are already on the move. Szaleresi insists that his benefactors stay for a drink, and the sight of Klári makes the young Ártándi, Pál, completely forget his previous haste. He rejoices, as does Klári, when Szaleresi suggests that all four should travel up to Buda together.

Alone with old Ártándi, Telegdi confides to him his fears: 'The bells which call the people to proclaim the crusade signify the storm gathering over our heads.' Telegdi had tried in vain to prevent the launching of the crusade, tried in vain to warn the Privy Council of the danger; now the only hope is that the right man be appointed to lead the army. With great reluctance Ártándi accepts Telegdi's offer of the command; but others have already formed other plans. Bakács's secretary has learnt, from a spy of his in Telegdi's service, of the proposal to give Ártándi the command, and must act quickly; his real reason for launching the crusade was not to fight the Turk but to check the ambition of Zápolya, so the army must be led by someone he can trust to comply with his wishes. Both Bakács's secretary and the parish priest of Cegléd, Mészáros Lőrinc (an historical character) urge that the command be given to Dózsa. Lőrinc impresses on the Cardinal the urgency of the situation; the crusaders, numbering over 10,000, are short of provisions, and if their desperate situation drives them to rebel, the lords will have an excuse for crushing them. Lőrinc also stresses the right of 'the free champions of Christ' to a say in the choice of their leader; they would refuse to fight under the command of a lord. Lőrinc represents the true crusading spirit, the reality, of which Bakács is the pretence; he is also a fearless spokesman of the people against their oppressors. Bakács agrees that Dózsa be appointed, and feels delighted at the prospect of humbling the proud lords who despise him for his peasant origin.

The party at Telegdi's palace was memorable also for another reason; Ártándi's son Pál and Telegdi's youngest (and only un-married) daughter Frusina, who were already on friendly terms, looked so radiant that all hoped they might marry, though Telegdi was determined that his daughter should freely choose her own husband. But Frusina was also the object of the true but hopeless love of Telegdi's young secretary Orbán, the son of a peasant who had given his life for Telegdi on the battlefield, and had asked him to care for his children. As Orbán was gifted, Telegdi had had him educated, and in time appointed him his secretary; throughout he was actuated by kindness and by the memory of Orbán's father, though the youth was understandably unhappy away from his home. Now Orbán guessed that Frusina was attracted to Pál, and he was right; shortly afterwards, in the garden of Telegdi's summer cottage in the hills above Buda, Pál declared his love to Frusina, and his love was accepted. But Orbán was also right in considering Pál unworthy of Frusina; for Pál could not bring himself to break off his affair with Szaleresi Klári, whose gratitude had quickly turned to love.

On one of his visits to Klári, Pál overhears a secret meeting of the leaders of the crusade, among whom is Szaleresi, at which they definitely decide to rebel against the lords. There is opposition from Dózsa's brother Gergely, and from Szaleresi, but it is overborne by Lőrinc with his visionary eloquence, his instant refutation of objections, and above all by his skill in playing on the emotions of Dózsa György. It is Lőrinc, too, who restores order when one Friar Márton draws his dagger against Gergely and Szaleresi. After this meeting, Lőrinc seeks to win over Szaleresi by informing him privately that his daughter is Pál's mistress, although Pál is engaged to Frusina. This is overheard by Klári; Pál denies it, though with difficulty. This piece of deceit stirs twinges of conscience in Pál, but these soon give place to dreams of winning fame by forestalling the revolt. So he informs Bornemisza, the highly respected tutor to the heir-apparent, the boy Prince Lajos, of what he has heard.

Eventually Pál steels himself to write a farewell letter to Klári, and tells her that he loves her but is marrying Frusina to please his father. Klári's love, however, is passionate; she forms a plan to organize a raid by crusaders on Telegdi's cottage in order to put pressure on Frusina to renounce Pál. Her conscience revolts, but only after she has set the wheels in motion, when it is too late. However, Orbán learns what is afoot and rescues the ladies of Telegdi's household, Frusina and Bebek Katalin, a relative of Telegdi's late wife who kept house for the widower. From a nearby inn they see Telegdi's cottage in flames.

The long raid scene is a memorable study of fanaticism and revenge. Significantly, the target is Telegdi; the lord who sympathized with the people in their sufferings is an object of particular hatred among the rebels, who know only that he opposed the crusade. Significant too is the fact that though Klári's purpose was to do Frusina no harm, only to make her promise not to marry Pál, the final outcome is that the cottage is stormed and every man, woman, and child in it killed. This outcome is due to a succession of mischances. Szaleresi (to whom Klári confesses) orders the raiders to disperse on pain of death, but only the moderates obey, so that the force which carries out the raid is composed wholly of fanatics. Then Gáspár, the Hussite peasant who had lost all his family, is shot dead by a servant of Telegdi's who did not know that the two sides were negotiating at the time. Finally, the moderate Szaleresi himself, after having cursed and disowned his daughter, learns the whole story and in his grief and remorse becomes as bitterly hostile to Telegdi, Frusina's father, as the raiders themselves.

When the news of the raid reached the rebel leaders, Lőrinc, aware of the danger created by the premature outbreak of the revolt, was in favour of seizing the capital at once; but Dózsa respected the Crown too much to approve such a plan, and was obstinately determined first to capture a town in southern Hungary. Outvoted, the priest began inwardly to doubt the effectiveness of the leadership, but fought his doubts as due to spiritual pride. As he prayed, a Franciscan of Buda named Villibald, came up to him with the news that the Primate—doubtless under duress—had ordered the crusaders to disband on pain of excommunication.

This order was read out to the crusaders as a royal proclamation. Dózsa formally rejected it, in terms respectful to the King, but disavowing loyalty to the 'usurping' lords, and pointing out that the crusade had been proclaimed by the Pope and all Christendom. At the same time he offered safe conduct to all who chose to obey the order; but Lőrinc followed with an inflammatory speech setting forth the grievances of the people, also defeating the Dominican provincial in theological argument; this was a time to render unto God the things which were God's. But when the Dominican announced the excommunication of all who refused to disband, adding a vivid description of the damnation of the disobedient, the people were terrified, and the cause of rebellion was saved only by a 'miracle' which had been rigged by Villibald, with Lőrinc's reluctant approval. When the dread rite of excommunication was performed, however, only Lőrinc remained unflinching; but he imparted his courage to the others, exercising over the whole camp the same power that had earlier swayed his colleagues in the debate. The great scene marks the climax of all that has preceded— civil war has now been declared, irrevocably. Already, too, we can discern portents of ultimate failure. The rebels' camp is a picture of want, squalor, and dissension; the leader, Dózsa, is a disastrous combination of scruples, obstinacy, and pride, and has already begun to rule by terror. The excesses of the rebels disgust Szaleresi to the point of negotiating with Bornemisza, who comes to the peasants' camp with a promise of full pardon, from the King himself, for those who disband. Szaleresi, and many others, do so; but Bornemisza cannot persuade the other lords to honour the promise, and in the event Szaleresi is kept in prison—a compromise proposed by the weak and vacillating King between his release and his execution.

Meanwhile Orbán had fled eastwards with the ladies, pursued by Klári, whose determination to seek out Frusina nothing could shake, and who had followed Orbán to the inn and overheard his plans for flight. These had to be changed more than once because of rebel successes; after a time the strain of the journey began to affect Frusina's health. Orbán then took his party to the cottage of his sister, who was married to a gamekeeper and lived in the forest near Temesvár,[1] which town was being besieged by Dózsa. Katalin, who was completely (indeed comically) lost away from the court, soon grew restive and vented her anger on Orbán, finally accusing him, a servant, of presuming to love Frusina. This quarrel released all the emotion in Orbán; he confessed his love to Frusina, then rushed out blindly, in horror at his failure to keep his resolution never to disturb her peace of mind; in his anguish he did not observe the approach of a rebel patrol. He was apprehended and brought to the rebel camp, where only the personal intervention of Lőrinc saved his life. The clash with Katalin, however, has convinced Orbán that his place is with the class into which he was born. Lőrinc tries to dissuade him from joining the peasants now; the priest whose fiery idealism had kept the rebel cause alive in more than one critical moment is now wholly disillusioned, not only because he sees the certainty of ultimate defeat, but still more as a result of Telegdi's fate. When Telegdi was taken prisoner, Dózsa, remembering with gratitude the kindness of the one lord who had shown a friendly attitude to him at the reception in the palace, ordered a reprieve: Lőrinc, feeling that the cause mattered more than any individual, and that unity must be preserved at all costs, yielded to a general demand and ordered, in Dózsa's absence, the execution of the captive:

[1] Now Timişoară in Rumania.

then the execution was carried out, on Friar Márton's instructions, in Lőrinc's own absence, in a manner which horrified Lőrinc when he heard of it.[1] So the priest now urges Orbán to hold himself in reserve for the better future which must come; but the young man replies 'Take me to Dózsa and give me arms'.

Meanwhile Pál, fighting in the army of Zápolya, has made a name for himself by his bravery, especially by his achievement in conveying a message from Zápolya to Báthori, whom Dózsa was besieging in Temesvár. In fact this achievement was Klári's; for Klári had found Pál, the two had reaffirmed their love, and Klári had insisted on carrying out Pál's dangerous mission for him. Agreement between Zápolya and Báthori, hitherto bitter enemies, and the resulting unification of the lords' forces, means certain defeat for the rebels; but they are not thinking of military preparations. When Frusina and Katalin are brought as prisoners into the rebel camp, Márton, Telegdi's executioner, inflames the mob—the captives will be spared only if someone volunteers to marry them. At the very last moment, when Márton definitely threatens to hand over Frusina to the executioner, Orbán comes forward, and Ollósi the court tailor, who has also fallen into rebel hands, similarly proposes marriage to Katalin. Frusina scornfully repels Orbán and wonders if he had planned everything from the outset—Katalin is certain that he had.

The weddings are celebrated on a scale which portends disaster —Zápolya attacks next day. Dózsa, fortified by class hatred, blind confidence, and drink, both performs and inspires miracles of valour; but eventually the peasant army is routed. Both Dózsa brothers are captured alive; Orbán is killed a moment after he has succeeded in informing Pál, who is fighting in the lords' army, that Frusina is in the rebel camp; so the ladies are saved.

At the same time Pál is deeply perturbed by a request from Bornemisza to intercede with Zápolya for the release of Szaleresi, who is still a prisoner and has been transferred to Temesvár. Worse, Klári produces Pál's farewell letter and threatens to show it to Frusina. But the life of Szaleresi, Klári's father, depends on Pál, who alone can intercede with Zápolya to arrange the release of the prisoner. Klári renounces her revenge, and thanks to Pál's good offices Szaleresi is freed, on condition that he leaves the country immediately.

[1] Eötvös departs from history here; the execution of Telegdi was in fact ordered by Dózsa.

Zápolya has also decided Dózsa's fate. The peasant leader receives the news of his sentence with a defiant dignity which confounds the mockery of his jailer, and moves those present to amazed admiration. 'A heavy load of sin lies on my soul; I have done deeds of which I have repented, and for which curses, perhaps, will be uttered over me, but my torments will atone for all. . . . I took up arms on behalf of the people, and as a living symbol of the people I shall sit on the burning throne which has been prepared for me; but the fiery crown which Zápolya will place on my head cannot be taken from my brow by his frail hand. The future will find it there and will bow before the man who could endure these things without complaint.' Left alone in his cell, Dózsa went off to sleep, on the last evening of his life, 'as deeply, as peacefully as he used to before a battle'; and that is the last we see of him.

Between 40,000 and 70,000 peasants perished, continues Eötvös, mostly in the reprisals which followed the victory of the lords. But a country, like a family, cannot survive without love; a building is enabled to withstand storms by the mortar, for which the pressure of the upper stones on the lower is no substitute. Bornemisza's prophecy that Hungary would disappear from the roll of free nations was soon fulfilled, at Mohács. The Turkish menace was near—had not Dózsa won nobility for his gallantry in battle against the Turk? But to relate the sequel of the revolt is the task of the historian; for the novelist, two events remain to be recorded. First, a magnificent reception was held at Telegdi's palace in Buda to celebrate the engagement of Pál and Frusina. It was overshadowed, though only for a moment, by the sound of Klári's voice outside, singing the same love-song which had once before touched Pál's heart. Secondly, Klári and her father departed into exile. On their way they meet a monk, who bids them farewell, in the last scene of the novel; it is Lőrinc. 'The way I have hitherto followed cannot lead us to our goal. The triumph of justice will not be achieved by savage violence. . . . But do not believe that I have abandoned my hopes. . . . God made man in His image; . . . how can divine justice remain for ever excluded from a world ruled by man? God be with you.'

To 'popularize history' becomes more difficult in proportion as the 'history' contains fewer events of the type which the reader of a novel normally expects. By this criterion the Dózsa rebellion is a most intractable subject, and *Hungary in 1514* is not so much an historical novel as a compound of history and novel, with both an historical plot describing the course of the rebellion itself, and a fictional plot relating the lives and loves of individuals. A few characters—notably Szaleresi—may be common to both plots, but this does not prevent the plots themselves from being largely separate. So Eötvös's energies are divided between the creation of his fictional characters and the quite different task of interpreting an important and controversial event in history. He devoted much thought to the difference between a history and an historical novel, and at one point he pulls himself up with the remark that he is 'not writing a history'. Yet there are long passages which could have come straight out of a history, especially the discussions of the chief figures in the revolt. These are written with power and penetration; but inevitably they retard the action. In addition, by describing his characters in detail before we see them, Eötvös sometimes deprives us of the pleasure of discovering for ourselves what manner of people they are. Indeed, he does this also with some of the fictional characters; in such cases the pleasure of discovering their nature is denied us, with no compensating service to the study of history.

In the last resort, then, *Hungary in 1514* is a joint production of Eötvös the novelist and Eötvös the historian, with a result very different from the superbly unified plot of *The Village Notary*; the reader, for his part, must alternately surrender to his imagination and apply his intellect—and this is not always easy. Moreover, because of Eötvös's scrupulous scholarship, the novelist is faced with a far harder task than the historian. The rebellion itself is presented with splendid vividness; not only does Eötvös know how to use his material, but the material is abundant. With a fictional plot, on the other hand, the historical novelist must risk anachronisms or leave gaps, as a traveller speaking an unfamiliar foreign language must risk solecisms or remain silent. This is possibly why the fictional characters, except Orbán, do not come fully to life, as the historical characters most certainly do.

There is, however, one most important link between the historical and the fictional plots; both portray the passion of revenge, its blindness, its ever-increasing intensity. But the two plots have contrasting climaxes. The historical plot culminates in the passing of sentence on Dózsa; in the fictional plot, on the other hand, Klári renounces her vengeance, when she finds that she can revenge herself on Pál only at the price of her father's life. By this contrast the novel achieves a fundamental unity.

Reform had opened with the words 'Our country cannot remain in its present condition', and *The Village Notary* had portrayed a system which must be changed; now we have seen what may happen when the victims of an evil system set about changing it by force. The conclusion is plain; Lőrinc had tried revolution and found it wanting. There is no evidence that the historical Lőrinc repented in this way;[1] and this one major departure from history is the more significant because Lőrinc's words at the end of *Hungary in 1514* epitomize Eötvös's own political career in the period following the completion of the novel. Between May and November 1847 he contributed to the *Pest Journal*, possibly in collaboration with others, a series of articles advocating radical reforms within the framework of the Monarchy. At the same time, mindful of the harm done by internal discord (of which both sides provided examples in 1514), he worked for opposition unity, and no longer wrote from a specifically centralist standpoint.

Then in March 1848 came the fall of Metternich, the historic demonstration by the youth of Pest on the 15th, and the granting by Vienna of the demands set forth in *Kossuth's draft address to the Crown, including independent government. Count *Batthyány Lajos, the provisional Minister President, formed a Government composed of all the ablest Hungarians of the day; Eötvös received the portfolio of Religion and Education. He had played a leading part in *Batthyány's prolonged negotiations in Vienna, and now applied himself to his ministerial duties with extraordinary energy; at the beginning of August 1848 he produced his draft Bill on elementary education.

He firmly accepted, at the outset, the principle that education is a State responsibility, while safeguarding the individual's right to educate his children as he wishes, subject to their taking an annual public examination. He made education, with a remarkably broad curriculum,[2] compulsory for boys aged 6–12 and girls aged 6–10. If it is to be compulsory, it follows that it must be free. The cost of the new scheme would be borne in the first instance by the

---

[1] Eötvös, however, is adhering to history when he makes Lőrinc flee from Temesvár and disappear.

[2] Reading and writing: mental and written arithmetic: physics: natural history, with special reference to the locality: Hungarian history and geography: citizenship: physical training: singing.

local authority, which was to have power to levy a small tax for the purpose if necessary. Instruction was to be given in the language spoken by a majority of the inhabitants of a district; Hungarian was to be a subject in the curriculum where it was not the majority language. Provision was also made for religious instruction to be given by a minister of the child's religion, and for Church schools.

Whatever its merits, the Bill could not have come before the Diet at a more unfortunate moment. Considerable Serbian forces had moved secretly into Hungary as early as April; on 16 May *Batthyány had appealed for 10,000 volunteers to defend the country against them, and on 11 July *Kossuth called for an army of 200,000 (40,000 to be equipped immediately) and a credit of 42 million forints, but these proposals did not come before the Diet till 16 August. Eötvös's Education Bill thus collided directly with the claims of national defence, and was even attacked as an instrument of deliberate obstruction. He replied that education was essential to the realization of the ideals of liberty and equality professed by the 1847–8 Diet; besides, was it reasonable to appoint a Minister and then expect him to do nothing? Eötvös might reasonably be criticized for confusing considerations of ultimate importance with immediate urgency; but to question his good faith was outrageous. *Kossuth, as Minister of Finance, could legitimately argue that the Bill was at present beyond the financial resources of the country; but his speech also clearly attempts to make Eötvös ridiculous, though it is free from the cruder forms of malice. The whole episode illustrates the Government's tragic lack of any concept of a collective policy or responsibility—its members appear throughout as individuals. Then in September *Jellačić crossed the Drave, and the Government resigned. Its successor existed only on paper; the country was in fact governed by *Kossuth. The Education Bill had eventually been passed, but was never put into effect.

On 28 September Count Lamberg, who had been appointed Royal Commissioner with full powers to negotiate a settlement, was lynched by a mob in Pest. Here was the 'spiritual darkness' which Lőrinc had declared to be incompatible with liberty; Eötvös, who had a wife and family (he had nearly lost his wife when their son was born on 27 July 1848) followed Lőrinc's advice to Orbán and 'reserved himself for the future'. He fled the country, arriving in Munich (where he had a married sister) on 12 October.

5

In exile Eötvös returned energetically to writing, though not to the novel. Out of material collected for a projected history of the French Revolution and for a history of Christian civilization there now grew a major political treatise, *The Dominant Ideas of the 19th Century and their Influence on the State* (*A XIX. század uralkodó eszméinek befolyása az álladalomra*). The first part appeared in 1851 a little over six months after Eötvös's return to Pest in December 1850, by which time the reign of military terror which had followed the suppression of Hungarian independence was over; the second part followed in 1854. Both parts appeared simultaneously in Hungarian and German.

The three dominant ideas of our age, says Eötvös, are *Liberty*, *Equality*, and *Nationality*.

Liberty is a condition in which man can use both his own powers, and the natural forces in his environment, to further aims of his own choosing, within the limits of what is possible.

Equality consists in so ordering the State that no citizen shall enjoy special privileges or bear special burdens. (Equality is, in fact, as Eötvös says later on in his treatise, the means by which all alike are enabled to enjoy Liberty.)

Nationality consists in the application of the principle of Liberty to a whole people; it manifests itself in the efforts of a people to achieve the status to which it considers itself entitled by virtue of historic rights, or for some other reason.

In practice, however, since the French Revolution,

Liberty has meant the absence of any power in the State exercised otherwise than in the name of the people.

Equality has meant that all are equally subject to, and contribute in equal measure to, the will of the people.

Nationality has meant the fusion of the previously separate parts of a 'nation' (by which is understood sometimes the State, sometimes a social or linguistic group), with the assimilation or elimination of foreign elements, and demanding sometimes equality, sometimes domination.

In this summary we shall refer to the former set of conceptions as the 'traditional' conceptions, to the latter as the 'revolutionary'.

The first part of the treatise is concerned to show that:

1. The revolutionary conceptions of the three dominant

ideas are mutually incompatible. (With the ideas of liberty and equality, however, Eötvös succeeds in establishing only that the revolutionary conceptions are incompatible with the traditional.) The revolutionary conceptions are absolutist, involving an increase in the power of the State, and a corresponding reduction in individual freedom; power may be exercised in the name of the people, but the individual is powerless. The revolutionary conception of nationality is incompatible with liberty and equality, for it is based on the desire to achieve a position analogous to that of a privileged class within the State. This is equally true whether we adopt the revolutionary conception of liberty and equality or the traditional.

2. The revolutionary conceptions of the three dominant ideas cannot be realized without breaking up all existing States. The revolutionary conceptions of liberty and equality postulate both complete social equality and a State so small that no part of it lies beyond the immediate reach of the government. The revolutionary conception of nationality, too, is incompatible with the existence of the states we know, because nationality has not been the basis of the growth of present-day Europe, and no nation could realize aspirations based on nationality without major changes in existing frontiers.

3. The realization of the ideas in their revolutionary conceptions would not bring the expected contentment; the revolutionary conceptions of liberty and equality attempt to substitute absolute State authority for individual rights, and ignore the fact that a 'people' is an aggregate of individuals, so that there can be no happiness of 'the people' other than the aggregate of every individual's happiness.

All the sufferings of our age have been caused by the clash between the revolutionary conceptions of the dominant ideas and those traditional conceptions on which our civilization has hitherto been based, not only the State, but the whole order of our society. We must choose between one set of conceptions and the other. If we decide—as is inevitable—in favour of the traditional conceptions which are the foundation of our civilization, how can we restrict the power of the State? The answer to this question forms the subject of the second part of the treatise, which thus suggests a remedy for the ills diagnosed in the first.

Eötvös begins with an historical survey tracing the traditional conceptions of liberty and equality to their Christian origins, and the revolutionary conception of liberty to the ancient Greek view of it as a share in the government. To win 'liberty' has been the objective of all ages; but the dissatisfaction with the revolutionary conception of liberty, where that has been achieved, shows that it is the traditional conception which represents men's true desire. Are the three dominant ideas, according to their traditional conceptions, compatible with the modern State? To answer this question we must examine the function of the State.

The State, unlike the need to live in some form of society, is not a basic requirement of man, but rather a means devised by him, when he has reached a certain level of civilization, for achieving certain ends which can be achieved in no other way. (It is not the product of any 'social contract'; history provides no evidence in support of any such contract. The notion of a 'social contract' is the result of purely abstract theorizing.) The object of the State is to secure (not to procure) the enjoyment of material and moral goods for the individual. Without drawing any rigid distinction between these two types of good, we may define a 'material' good as one apprehended by the senses, a 'moral' good as one which satisfies our religion or code of ethics. Liberty, a dominant idea, is one of the greatest moral needs of the individual; so to secure it becomes one of the chief obligations of the State.

A State must be independent in its relations with foreign powers, and strong enough to protect the material and moral goods of its individual citizens against attack. (Many thinkers, adds Eötvös, have discussed the State as if there were to be only one State in the world.) A State can be stronger than its parts only if those parts coalesce into a single moral personality, possessing both a will and the strength to carry that will into effect. It needs, in fact, a united and centralized legislature (to which the executive must be subordinate), government, and system of representation, which must be closely interconnected, like the parts of the human body.

But centralization must be limited to the extent prescribed by the function of the State. An excessively centralized State is more likely to suffer from internal conflict (for the more power is centralized, the more acute does the struggle for that power become), more vulnerable to outside attack, and, because of the importance of specialized knowledge of local conditions, less efficient. Moreover, 'the object of all centralization is the establishment of absolute power' (Part II, Book 4, ch. XIV (D))—which can, however, be prevented by the existence of a flourishing political life in closely knit local communities. Eötvös here attacks excessive centralization in a long discussion written with a power and conviction surprising in the former 'centralist'; yet it is the times which have changed, and consequently the emphasis— Eötvös's views remain virtually the same, and here too he insists that no local authority must be so independent as to endanger the State. The State must, in fact, possess certain guarantees of its own power. These are, first, the desire for individual liberty, which the existence of the State protects against possible encroachments by the local authority: secondly, the interests common to all citizens of the State, to secure which the State came into being in the first place.

Clashes between the State and its component parts can be avoided, if 'natural rights' are respected by the State as the individual respects the law. This respect is secured by the existence of (1) a judiciary with supreme authority, and (2) a Church—both independent of the State. The former will avert clashes between the State and its parts; the independence of the Church will ensure that the power of the State is confined within its proper limits. By respecting these institutions the State will set an example of respect for rights, thereby implanting a similar respect in the minds of its citizens, which in turn will strengthen, as nothing else could, the structure of the State itself. A State can be secure only if it satisfies the convictions of its citizens, and the States of today must meet the demands made on them in the name of liberty, the dominant idea of our age.

Is it possible for the modern State to grant its citizens the measure of liberty they demand? To give a practical, as opposed to a utopian, answer to this question, we must first examine the nature of human development and progress, and their influence on the structure of the State.

Progress is a fact, attested by palaeontology, history, and religion; the greatest achievements of past ages are untypical of the general level. Those who deny the fact of progress forget that the concept does not imply perfection in the present; moreover, like the growth of a man, progress is slower in its later stages and consequently less conspicuous.

Progress can be measured by man's power over the forces of the physical world, and by the growth of respect for human dignity. Its nature may be formulated in the following three laws (Book 6, ch. IV–VI):

1. All progress depends on contact between different individuals who embody some conflict between different forces or ideas.

2. The direction of progress in any age depends on the dominant ideas of that age.

3. The extent of progress depends on need, which provides the impulse to overcome that conservative instinct which operates as inertia does in the physical world.

Since progress is the purpose of man's life on earth, only those State institutions which conform to the laws of progress can be lasting. In practical terms: (1) the first law of progress requires that there shall be individuals capable of self-expression, and opportunities for the necessary contacts; (2) the second law requires the establishment of that liberty and equality which man really desires, i.e. the traditional conception; (3) as regards the third law, we must show that certain changes are needed, that the power of the State must be limited; only when convinced of the necessity of such a change can we inquire how it may most easily be effected. Political philosophy is of practical value only in so far as it is able to meet the needs of the present age, and on ability to solve this last problem 'the whole value of my work depends' (Book 6, ch. IX).

To limit the power of the State is necessary, in its own interest; not only will it then better fulfil its task of securing the material and moral goods of the individual, it will command the individual's loyalty. Again, only by limiting the power of the State can we meet the demands made on it in the name of nationality;[1] and to meet those demands is as essential in our century as religious reform was in the sixteenth, and political reform in the eighteenth, centuries. The demands of nationality cannot be met in the revolutionary State, for the 'freer' (according to the revolutionary conception of liberty) the State, the greater the injury inflicted on all national minorities. It would be impossible to redraw the map of Europe in accordance with the principle of nationality; the solution is to be found in a measure of local autonomy (as in Switzerland and the U.S.A.), sufficient to prevent the principle of nationality from endangering the State.

The enthusiasm for the principle of nationality which we have witnessed is a protest by all peoples in the name of the Christian

---

[1] The word is used here in its ethnical sense.

principle of individual liberty, against the pagan belief in the absolute power of the State; it is the instrument by which Providence is leading us back to the path of peace and progress. The victory of the traditional conception of nationality over the revolutionary would consolidate order and peace; now that the events of 1848 have shown that no European nation can be oppressed with impunity, the guarantee of peace is to be sought in the enjoyment of equal rights by all peoples. When this has been achieved, when the belief that the map of Europe can be redrawn on the basis of nationality has been abandoned as an illusion, the bond between members of the same nationality in different countries will bring all States closer together, and, as a result, the need for peaceful coexistence[1] will be more widely felt.

Eötvös concludes the treatise by reaffirming that all the unrest and suffering of the age are due to the clash between the two conceptions of the dominant ideas. One set of conceptions or the other must, in the end, win complete victory. We may look forward with confidence to the final outcome, for the results achieved by the natural development of mankind can never be permanently destroyed.

The Dominant Ideas, like *The Village Notary*, attracted considerable attention abroad, not only in Germany but also in France, where Édouard Laboulaye discussed it fully in *L'État et ses limites*[2] and in Britain, where it was warmly praised by the *Westminster Review*.[3] Noteworthy also is the extent of Eötvös's agreement with the ideas which J. S. Mill was to propound five years later in *On Liberty*—a fact which gave the Hungarian great pleasure; he sent Mill a copy of *The Dominant Ideas* in 1869.

At home, Eötvös's attitude since 1848 had pained some of his contemporaries, less on account of any particular passage in *The Dominant Ideas* than because he seemed to view the problems of the nationalities in the Monarchy from the Austrian standpoint. In 1850 he had published[4] a pamphlet in German entitled *Über die Gleichberechtigung der Nationalitäten in Österreich* (*On the Equality of Status of the Nationalities in Austria*) in which he showed that

---

[1] Eötvös here employs the same phrase which modern Hungarian (in all probability by coincidence) has adopted for use in a present-day political context.

[2] In *Revue nationale et étrangère*, I (1860), pp. 5–33, 169–203. On Eötvös see especially pp. 182 ff.   [3] N.S. 7 (1855), p. 230.

[4] The first edition was published anonymously at Leipzig; a second, in the author's name, appeared at Pest in the following year.

equality of status for all nationalities was incompatible with the survival of the Monarchy, and advocated a combination of a centralized Reichstag and government with a separate, independent internal administration for each of the various provinces. This was, in fact, an application to the Monarchy of the principles he was to expound in *The Dominant Ideas*. In the larger work most of the examples are drawn from France (a natural result of the origin of the treatise in a study of the French Revolution) and Britain; references to Austria are very rare, those to Hungary still rarer. But what Eötvös says in *The Dominant Ideas* is implicitly relevant to the centralized absolutist administration which Austria imposed on Hungary in 1850, and his argument is strengthened by being based not on the particular case, but on universally valid principles. Here is a warning to Austria that her policy must fail; and by 1860 Laboulaye could say that 'the ideas of the despised theorist [Eötvös] are winning the day'.

6

Immediately after completing *The Dominant Ideas*, Eötvös wrote three short stories, all set in contemporary Hungary, all unconnected with politics. The first two, *A Slovak Girl in the Lowlands* (*Egy tót leány az alföldön*) and *The Miller's Daughter* (*A molnárleány*) appeared together in 1854; the third, *Winter Market* (*Téli vásár*) was written in 1855 and published in 1859.

The first pair are well contrasted. The *Slovak Girl* relates how a Hungarian peasant decides to adopt a little Slovak girl whose father was dying, and how she grew up to marry the son of her adoptive father—a delectably warm-hearted story, with no mention of the bonds of common humanity which transcend nationality. In the second tale, the miller's daughter is driven to suicide by her father, who forces a marriage on her (in her own interest, as he persists in believing) without regard for his previous promise that she shall marry the friend of her childhood whom she loves. *The Miller's Daughter* is twice as long as the *Slovak Girl* and more richly adorned with the resources of the literary artist; but the latter story cannot fail to endear itself to the reader who has no automatic preference for a tragic ending.

The heroine of *Winter Market*, Vikta, caught in a snowstorm after having sold her mother's cow at the market, is befriended by an old herdsman, Péter. Her lover is about to join the army in despair at her disappearance and his parents' refusal to allow him to marry her, because she is poor; Péter, hearing this story by chance in an inn, realizes that the girl in question is Vikta and reunites the lovers, roaring with laughter in which the delighted reader joins; then he takes her home and recognizes her as his long-lost daughter. This delicious story combines the warmth of the *Slovak Girl* and the art of *The Miller's Daughter*; the description of the snowstorm is an outstanding passage—not self-consciously microscopic as a twentieth-century writer might make it, but vividly portraying Vikta's experience. Péter the herdsman is one of Eötvös's most memorable characters; he has mellowed since the days when he behaved to his daughter like the miller (with the result that she eloped with her soldier lover and disappeared), yet the Péter whom we see has retained just enough obstinacy to make his previous self credible.

These stories originated in a project for translating Auerbach's *Village Tales* (*Dorfgeschichten*), but Eötvös decided to write original stories instead. He was now the father of four young children,[1] and the relationship between parents and children is a theme common to all three stories.

In 1855 Eötvös was elected Vice-President of the Academy, and in the following years he also revived the *Kisfaludy Society, which had played a major part in Hungarian literary life before 1848. At the same time he was at work on a new full-length novel, *The Sisters* (*A nővérek*), which appeared in the summer of 1857.

At the opening of *The Sisters* we see the two little daughters of Count Ormosy, the two-year-old Margit and her baby sister Ninácska (Anna), in the garden of Ormosy's castle in northern Hungary. Margit is playing with her mother, while Ninácska is sleeping in her basket, fanned by her nurse Kati. This idyll, however, is soon shattered when the Count announces the outbreak of a peasant revolt, the 'cholera-rebellion'[2] of the summer of 1831. He had made preparations for flight; and the Countess having (not

---

[1] His daughters Ilona, Jolán, and Mária were born in May 1846, July 1847, and September 1851 respectively; his son Lóránd (the future physicist) was born in July 1848 (cf. pp. 197, 226 f.).

[2] The peasants believed that the lords had deliberately caused the epidemic by poisoning the wells. It was in the suppression of this rising that Eötvös's father became notorious for his ruthlessness (cf. p. 160), though this fact is not relevant in the novel.

without difficulty) accepted his plan, they all set out for their first stopping-place, the cottage of Kati's husband, the gamekeeper Miska.

Miska has to hide his guests in the attic soon after their arrival, for a band of peasants approaches the cottage determined to extirpate the whole Ormosy family. The Count and Countess overhear this with horror—the Count even regrets his kindness to his peasants—and to horror is added dread when footsteps are heard on the stairs. However, the fugitives remain undetected, and when Miska has given the 'all clear' they set out on their journey as planned, the baby, wrapped in a peasant's swaddling-clothes, travelling separately with her nurse. Soon after their departure Miska learns that Ormosy's castle has been raided by the rebels and that he himself is suspected of having sheltered the hated lord and his family; indeed, the peasants soon return, to overrun the cottage, and Miska is killed defending his home.

When the rising was crushed Kati and the baby could not be traced, though the Countess remained convinced that her little daughter was still alive. To give her a change of environment Ormosy took his wife on a tour of Europe. Their happiness, however, had ended, not only because of their loss, but a rift between them, which had first opened when the Count showed impatience with his wife's attempts to postpone the parting from her baby, now widened till both lacked the courage to confide in each other. Seven years later, when they were in Italy, the Count died (after laying bare his heart to his wife), and eventually homesickness and the appeals of the parish priest Farkas, who urged that the continuous travelling was bad for Margit, decided the Countess to return home to another of the Ormosy estates.

Margit had all the liveliness a child should have, but also strong emotions which augured ill for her permanent happiness. She had also lacked the company of other children; but now she had an ideal playmate in Mariska, the granddaughter of the Countess's housekeeper. The two girls had well-contrasted temperaments, and were truly happy together.

When Margit was nearly eighteen Farkas urged her mother to take her out into the world—'only life is a training for life'. As the Countess and the priest discuss the upbringing of children, a storm comes on and the Countess is appalled at the thought that Margit, who had gone for a walk with Mariska, is out in it. During the walk

Margit confides to Mariska her thoughts; she feels cramped at home, and unloved—she cannot compensate her mother for the loss of Ninácska; even Mariska she may have to share with Fekete András, whom Mariska loves. Mariska blushes at this—András is no longer interested in her, she says, and his father, old Fekete, the most prosperous farmer in the district, will never let him marry a girl like herself, who, though noble, is so poor. By now the storm has compelled the girls to turn back, but they find their way barred by the collapse of a bridge. As they shelter under a rock a man approaches; it is Count Káldory, a neighbouring landowner, who now offers to take them to his mill, from where he can arrange for their transport home. At the miller's we meet András; Mariska's notion that he has lost interest in her is certainly not shared by the miller's daughter Vikta, who is resisting her parents' desire to marry her to him—precisely because she knows that he loves Mariska.

Margit, for her part, quickly realized that she had fallen deeply in love with Káldory, about whom we now learn a good deal. The last of a rich and illustrious family, he had been orphaned in childhood and spoilt by the aunt who brought him up, so that he became temperamentally incapable of exerting himself; contemptuous of pleasure, he yet found nothing to strive for and became bored with life. He had no desire to marry and perpetuate the family as his aunt hoped he would; he had had many affairs which had ended painlessly, but his present liaison with Countess Dárday Irma was another matter. At first she had been indifferent to him, and he had taken up what he saw as a challenge; then she fell desperately in love with him, while success changed his feelings—though in her company he could still persuade himself that love, and not vanity, had drawn him to her. She was married to a man twice her age, whose health was failing, and Káldory foresaw that she might soon be free to marry him, in circumstances in which he would find it impossible to extricate himself. So he went away to his country estate for a time in the vain hope that his absence would kill her love. At the same time his visits to Margit became steadily more frequent, and her visible radiance in his company eventually overcame even Farkas's doubts.

One day, when out hunting, Káldory caught sight of Irma's brother Vilmos, and the suspicion that Irma had sent Vilmos to spy on him stung him into proposing marriage to Margit; his love was accepted, and the Countess gave them her blessing. Just then Mariska announces that András loves her, and that the priest has persuaded András's father to consent to the union. Margit and Mariska are overjoyed; the weddings shall take place on the same day.

Shortly before that day, however, the Countess's housekeeper, Mariska's grandmother, is visited by an old beggar-woman from whom she had received Mariska as a baby; for, as we now learn, Mariska is not really the housekeeper's granddaughter, but an adoptive child. Now the old beggar-woman blackmails the housekeeper into parting with all her savings by threatening to reveal to Fekete, Mariska's future father-in-law, an important secret about the girl his son is going to marry. The couples themselves, however, felt supremely happy—except Káldory. Mariska might be keenly aware of her new responsibilities, which made her quieter and more serious; but this feeling was something very different from Káldory's conscience about his treatment of Irma. He wrote Irma a letter saying that she was the true love of his heart, but he was marrying Margit in obedience to the dictates of his reason and at the instance of his relatives. However, the only reply he received was a formal announcement of the death of Irma's husband; and Irma herself, in deep mourning, appeared at his wedding.

So the two marriages took place. The Káldorys went abroad for their honeymoon, staying away longer than they had originally intended, because of the events of 1848. We next see them nearly three years after their marriage, in Ems, where they have taken a house. Káldory returns from a short absence visiting acquaintances in Frankfurt to find that his wife has become a close friend of Irma, who was in Ems with her brother Vilmos. Vilmos soon fell violently in love with Margit, and even Irma, who knew what a butterfly her brother was, became convinced that this time his feelings were genuine. Moreover, Margit and Káldory were unhappy; Káldory had no desire to become a father, though he came to see more and more clearly that nothing would compensate his wife for the lack of children; and now his anxiety about what Irma might do showed itself in a moodiness which made Margit (who knew nothing about her husband's previous relationship with Irma) first suspect, then accuse, him of loving another; but he was able to allay her suspicions on this score.

Irma, though mercy restrained her from destroying Margit's peace of mind at one stroke, realized that by working to break up the marriage she might both achieve happiness for her brother and avenge herself on Káldory; besides, she could truthfully tell herself that the marriage was a potential failure for other reasons. So she encouraged her brother, and indirectly advised Margit to make Káldory jealous; Margit began to show friendliness towards Vilmos, and Vilmos declared his love. Margit repelled him, horrified, and without revealing her reason, succeeded in persuading her husband to leave Ems and return home at once.

Margit arrived home, after a three years' absence, to find Mariska and András happy and prosperous, with two small daughters, Margit and Mariska. Countess Ormosy greeted her daughter with unbounded joy, which, however, soon gave place to anxiety at Margit's visible unhappiness; but Margit confided only in Mariska. Worse, Vilmos reappeared, having accepted, at the instance of his sister, Káldory's invitation to stay with him for a few days' hunting. The miller's daughter Vikta had fallen hopelessly in love with Vilmos, threatening to drown herself if he forsook her; so, in order to oblige, Vilmos pretended he still loved her, and the two met—in secret, because when he made no definite proposal Vikta's parents forbade her to see him. At the same time Vilmos saw Margit almost every day.

In the autumn, when the Káldorys moved to Pest, matters came to a head. Káldory and Margit had a major quarrel, and soon after, Vilmos, who till then had controlled himself, burst out with the remark that Káldory had never loved his wife, and that Irma possessed letters proving this. Irma, though she had long ago prepared for this moment, still hesitated, but when Margit accused her of intriguing to break up the marriage she produced Káldory's letters. Thereupon Margit, without waiting for her husband's return (he was away in Vienna on business), went back to her mother.

Vilmos wrote to Margit imploring her to give him an opportunity of explaining his conduct, and in reply to his third letter she agreed to see him. But his servant, bringing back her reply, took it into his head to call at the mill (where he had been given many a good lunch), with the result that the letter fell into the hands of Vikta, who immediately set out revenging herself on her lover for his duplicity; she told Káldory that Vilmos was in love with

Margit. However, Margit's cold, composed dignity and her obviously clear conscience left her husband in no doubt that his accusations of infidelity were groundless. She also confronted him with his letter to Irma (which shocked Káldory himself) and finally repudiated him.

Now, however, Vikta tells Margit that she has overheard Vilmos challenge Káldory to a duel, and begs for her help in preventing it. Regardless of her now delicate health, Margit rides straight off through the snow to Káldory's estate, where she finds a letter from her husband amply confirming Vikta's statement that he still loves her. She then goes on to Vilmos's estate, where the duel was to take place, and arrives there to find Vilmos dead, his pistol having accidentally gone off when Vikta had tried to snatch it from him. All this excitement had an effect on Margit's health which proved fatal in a few weeks; Káldory nursed her in her last illness with a devotion which proved the sincerity of his love ('wholly consistent characters exist only in novels', remarks Eötvös) and she died with his name on her lips.

Three months later, Irma had disappeared—it was rumoured that she had become a nun: Vikta, who felt that she had murdered her beloved Vilmos, threw herself into a well; the old housekeeper fell ill and died. After her death the priest Farkas, who had observed that setbacks in her condition coincided with visits from the old beggar-woman, investigated her affairs and found proof that Mariska was the Countess's long-lost child.

On hearing this wonderful news the Countess went to Mariska's home, and found the elder child playing in the garden, while the younger slept in her basket—just like her own children on the day when her husband had brought the news of the cholera-rebellion. She realizes that Mariska must remain in her present mode of life and asks only that Mariska shall regard her as her mother. To accede to the request crowns Mariska's happiness.

In the course of The Sisters Eötvös indulges in a few incidental remarks which make it plain what kind of novel he was now writing. Midway through his story (ch. 26), he pauses to express his fear that some of his readers may be bored by the absence of those 'nerve-shattering events with which the novelist who is conscious of his obligations pleases his reader nowadays'. 'My only hope', he continues, 'is that the silent flow of my novel will make some impression on the reader accustomed to great sensations, as the miller who fell asleep to the noise of the wheels woke suddenly when they stopped.' Lastly 'I cannot help my inability to create characters from my imagination; I can describe only such people as my readers and I have known. Most of these become unhappy without any extraordinary occurrences, quite quietly.' Why do they become unhappy? Describing Káldory's personality when we first meet him (ch. 13), Eötvös observes that 'the novel, which in our time exercises almost the same influence which Plutarch's lives once wielded, has set up peculiar ideals. Instead of *Weltschmerz* . . . it has set up boredom with the world as an ideal.' Káldory exemplifies that boredom, and this is the most important fact about him.

The Sisters, then, is a psychological novel, demonstrating 'world-boredom' and its consequences, as *The Carthusian* treated *Weltschmerz* (though the style has none of the emotionalism so conspicuous in the earlier work). Káldory and Gustave have much in common, and Vilmos's nature is similar though more emotional, but whereas Vilmos never faces the facts about his relationship with Vikta, Káldory in the end not only understands (as Gustave does) but acts on his understanding, and tends Margit devotedly in her last illness.

The man who 'lives for himself' and enjoys a private income will play no part in public affairs. In the cholera-rebellion, Ormosy thinks first of flight; Káldory stays abroad in 1848, not only playing no part in events, but despising those who did otherwise. To criticize Eötvös for remoteness from events is to miss one of the main points of the novel; it is Ormosy and Káldory who stand aloof, not Eötvös. The novelist shows the limitations of his characters in the most effective way possible, by omitting what lies beyond their horizons. Indeed we may detect here Eötvös's misgivings about his own flight as early as September 1848; the parallel between characters and novelist cannot be extended beyond the one point, that both absent themselves from the scene of action; but still Káldory's attitude to the events of his time constitutes a most important element in the plot, because of its effect on Margit: 'The February revolution, and still more its consequences in our country, deeply moved Margit's imagination, and the passionate lady . . . could not understand her husband's aloofness . . . the thought that in this great period he stood idle, pained her heart'; she loves him, indeed idealizes him, and knows, as his own better self knows, that he is not realizing the best of which he is capable. So Countess Ormosy at first opposes her husband's decision to flee immediately, for her conscience is clear about their treatment of the peasants. But though in this respect the Countess and Margit are right, the dangers of the leisured life apply also to them; for they reflect on their own emotions till the 'first drop of bitterness', which events have injected into their marriages, becomes a flood. But Eötvös not only indicates the mistake and its consequences; he shows us its causes, in heredity and upbringing. Káldory could not have been other than what he was; Margit, the child of unhappy parents, born with strong emotions (including, from the very beginning, a streak of possessive jealousy), the object of a mother's love dangerously intensified by the loss of the other child, spending her early, formative years in a succession of hotels and lacking the company of other children—here if anywhere is someone born to tragedy, and although, when she returns to Hungary after the death of her father, she has the companionship of Mariska, it is too late.

All this adds up to a most damning indictment of the aristocratic life of ease and leisure; it is self-destructive, even without any external pressure. The peasants are defeated, but the victors, through their own egoism, risk a ruin as complete as would have resulted from a successful revolution. However, *The Sisters* does not end tragically; just as *The Village Notary* promises a better future, so now Countess Ormosy's unselfish love for Mariska ensures her own happiness—an outcome far more convincing than if she had remained blind and initiated another tragedy. Instead, she sees things as they are, and faces the fact that it is the sister whom she herself has *not* brought up who has achieved happiness.

A conspicuous feature of *The Sisters* is Eötvös's interest in feminine psychology. Not only do the women outnumber the men, but we see the men through the eyes of the women; indeed the whole plot revolves round the emotions of the female characters. This consideration for women readers, however, is no isolated phenomenon, but part of a long-established tradition in Hungarian literature. *The Village Notary* contains several references to 'my lady readers': *Széchenyi in 1830 dedicated *Credit* (*Hitel*) to 'the noble-hearted ladies of our country';[1] and the tales of

---

[1] See p. xxv f.

adventure—sometimes with no specifically feminine interest at all[1] —which were popular towards the end of the eighteenth century, played a vital part in the revival of Hungarian literature. In addition, many important works appeared first in fashion magazines.

The other main psychological theme of *The Sisters* is the upbringing of children, a subject which preoccupied Eötvös's mind at this time. Although *The Sisters* contains far fewer reflections by the author than its predecessors, a discussion of upbringing is attached to the description of Margit's character when she returns to Hungary with her mother, and the problem is also the subject of lengthy talks between Countess Ormosy and the priest Farkas, who is most often the mouthpiece of Eötvös's own opinions. These latter discussions arise naturally out of the situation and hardly obtrude.

A psychological novel, however, cannot be all psychology. Although the humour which brightened *The Village Notary*, and of which there were occasional glimmers in *Hungary in 1514*, is totally absent, possibly because Eötvös felt it would seem incongruous, dramatic excitement abounds, though the identity of Mariska as the lost sister is almost revealed by the title alone, even without the other clues which Eötvös liberally scatters. But the scene in Miska's cottage, where the Ormosy family are hiding from the peasants, is a masterpiece of tension and suspense. Some of the later chapters, too, are vividly dramatic; indeed the episode of Vilmos's death is open to Eötvös's own criticisms of gratuitous melodrama. Nor is the excitement lessened by the close parallels— notably in the character of the rebel peasants—with *Hungary in 1514*.[2] There are other parallels, too, with the earlier novel; Káldory and Vilmos both involve themselves with two women, as Pál does, and Káldory's letter to Irma recalls Pál's to Klári. Vikta, too, resembles (and also surpasses) Klári in the uncontrolled vehemence of her passion. Now, however, the psychology is far more profound and subtle than was possible in *Hungary in 1514*, where

---

[1] For example, *Rontó Pál*, the picaresque narrative in verse describing the adventures of the rascally soldier Rontó Pál, who became the servant of Count Benyovsky, and accompanied him into captivity in Kamchatka and in flight to Madagascar. The author, the retired cavalry general Gvadányi (see p. xx), wrote it (in 1793) for 'the ladies of our country'.

[2] Only the religious justification for the peasants' extremism ('an eye for an eye is God's command') seems less relevant here than in *Hungary in 1514*, where Eötvös was concerned to bring out the Hussite influence on the rebels.

the novelist had set himself other tasks in addition to the portrayal of fictional characters.

When we turn back to *The Village Notary*, however, we are struck by a blazing vitality which *The Sisters* almost entirely lacks. Even the features of *The Village Notary* most open to criticism, the length,[1] the luxuriant periods, the digressions, were also signs of that vitality. At the same time, *The Sisters* is what its characters have made it; to depict the boredom with the world which is his main theme, Eötvös had to deny himself the use of those qualities which make *The Village Notary* his masterpiece.

7

Eötvös was not going to make Káldory's mistake now. He returned to politics, and wrote, in successive years, two political pamphlets in German, *The Guarantees of the Power and Unity of Austria* (*Die Garantien der Macht und Einheit Österreichs*) (1859) and *The Special Position of Hungary from the point of view of German Unity* (*Die Sonderstellung Ungarns vom Standpunkte der Einheit Deutschlands*) (1860). The former of these follows directly from the *Gleichberechtigung* of 1850, which had argued that the 'power and unity' of Austria were indispensable for Europe. The 'guarantees' of that necessity Eötvös now finds in a constitution suiting a multi-national state, placing all its component parts on an equal footing, with a large measure of local autonomy, in order to respect the principle of nationality. He believed that the problems of the Monarchy—like all political problems—could be solved only by constitutional means, and that this could not be done by a movement confined to Hungary;[2] his object was to show all believers in constitutional procedures that they had a common interest, by advocating proposals beneficial to both Austria and Hungary. Then came Solferino; the achievement of Italian unity, together with the movement towards German unity, confronted Austria with a new and grave problem; the *Guarantees* became out of date in less than a year. Eötvös now advocated, as the only practical solution, that Austria should enter the German federation, but with her German territories only; the non-German areas

---

[1] *The Sisters*, the shortest of Eötvös's novels, is little more than half the length of *The Village Notary* or *Hungary in 1514*.

[2] Cf. the entry in his diary (headed *Nationality*) for 18 July 1866.

should be joined to the Monarchy by the revival of the personal union which for centuries had linked the lands of the Hungarian Crown with Austria. Thus, again, a solution advantageous to Hungary (now, however, recognizing her rights as a country with her own Crown and constitution) appears as equally advantageous to Austria, for the personal union would save Austria from a dangerous isolation. The Emperor, too, had seen that some concessions must be made to Hungary, and a royal decree of April 1860 abolished the centralized, absolutist administration.

The equally difficult problem of the relations between Hungary and the other non-German nationalities was treated by Eötvös in *The Nationality Question* (*A nemzetiségi kérdés*), which appeared in 1865. He had, however, begun it as early as 1861, and (like the German pamphlets) it is plainly the work of the author of *The Dominant Ideas*.

The concept of nationality, says Eötvös, is 'the consciousness of affinity which arises among a multitude of men by virtue of their memories of their past, their present situation, and the resulting interests and sentiments'. It corresponds to the individual's consciousness of his own personality; a nation is, in fact, a group of people who have awakened to their existence as a separate personality. This feeling has never been stronger, because it is intimately connected with the dominant ideas of the eighteenth century, and because Europe is now reacting against its suppression as a result of the Napoleonic Wars and the Congress of Vienna. It is not the product of artificially fomented agitation, but the inevitable outcome of the advance towards individual liberty.

No country has been more profoundly affected by these developments than Hungary. In earlier ages the causes of strife in Hungary were political, religious, or social, not national; recently, however, national questions have come to the fore, as a result of progress in language and literature, and the end of Latin as a universal official language. Moreover, national movements have spread from neighbouring countries, and the advance of democracy has made it possible for representatives of all nationalities to influence the conduct of affairs.

The best guarantee of security in this part of Europe is a unified State comprising the lands ruled by the Crown of St. Stephen; but to achieve the necessary unity, the claims of all nationalities must be satisfied, just as the satisfaction of those claims is possible only if the unity of the State is guaranteed. The proper starting-point for finding the way to a solution is not to consider oneself above all national feeling, but to be devoted to one's own national interests, while realizing that others are no less devoted to theirs. Absolute equality of rights must be the guiding principle, and only those national claims must be rejected which endanger the unity of the State.

All the solutions to the problem which have been proposed belong to one of two types, those which require the rights of all the nationalities to be precisely defined by legislation, and those which depend on the free will of the individual, all individuals enjoying complete liberty. Solutions based on legislation (mandatory, not merely permissive) inevitably involve infractions of individual liberty, whereas the problem can be solved only if the liberty of all individuals is guaranteed. Attempts to solve by legislation the problems raised when the religious movements of the sixteenth century emerged, resulted in endless friction and oppression of minorities, in exact proportion to the thoroughness of the legislation. In the nineteenth century the principle of liberty has been adopted, and the problem thereby solved; so with the national movements of the time—only the granting of liberty will satisfy them, for they are born of the need of liberty. The State which grants liberty will be regarded by its citizens not as a menace, but as the best guarantee of their free development.

The only advantage which will accrue to a particular nationality is the adoption of its language as the official language of the legislature and the central government. Eötvös is convinced that all the nationalities will agree in choosing Hungarian. This will not impede the free development of the other nationalities, because their representatives will be able to speak in the legislature in their own tongue, and the central government will accept and act on petitions addressed to it in any language.

Throughout its history, the human race has developed consistently towards the Christian ideals of liberty, equality, and common well-being. The only acceptable solution to the nationalities question is one consonant with that development and with the spirit of Europe. It is not in isolationism, but in advancing alongside Europe, that Hungary's own salvation lies—and progress is irresistible.

One of Eötvös's greatest virtues as a political thinker, perhaps, lies in his continual awareness that the State is a multitude of human beings; and *The Nationality Question* contains what is perhaps the best expression of his conception of the State:

Many regard the State as no more than a great machine. One sees in it an enormous cuckoo-clock which can be kept going only if huge weights are hung on it; another sees it as a gigantic loom, whose function is to weave warm and soft rugs for individuals from the threads on which the lives of millions hang. As in a clock one wheel fits into another, and all revolve on their axles, such should be the State, and so it should function. If the result does not match the expectations, the fault lies in the machinery. . . . My conviction is that no greater mistake can possibly be imagined than such a conception of the State. . . . The effectiveness of the most perfect machinery depends on the strength of the driving force, and the driving force, in all States, can be found only in the feelings of their peoples. (ch. 12.)

Eötvös's practical common sense and his humanity come through on every page; the two qualities are closely connected, for to him repression is futile as well as wicked. About the capacity of the non-Hungarian peoples to feel enthusiasm for the Hungarian State, however, his optimism was unrealistic; more than one passage of *The Nationality Question* suggests the prophet pointing to an ideal future rather than the statesman solving the problems of the present. His proposals could scarcely have failed to win acceptance—except from the nationalists to whom they were addressed.

The period of composition of *The Nationality Question* was also a period of intense political activity. Eötvös was elected a deputy for Budavár in 1861, and in a great speech in the Diet, delivered on 17 May of that year, he firmly supported *Deák's refusal to accept the 'February Patent' (1861) which, though in some respects an advance on the absolutism of the fifties, denied Hungary her constitutional rights and required her to send deputies to a newly established Reichsrat in Vienna; in this respect the 'Patent' was less liberal than the 'Diploma' of the previous October. 'An oak which has stood for centuries can be felled by the axe;' said Eötvös,[1] 'its remains can be removed, so that the place where its mighty trunk stood is scarcely visible; but to plant another sapling there is not within the power of anyone. The deep roots come up as soon as the axe is still, and kill the frail plant; so it is with constitutions. We can cite from world history abundant

[1] Révai ed., vol. 10 (= *Beszédek* III), p. 4 f,

examples of the destruction of freedom; but we shall not find a single one where anything has taken its place except despotism, or where freedom has been restored otherwise than in its old forms.' The peroration, too, expressing Eötvös's conviction that the Hungarian cause was closely linked to the cause of the other peoples in the Monarchy, and to the struggle for liberty throughout Europe, expressing also his faith in the future, has a resolute dignity which makes it one of the finest passages in all his speeches.

Throughout this period Eötvös continued his work for Hungarian literature; in 1860 many years of patient effort were rewarded when the constitution of the *Kisfaludy Society was approved, and in the following year he became the first President of the 'Hungarian Writers' Benevolent Society' (Magyar Írók Segélyegylete). A charitable project also provided the inspiration for his next works; when the poet Vachott[1] died, Eötvös helped generously to support the widow and her children, and contributed to a magazine which she edited, notably the *Novella* which appeared in 1861. In addition, her plan (to which he readily consented) to publish an anthology of the reflections contained in his works prompted him to bring out a similar collection of those *Thoughts* (*Gondolatok*), as the book was entitled, which had not yet appeared in print; this volume was published in 1864.

In the *Novella* (which has no further title) the narrator describes how, when out on an Alpine ramble, he met a Hungarian. Delighted at thus unexpectedly meeting a compatriot, the Hungarian took him into his home, welcomed him with real Hungarian hospitality, and recounted his life-story. He had loved the same girl as his brother; but when he saw that it was his brother whom the girl really loved he joined the army, determined not to stand in the way of his brother's happiness. He fought in the Hungarian Army in 1848-9, was then re-enlisted by the Austrians as a private and fled to Switzerland, where he obtained work on a farm. Then he saved his employer's life in an avalanche, and married the daughter. 'God has given me every happiness; my one grief, which will be with me till my dying day, is that I cannot live in my country.' So he sums up his life; and at the end his voice is heard in the distance singing the famous words of *Kisfaludy Károly: 'Fair

---

[1] Vachott Sándor (1818-61), a friend of Vörösmarty and Petőfi, was imprisoned by the Austrians in 1852 for sheltering a wanted man, and lost his reason as the result of his sufferings.

lands of my native country, shall I ever see you again?'[1] This
introduction of patriotic feeling may well offend a reader who has
not known exile; but the story as a whole, though overlong, can
scarcely fail to arouse feelings of regret that Eötvös abandoned
narrative. And there are splendid descriptions of Alpine scenery.

The *Thoughts* are the final expression of the philosophical,
reflective side of Eötvös's temperament, attested by so many
passages in his earlier works, which designated him as a likely
successor to Pascal and La Rochefoucauld; indeed, as early as
1833 he had contributed to a magazine[2] a similar collection, entitled *Inner and Outer World* (*Bel- és külvilág*). Such a work as the
Thoughts cannot be read as a continuous essay, but some themes
recur with significant frequency. There are four main sections,
headed *Faith and Religion, Man and the World, Literature and
Science, State and Politics*, followed by a set of miscellaneous
Observations and Maxims.

In the first section Eötvös is concerned mainly with the position
of religion in his own day, with emphasizing that 'our religion is
not endangered by the progress which recent years have made in
the natural sciences. Since every secret which we have discovered
leads only to a new secret...science... will finally lead men back
to religion.' Eötvös writes as a Christian, though he is not primarily
concerned with specifically Christian doctrines. 'The different
religions only prove the uniformity of human nature, its uniformity in the highest desires and noblest aspirations of the soul.'
At the same time, 'one of the principal causes of that great and
lasting influence which Christianity has exercised over man's moral
development may be found in the fact that it takes into account
one of our main and most widespread characteristics, egoism.'
Christianity replaces egoism by a nobler emotion which 'labours
to satisfy our highest inclinations and desires, and through which
we do not come into conflict with others'. Religion is a cohesive
force in society, and in that, not in its power as a deterrent, lies
its importance.

The second section, *Man and the World*, includes all human re-
lationships—love, marriage, parenthood—as well as the pursuit and
achievement of ambition; there are also some general reflections

---

[1] Szülőföldem szép határa
Meglátlak-e valahára?
[2] *Muzárion*, 1833.

on life. 'Our life is like a burning torch, which is consumed, now more slowly, now more quickly, but ceaselessly. Happy is he who, when he reflects on this transitoriness of his being, can console himself with the thought that he provided light for many.' The secret of life is activity: 'the mother by the grave of her child, when she remembers that she still has to cook for her other children, is snatched out of her grief more effectively than if she heard the consolations of all the philosophers in the world.' 'Every man toils for his own happiness, and every man can find it only in another'— again, egoism is the greatest obstacle to happiness. At the same time, 'our own self never takes a greater place in our thoughts, than in our youth', but 'the privilege of this happy period is only that the egoism of the young has not yet clashed with the interests of others'. Our youth is the time when we acquire a self-confidence which is a necessary equipment for life: 'he who at the start of his career does not feel himself called to play the part of a Mirabeau or a Napoleon, rarely attains even mediocrity.' But when he considers the man who has fulfilled the dreams of his childhood (and fame is the subject of more 'thoughts' than any other single topic in this section), Eötvös becomes pessimistic: brilliant careers, like lighthouses, point out dangers to be avoided as well as harbours to be sought. To fling away ambition, however, is no solution: 'every advance is accompanied by restlessness, and without progress there is no satisfaction. That is why he who seeks happiness in rest is never happy.'

There are many parallels between the *Thoughts* and the novels; this is because 'the task of all art is to express truth in a beautiful form' as the opening observation of the third section *Literature and Science* states. Art does not, 'like the flowers in the field, develop without cultivation; . . . Nature, even to those whom she has endowed most richly, has given only the possibility of becoming artists; serious work, prolonged effort and manly endurance are necessary' in order to realize that possibility, although 'there are two things for which effort and study are no substitute: in life, a fine moral sense, and in art, taste.' Matter, however, is more important than manner; only that style is good to which 'le style, c'est l'homme' is applicable. Of artistic qualities in the narrower sense, Eötvös attaches particular importance to clarity: 'There is no light without clarity.' Again: 'it is my absolute conviction that when we are quite clear in our own minds, the proper expression is never lacking.' No less vital is the structure of a work of art: 'as the firmness and magnificence of a building do not depend on the hardness or size of individual stones, so the effect and permanence of every work of literature depend not on the perfection and magnificence of single parts, but on whether the single parts . . . stand indissolubly united to one another.'

On science, Eötvös is chiefly concerned, as in the first section, with the dangers of overestimating its achievements, especially in relation to religion. 'However proud we may be of our science, it is only a torch by which we can illuminate a restricted area, and particular objects; but our whole horizon can be illuminated adequately only by the sun, which is in Heaven.' 'A natural science in which Man appears only as one of the mammals . . . will never lead to a knowledge of the truth.'

But whatever the dangers of materialism, to complain with Rousseau and others that civilization has resulted in loss to mankind is futile; man must advance no less than a child or a tree must grow, and to emphasize the inevitability of progress is one of the main concerns of the next section, *The State and Politics*. Every State reaches the logical conclusion of its dominant ideas; so our civilization will move towards individual liberty. Liberty, in fact, is a condition of all other goods, and the more human civilization progresses, the more essential it becomes. To guarantee it, both for the individual and the community as a whole, is the function of the State; but it can be established only by order—liberty and order, like the oxygen and the nitrogen in the air, are both lethal in isolation. In addition, the main task of our age is to establish democracy; but to do this we must devise institutions which enable all classes to exert influence, and 'the great transformation through which we are passing' must in time involve a change 'in the State, in its forms, and in its whole structure'.

Government is above all a practical matter: 'In a State governed by philosophers . . . we might find the best laws, but as regards putting them into effect, and the practical conduct of affairs, my conviction is that a State governed by philosophers would be the worst governed in the world.' Political science has, however, a definite part to play, but it acts at long range; like the artillery in a siege, it makes the breach through which others come to grips with the enemy. The first duty of any man in public life is to speak out his convictions; the second is to fulfil his civic obligations in collaboration with those whose views come nearest to his own, if his own are rejected. 'I can look back with satisfaction on two things', ends this section; 'one is ... that I have never ... lost my faith in certain ideas; the second is that my whole life was devoted to the realisation of those ideas, and I regarded both myself and all my abilities solely as their instruments.'

The last, the miscellaneous section begins with Eötvös's reflections on man and ends with those on God. 'Man is both good and bad, but always weak', and differences of opinion about individuals are due to generalizing from either the good or the bad. The discovery of chemistry that substances which appear to be totally different from one another are formed from the same elements applies equally to the ingredients in human nature; 'since the qualities we honour and the qualities we despise in men stand so near to each other, no one has cause for over-confidence, or for despair'. Progress may be difficult, but to deny it is as foolish as to look only at the pendulum of a clock and not at the hands; 'No one believes how far we can advance by stumbling, if we stumble always in one direction, making for the same goal.' The key to success is to be convinced of the importance of what we are doing, and to pursue our aim with single-mindedness combined with the tolerance that proceeds not from indifference but from respect for the opinions of others: to regard life not as a source of enjoyment but as an obligation: and to consider all that life gives us to be the immutable decree of a superior Power. The last 'thought' of all discusses the illogicality of combining a belief in God with disbelief in Providence. The only argument which can be brought against a belief in Providence is the difficulty of reconciling the afflictions of the innocent and the prosperity of the wicked with God's infinite goodness. 'The sole, but at the same time the perfect, solution of the apparent contradiction is the idea of immortality'; Divine Providence and the immortality of the soul are closely connected with, and follow directly from, the fact of God's existence.

Taken as a whole, the *Thoughts* seem uneven—perhaps largely because such a collection should not be taken as a whole. Eötvös's ideas, however, are remarkably consistent,[1] both within the book

---

[1] The nearest approach to a real inconsistency is in Eötvös's views on monarchy. In *The State and Politics* he praises monarchy as providing a suitable object for both the educated classes' devotion to principles and the loyalty of the uneducated to persons; but in the last section he criticizes Cousin, Hegel, and Benjamin Constant for forgetting that a monarch is only a man, who differs from

and in relation to his other works and his life. Some of his reflections seem obvious, though there is a difference between what is obvious and what seems obviously true once it has been said. Not all are expressed in an equally memorable form, and some similes (especially tree-similes) are overworked. Nevertheless, with the unevenness goes variety; here are both aphorisms and extended arguments, both reasoned prose and flights of poetic imagery, from a man who reconciled with rare success the rival claims of heart and mind.

The *Thoughts* was Eötvös's last published contribution to literature, though he was continually noting further similar reflections, which were incorporated in later editions of the work. In addition, he left behind some fragments of novels, and, in nearly complete form, a pleasant though not outstanding short story of uncertain date, *Pusztalak*,[1] which relates how two young people who had been indifferent to each other while their parents were friends fell in love when an officious lawyer stirred up trouble between their widowed mothers. Then the young man, waiting for his beloved at their secret meeting-place, overhears her mother's lawyer describing to his client how the couple might elope. The lovers put this plan into effect, and their marriage happily ends the feud between their mothers.

The rest of Eötvös's life was devoted entirely to public service. Franz Josef's reply to Hungarian resistance in 1861 had been to dissolve the Diet, which did not meet again till 1865. In his adoption speech (1 October 1863) as deputy for Budavár in the forthcoming Diet, Eötvös urged the importance of achieving a permanent and not a provisional solution; the relationship between Hungary and the Empire must be precisely defined, for the failure to do this was the root cause of the conflicts of the past. The present age was one of union, not of separation; Hungary must make her contribution to the strength of the Empire, in her own interest; but it was also an age of liberty, in which 'all that is great and all that we wish to be permanent, can only be the work of free individuals'—no solution could last which did not accept Hungary's constitutional freedom as guaranteed by laws of 1790 and 1848.

others 'solely in having, as heir to the throne, usually learnt less about life than others, and in having received an education far inferior as a preparation for performing a serious task'.

[1] A place-name, meaning literally 'Dwelling in the Puszta'.

Nor would it add to the lustre of the Emperor if he 'tore to pieces one of the two crowns which Providence had placed on his head, in order to decorate the other with the fragments'.[1] Finally, while Hungary must remain steadfast in defence of her legal rights, she must be just to the other peoples, with whom she had lived in alliance for centuries. Only a solution satisfactory to all could last, but if Hungary remained steadfast and just, 'the future, and I am convinced the near future, will bring the reward of our efforts'.

Agreement with Austria was reached in 1867, and in the new Government under *Andrássy, Eötvös, whose personal standing was second only to that of *Deák himself, returned after nineteen years to the Ministry of Religion and Education. Following, as always, the principles expounded in his writings, he worked first to achieve equality of rights for all nationalities and religions, secondly to expand and democratize education. He was, however, only partially successful, because the beneficiaries of his liberal outlook under the first of these heads failed to respond, and did much to frustrate his achievement under the second.

The Nationalities Act, which became law in November 1868, was essentially an attempt to put into practice the ideas Eötvös had expounded in *The Nationality Question*—an interesting example of his own 'thought'[2] on how political philosophers prepare the way for governments. The principles on which the Act was based were stated by *Deák in the draft version of the measure: 'All citizens of Hungary constitute politically a single nation, the Hungarian nation, one and indivisible. Every citizen of the country, to whatever nationality he may belong, is a member of the nation possessing parity of rights.' Thus all the nationalities would be independent in their local government and magistrates' courts, in their religious, cultural, and educational life (the Act secured Church autonomy, including independent schools, for the nationalities), in all of which fields they would enjoy the right to use their own language. Only at the highest level, where centralization was a necessary condition of the existence of the single State, was the Magyar language to be used; laws were to be drafted in Magyar, and Magyar was to be the language of the legislature, just as in the British Parliament, for instance, English is spoken and not Welsh or Gaelic. But the Act could succeed only if the nationalities

[1] Révai ed., vol. 10 p. 46.   [2] See p. 221.

accepted the premiss that the existence of a strong, unified State in the lands of the Hungarian crown was in their own interest, and they rejected it, insisting instead on carving out territories for themselves in which they could rule with absolute authority. Whether or not they were right, there can be no doubt about the goodwill of those who conceived the Act.

Eötvös's own Ministry produced a new Education Act in 1868, and it became law, after a long struggle, on 8 December of that year. The Minister expounded his principles in his speech to the Upper House on 1 December: In a constitutionally governed country, the general level of education directly affects the government, well-being, and development of the State; education is thus a particular obligation of the State. It cannot be entrusted entirely to the parents, who are not always aware of their obligations, or capable of fulfilling them; nor entirely to the Church, as experience in France and England, for instance, has shown. The duty of the State remains to bring children up to be good citizens, as the Church brings them up to be good Christians. But no constitutional State has the right to a monopoly of education; its concern is not to enforce particular beliefs, but to raise the general level. Education should, in fact, be as free as the Press, and the possibility of abuses in individual cases does not constitute an argument for destroying either liberty. So the State schools for which the Act provided were to supplement, not supplant, the Church schools, and specific provision was made for religious instruction to be given by priest or pastor.

If education is a national necessity, the State must provide financial aid. The necessary taxation was to be organized on a local basis, as in 1848; Eötvös stood by the arguments of *The Dominant Ideas* that decentralization was more economical. From the start he had tried to stimulate local interest in education—as early as July 1867 he had mooted the establishment of 'People's Educational Associations', but the scheme was a failure. This was partly due to apathy, but far more to its opposite—a statement which applies to Eötvös's whole educational programme. The national minorities were hostile—in vain did the Minister issue educational periodicals and textbooks in seven languages. The Roman Catholic Church from the beginning saw Eötvös's educational reforms as an attack on itself, and opposed them with determination and ferocity; in vain did the Minister provide for religious instruction in the

State schools, he was accused of subverting religion. This was the age of ultramontanism, of the *Syllabus*, of the 1869–70 Vatican Council; an age in which a liberal Catholic Minister of Education, working for Church autonomy, for 'l'Église libre dans l'État libre' (in the phrase of Eötvös's friend and correspondent Montalembert, also a devout Catholic) was an absurd anomaly.

Eötvös followed up his Act with a survey of the educational situation, which was completed early in 1871, and revealed the full size of his task. In Hungary only some 50 per cent. of the children legally obliged to attend school were in fact receiving education, in Transylvania only 40 per cent.: of the children in Hungary only 16 per cent. could read and write well when they left school, of those in Transylvania, 15 per cent. The pay and working conditions of the teachers were pitiful. Eötvös applied himself not only to remedying this state of affairs, but to the improvement of all branches of education. He reorganized the curriculum in the grammar schools, providing a preparatory final year for those about to enter a university; he incorporated technical courses in the school curriculum, as a prelude to the foundation of technical colleges; he established teachers' training colleges, and law academies; he enriched Pest University by expansions in the staff, by the provision of scholarships for study abroad, by new buildings and a new chemical laboratory. No less impressive were his services to education in Transylvania which he toured in 1869; his major project there was the foundation of a university at Kolozsvár,[1] but this came into being only after his death, in 1872. It is pleasant to record that his future biographer Ferenczi[2] was a student and later University Librarian there. In addition to his work for schools and universities, Eötvös acquired for the nation the Esterházy collection of pictures, and reorganized the National Museum, including its library.

Relief from the task of raising the educational level of his country, and from the conflict with ultramontanism, came in the happiness of Eötvös's family life. The son who had been born in the critical days of 1848 had been destined by his father for politics, but chose instead a scientific career. Parental authority did not intervene—except once, to prevent a proposed expedition to the North Pole. Eötvös Lóránd (1848–1919) achieved fame as a physi-

---

[1] Now Cluj in Rumania.
[2] Ferenczi Zoltán (1857–1927), also the biographer of Petőfi and *Deák.

cist, and did work of lasting value on gravitation;[1] the University of Budapest was renamed after him in 1945. His father found in him a friend to whom he could confide his innermost feelings, a correspondent whose letters express not only affection for a father but understanding of the burdens of a Minister. Through his son, Eötvös developed a keen interest in science, and in one letter we find him recording a benevolent suspension of judgement on Darwin.

As early as December 1867 Eötvös wrote to his son: 'there are moments when I am seized by a feeling that I see before me a huge boulder which I must lift, but to lift it my own strength is inadequate, and I cannot count on the help of others'; and such moments became more and more frequent. True, the esteem in which *Andrássy held him, and his personal standing in the Government (he acted as *Andrássy's deputy when the Prime Minister was in Vienna) gave him an influence extending far beyond the province of his own portfolio. But his energies were continually drained, not only by the size of the 'boulder' but also by the bitter political struggles in which he became involved; he was not only almost overwhelmed by the quantity, but taken aback by the quality of the opposition he encountered. Besides, his substantial concessions to his Catholic critics cost him liberal support; some even came to see him as a man who tried to please everybody. Perhaps his character had something of old Kislaky in *The Village Notary*; perhaps his 'thought' that philosophers make the worst practical statesmen was not without relevance to his own scrupulous intellectual honesty, his benevolent accessibility to criticism. It was his tragedy, too, to find that his educational work, which had been stillborn in 1848, was now being frustrated again, for quite a different reason. Eventually overwork and depression began to affect his health, which by early 1870 was causing concern; on 2 February 1871 he died. On his death-bed he told his son that he would be happy as a scientist; only let him steer clear of politics.

He had ceased to hope for what he considered success; yet thoughts of what he might have achieved cannot obscure what he did achieve, for religious and civil liberties as well as for education. The full emancipation of the Jews, for which he had campaigned

---

[1] I am grateful to Dr. Nicholas Kürti of the Clarendon Laboratory, Oxford, for information on this point.

almost thirty years earlier, was realized in December 1867. In literature, in addition to the *Thoughts* and *The Dominant Ideas*, he wrote four novels, differing widely from one another, of which the first two at least broke new ground in Hungarian literature. *The Village Notary*, his masterpiece, succeeds, as Dickens succeeded, in 'entertaining' while also 'being of service', striking one of its author's hardest blows in his fight against cruelty and oppression. To this fight Eötvös devoted his life; as he said in his poem *Testament* (*Végrendelet*) of 1848, 'let the victory of my ideas be my memorial'.

V

PETŐFI (1823–1849) * LYRIC

I

IN February 1844 an unsuccessful, young actor of twenty-one, who dreamt of fame as a poet, found himself facing total destitution. 'After a week's painful wandering I reached Pest', he wrote.[1] 'I did not know to whom to turn. . . . A desperate courage seized me and I went to one of Hungary's greatest men, with the feeling of a card-player staking all he had left, for life or death. The great man read through my poems; on his enthusiastic recommendation the Circle[2] published them, and I had money and a name. This man, to whom I owe my life, and to whom the country owes any service I have done or will do her—this man was Vörösmarty.' Vörösmarty thereby showed not only insight, but magnanimity; for these poems represented a revolution in Hungarian lyric. Two years earlier the same young poet, in *Ideal and Reality* (*Ideál és való*) (April 1842), had written: 'Magic shape of my imagination! Vanish into your heaven, vanish away; the son of earth needs reality, and the poet—is he not the son of earth?'—expressly renouncing the older generation's view of the poet and his art. Vörösmarty himself had begun *The Island of the South*[3] with the words 'Remain far hence, far far hence, ye profane ones! I have neither wish nor time to write of everyday things.'

Ideal and Reality was one of four poems which an unknown poet of Slovak parentage named Petrovics Sándor submitted to *Bajza for publication in *Athenaeum*. Three were rejected, but the fourth, *The Wine-bibber* (*A borozó*) (April 1842) appeared, in the leading literary periodical of the day, on 22 May 1842.

---

[1] In *Traveller's Letters* (*Úti levelek*), no. XI (July 1847). Cf. p. 275.
[2] The 'National Circle' (Nemzeti kör), of which Vörösmarty was the first chairman.
[3] See pp. 114 f.

The Wine-bibber[1]

With a draught of wine by my side to banish care, my life flies gaily
on: with a draught of wine by my side to banish care, I laugh at your
power, Fate.

Why are you all surprised when I say that the god of wine alone do I
worship, he is all to this breast.

And in the gay warmth of wine I whistle in your face, grim world!
where the scorpions of so many torments have rent my heart.

Wine taught me to coax a gentle song on to my lyre; wine taught me
to forget you, false maidens.

One day, when Death comes to drive me from my place beside my
wine: another draught—and with a laugh I plunge into thy bosom of ice,
O grave!

This is not the first drinking-song in Hungarian literature, but
the 'son of earth' has already stepped off the pedestal from which
his predecessors had so often stood before the nation as seers;
there are conspicuously few patriotic poems in the collection which
aroused Vörösmarty's enthusiasm in 1844. Yet the young poet
loves his country: *In my Country* (*Hazámban*) (October 1842)
had been published in *Athenaeum* in November 1842, and was
the first poem to appear over the poet's Magyarized version of his
name, Petőfi. But only rarely does he lament past tragedy or
present decline, preferring rather to express his love for the actual
sights he sees around him, the 'plains decked with golden ears of
corn', the 'letter V of the migrant cranes flying through the autumn
air'. This is a fact of the first importance. His seniors, too, were
beginning to feel that they had had enough rhetorical patriotic
poetry; 'one cannot be always and continuously roused to enthu-

[1]   *A borozó*

Gondüző borocska mellett
Vígan illan életem:
Gondüző borocska mellett,
Sors, hatalmad nevetem.

És mit ámultok? ha mondom,   5
Hogy csak a bor istene,
Akit én imádok, aki
E kebelnek mindene.

És a bor vidám hevében
Füttyentek rád, zord világ!   10

Szívemet hol annyi kínnak
Skorpiói szaggaták.

Bor taníta húrjaimra
Csalni nyájas éneket;
Bor taníta elfeledni,   15
Csalfa lyányok, titeket.

Egykor majd borocska mellől
A halál ha űzni jő:
Még egy korty — s nevetve dűlök
Jégöledbe, temető!   20

siasm by an abstract idea' said *Toldy in 1843. *In my Country* thus came at an opportune moment, and its artistic qualities are sufficiently attested by the fact that Vörösmarty, whom the plains themselves left unmoved, was so impressed by this poem about them as to suspect that 'Petőfi' was the pseudonym of an experienced and established writer.

Stylistically, however, the new poet is still working within the conventions of his day. 'The scorpions of so many torments' and the 'bosom of ice' in *The Wine-bibber* are examples of just that stock poetic diction which Petőfi's spontaneity was to banish from Hungarian poetry, and the luxuriance of epithets in *In my Country* was to be replaced by the directness and conciseness which went closely with that spontaneity. These qualities had already appeared in some earlier poems, which remained unpublished, and not least in a translation of Schiller's *Der Jüngling am Bache* (*The Boy by the Brook*) dating from February 1842, where Petőfi strikingly exhibits the effortless simplicity of genius. Here already are the beginnings of a practical demonstration that 'there neither is, nor can be, any *essential* difference between the language of prose and metrical composition'.[1]

The foundation of Petőfi's mature style was the folk-song. Its importance for literature had already been emphasized by *Kölcsey in his essay *National Traditions* (*Nemzeti hagyományok*) (1826), and the leading poets of the period, including Vörösmarty,[2] had all, in their different ways, written in a popular vein, but as a temporary and conscious departure from a 'poetic' style. As Petőfi himself later put it, in conversation, 'the older poets, even Vörösmarty, when they write in the popular style, are like a swallow flying over water. Sometimes it almost grazes the surface, as if it would dive below and were in its element; but immediately it shoots upwards and soars on high.' It is for this reason that their relation to their folk-song models can be formulated more easily and precisely than that of Petőfi, because he was making his home in territory to which they only paid occasional visits. And as 'instinct was his guide',[3] his abandonment of poetic diction did not mean that poetic phrases were replaced by obtrusively 'popular' ones,

[1] Wordsworth, Preface to *Lyrical Ballads* (1798).
[2] See pp. 120 ff.
[3] 'Instinct is my guide' were Petőfi's own words in the preface to the edition of his *Complete Poetical Works* which appeared in 1847.

though his earliest poems in the 'popular' style can fairly be described as imitations of folk-song, and some are strongly 'popular' in flavour. One of the first, dating from October 1842, was actually incorporated by *Erdélyi in his collection of folksongs. In it some gay tramp travelling over the Hortobágy has stopped at an inn, and is calling on the innkeeper's wife to give him a drink. It is as 'popular' (notably in the terms of endearment with which the visitor addresses the innkeeper's wife) as *The Wine-bibber* and *In my Country* are 'literary':

The Hortobágy Innkeeper's Wife[1]

My angel! Give me a glass of wine, let me drink; the Great Hortobágy is far from Debrecen, I have been thirsty from Debrecen to the Hortobágy.

Wild is the tune the winds whistle, the cold will soon take my body and soul: look on me, my violet! I will warm in the rays of your blackthorn-dark eyes.

Where does your wine come from? It is as sour as an unripe crabapple. Give me lots of Kisses; the kiss is sweet, it will sweeten my lips.

Lovely girl ... sour wine ... sweet kiss ... my legs are almost reeling; embrace me, my sweet! Don't wait for me to fall right down on the spot.

My dove, how soft is your breast! Let me rest on it, just a little. My bed will be hard enough tonight anyway—I live far off and shan't reach home today.[2]

[1] The opening words of the poem mean literally 'Hortobágy innkeeper's wife! My angel!', 'innkeeper's wife' (kocsmárosné) being a perfectly natural form of address in Hungarian.

[2]   *Hortobágyi kocsmárosné* ...

(This poem, like many by Petőfi, has no title apart from its opening words.)

Hortobágyi kocsmárosné, angyalom!
Tegyen ide egy üveg bort, hadd iszom;
Debrecentől Nagy-Hortobágy messze van,
Debrecentől Hortobágyig szomjaztam.

Szilaj nótát fütyörésznek a szelek,   5
Lelkem, testem majd megveszi a hideg:
Tekintsen rám, kocsmárosné violám!
Fölmelegszem kökényszeme sugarán.

Kocsmárosné, hej hol termett a bora?
Savanyú, mint az éretlen vadalma.   10

Csókolja meg az ajkamat szaporán,
Édes a csók, megédesül tőle szám.

Szép menyecske ... savanyú bor ...
édes csók ...
Az én lábam idestova tántorog;
Öleljen meg kocsmárosné édesem!   15
Ne várja, míg itt hosszában elesem.

Ej galambom, milyen puha a keble!
Hadd nyugodjam csak egy kicsit
fölötte;
Úgyis kemény ágyam lesz az éjszaka,
Messze lakom, nem érek még ma
haza.   20

The characteristics of Petőfi's fully developed style may appear
negative; an account of them is primarily an enumeration of
absent features—his best poems have neither the poetic diction of
The Wine-bibber nor the obvious reminiscences of folk-song found
in the *Hortobágy Innkeeper's Wife*. But precisely this negative
appearance is the measure of the poet's success in instinctively
finding the common ground between the language of the man of
letters and that of the people. Nor is it only the style which exhibits the art that conceals art; as early as the *Hortobágy Innkeeper's
Wife* the monologue brings out quite naturally not only the whole
background to the story, but the action itself—the point at which the
innkeeper's wife serves the wine, the moment when she kisses her
guest. Again, in *I looked into the kitchen* (July–August 1843) the
speaker is telling us how he looked into the kitchen on the pretext
of lighting his pipe, but really to see the beautiful girl who was in
there.

I looked into the kitchen . . .[1]

I looked into the kitchen, I lit my pipe . . . that is to say, I should
have lit it, had it not been already alight.

My pipe was going nicely, that is not why I went! I went because I
noticed there was a lovely girl in there.

She was making up the fire, the darling; it blazed up as she did it;
but oh! her two eyes—how bright was their flame!

I walked in, she looked at me—she must have cast a spell on me! My
glowing pipe went to sleep, my sleeping heart caught fire.

To dissect this little drama would kill it; but we may perhaps
just note how perfectly the false start reflects the speaker's am-
biguity of purpose.

All the poems so far mentioned, the 'literary' as well as the
'popular', are written in the first person; but the relation between

[1] *Befordúltam a konyhára* . . .

Befordúltam a konyhára,
Rágyujtottam a pipára . . .
Azaz rágyujtottam volna,
Hogyha már nem égett volna.

A pipám javában égett,   5
Nem is mentem én a végett!
Azért mentem, mert megláttam,
Hogy odabenn szép leány van.

Tüzet rakott eszemadta,
Lobogott is, amint rakta;   10
Jaj de hát még szeme párja,
Annak volt ám nagy a lángja!

Én beléptem, ő rámnézett,
Aligha meg nem igézett!
Égő pipám kialudott,   15
Alvó szívem meggyúladott.

the speaker and the poet himself is obviously different in each poem. *In my Country* plainly expresses Petőfi's own feelings, and raises no problems. *The Wine-bibber* may convey a particular mood of the poet, and certainly the speaker's references to his sufferings and to his defiance of Fate accurately reflect Petőfi's perseverance in his career as an actor and the hardships he suffered as a result. Sometimes, however, we do wonder if this convivial character can be identified with the poet, partly because of the high proportion of drinking-songs in this first collection of Petőfi's poems (especially in those dating from 1844), but still more because of particular examples. For instance, in *All along the village street . . . (A faluban utcahosszat . . .)* the speaker tells us that 'All along the village street I make music for myself; with a full bottle in my hand, I dance like a mad wild beast' while a gipsy fiddler serenades 'my' faithless lady-love on 'my' behalf. The *Hortobágy Innkeeper's Wife* seems to be put into the mouth of some tramp, cowboy, or horse-thief, though the wandering actor was certainly travelling over the Hortobágy plain at the time he wrote the poem. The man who 'looked into the kitchen' gives no definite clue to his identity with the poet. In many other poems of this period in Petőfi's career the relation between speaker and poet cannot be definitely established; and it scarcely matters.

It scarcely matters, because of the width of Petőfi's human sympathy; it is this quality—far more than the fact that he was an actor—which enables him to identify himself with all the characters he knows and portrays. This stands out just as clearly when there can be no question of a self-portrait—especially, perhaps, in his pictures of the criminals, the highwaymen and horse-thieves. He makes no romantic attempt to idealize them, only sees to it that when they speak in the first person they are sympathetic characters. We learn of the villainies of the 'godless bandit' Büngösdi Bandi,[1] but from one of his victims, whose horse and sweetheart he has stolen. A similar type to Büngösdi Bandi, in all probability, is the native of Kecskemét who tells us (uniquely, in his broad dialect)[2] that he has made, and is making, a good living, and will do so as long as his 'two eyes see a traveller in the Puszta'; he pays his bills

---

[1] *Hej Büngösdi Bandi* (June 1844).

[2] In *Kecskemét is a famous town in the Lowlands . . . (Hirös város az aafődön Kecskemét,* for which standard Hungarian would be *Híres város az alföldön Kecskemét* (January–February 1844).

at the inn, and upholds his honour. However, we hear no details
of his activities, only that he has a horse swifter than the wind
which he 'did not buy', which knows the representatives of the
law as well as he does himself. 'When they come, he neighs loudly—
I jump on him; and when I'm on him, those gentlemen can come!'
But the tragedy is there too; in *Moonlight bathes in the sea of
Heaven* . . . (*Fürdik a holdvilág az ég tengerében* . . .) (April 1844) we
see a brigand in the forest weeping at his own folly in having left
home, against his mother's advice, to become an outlaw. 'I would
gladly leave this gang, but now it is too late: my mother is dead . . .
our little house has long since crumbled . . .[1] and there stands the
gallows.' Sentimental, certainly; yet not the least important point
is that this man has, after all, a tenderer side to his character.

By no means all these poems, however, are monologues; sometimes, indeed, the principal character does not speak at all:

The shepherd rides his donkey . . .[2]

The shepherd rides his donkey, his legs reach to the ground; he is a
great big fellow, but his sorrow is greater.

He was playing his pipe on a grassy mound, his flock was grazing.
Suddenly he hears that his sweetheart is dying.

He jumps on to the donkey and gallops for home. But he arrived too
late, he can see only a dead body.

In his despair what could he do? He struck the donkey a mighty
blow on the head with his stick. (July 1844)

These folk-song poems, then, portray a whole people, a people
to whom the poet belonged so intimately that we often cannot tell
whether he is speaking in his own person or not; but Petőfi's

---

[1] These dots are in the original text, and do not denote omissions in the quotation.

[2] *Megy a juhász szamáron* . . .

Megy a juhász szamáron,
Földig ér a lába;
Nagy a legény, de nagyobb
Boldogtalansága.

Gyepes hanton furulyált,   5
Legelészett nyája.
Egyszercsak azt hallja, hogy
Haldoklik babája.

Fölpattan a szamárra,
Hazafelé vágtat;   10
De már későn érkezett,
Csak holttestet láthat.

Elkeseredésében
Mi telhetett tőle?
Nagyot ütött botjával   15
A szamár fejére.

first collection also includes poems—mostly, like *In my Country*, not in a popular vein—in which the first person does clearly represent the poet himself. From the beginning poetry was the natural outlet for his feelings; this is perhaps especially clear from a poem which has not survived, *The Prompter* (*A súgó*) (November 1842). Disliking the nasal timbre of Petőfi's voice, the manager of the company of actors to which he belonged tried to sidetrack him into prompting, in which capacity he had successfully deputized when the regular prompter was ill. The poet went home, furious, composed *The Prompter* and, having by this truly cathartic method worked off his feelings, tore the poem up. He has in fact described this catharsis himself, in *To blazes!* ... (*Lánggal égő teremtette!* ...) (May 1843). 'To blazes! Great is the anger in my heart! I storm and toss as if I were the Balaton.... Heh, weeping is not my bread! Let him whimper who likes. I utter a mighty curse, that is how my anger subsides.' In his poem *I* (*Én*) (March 1843) Petőfi says: 'The way of my soul in what I do is as open as the plains where I was born', and he gives us true pictures of his personality, the antithesis of the self-dramatization typical of the Romantic period. When Berlioz, for instance, wrote a symphony about himself, he called it (with good reason) *Symphonie fantastique*.

This does not, however, mean that we need expect even obviously autobiographical poems to be factually true in every detail. A delightful example of one that is not is *My Career as Scholar* (*Deákpályám*) (April–May 1844). The Hungarian word *deák*, derived (through Old Church Slavonic) from the Latin *diaconus*, means both *student* and *Latin*, which gives added point to the hybrid Hungarian-Latin of these reminiscences of the poet's schooldays, written just when Latin had ceased to be the official language in Hungary. The poem refers to Petőfi's expulsion from school:

So the quarrel[1] between us[2] went on *ad infinitum*, and in short the end of it was[3] *consilium abeundi*.[4]

However, Petőfi was never in fact expelled from school, though he had been to eight schools before he was sixteen (when he joined

---

[1] 'per' in the poem is the Hungarian word for 'quarrel' or 'lawsuit'.
[2] i.e. between Petőfi and his schoolmasters.
[3] 'advice to leave', i.e. expulsion.
[4] Csak denique mi közöttünk   S consilium abeundi
     Sine fine folyt a per,   Lett a vége breviter.   20

the army in desperation). The reasons for these frequent changes were, first, the restless determination of his butcher-innkeeper father (who at this time was prosperous) to find the best possible education for his son, then clashes between Sándor and his masters, of whom one kept him incarcerated to prevent him from joining a company of actors (and also reported him to his father), and another was an anti-Hungarian Slovak nationalist.

The conflicts with his father—who, on receiving the schoolmaster's report about his son's attempt to join the company of actors, promptly came and thrashed him, then two years later, in 1839, disowned him for unsatisfactory school results—had no effect whatever on Petőfi's affection for his parents. When the visit to Vörösmarty in February 1844 led not only to the publication of his poems, but also to his securing a post as assistant editor of a new paper to be launched in July, nothing gave Petőfi more pleasure than the fact that he could now face the parents of whom he had thought continually during his wanderings. Being the spontaneous artist he was, he naturally gave expression in his poems to his feelings for his parents—thereby making a major break with literary convention. *In my Country* already contains a reference to his mother: in the emotional *From Afar* (*Távolból*) (May 1843) he had recalled the sadness of the parting from her when he left home, and adjured visitors to the house to tell her that 'Fortune is favouring her son—Ah if she knew in what misery I am living, her poor heart would break!' Now he returned to his parents for Easter.

A Plan which came to Nothing[1]

All the way home I thought about what to say to my mother—it was so long since I had seen her.

What sweet, kind things shall I say to her first, when she stretches out the arms that rocked my cradle?

And innumerable thoughts, each sweeter than the others, came into my mind; time seemed to stand still, although the wagon was speeding along.

[1]   *Füstbement terv*

Egész uton — hazafelé —
Azon gondolkodám:
Miként fogom szólítani
Rég nem látott anyám?

Mit mondok majd először is   5
Kedvest, szépet neki?

Midőn, mely bölcsőm ringatá,
A kart terjeszti ki.

S jutott eszembe számtalan
Szebbnél-szebb gondolat,   10
Míg állani látszék az idő,
Bár a szekér szaladt.

And I appeared in the little room . . . my mother flew towards me . . .
and I hung on her lips . . . silent . . . like the fruit on the tree. (April
1844)

The next poem, *An Evening at my Home* (*Egy estém otthon*)
(April 1844) describes how the poet recited one of his drinking-
songs to his father. 'I was very, very happy that it made him laugh.
But he is not very proud of having a poet for a son; to him all
that sort of thing is useless. Later . . . my mother came out with a
hundred questions; I had to answer them—I left off my writing.
There was no end to her questions; but I enjoyed them all so much,
because each question was a mirror in which I could see that I
have the most loving mother on earth!' Then the poetic epistle
To my younger brother István (*István öcsémhez*), written from Pest
in June 1844, shows that when Petőfi was away from home his
concern for his parents equalled his delight in their company, and
refers particularly to the disastrous change in his father's financial
position that had taken place in 1838, as a result of the flood and an
incautious attempt to expand his business: 'Our poor father! had
he not trusted men so, they would not have thus tricked him. . . .
He became the victim of his faith in them, losing all he had earned.
Now another eats the fruits of the sweat of his hard-working life.
Why does God love me so little? If I could, I would ease his lot.' In
a more playful mood, *To my Parents* (*Szülőimhez*) (August 1844) describes what a wonderful time they will all have if the poet makes a
fortune. By contrast, Vörösmarty did not reveal to the public (even
in 1847) that the subject of *The Poor Woman's Book*[1] was his mother.

Petőfi bade an affectionate, but final, farewell to the 'romantic
life' and 'adventures' of the stage[2] and now devoted himself wholly
to his 'one friend, poetry, who was ever with me—I wrote poems
amidst all my woes on the stage and in the guard-room'.[3] The collection of his poems, whose publication had been arranged (not
without difficulty) by Vörösmarty, contained nearly all he had
written between April 1842, the date of *The Wine-bibber*, and
July 1844; it appeared the following November.

S a kis szobába toppanék . . .	S én csüggtem ajkán . . . szótlanúl . . .15
Röpűlt felém anyám . . .	Mint a gyümölcs a fán.

[1] See p. 153.
[2] *Farewell to the Stage* (*Búcsú a színészettől*) (end of June 1844).
[3] *In my Room* (*Szobámban*) (July–August 1844). Petőfi had volunteered for
the army in September 1839, but was invalided out in February 1841.

One of the latest poems to be included in this edition was *The Lowlands* (*Az alföld*) (July 1844), generally agreed to be one of his masterpieces. The sense of form—the portrayal of all the various manifestations of life in the Hungarian plains, within the framework of a view of the whole scene (given in stanzas 3 and 11): the presence of the poet himself, outside this framework and without affecting the unity of the poem: the absence of any of the licence with word-formation and grammar which betrayed the inchoate technique of *In my Country*, which in its theme is a forerunner of *The Lowlands*: all these things show how far Petőfi has advanced in two years.

The Lowlands[1]

What do you mean to me, region of the grim Carpathians, wildly romantic with pine-forests? I may admire you, but I do not love you, and my thoughts do not range over your hills and valleys.

Down in the Lowland country, flat as the sea, there I am at home, there is my world; my soul is freed from its prison like an eagle, when I see the infinity of the plains.

Then I soar in thought beyond the earth almost to the clouds, and the picture of the plain stretching from Danube to Tisza looks on me, smiling.

Beneath the sky with its mirages a hundred fat herds of the Kiskunság[2] ring their bells; as they rest in the midday heat the two branches of the broad trough wait for them, by the well with its long sweep.

The galloping of the horses on the stud-farms sounds in the wind, their hooves clatter, and the shouts of the cowboys can be heard, and the crack of loud whips.

[1]   *Az alföld*
Mit nekem te zordon Kárpátoknak
Fenyvesekkel vadregényes tája!
Tán csodállak, ámde nem szeretlek,
S képzetem hegyvölgyedet nem járja.

Lenn az alföld tengersík vidékin   5
Ott vagyok honn, ott az én világom;
Börtönéből szabadúlt sas lelkem,
Ha a rónák végtelenjét látom.

Felröpűlök ekkor gondolatban
Túl a földön felhők közelébe,   10

S mosolyogva néz rám a Dunától
A Tiszáig nyúló róna képe.

Délibábos ég alatt kolompol
Kis-Kunságnak száz kövér gulyája;
Deleléskor hosszú gémű kútnál   15
Széles vályu kettős ága várja.

Méneseknek nyargaló futása
Zúg a szélben, körmeik dobognak,
S a csikósok kurjantása hallik
S pattogása hangos ostoroknak.   20

[2] Petőfi's native district, called after the Cumans (Kunok) who settled in that part of Hungary in the 13th century.

On the farms, the ears of wheat are rocked in the soft lap of the breezes, and gaily crown the land with the bright colour of the emerald.

Here pass the wild geese from the neighbouring reeds in the grey of evening, and rise in alarm on to their path through the air, when the rushes are stirred by the wind.

Beyond the farms, in the depths of the plain, stands a lonely inn with a tumbledown chimney; the thirsty highwaymen visit it on their way to the market at Kecskemét.

By the inn, a wood of dwarf poplars turns yellow in the sand, where caltrops grow; there the screeching kestrel goes to build its nest, undisturbed by children.

There thrive the sad feather-grass and the blue flower of the globethistle; brightly coloured lizards go to its cool roots to rest in the heat of the noonday sun.

Far away, where the sky touches the earth, the tops of blue fruittrees peer out of the haze, and behind them, like a faint column of mist, the tower of a town church, here and there.

You are beautiful, Lowlands! at least to me you are beautiful. Here my cradle was rocked, here I was born. Here may the shroud cover me, here may the grave rise over me.

2

1844 also saw the appearance of Petőfi's first longer narrative poem—an epic in four cantos entitled *The Hammer of the Village* (*A helység kalapácsa*) (August). The hero is the village blacksmith Fejenagy, for whom 'the hammer of the village' was

A tanyáknál szellők lágy ölében
Ringatózik a kalászos búza,
S a smaragdnak eleven szinével
A környéket vígan koszorúzza.

Idejárnak szomszéd nádasokból 25
A vadlúdak esti szürkületben,
És ijedve kelnek légi útra,
Hogyha a nád a széltől meglebben.

A tanyákon túl a puszta mélyén
Áll magányos, dőlt kéményű csárda; 30
Látogatják a szomjas betyárok,
Kecskemétre menvén a vásárra.

A csárdánál törpe nyárfaerdő
Sárgul a királydinnyés homokban;
Odafészkel a visító vércse, 35
Gyermekektől nem háborgatottan.

Ott tenyészik a bús árvalyányhaj
S kék virága a szamárkenyérnek;
Hűs tövéhez déli nap hevében
Megpihenni tarka gyíkok térnek. 40

Messze, hol az ég a földet éri,
A homályból kék gyümölcsfák orma
Néz, s megettök, mint halvány ködoszlop,
Egy-egy város templománnak tornya.

Szép vagy, alföld, legalább nekem
szép! 45
Itt ringatták bölcsőm, itt születtem.
Itt borúljon rám a szemfödél, itt
Domborodjék a sír is fölöttem.

a description, in the best epic tradition, given him 'poetically, by the richly imaginative people'. (I. 14–15.) In the first canto we see him alone in the village church, left behind after the service.

Ah, but what terrible noise, what sudden din disturbs the sepulchral calm of the church? Thunder? Or porridge boiling in a pot? No! There a man is snoring. It is so! this is a human form. In a corner, leaning on his two clenched fists, he sleeps . . . but lo! he is awake, when he has had his fill of snoring. He yawns . . . he rubs his eyes and looks round. He sees and suspects . . . heathen are his suspicions. He goes to the door; he shakes the handle, and he shook it invain. With his keen mind he saw at once the position, and said: 'I am shut in.' And yet again he said: 'I am shut in.' Then, as befits a man, he called thee to his aid, Presence of Mind. And he asked thee not to desert him. And thou didst not desert him.[1]

So he climbs into the belfry and escapes through the belfry window, letting himself down on the bell-rope. He makes for the village inn, where the landlady, 'chaste Erzsók', has the 'leasehold in perpetuity of the workshop of his heart' (III. 79–80), but arrives just when the 'tender-hearted local cantor' (II. 81) was himself declaring his love to Erzsók, on his knees, begging her 'virgin lips' to say 'at once whether the green garland of hope shall wreathe my brow, or the club of despair batter me to death'.

' "I will batter you to death . . . I am Despair!" said . . . no! thundered a voice, the voice of broad-handed Fejenagy: and with his broad hands he seized the collar of the tender-hearted cantor, and raised him from his knees, so that not even his heels touched the ground: then dropped him, so that his nose did touch the ground.' (III. 173–88.) 'His howls were the cause of tumult among the merrymakers'; the dancers stood still, the gypsy trio

---

[1] Hah, de mi szörnyű zaj,
Mily lárma riasztja
Egyszerre az egyház   50
Temetői nyugalmát?
Mennydörgés?
Vagy kásának forrása fazékban? . . .
Nem!
Ott ember hortyog.   55
Úgy van! ez emberalak.
Egy zugban két öklére hajolva
Alszik . . . hanem íme fölébredt,
Miután elhortyantotta magát.
Ásít . . . szemeit dörzsölve
   körülnéz.   60

Lát és sejt . . . sejtése pogány.
Megy az ajtóhoz; megrázza kilincsét.
És rázta hiába.
Éles eszével
Átlátta azonnal   65
A dolog állását,
És ezt mondta: 'Bezártak.'
S még egyszer mondotta: 'Bezártak.'
Azután, mint férfihoz illik,
Téged híva segédül,   70
Lelki jelenlét!
S kére: ne hagyd el.
S te nem hagytad el őt. (I. 48–73)

'forgot to make the heavenly music of their instruments any more.'
(III. 245-53.) The cantor told how the 'scheming-souled sexton'
(II. 112) had 'inflamed the fires' of his love, and plotted to lock
the blacksmith up in the church; so 'the hammer of the village'
set upon the sexton and punched his nose, to which the sexton
replied by seizing the blacksmith's hair and pulling it like the bell-
rope. 'This horrible sight gripped the tender nerves of chaste
Erzsók, and the poor dear fell into the whirlpool of unconscious-
ness.' (III. 376-80.) Another of the company placed her tenderly
on her bed—and went off to tell the judge that 'war has broken
out, and rages; the pub of chaste Erzsók has become a battlefield ...
men are dropping down like flies in autumn.' (IV. 55 ff.) So the
'hammer of the village' ended up in the stocks, while the cantor was
hauled off by his formidable wife, 'Márta of the Amazon stature'.

Even without the title to tell us that this is a 'heroic poem' it
would be clear that it is primarily a parody of epic; clear from the
style, from the use of descriptive formulae peculiar to epic, from
the similes. It is written not in hexameters but in fragments of
hexameters; for (like Mozart's *Musical Joke*, to which it is in
many respects parallel) it makes fun of inept execution as well as of
inane conception—not only in the language, the attempts at sublimity mingled with the grossest bathos, but also in the helplessness
of construction and the endless retardations of the action caused
by the fatuous apostrophes, descriptions, and digressions. Well
may the poet exclaim (II. 40-42) 'And . . . but whither hast thou
transported me, swift wheelbarrow of ardour?'

The Hammer of the Village was prompted by a current literary
debate on whether epic was obsolete, though it cannot have been
intended as a positive contribution to the discussion. The parody
is firmly rooted in epic, but has also wider implications as a more
general satire on the false sublime and incongruity between style
and matter—implications with meaning for some of Petőfi's
minor contemporaries. It certainly cannot be interpreted as an
attack on Vörösmarty, who had long ago abandoned epic and for
whom Petőfi felt an admiration as a writer fully equal to his gratitude to and affection for the man. When he passed near Eger, in
February 1844, Petőfi wrote, in the poem *Near Eger* (*Eger mellett*),
'I will see the place where the great spirit of Dobó fought; and I
will drink to him who sang of Dobó so nobly.'[1]

[1] On Vörösmarty's *Eger* see pp. 111 f.

Again, in November and December, when he wrote his master-piece of narrative poetry, *Sir John (János vitéz)*, Petőfi drew inspiration from several of Vörösmarty's works, especially *The Valley of the Fairies*,[1] and Vörösmarty was one of the delighted company to whom he read his new poem.

Sir John cannot be better described than by quoting the words of F. L. Lucas about the *Odyssey*: it is 'not merely a tale of changes and chances in perilous seas; it is a tale of loyalties that all those changes and chances failed, in the end, to break.' It is the story of a foundling shepherd-boy, named Kukorica Jancsi (Johnny Maize) because he was discovered in a field of maize as a baby (XIV).[2] He has fallen in love with Iluska, a lovely fair-haired girl, who like him is an orphan, and whose stepmother is as cruel to her as Jancsi's foster-father is to him. At the opening of the poem they meet by a brook where Iluska is washing clothes; then in protecting her against the fury of her stepmother at the delay in completing the washing, he fails to notice that his flock has strayed and that many of the sheep have been lost. For this negligence his enraged foster-father drives him out of the house (III). Jancsi bids a pathetic farewell to his beloved and sets forth into the world.

He trudged on, trudged on in the dim night, only his heavy cloak rustled about his neck. Poor Jancsi thought his cloak was heavy, but the weight was in his heart.[3]

But he keeps going, and at length sees what he believes to be an inn, and enters. The house, however, is occupied by bandits, and their leader replies to Jancsi's greeting in threatening words which are also full of poignant dramatic irony:

'Man of misfortune, who are you, that you dare to set foot on this threshold? Have you parents? have you a wife? Whatever you have, they will never see you again.'[4]

---

[1] See p. 113.
[2] References are to cantos.

[3] Ballagott, ballagott a halk éjsza-
   kában,
   Csak nehéz subája suhogott
   nyakában;
   Ő ugyan subáját gondolta nehéz-
   nek,
   Pedig a szive volt oly nehéz sze-
   génynek. (IV)

[4] 'Szerencsétlenségnek embere, ki vagy
   te,
   Hogy lábadat mered tenni e
   küszöbre?
   Vannak-e szüleid? van-e feleséged?
   Akármid van, nem fog többé látni
   téged.' (VI)

Jancsi replies to these threats with an indifference and bravery which win over the bandit chief, who shows him a barrel of silver and another of gold, and invites him to join them. Jancsi accepts (though 'with feigned good humour'), his mind filled with thoughts of how happy he will make Iluska with this treasure; but soon he pulls himself up sharply, and instead of joining the bandits, sets fire to their house the same night. It is as dramatically effective as it is unexpected that Jancsi's first adventure should be not an obstacle but a temptation, and the effect is the greater because the poet resists the temptation to moralize. And nothing could show more vividly the depth of Jancsi's love for Iluska than his rejection of the short cut. Nor are the bandits sympathetic characters, even in their fate; Petőfi intentionally calls them 'bandits' (zsiványok), using a word which is purely pejorative, with none of the glamour attaching to the 'betyár'.

Jancsi now meets, and joins, a force of hussars who are on their way to defend France against the Turkish invader. They make the journey to France by way of the land of the Tartars, Italy, Poland, and India; when battle is joined Jancsi kills the Turkish general who has abducted the King's beautiful daughter. In gratitude the princess offers him her hand in marriage (XII), whereupon 'a violent struggle arose in his heart, but he quelled that struggle, remembering his Iluska' who has not been mentioned since Jancsi set out for France with the hussars.

The opening canto of the poem, where Jancsi meets Iluska as she is washing clothes in the brook, already suggests a parallel with the meeting of Odysseus and Nausicaa in the *Odyssey*; but it is the fair French princess who is the Nausicaa of *Sir John*. The whole passage in fact closely resembles the Phaeacian episode of the *Odyssey*, not least in the superbly delicate touch with which Petőfi handles it.

Thus he [Jancsi] spoke gently to the fair princess: 'Let us go, my rose, first to your father. There we will consider the matter more closely.'[1]

So Jancsi tells the King his story, of his love for Iluska which needed no oath to seal it. The Princess herself is moved to tears of

---

[1] Nyájasdadon így szólt a szép   Ott majd közelebbről vizsgáljuk a
   királylyányhoz: dolgot.'   (XII)
'Menjünk, rózsám, elébb az édes-
   atyádhoz.

'sorrow and pity' (xv), and her father, rejecting at once any idea of forcing Jancsi into marriage, knights him (so that from now on he is no longer Jancsi (=Johnny) but János vitéz (=Sir John)) and sends him on his way in a ship laden with treasure.

When Odysseus leaves Alcinous's island, his contests with superhuman forces are over; but those of János are now about to begin. His mind full of the words with which he will greet Iluska on his return, he sets sail; the migrant storks, too, remind him of his home, but

> The next day, just as the horizon had prophesied, a wind arose—and no feeble one: the tossing waves of the sea sobbed under the lash of the roaring storm.[1]

The ship is struck by lightning and destroyed, but

> The water carried him away on high, on high, so that the fringe of the cloud touched its crest; then Sir John swiftly seized the cloud with both hands.[2]

This same wave transports the reader into Fairyland; János clings to the cloud till it brings him to a rock where a gryphon has its nest. On the bird's back he rides to his home village. 'I bring no gold, I bring no treasures,' he thinks, 'but I bring the same faithful heart.' However, he finds Iluska's house inhabited by strangers, and learns that she is dead. Plucking a rose from her graveside, he sets out again into the world, with two companions, his grief and his sword.

In the depths of a forest he meets a potter whose wagon is stuck in the mud. To extricate it is child's play for the knight; nor can the potter deter him from the road which leads to the land of the giants, a road by which none have returned—for János intends to 'wander to the end of the world, till the day of my death for which I long' (xviii). Yet it is not really death which the knight is seeking; when the giants' frontier-guard comes to crush the intruder beneath his feet, János defends himself, holding his sword above his head. The giant treads on the blade, and his prostrate

---

[1] Másnap, amint az ég alja jövendölte,
  Csakugyan szél támadt, mégpedig
    nem gyönge,
  Zokogott a tenger hánykodó hulláma
  A zugó fergeteg korbácsolására.
                                (xvii)

[2] Ragadta őt a víz magasra, magasra,
  Hogy tetejét érte már a felhő rojtja;
  Ekkor János vitéz nagy hirtelenséggel
  Megkapta a felhőt mind a két
    kezével.   (xvii)

body serves as a bridge over which János crosses the brook into Giant-land.

Boldly entering the royal palace he finds the giant king and his sons eating rocks for lunch; the King tears off a piece as a 'dumpling' (galuska) for János, who hurls it straight back, striking the King a fatal blow on the forehead. The giants beg the knight to show mercy and accept their allegiance; he agrees to acknowledge them as his vassals, but only on condition that he instal a viceregent and continue his travels. The giants are not told, and we do not need to be told, why he makes this condition. János's new subjects give him a whistle, with which he can summon them at will. The first task for which he thus invokes their aid is the destruction of the witches, whose land he has entered. The last surviving witch turns out to be Iluska's stepmother (who had been described in the opening scene of the poem as a 'furious witch', though only incidentally), and her end marks a turning-point in the story.

My knight János wandered on, his heart was now quite cured of grief, for when he looked at the rose on his breast, what he felt was grief no more.[1]

When János reaches the coast, the sea too (which, it need hardly be said, Petőfi had never seen) takes on a different aspect:

The sea stirred not, but now and then brightly coloured little fish sported on its smooth surface, and when a ray of sunlight caught their scaly bodies, it quivered like the light of a flashing diamond.[2]

But this sea is the Ocean (Óperenciás tenger), and the old fisherman whom János meets cannot convey him across it; the lord of the giants must again summon his faithful vassals. A giant comes and carries him over the waters, with mighty strides, 'at terrible speed'. Even so it is three weeks before land appears, and then the land they reach is 'only an island', as the giant says, not the further shore of the Ocean which János hails. But this island is Fairyland, and

[1] Vándorolgatott az én János vitézem,
Meggyógyult már szíve a bútól
egészen,
Mert mikor keblén a rózsaszálra
nézett,
Nem volt az többé bú, amit akkor
érzett.   (XXII)

[2] Nem mozdult a tenger, de fickándoztanak
Sima hátán néha apró tarka halak,
S ha napsugár érte pikkelyes
testöket,
Tündöklő gyémántnak fényeként
reszketett.   (XXIII)

János is curious to see it, though first he must kill the monsters which guard its gates. When he is victorious, and enters, the blissful happiness which he alone cannot share brings back his despair —but only for a moment; seeking guidance from his rose he throws it into the lake situated at the centre of Fairyland. The flower is transformed into Iluska.

> I could tell all splendidly, only not what the knight János felt then.[1]

The fairies are enraptured by Iluska's beauty, and the lovers are hailed as King and Queen of Fairyland.

Sir John is essentially a folk-tale, and Petőfi establishes the same friendly relationship with his readers as does the teller of a folk-tale with his audience, by the same informal, improvisatory style:

> I'm not telling fibs, but the gate [of the fortress of the giant king] was so big that, that... well, I really don't know how big it was, but you can imagine; the giant king doesn't have his building done on a small scale.[2]

As so often in folk-tales, the action is divided between a natural and a supernatural world, but this is the least important fact about the poem, because Petőfi ignores the distinction; he has instinctively grasped that calculated transitions would kill the story stone dead. Above all, the poem succeeds because the story, and the verse, move swiftly; and the poet completed its 370 stanzas in about a month. It achieves artistic unity, too, from the constancy of János's love for Iluska, and also from the consistency with which he moves towards his final triumph by overcoming ever greater difficulties, not only extraneous obstacles but the grief and deathwish in his own heart. However, the assurance of ultimate victory, though unobtrusive, was there from the start; the despair of János's thoughts was never translated into action. When he first sets out on his travels, as he 'trudges along, with the dark shadows and dark thoughts in his mind', 'when the sun reached the highest point of heaven, it occurred to him that he ought to have a bite' (v). And he remains the same, till the destruction of the witches finally 'heals his heart'.

---

[1] Mindent el tudnék én beszélni ékesen,
Csak János vitéznek akkori kedvét nem. (xxvii)

Nem hazudok, de volt akkora kapuja,
Hogy, hogy ... biz én nem is tudom, hogy mekkora,

Csakhogy nagy volt biz az, képzelni is lehet;
Az óriás király kicsit nem épittet. (xx)

3

Settled in Pest, Petőfi rapidly became famous as the poet of wine and good cheer, conspicuous in the street as a 'character', parading his traditional national dress as befitted the writer of folk-songs. Even his slighter poems, however, sometimes betrayed that this was not the whole story: in *To the Girls* (*A leány-kákhoz*) (October 1844) he wrote: 'Don't be cross with me, girls, my dears! because my verses speak so often of wine. . . . While you read funny songs by me, you have no idea that my heart is sometimes almost breaking.' The editor for whom Petőfi worked, Vahot Imre,[1] a man with a shrewd commercial sense, found it profitable to encourage the poet to write as many drinking-songs and light folk-songs as possible; in these circumstances Petőfi might easily have continued indefinitely producing 'spontaneous' poems of this type, with an ever-decreasing degree of spontaneity.

His appearance before the public as the embodiment of the Bohemian not only distorted his natural development, but also carried him still further from the upper strata of literary and social life. The occurrence of the mildest of expletives in a humorous convivial poem[2] caused one critic[3] to recall having heard his coachman use a similar expression and to comment, in the course of a lengthy disquisition on taste, 'it is a pity that criticism is silent . . . and does not try to extirpate everything which does not speak in the heavenly voice of poetry'. But there was certainly no cause to complain that 'criticism is silent'; Petőfi was assailed by a most vigorous campaign in fashionable literary magazines. More than one critic judged *The shepherd rides his donkey* from the point of view of the donkey; *The Hammer of the Village* aroused sarcastic indignation[4] —'it is named a "heroic poem", and rightly, indeed, inasmuch as a brawl in a low inn may be named a heroic deed!'—a verdict which assumptions of genuine incomprehension and of deliberate malice are equally powerless to explain. The same critic, though

---

[1] Vahot Imre (1820–79), journalist and playwright, was the brother of Vachott Sándor, on whom see p. 218, n. 1.

[2] *My Economic Views* (*Gazdálkodási nézeteim*) (April–May 1844).

[3] 'Dardanus' (Pompéry János) in *Életképek* (*Pictures of Life*), 11 December 1844.

[4] Császár Ferenc in *Irodalmi Őr* (*Literary Guardian*), 16 August and 6 September 1845. The above quotations are taken from the second instalment.

he admired some parts of *Sir John*, simply refused to believe that
Vörösmarty had said that it would 'be an adornment to any
literature', and reproached the poet, among other things, for
misleading the 'simple peasant' by telling him that France and
India were contiguous, and for using exclamations which were
proof of moral decay.

Long before the campaign against him reached its climax,
Petőfi was stung into replying to his critics (naturally in verse),
which he did with an anger conspicuously different from the
humour with which he so often faced adversity. In *The Wild
Flower of Nature* (*A természet vadvirága*) (December 1844) he
warns the 'base curs' who bark at him and bite him that he, the
'wild flower of Nature', has thorns; and in *The World and I* (*A
világ és én*) (January 1845) this anger has intensified into a more
general misanthropy. Yet, even as he cursed the moment of his
conception, there could be no question of his abandoning poetry
(*To Be or not to Be a Poet*) (*Költő lenni vagy nem lenni*) (January 1845),
and the lighter *On My Bad Verses* (*Rossz verseimről*) (February–
March 1845) provides a welcome reminder that the dark hatred of
The World and I was not the poet's only mood. Yet the darkness
was there, and it was deepened by contemplation of the political
scene. Petőfi still wrote few political poems, but now that he was
living at the centre of political life he soon came to feel closer to
current affairs than ever before. True, he had once spent six
weeks (in May–June 1843) in the capital, Pozsony,[1] where he
earned a small sum by copying out the minutes of the Diet; but,
possibly because of the remoteness of so many speakers from the
life and problems of the people he knew, his stay there had not
proved stimulating. In the following year his hopes of reform ran
high, but when the 1843–4 Diet ended in November 1844, only
thirteen out of the 100 measures it had prepared had become law.
So in *Farewell to 1844* (*Búcsú 1844-től*) (December 1844) he wrote:
'You tore to shreds the garland of my country, which her youthful
hopes had placed upon her head; for this reason I will not inscribe
you where my happy years are recorded', although 'the star of
Fame has cast a ray on me', although 'I stand on the threshold of
Heaven'. Now to political disappointment and the hostile campaign of the critics was added a personal sorrow.

In November 1844 Petőfi had made the acquaintance of Csapó

---

[1] Now Bratislava in Czechoslovakia.

Etelke,[1] a girl of fifteen whose fair hair, blue eyes, and happy,
childlike smile immediately attracted him, at a time when he felt
at odds with a dreary and hostile world. Whether his feelings for
her would have deepened into love it is impossible to say, but there
is no doubt that he was profoundly stirred when she died on
7 January 1845. Moreover, for four days there was doubt whether
she was indeed dead, a circumstance which exposed the poet to
the morbid side of Romantic emotion: 'For two long days I saw
your cold frame, the speechless lips, the closed eyes; I kissed the
ravaged Eden of your brow,—that was my first kiss, and you did not
even feel it!' (*For two long days I saw*. . .) (*Láttam két hosszú nap* . . .)
(January 1845). On 20 March there appeared a new volume of
Petőfi's poems, *Cypress-leaves from Etelke's Grave* (*Cipruslombok
Etelke sírjáról*)—but already one of the later poems in it begins
Time is a powerful healer . . . (*Hatalmas orvos az idő* . . .) (January–
February 1845).

Nevertheless a deep feeling of emptiness and discontent remained, of which one symptom was the poet's resignation of his
assistant editorship, at the beginning of April, though he consented
(after some discussion) to give Vahot exclusive publishing rights
for his poems. He felt bored and cramped by city life; in addition
to his recent experiences and earlier wanderings, there was a
streak of restlessness in his nature, inherited from his father.
He set out on a tour of northern Hungary, having written, just before he left, a farewell *To those good friends of mine in Pest* (*Azokhoz
az én jó pesti pajtásaimhoz*) (end of March 1845): 'Ha, the door of
my prison has opened—is not an office a prison?—Dear Freedom
continually kisses me with her sweet, fiery lips. . . . To depart!
the thought hurts so, hurts me so—and why? I had a beloved
here, but she is gone into the night of the grave. To no one am I
dear; my soul loathes that barren, empty word.'

Though his output of poetry during his twelve weeks' absence
from the city was relatively small, his *Notes on a Journey* (*Úti
jegyzetek*) in prose clearly reflect the return of the gay extrovert
of his earlier days—they are written with a lightness of touch
scarcely paralleled in earlier Hungarian prose. Passing through
Aszód,[2] where he had been at school for three years (1835–8), he
recalls his 'first love', for the daughter of the pastor's widow with

---

[1] Her sister was the wife of Vahot's elder brother, Vachott Sándor (cf. pp.
218, n. 1, 248, n. 1).   [2] Some twenty-five miles east-north-east of Budapest.

whom he lodged, which he had described in his poem *My First Love* (*Első szerelmem*) (July 1844). There he relates how his sweetheart gave him ham and other choice delicacies to take with him to school, and recalls their blissful evenings together by moonlight in the garden, but now

Ah, happy times, you are gone, and perhaps for ever; now I have no ham, no girl.[1]

In a similar vein he recalls the episode now—his love was as deep, he says, as the mud in which their wagon got stuck. It was at Aszód, too, that his father, to save him from the 'whirlpool of hell', had given him 'advice' against becoming an actor which 'was visible, weeks later, on my back'.

These *Notes* leave us in no doubt of the fact of Petőfi's recovery from the despair of the period immediately before he set out on his travels; the slight but revealing poems in which he hails the beauties of Nature tell us, with equal clarity, what healed him. The birds whose home is the forest, he says, 'know of themselves how sweet is the pure air of freedom. . . . God is good, His anger is short-lived.' (*The Forest Home*) (*Az erdei lak*) (April 1845). In addition, the poet was accorded the great honour of being appointed a judge in Gömör County, one of the counties through which he passed on his journey.

But immediately on his return to Pest, in June, the mood changed.

I wandered far . . .[2]

I wandered far, my sweet departed beloved, but always, in all places, wherever I came and went, your sorrowful memory, like a dark veil, spread out behind me from the mound of your grave.

I came back to you. I could give you no kiss as a gentle greeting; you are deep beneath me. I bow my head like a weeping willow, not on your soft breast, but on the hard wooden cross over your grave.

---

[1] . . . Ah, szép idők! ti elmulátok
És mindörökre tán,
Már nem terem számomra többé 35
Sem sonka, sem leány.

[2]   *Messze vándoroltam . . .*

Messze vándoroltam, elhunyt édes lelkem,
De mindig, mindenütt, ahol jártam-keltem,

Bánatos emléked, mint egy sötét fátyol
Huzódott utánam sírodnak halmától.

Visszajöttem hozzád. Csókot nem adhattam 5
Nyájas idvezletül; mélyen vagy alattam.
Lehajtom fejemet árvafűz módjára,
Nem lágy kebeledre, de kemény fejfádra.

My playful fingers stroke, not your fair locks, but blades of grass which perhaps have sprung from your ashes; and I hear the whisper, not of your dear lips—I hear the whispering only of the wind in the graveyard.

Thus I meditate, on the quiet mound of your grave, thinking calmly of times past. Now my breast is calm. The storm of my pain has spent its fury; it roars no more, it has ceased, expired.

The past is a sea asleep. Your death is the rock on which the boat of my hopes snapped in two. This grim rock now stands so beautiful on the horizon in the blue distance;

And it will ever stand before my eyes, your picture will be in my heart unto death, my Etelke! Your picture will hang from my heart as this withered garland hangs from the cross over your grave.

At the same time, however, his 'longing for love' asserted itself. 'What is the garden worth, if it grows no roses? If it is not adorned with love, what is life, what is youth worth to me?... But though I long to love anew, I have not forgotten the dead maiden. . . . The snow of winter is still lying on the mountain peak when the flower at its foot opens out.'[1] (*Longing for Love*) (*Szerelemvágy*) (June–July 1845). The conflict was real, and painful; but in the autumn, when staying with a friend in the country, Petőfi met another fair-haired, radiant girl in the person of Mednyánszky Berta, the daughter of an estate-manager, began a new collection of poems entitled *The Pearls of Love* (*Szerelem gyöngyei*), which appeared in October, and in September asked Berta's father for her hand. Mednyánszky refused, saying that he owed it to his ancestors not

Játszanak ujjaim, nem szőke hajaddal,
Tán már hamvaidból sarjadt fűszálak-
    kal;   10
És hallok suttogást, nem kedves
    ajkadét,
Hallom suttogni csak a temető szelét.

Ekképen merengek sírod csendes
    halmán,
A lefolyt időre nyugodtan gondolván.
Nyugodt már kebelem. Fájdalmam
    szélvésze   15
Kitombolt, elzúgott, megszűnt, el-
enyésze.

Alvó tenger a mult. Halálod a kőszirt,
Amelyen reményim sajkája kettétört,
Ez a durva kőszirt most már olyan
    szépen
Áll a látkör végén a kék messzeség-
    ben;   20

És állani fog az szemem előtt váltig,
Szívemen lesz képed, Etelkém, halálig!
Függni fog szívemen képed, mint
    domború
Sírodnak fejfáján e hervadt koszorú.

[1] In this quotation, the dots after 'me?' indicate an omission; those after 'maiden' are in the original text.

to give his daughter in marriage to an actor or a poet; but the refusal
was scarcely contrary to Berta's wishes. She liked Petőfi the man,
and took an interest in Petőfi the poet, but no more. Petőfi accepted
the rebuff with composure; perhaps the experience had not been
so deep after all, though it combined with a renewed offensive
by his literary enemies to produce a mood of gloom and bitterness
which reached a frightening intensity, though it lasted only some
six months. His next collection of poems, which appeared in
April 1846, was entitled *Clouds* (*Felhők*).

4

... Why do you disturb me? Clear out, the lot of you! I am engaged in
a great task. I am in haste. I am weaving a whip, a whip of flame, from
the sun's rays; I will flog the world! They shall wail, and I will laugh, as
they laughed while I wailed. Hahaha! For such is life. We wail and we
laugh. But Death says: Hush! I too have died once already. Those
who drank my wine poured poison into the water I drink.[1]

The above lines are the opening of the dramatic monologue
The Madman (*Az őrült*) (January 1846). Though not one of the
Clouds, it well illustrates the pervading mood of that collection,
from which it differs only in degree. The *Clouds* themselves are a set
of sixty-six short aphoristic poems, modelled on Shelley's *Fragments*.
Many express the poet's despair and fury, but there is pathos too:

Grief? A great ocean[2]

Grief? A great ocean. And joy? A small pearl in the ocean.
Perhaps even while bringing it to the surface, I break it. (Early 1846.)

Petőfi's debt to Shelley in the *Clouds* is only one of many
examples of the markedly literary quality of his work in the whole
of this period; the stream of folk-songs has almost run dry. His

---

[1] ... Mit háborgattok?
Takarodjatok innen!
Nagy munkába' vagyok. Sietek.
Ostort fonok, lángostort, napsuga-
  rakból;
Megkorbácsolom a világot!   5
Jajgatnak majd és én kacagok,
Mint ők kacagtak, amikor én jajgat-
  tam.
Hahaha!
Mert ilyen az élet. Jajgatunk s
  kacagunk.

De a halál azt mondja: csitt!   10
Egyszer már én is meghalék.
Mérget töltöttek azok vizembe,
Akik megitták boromat.

[2]   *A bánat? Egy nagy óceán*

A bánat? Egy nagy óceán.
S az öröm?
Az óceán kis gyöngye. Talán,
Mire fölhozom, össze is töröm.

patriotic poems written towards the end of 1844 show him moving towards the style of Vörösmarty's odes: *I wandered far* marks a conspicuous return to the poetic diction which he had apparently abandoned. Moreover, his reading reinforced the effect of his experiences, and made him a typical Romantic. In this period the main influences are those of Shelley and Byron, also Shakespearian tragedy, with which Petőfi was familiar from his career as an actor—one of his few successful roles had been the Fool in *Lear*, which he had acted in his benefit performance at Kecskemét in March 1843.

In spite of these changes in the character of his work, the personality of the earlier Petőfi still shows through, even though the treatment is different. For example, *Moonlit Night* (*Holdvilágos éj*) (July 1845) no doubt exhibits the influence of Heine, but its spirit is that of Petőfi:

Moonlit Night[1]

The moon in the heavens is a silver lute, its beams are so many strings; on the moon's silver lute the breezes play with ghostly hands.

The wanderer draws near to a village, perhaps he is also a poet? For he hangs so dreamily on the moon and its flooding rays.

He walks on, on, the musing wanderer, and finally reaches the village; in the village is silence, mute silence, the people have long ago gone to sleep.

By the gate of the cantor's house, a beautiful maiden is sobbing; the evening is cool . . . she is in her night-gown . . . the tender limbs are trembling.

The wanderer trudges along that way, and speaks: 'What is the matter, what is the matter, fair maiden? Answer, most beautiful moonbeam, can I help you in your woe?

[1]   *Holdvilágos éj*

A hold az égen egy ezüst lant,
Megannyi húr a sugarak;
A hold ezüst lantján a szellők
Szellemkezekkel játszanak.

Egy faluhoz közelg a vándor,   5
Egyúttal költő is talán?
Mert úgy elandalodva csügg a
Holdon s elömlő sugarán.

Megy, megy tovább a méla vándor,
S eléri végre a falut;   10

A faluban csend, néma csend van,
Népsége régen elaludt.

A kántor háza kapujánál
Szép hajadon leány zokog;
Az este hűs . . . ő pongyolában . . . 15
Reszketnek a gyöngéd tagok.

A vándor arra ballag és szól:
'Mi lelt, mi lelt, szép hajadon?
Felelj, legszebbik holdsugár te,
Segíthetek-e bajodon?   20

'Perhaps you are mourning a faithless lover? If I could be your lover, the world would never have seen one so faithful.

'Be my moonlight, fair maid! I care not whatever Fate may bring, let my life be eternal night . . . that I may look on my moon for ever!'

So spoke the wanderer, ardent, but the maiden does not reply; she just stands still, and silently weighs down her small handkerchief with her tears.

Now the moon casts its rays into the cantor's room; the cantor, the girl's drunken father, is beating his wife in there.

Not surprisingly, the persistence of the earlier Petőfi is particularly marked in those happy weeks when the poet was looking forward to a future with Berta. For example, in late August or September 1845 he wrote a poem about *The Good Old Innkeeper* (*A jó öreg kocsmáros*) with whom he was staying, contented and happy. Only at the end of the last (the fifth) stanza does he tell us that 'This good old innkeeper is my father; may God bless him with both hands!'

The period of the *Clouds* also saw the production of six works on a larger scale: the poems *The Curse of Love* (*Szerelem átka*) (September–October 1845), *Fairy Dream* (*Tündérálom*) (February 1846), *Wild Stephen* (*Szilaj Pista*) (April 1846), and *Salgó* (the name of a castle in northern Hungary) (May 1846): also the tragedy *Tiger and Hyena* (*Tigris és hiéna*) (January 1846) and the short novel *The Hangman's Rope* (*A hóhér kötele*) (February 1846).

The *Fairy Dream*, the only work in this group to be concerned explicitly with the poet himself, is paradoxically free from the savagery characteristic of Petőfi's Romantic imagination in this period. It is an allegorical lyric autobiography, in general terms, of a type similar to Shelley's *Alastor* or Byron's *Dream*; Petőfi describes the happiness of childhood, then the feeling of emptiness and indefinable longing which followed it. He withdrew 'far, far

Hűségtelen kedvest siratsz tán?	Igy szólt a vándor lelkesedve,
Ha én lehetnék kedvesed,	De a leányka nem felel; 30
Olyan lennék, hogy a világ még	Csak áll és némán nehezíti
Nem láta oly hűségeset.	Kis kendejét könyűivel.
Légy holdvilágom, szép leányka! 25	A hold a kántor szobájába
S nem bánom: a sors bármit ad;	Sugárait most beveti;
Legyen örök éj létem . . . csak hogy	A kántor, a lyány részeg apja, 35
Örökké lássam holdamat!'	Benn feleségét döngeti.

from the din of life, as one pursued by a host of spectres' (9)[1] to seek solitude in the depths of a forest; the 'fairy beings' half-remembered from the tales of his childhood 'came forth from' his heart and were gone for ever (10). 'Then I grew tired of this earthly life, which had lost its beauty in my eyes. Up, up! I said, to Heaven, where fly the fairies of my aching heart' (13). The poet was on the point of hurling himself from a mountain peak when an angel held him back, and he grasped her hand. '"I am a maiden," she said, "an earthly maiden, not an angel"' (19), and her kiss restored his soul. Their happiness lasted through spring and summer, but in autumn, 'that savage tyrant of Nature' (28), they were parted. So we reach the last stanza:

> Since then my face and my hands have healed, my face and my hands which thorns had hurt, and the wounds of parting are now effaced from my heart; but now I feel a wound far greater than these, far greater, for I know that I am near to forgetting the sweet salvation that thy fancies gave me, O fairy dream, first love![2]

The other poems of the group are narrative. The relatively unimportant *Curse of Love*, written immediately after Petőfi's rejection by Berta, tells how a spurned lover curses his former beloved and her husband, so that they are turned into rocks, and he himself into a 'dark storm brooding over the two accursed peaks'. *Wild Pista* tells of a ferryman's son who drowns his former sweetheart, a fisherman's daughter, and the young gentleman from the city for whom she has forsaken him, then follows them himself. Both these works are typical minor Romantic productions; the latter, however, has its relevance to the poet's future, because of its unmistakable political overtones. The style is popular, but the supernatural element of the folk-tale is absent, as the subject requires.

The castle of Salgó[3] made a deep impression on Petőfi when he visited it on his tour of northern Hungary in 1845. 'It was as well that we took on a guide, for otherwise we might not have even

---

[1] References are to stanzas.

[2] Azóta arcom és kezem begyógyult,   De e sebeknél jobban fáj nekem most,
Arcom s kezem, mit tüske sérte meg,   Jobban fáj az, hogy már-már feledem
S szívemből is ki vannak irtva már   Ábrándjaidnak édes üdvességét,
Az elválástól támadott sebek;   Oh tündérálom, első szerelem!   30

[3] In the Mátra mountains, near the town of Salgótarján.

located the castle. It stands in so extraordinary a position that the very thought of building there was madness. It is surrounded by a mighty forest of beech, oak, and other trees. The top of the mountain is a huge rock of granite and on that rock stood the castle; little of it now remains. The highest wall is only some twelve feet high. Perhaps there never was a castle in Hungary so close a neighbour to the stars as Salgó. I sat for long on the topmost peak of its ruins; my gaze roamed over miles, my soul over centuries.' So he had written in the *Notes on a Journey*; now in May 1846, he took Salgó as the setting for a story which, whatever its debt to *Kisfaludy Sándor's narrative poems, which brought the Romantic interest in ruined castles into Hungarian literature, and to Vörösmarty's *The Two Neighbouring Castles*,[1] epitomizes this period of Petőfi's own development as perfectly as *The Hammer of the Village* reflects his abandonment of high-flown poetic diction, or *Sir John* his affection for his people and their store of folktale.

The atmosphere of *Salgó* is established immediately at the opening of the poem, in the description of the castle itself:

Here stood Salgó . . . so near to heaven, yet in it dwelt hell. The ruinous feet of the centuries long ago trampled down the towers of this castle. Only one or two broken walls remain, passing their days in gloom, like one who after a riotous youth grows weary of his life and becomes a hermit.[2]

At the time when the house of *Árpád died out with King András III in 1301, the lord of Salgó was Kompolti Péter, the terror of the district. With his two sons Dávid and Jób he attacked the neighbouring castle of Gedővár one night as its lord Gedő Simon lay awake, thinking not of internecine strife but of his country; Gedő's wife Perenna also was praying for Hungary, and so for her husband's happiness. In the attack Gedő was killed attempting to protect his wife, who was taken back to Salgó as a prisoner by Dávid. The swooning Perenna does not understand what has happened till Jób shows her her husband's blood on his sword and exclaims

---

[1] See pp. 116 ff.

[2] Itt állt Salgó... az éghez oly közel,   15
És benne mégis a pokol tanyázott.
A századoknak döntő lábai
Elgázolák rég e vár tornyait.

Belőlök egy-két csonka fal maradt,
  mely
Szomorkodással tölti idejét,   20
Mint aki lármás ifjúság után
Éltét megunva remetéskedik.

'Now you are free, fair lady, free! The servile bonds of woman's loyalty constrain your soul no longer' (288-90).

Now, however, a dispute arises between the two Kompolti brothers for the prize, and soon 'instead of their tongues, their swords were speaking' (346). But as they fight their father intervenes to assert his rights and claim Perenna for himself. In a voice 'like the Angel of Death' (395), she accepts his offer of marriage; but at the same time she asks Dávid if he loves her—if he does, let him prove it by freeing her from his father and brother. Dávid successfully curbs his conscience till the deeds are done, but then (as Perenna sees) it torments him into madness. He embraces her and plunges over the battlements with her in his arms.

Salgó is a direct descendant of *The Two Neighbouring Castles*, but the two poems have little in common except the attack itself. Petőfi's plot is far more varied than Vörösmarty's, and holds our interest in a way scarcely possible for Tihamér as he works systematically through his list of victims; besides, Petőfi's iambics move so much more swiftly than his predecessor's hexameters.

The story of *Salgó* is perhaps too studiously horrific; but at least the horror does not overspill into absurdity, as happens in *Tiger and Hyena*, a tragedy on the attempt of Borics, the illegitimate son of the ex-queen Predszláva, to usurp the throne of King Béla II (Béla the Blind) on the King's accession in 1131. The title derives from a scene between mother and son (I. x) at the end of which Predszláva calls Borics a tiger, to which he replies by calling her a hyena; she has in fact already attempted to murder him. She appears to be the product of a desire to outdo Hugo's Lucrezia Borgia, and the play lacks nothing in Romantic fury; on the other hand, it shows no signs of having been written by a man with considerable experience of the stage. Equally devoid of feeling for its literary form (even if we make allowances for the extreme haste in which it was written), still more frenzied, and more absurd, is the novel *The Hangman's Rope*, a story of the vengeance taken by Andorlaki on his rival Ternyei, who has prevented Andorlaki's marriage by revealing, on the wedding-day, that Andorlaki was already a father by another woman. The 'hangman's rope' of the title is the rope with which Ternyei's grandson, driven to suicide by Andorlaki, hangs himself on the same gallows where Andorlaki's son had been executed as the result of Ternyei's devilish machinations. Both these works have their moments of relief, their sympathetic characters, especially the blind king in *Tiger and Hyena*; but in the last resort both are of interest solely as proof that Petőfi's genius could express itself only through lyric and narrative poetry, and they are his only completed attempts at drama or novel. They also illustrate his state of mind at the time; and no doubt to write them helped to relieve his feelings and to pave the way for the change in him which was about to take place.

5

'I have left the city ... my good fortune has placed me in the happy bosom of Nature ... I have come here to dispel the mist which so long brooded, gloomy and dark, over my wan countenance' wrote Petőfi in *I have left the city ...* (*Elhagytam én a várost ...*) (April 1846). He returned to Pest after a fortnight in the country with his parents, in a mood of horror at his own recent self, which he knew instinctively was not his true self. 'What has become of the earth? ... In every bush is hatred of mankind. ... I too hated— I had good reason; but since seeing these blackguards making Byron-faces, my hatred has snapped. ... Truly the world is beautiful, very beautiful; every year spring covers it, every village has its lovely girl, and if one man weeps, another laughs. How comic is grief itself! How different its effect on heart and hair! It darkens a white heart, and whitens dark hair!' (*World-hatred*) (*Világgyűlölet*) (late April 1846).

These poems are of the greatest importance in Petőfi's development, not only because they show him regaining his composure (in this connexion the relaxation of tension in the flippant epigram which ends *World-hatred* (the last sentence in the above quotation) is significant) but because they mark the maturing of the absolute spontaneity which his best work presents. In his first period the disproportionately large output of drinking-songs suggests that the coincidence between his literary self and his real self was not yet complete, and in 1845-6 his bitterness, though it originated in his own state of mind, had tended to be generalized into a conventional Romantic misanthropy, largely under the influence of his reading. The border between the conscious and the unconscious is both fluid and indistinct, and a discussion of the poet's 'sincerity' might well prove impertinent as well as inconclusive; what is clear, however, is that a biography of Petőfi constructed from his poems alone would become far fuller and far more accurate when it reached the early summer of 1846; and for a genius like this poet whose natural gifts enabled him to write, on an average, a poem almost every other day, with no more difficulty than an ordinary man has in keeping his diary, this means that for the first time Petőfi has found himself.

But recovery from his 'world-hatred' meant no passive acquiescence in the existing state of affairs, no contemplation of a calm and uneventful future. Even earlier, by October 1845, the wide open spaces which had freed the thoughts of the poet of *The Lowlands* from their 'prison' had been transformed into a symbol of an explicitly political liberty: 'Plains, you are the picture of freedom, and Freedom, you are the god of my soul! Freedom, my God, I live only that one day I may die for you!' (*The Ruined Inn*) (*A csárda romjai*) (October 1845). We cannot trace fully the development of Petőfi's ideas on this subject (largely, no doubt, because of the censorship which he had to bear in mind) or say whether 'Freedom' here implies more than Hungarian freedom; but it is certain that six months later his cause is one which transcends all national boundaries. 'Fate, open for me a field, let me render some service to humanity! Let this noble flame which so fires me not burn away uselessly to ashes. There is flame in my heart, flame descended from Heaven, causing every drop of blood to seethe; every beat of my heart is a prayer for the happiness of the world. Would that I could say this not only in empty speech, but in deeds! Let the reward for my deeds be a new cross, on a new Golgotha! To die for the good of humanity!' (*Fate, open for me a field . . .*) (*Sors, nyiss nekem tért . . .*) (April 1846). And in a poetic epistle of 22 May to a friend, Várady, Petőfi describes how his hatred of the world has given place to wrath that 'the sufferings of thousands of years' are not avenged, and says (84 ff.) that he is 'beginning to believe' (no more than that) that the world will soon be purged in a Flood of blood, a final conflict which shall deliver the oppressed from their oppressors. Then in *One thought torments me . . . (Egy gondolat bánt engemet . . .)* (December 1846) the final struggle for World Freedom (*Világszabadság*) is identified with the poet's own destiny, and the battle described, in one long sentence (21–30) whose division into short sections reinforces the effect of the galloping anapaestic rhythm to convey an unsurpassed drive and energy.

One thought torments me . . .[1]

One thought torments me—to die in bed, among the pillows! To wither away slowly, like a flower gnawed by the tooth of an invisible worm; to be consumed slowly, like a candle in a deserted, empty room. Give not such a death as this, my God, give not such a death to me! Let me be a tree through which lightning darts, or which a hurricane tears up by the roots; let me be a rock which thunder, shaking heaven and earth, hurls down from hill to valley . . .—When every enslaved people, tired of its yoke, enters the lists with countenance aglow, with glowing red banners, and on the banners this holy watchword: 'World Freedom!' and this they trumpet forth, trumpet forth from East to West, and tyranny clashes with them: there may I fall, on the field of battle, there may the young blood flow out from my heart, and when the last words of my lips resound, full of joy, let the clash of steel drown them, the voice of the trumpet, the roar of the cannon, and let steeds gallop panting over my dead body to the triumph won, and let them leave me there crushed beneath their hooves.—There may my scattered bones be gathered, when the great day of burial comes, where with solemn, slow funeral music and crape-covered banners those heroes are committed to one common grave, all those who died for thee, holy World Freedom!

Petőfi's concept of self-sacrifice in a final battle with tyranny is thus inspired by the union of his patriotism, his willingness to lay down his life for his country, and his democratic ideals. The former

---

[1] *Egy gondolat bánt engemet . . .*

Egy gondolat bánt engemet:
Ágyban, párnák közt halni meg!
Lassan hervadni el, mint a virág,
Amelyen titkos féreg foga rág;
Elfogyni lassan, mint a gyertyaszál,   5
Mely elhagyott, üres szobában áll.
Ne ily halált adj, istenem,
Ne ily halált adj énnekem!
Legyek fa, melyen villám fut keresztül,
Vagy melyet szélvész csavar ki
  tövestül;   10
Legyek kőszirt, mit a hegyről a
  völgybe
Eget-földet rázó mennydörgés dönt
  le . . . —
Ha majd minden rabszolga-nép
Jármát megúnva síkra lép
Pirosló arccal és piros zászlókkal   15
És a zászlókon eme szent jelszóval:
'Világszabadság!'

S ezt elharsogják,
Elharsogják kelettől nyugatig,
S a zsarnokság velök megütközik: 20
Ott essem el én,
A harc mezején,
Ott folyjon az ifjui vér ki szivembül,
S ha ajkam örömteli végszava zendül,
Hadd nyelje el azt az acéli zörej,   25
A trombita hangja, az ágyudörej,
S holttestemen át
Fújó paripák
Száguldjanak a kivivott diadalra,
S ott hagyjanak engemet
  összetiporva. —   30
Ott szedjék össze elszórt csontomat,
Ha jön majd a nagy temetési nap,
Hol ünnepélyes, lassu gyász-zenével
És fátyolos zászlók kiséretével
A hősöket egy közös sírnak adják,   35
Kik érted haltak, szent világszabadság!

of these appears as early as the *Patriot's Song* (*Honfidal*) of January or February 1844, where the poet had also observed 'I do not proclaim it aloud that you, my country, are dearer to me than anything in the world'—and his references to the subject are in fact rare, though they recur at regular intervals. His democratic sympathies, too, like those of many of his countrymen, had grown up over a considerable period. The poems in which he expressed them are of two main types, the contrast between which can be illustrated by a comparison of *The Noble* (*A nemes*) (January–February 1844) and *The Hungarian Noble* (*A magyar nemes*) (September–October 1845).

The Noble[1]

They are placing the villain on the whipping-post, to expiate his crime by a beating; he has robbed, plundered and the devil knows what else he has not done.

But he shouts, resisting: 'Do not touch me! I am noble . . . you have no right to beat a noble.'

Do you hear this, spirit of his dishonoured ancestor? Now he should be placed not on the whipping-post, but on the gallows!

The Hungarian Noble[2]

The bloodstained swords of my ancestors hang on the peg, rust eats them away; rust eats them away, they do not shine. I am a Hungarian noble!

Doing no work—that is life. I am idle, therefore I am alive. Work is for the peasant. I am a Hungarian noble!

Prepare well the road, peasant, because it is your horse which draws my carriage. I just can't walk. I am a Hungarian noble!

[1] *A nemes*	[2] *A magyar nemes*
Deresre húzzák a gazembert,	Őseimnek véres kardja
Bűnét botokkal róni le;	Fogason függ, rozsda marja,
Lopott, rabolt, és tudj' az ördög,	Rozsda marja, nem ragyog.
Még mit nem mívele.	Én magyar nemes vagyok!
De ő kiált ellenszegűlve: 5	Munkátlanság csak az élet. 5
'Hozzám ne nyúljatok!	Van életem, mert henyélek.
Nemes vagyok . . . nincs nemesembert	A paraszté a dolog.
Botozni jogotok.'	Én magyar nemes vagyok!
Hallottad e szót, meggyalázott	Jól készítsd, paraszt, az útat,
Ősének szelleme? 10	Mert hisz a te lovad vontat. 10
Most már őt húzni nem deresre:	Csak nem járhatok gyalog.
Akasztófára kellene!	Én magyar nemes vagyok!

Perhaps I should live for learning? The learned are all poor. I don't write, I don't read. I am a Hungarian noble!

True, of one branch of knowledge I am a master; in it I rarely see my peer. I know well how to eat and drink. I am a Hungarian noble!

What a good thing I don't pay taxes. I have estates—not many; and I have debts—many. I am a Hungarian noble!

What do I care about the country? The hundred troubles of the country? The troubles will soon pass off. I am a Hungarian noble!

When I have piped away my life on my ancestral rights, in my ancestral home: angels will carry me to Heaven. I am a Hungarian noble!

Any reader who prefers the fury of the first of these poems to the irony of the second will find plenty in Petőfi to suit his taste; indeed the former type is far commoner, especially in the poems written during the 1848 revolution. Petőfi was a young man; in the Hungary of his time there was enough misery and social injustice to make any young man angry, and he had seen it at first hand. Moreover, it is an essential feature of his spontaneity that his poems should express all his feelings, not just a selection made on artistic grounds. He knew no barrier between thought and its expression; he was downright, because he was upright. (Nevertheless even his most furious outbursts are often far more carefully constructed than is apparent at first sight.) At the same time, a taste which finds the irony of the second of these poems more convincing, because the poet has kept his temper, can delight in the subtlety with which he has chosen the most effective form for his purpose, the monologue—the noble just talks, and at no point is he shown as doing anything, or as ever having done anything beyond eating, drinking, smoking and riding in his carriage—and we can relish also the expressive portrayal of his character in the heavy, slow trochaic rhythm and long syllables of the opening line. Here is the full

Tán a tudománynak éljek?
A tudósok mind szegények.
Nem írok, nem olvasok.   15
Én magyar nemes vagyok!

Van, igaz, egy tudományom,
Ebben párom ritkán látom:
Enni, inni jól tudok.
Én magyar nemes vagyok!   20

Milyen jó, hogy nem adózok.
Gazdaságom van, de nem sok,

S van adósságom, de sok.
Én magyar nemes vagyok!

Mit törődöm a hazával?   25
A hazának száz bajával?
Majd elmúlnak a bajok.
Én magyar nemes vagyok!

Ősi joggal, ősi házban
Éltemet ha elpipáztam: 30
Mennybe visznek angyalok.
Én magyar nemes vagyok!

realization of those powers of character-drawing which Petőfi first revealed in his early folk-songs. The poem has stood the test of time, and it is on record that the son of the noble whom Petőfi had in mind retained into old age his great pride that his father had inspired the poet, a pride which the satire in the poem could not affect.

Now the time had come for action in the cause of democracy; not for asking, as the poet had done in November 1844, 'Why was I not born a thousand years ago?' 'The nightingale is the bird of twilight; now the night is drawing to its close, dawn is approaching; now the world needs not nightingales, but skylarks.'[1] Petőfi was keen to acquaint himself more closely with conditions in various parts of the country, so in August 1846 he set out for Szatmár[2] in the north-east, where some friends had invited him to stay with them, with a view to going on to Transylvania. Then at a county ball at Nagykároly[3] on 8 September, he met Szendrey Júlia, the seventeen-year-old daughter of a well-to-do estate manager. 'Ruddy cheeks, ruddy lips, brown curls, brown eyes; and in that face, in those eyes, how great a soul, my God! O if that soul, if the girl with that soul, could be mine! Speak, and say that you are still untroubled by love. No, no! say that now you do love, that you love me, and that word will be the creator of a new life for me. I love you, and my love, that infinite flood, has buried my past as a deluge buries the earth. I know not what I was before, or what I shall be; it depends on you whether I become a dark shadow or a shining ray.' (*To Julia*) (*Júliához*) (8–10 September 1846). On 27 September he wrote a poem beginning 'All my feelings before now were a poet's dream, a poet's dream and not love' (*Költői ábránd volt, mit eddig érzék* . . .) and all his work in this period shows that he was right. The Julia lyrics are dynamic, spontaneous, full of particular references; by comparison those on Etelke and Berta are static, literary, and generalized. Significant, too, is the fact that Petőfi now returns, after a long interval, to the folk-song, which had been so fruitful a source of inspiration in the past; nearly all the poems written in the weeks following his meeting with Julia are of this type.

---

[1] *Why was I not born a thousand years ago?* . . . (*Miért nem születtem ezer év előtt* . . .) (November 1844): *Nightingales and Skylarks* (*Csalogányok és pacsírták*) (September 1846).

[2] Now Satu Mare in Rumania.

[3] Now Carei in Rumania.

Julia, for her part, though not unresponsive, was cautious; on 21 October she wrote in her diary: 'I admit that I like you, better than anyone; but I dare not be confident that I shall feel this later. . . . I will make no promises, I will say only that if you return in the spring and we both feel the same, I shall regard us as in duty bound to seek in each other the foundations of our future happiness—not, however, of that happiness which lasts only as long as the first intoxication of love, but the happiness of a whole life. Oh, if only you were not so passionate! I have always feared the flames of such a passion, which, just because it blazes so fiercely, consumes not only everything which approaches it, but itself too, very soon.' When they met again, on the following day (by this time the poet had returned from his visit to Transylvania, which he had temporarily postponed after meeting Julia, to see more of her) she communicated to him the suggestion she had recorded in her diary. 'No wonder I live again, for I have seen her again. . . . Soon we shall be looking at all the flowers as their buds open out. When you see the flowers opening, perhaps your heart will open too' he wrote in a poem dated 22–23 October (*No wonder I live again . . .*) (*Nem csoda, ha újra élek . . .*).

'He looked for politics and found love'[1] but this was no time to give up politics. On the contrary, the nation must revive if she was to survive, and no one felt this more keenly than Petőfi. His first poem of 1845, *The Hungarian Nation* (*A magyar nemzet*) (January 1845), had denied that the nation did deserve to survive, and when Petőfi wrote another poem with the same title, in December 1846, though past such bitterness, he still saw a country which could inspire only pity or contempt, a tragedy of untapped resources: 'If the earth is the hat of God, our country is the garland on it! So fair a country, so fertile, enchanting to eye and soul, and so rich!—the ocean of ears of corn billows golden on its plains, and in its hills how much treasure!—more than you see in your dreams. Yet in spite of such blessings the nation is still orphaned, still ragged, still starving, near to destruction. . . . O my country, when will you awake?' That the tragic tone of this poem springs from deep personal involvement is made even clearer by *I am a Hungarian* (*Magyar vagyok*) (February 1847): 'I am a Hungarian. My country is the loveliest land in the great expanse of the five continents. It is a little world in itself; the beauties in its rich

[1] Horváth.

bosom are past counting. It is crowned by peaks which cast their gaze beyond the waters of the Caspian, and its plains stretch so far, so far, as if they were searching for the end of the earth.'

I am a Hungarian. I am serious by nature, like the deepest sounds of our violins; now and then a smile rises to my lips, but my laughter is rarely to be heard. When joy most colours my countenance, in my high spirits I burst into tears; but my face is gay in time of grief, because I do not wish to be pitied.[1]

The poet now proceeds to contrast the pride with which he looks out over 'the sea of the past' and the dismal present, in a manner reminiscent of *Zalán*[2] and the poets of the previous generation; but he ends with the positive affirmation that 'for no treasure, no fame in the world, would I abandon the land of my birth, because I love, fervently love, adore my nation even in her shame'.

His love for the natural beauties of his country, expressed both in *The Hungarian Nation* of 1846 and in *I am a Hungarian*, also inspired about the same time the poem on the river Tisza which ranks second only to *The Lowlands* among his landscapes, with the addition of a dramatic element absent from the earlier poem:

The Tisza[3]

At sunset on a summer's day I stopped by the winding Tisza, where the little Túr rushes into it[4] like a child on to its mother's lap.

The river glided on, so smoothly, so gently in its bed, edged by no banks; it did not wish the rays of the sun to stumble in the ripples of its waters.

[1] The original of the second stanza is as follows:

Magyar vagyok. Természetem komoly,
Mint hegedűink első hangjai; 10
Ajkamra fel-felröppen a mosoly,
De nevetésem ritkán hallani.

Ha az öröm legjobban festi képem,
Magas kedvemben sírva fakadok;
De arcom víg a bánat idejében, 15
Mert nem akarom, hogy sajnáljatok.

[2] See pp. 103 ff.

[3]   *A Tisza*

Nyári napnak alkonyúlatánál
Megállék a kanyargó Tiszánál
Ott, hol a kis Túr siet beléje,
Mint a gyermek anyja kebelére.

A folyó oly símán, oly szelíden 5
Ballagott le parttalan medrében,
Nem akarta, hogy a nap sugára
Megbotoljék habjai fodrába'.

[4] In north-east Hungary.

The red rays danced on the smooth mirror of its surface like so many fairies; the ringing of their steps almost sounded, like the jingle of tiny spurs.

Where I stood, a yellow carpet of sand was spread out; it stretched as far as the fields, where the cut swathes lay, like the lines in a book.

Beyond the meadow stood a lofty forest in silent dignity; beneath the trees, it was already dark, but the twilight cast embers over them— they seemed to be ablaze, their blood flowing.

In another direction, on the further bank of the Tisza, grew brightly coloured hazel and furze-bushes; among them there was just one opening, through which you could see in the distance the church tower of a little village.

As a fair memory of happy hours, rose clouds floated through the heavens. From the furthest distance the peaks of Mármaros[1] looked at me thoughtfully through the mist.

No noise. Just now and then a bird whistled into the solemn silence. Far, far away the whirring of the mill was no louder than the buzzing of a mosquito.

On the other side, straight opposite me, a young peasant's wife came, with a pitcher in her hand. As she dipped her pitcher in the river and filled it, she looked across at me, then she went hurriedly on her way.

I stood there silent, motionless, as if my legs had taken root. My soul collapsed, reeling, into sweet, deep intoxication before the eternal beauty of Nature.

Síma tükrén a piros sugárok
(Mint megannyi tündér) táncot jártak, 10
Szinte hallott lépteik csengése,
Mint parányi sarkantyúk pengése.

Ahol álltam, sárga föveny-szőnyeg
Volt terítve, s tartott a mezőnek,
Melyen a levágott sarjú-rendek, 15
Mint a könyvben a sorok, hevertek.

Túl a réten néma méltóságban
Magas erdő; benne már homály van,
De az alkony üszköt vet fejére,
S olyan, mintha égne s folyna vére. 20

Másfelől, a Tisza túlsó partján,
Mogyoró- s rekettye-bokrok tarkán,
Köztök egy csak a nyílás, azon át
Látni távol kis falucska tornyát.

Boldog órák szép emlékeképen 25
Rózsafelhők úsztak át az égen.
Legmesszebbről rám merengve néztek
Ködön át a mármarosi bércek.

Semmi zaj. Az ünnepélyes csendbe
Egy madár csak néha füttyentett be. 30
Nagy távolban a malom zugása
Csak olyan volt, mint szúnyog dongása.

Túlnan, vélem átellenben épen,
Pór menyecske jött. Korsó kezében.
Korsaját mig telemerítette, 35
Rám nézett át; aztán ment sietve.

Ottan némán, mozdulatlan álltam,
Mintha gyökeret vert volna lábam.
Lelkem édes, mély mámorba szédült
A természet örök szépségétül. 40

[1] Now Maramureş, in Rumania.

O Nature, O glorious Nature! What tongue might dare to rival thee?
How great art thou! The more thou remainest silent, the more, the
fairer are thy words.

Late at night I reached the farm for supper—fresh fruit. We talked at
length, my friends and I; the fire of twigs blazed beside us.

Among other things I said to them: 'Poor Tisza, why do you all
malign it? You shout so much evil about it, and it is the meekest river
on earth.'

Two days later the tolling of the bell roused me from my dozing.
'The flood is coming! the flood is coming!' it rang. And I saw a sea when
I looked out.

Like a madman who has torn off his chains, the Tisza galloped over
the plain. Roaring, bellowing, it burst through the dam, it wanted to
swallow up the world! (February 1847)

These natural beauties were an essential part of the country
which the poet must now help to achieve liberty. This liberty was
one of the two main sources of inspiration which he noted in a
short poem written on 1 January 1847:

Liberty, Love![1]

Liberty, Love! These two I need. For my love I will sacrifice life, for
liberty I will sacrifice my love.

6

'If (as I fear) his unlimited freedom means more to him than
my love', wrote Julia to a friend on 1 May 1847, 'then we shall

Oh természet, oh dicső természet!
Mely nyelv merne versenyezni véled?
Mily nagy vagy te! mentül inkább
    hallgatsz,
Annál többet, annál szebbet mondasz.-

Késő éjjel értem a tanyára   45
Friss gyümölcsből készült vacsorára.
Társaimmal hosszan beszélgettünk.
Lobogott a rőzseláng mellettünk.

Többek között szóltam én hozzájok:
'Szegény Tisza, miért is bántjátok? 50
Annyi rosszat kiabáltok róla,
S ő a föld legjámborabb folyója.'

Pár nap mulva fél szendergésemből
Félrevert harang zugása vert föl.

'Jön az árvíz! jön az árvíz!' hangzék, 55
S tengert láttam, ahogy kitekinték.

Mint az őrült, ki letépte láncát,
Vágtatott a Tisza a rónán át,
Zúgva, bőgve törte át a gátot,
El akarta nyelni a világot!   60

    1   *Szabadság, szerelem!*

Szabadság, szerelem!
E kettő kell nekem.
Szerelmemért föláldozom
Az életet,
Szabadságért föláldozom
Szerelmemet.

part for ever'; and she was right to connect Petőfi's political creed with his lifelong refusal to accept restrictions on his own personal freedom.[1] This time, however, freedom did not come first.

The bush trembles . . .[2]

The bush trembles, because a little bird has alighted on it. My soul trembles, because I have thought of you, I have thought of you, little love, the greatest diamond in the great world!

The Danube is high, perhaps it is even bursting its banks. My heart can scarce contain its feelings. Do you love me, my rose? I love you, your father and mother cannot love you more.

When we were together, I know, you loved me. Then it was warm summer; now it is winter, cold winter. If you do not love me any more, God bless you; but if you still love me, may He bless you a thousand times! (November 1846)

Julia read these lines (in print) in January 1847, at a time when mutual misunderstandings and the opposition of her parents seemed decisive; and the poem surprised her as much as the news that his feelings were reciprocated surprised the poet. Then in May, finally reassured by a friend of Julia's, Petőfi asked Szendrey for his daughter's hand. 'The dust on the road flies, the ground re-echoes, the maddened steed gallops with a poor rider . . . I love my rose. . . . I asked your father for you, I asked in vain' (*The dust on the road flies . . .*) (*Röpül az úti por . . .*) (May 1847). Szendrey fought every inch of the way; finally, though he stopped short of forbidding his daughter to marry the poet, he boycotted the engagement and the wedding, which took place on 8 September 1847, the

[1] Cf. *My First Oath* (*Első eskü*) (April 1847).

[2] *Reszket a bokor, mert . . .*

Reszket a bokor, mert
Madárka szállott rá.
Reszket a lelkem, mert
Eszembe jutottál,
Eszembe jutottál, 5
Kicsiny kis leányka,
Te a nagy világnak
Legnagyobb gyémántja!

Teli van a Duna,
Tán még ki is szalad. 10
Szívemben is alig
Fér meg az indulat.

Szeretsz, rózsaszálam?
Én ugyan szeretlek,
Apád-anyád nálam 15
Jobban nem szerethet.

Mikor együtt voltunk,
Tudom, hogy szerettél.
Akkor meleg nyár volt,
Most tél van, hideg tél. 20
Hogyha már nem szeretsz,
Az isten áldjon meg,
De ha még szeretsz, úgy
Ezerszer áldjon meg!

anniversary of their first meeting. A month later Petőfi described their departure on their honeymoon, in *That was the great, great task . . . (Az volt a nagy, nagy munka . . .)* (October 1847): 'That was the great, great task, darling wife, before you were mine, before I could come away with you. . . . True, such a girl does not grow on every bush, and my goodness, a poet, a poet in rags for a son-in-law! . . . The wheel of our carriage broke on the road, but I don't think it was broken by the great weight of the blessing with which my father- and mother-in-law sent me off. But at this I am indeed surprised, even now, that I came out throught he door and not the window.'

'In one smile of yours, there is more poetry, my darling, than in all the five hundred and fifty poems I have written' said Petőfi in *I am thought a good poet . . . (Jó költőnek tartanak . . .)* (August 1847) and with his marriage came a new source of inspiration. As he expressed in his poetry his affection for his parents, so his spontaneity disregarded the convention which has made married happiness so rare a subject for poets, though a Hungarian poet had a precedent in the *Happy Love* of *Kisfaludy Sándor's *Himfy*:[1]

Rosebush on the hillside . . .[2]

Rosebush on the hillside, fall on my shoulder, my angel, whisper in my ear that you love me! O how happy that makes me!

Down in the Danube is the image of the sun, the river trembles in its joy, it cradles the sun quietly, just as I cradle you, my love.

Of what do evil men not accuse me, saying that I deny God! Yet even now I am praying... I hear the beating of your heart. (November 1847)

This ecstasy was punctuated by one dramatic premonition (or rather prophecy[3] of tragedy:

[1] See p. xxii.

[2] *Rózsabokor a domboldalon . . .*

Rózsabokor a domboldalon,
Borúlj a vállamra, angyalom,
Súgjad a fülembe, hogy szeretsz,
Hej, milyen jólesik nekem ez!

Lenn a Dunában a nap képe,   5
Reszket a folyó örömébe',

Ringatja a napot csendesen,
Épen mint én téged, kedvesem.

Mit nem fognak rám a gonoszok,
Hogy én istentagadó vagyok!   10
Pedig mostan is imádkozom . . .
Szíved dobogását hallgatom.

[3] Julia remarried in July 1850, a few days under a year after her husband's death.

At the end of September[1]

The garden flowers in the valley are still blooming, the poplar in front of the window is still green, but do you see the wintry world over there? Snow has already covered the mountain peak. In my young heart the flaming rays of summer still burn and the whole of spring is still in flower, but see! my dark hair is mingled with grey autumn, the frost of winter has already touched my head.

The flower falls, life flies past. . . . Come here, my love, come here and sit on my lap! You who now have placed your head on my shoulder, to-morrow will you not throw yourself down over my grave? O tell me, if I die first, will you weep as you draw the shroud over my body? And can a young man's love ever persuade you to abandon my name?

If one day you throw away the widow's veil, hang it as a dark banner over the cross of my grave; I will come up for it from the land of the tomb, at midnight, and will take it down there to wipe away my tears for you, who light-heartedly forgot your faithful one, and to bind up the wounds of this heart, which loves you for ever, even there, even then!
(September 1847)

But spontaneity also means variety:

My sweetheart's a stubborn little girl, and I too don't bow my head at every word; our blood is a fiery brook, but still we get on, somehow.
(*Somehow*) (*Valahogy*) (August 1847)[2]

Another stanza of the same poem, on the poet's poverty, ends: 'Trouble, trouble! but not so very much trouble, still we live,

---

[1] *Szeptember végén*

Még nyílnak a völgyben a kerti virágok,
Még zöldel a nyárfa az ablak előtt,
De látod amottan a téli világot?
Már hó takará el a bérci tetőt.
Még ifju szivemben a lángsugarú nyár
S még benne virít az egész kikelet, 6
De íme sötét hajam őszbe vegyül már,
A tél dere már megüté fejemet.

Elhull a virág, eliramlik az élet . . .
Ülj, hitvesem, űlj az ölembe ide! 10
Ki most fejedet kebelemre tevéd le,
Holnap nem omolsz-e sirom fölibe?
Oh mondd: ha előbb halok el, tetemimre
Könnyezve borítasz-e szemfödelet?
S rábírhat-e majdan egy ifju
    szerelme, 15
Hogy elhagyod érte az én nevemet?

Ha eldobod egykor az özvegyi fátyolt,
Fejfámra sötét lobogóul akaszd,
Én feljövök érte a síri világból
Az éj közepén, s oda leviszem azt, 20
Letörleni véle könyűimet érted,
Ki könnyeden elfeledéd hivedet,
S e szív sebeit bekötözni, ki téged
Még akkor is, ott is, örökre szeret!

[2] Menyasszonyom akaratos 15
    Kisleány,
Én sem hajtok fejet minden
    Szó után,
Tüzes patak a mi vérünk,
Hanem azért csak megférünk 20
    Valahogy.

somehow.' Petőfi's main source of income was the royalties from the edition of his complete works (dedicated to Vörösmarty) which had appeared in March, and sold out almost at once; this success was a landmark in his career. In the preface to this edition, dated 1 January 1847, Petőfi's twenty-fourth birthday, the day on which he attained his majority, he described himself as 'the faithful child of my century', and this January he also wrote the poem which best sums up his artistic creed. It is entitled, significantly, *The Poets of the 19th Century*:

The Poets of the 19th Century[1]

Let no one thoughtlessly touch the strings of the lyre! He undertakes a great task who now takes the instrument into his hands. If you can do nothing but sing of your own joys and sorrows, the world has no need of you; so lay aside the sacred lute.

We wander in the wilderness as Moses once wandered with his people; he followed the pillar of fire which God sent to guide him. In later days, God has appointed poets to be just such a pillar of fire, that they may lead the people towards Canaan.

Onward then, whosoever is a poet, with the people through fire and water! A curse on him who flings away the banner of the people from his hand; a curse on him who through cowardice or sloth hangs back to rest beneath the shade while the people struggles, toils, sweats!

False prophets there be, who most wickedly proclaim that here we may halt, for here is the Promised Land. A lie, a shameless lie, which millions refute who drag out their lives despairing in the heat of the sun, hungry and thirsty.

[1] *A XIX. század költői*

Ne fogjon senki könnyelműen
A húrok pengetésihez!
Nagy munkát vállal az magára,
Ki most kezébe lantot vesz.
Ha nem tudsz mást, mint eldalolni 5
Saját fájdalmad s örömed:
Nincs rád szüksége a világnak,
S azért a szent fát félretedd.

Pusztában bujdosunk, mint hajdan
Népével Mózes bujdosott, 10
S követte, melyet isten külde
Vezérül, a lángoszlopot.
Újabb időkben isten ilyen
Lángoszlopoknak rendelé
A költőket, hogy ők vezessék 15
A népet Kánaán felé.

Előre hát mind, aki költő,
A néppel tűzön-vízen át!
Átok reá, ki elhajítja
Kezéből a nép zászlaját, 20
Átok reá, ki gyávaságból
Vagy lomhaságból elmarad,
Hogy, míg a nép küzd, fárad, izzad,
Pihenjen ő árnyék alatt!

Vannak hamis próféták, akik 25
Azt hirdetik nagy gonoszan,
Hogy már megállhatunk, mert itten
Az ígéretnek földe van.
Hazugság, szemtelen hazugság,
Mit milliók cáfolnak meg, 30
Kik nap hevében, éhen-szomjan,
Kétségbeesve tengenek.

When all alike can draw on the basket of plenty, when all alike take their place at the table of justice, when the sunlight of the spirit shines through the window of every house, then we can say, 'let us halt, for here now is Canaan!'

And till then? Till then there is no rest, till then we must continually struggle. Perhaps life will pay us no reward for our toil, but Death will close our eyes with a tender, gentle kiss and will send us down to the depths of the earth with garlands of flowers on a pillow of silk.

Again, 'the true poet is he who lets fall his heavenly manna on to the lips of the people' (*To *Arany János*) (*Arany Jánoshoz*) (February 1847). But this prophet is not addressing the people from outside. Not only does the voice warn the nobles 'in the name of the people'[1] that the flames which consumed *Dózsa's body did not overcome his spirit, and that his spirit, being fire, will consume his enemies, but the hand is ready for action: 'in my breast slumber so many songs, the seeds of a whole forest, which will give cool shade to many a traveller. So far I have only written: where are deeds?' (*The old woe has returned . . .*) (*Újonnan visszajött a régi baj . . .*) (March 1847).[2] And the time for action is drawing nearer: in *The sad wind of autumn talks with the trees . . .* (*Beszél a fákkal a bús őszi szél*) (September 1847) the poet holds in one hand the history of wars of freedom which he is reading, and each successive stanza brings nearer the day when the foes of freedom shall be destroyed—a graphic contrast to the picture of the poet's wife sleeping 'deeply, quietly' on his other shoulder, as we see her in the refrain which remains unchanged through the whole poem.

But Petőfi knew also how to 'touch the strings of the lyre' lightly, even in a poem with a political point:

Ha majd a bőség kosarából
Mindenki egyaránt vehet,
Ha majd a jognak asztalánál 35
Mind egyaránt foglal helyet,
Ha majd a szellem napvilága
Ragyog minden ház ablakán:
Akkor mondhatjuk, hogy megálljunk,
Mert itt van már a Kánaán! 40

És addig? addig nincs megnyugvás,
Addig folyvást küszködni kell. —
Talán az élet, munkáinkért,
Nem fog fizetni semmivel,
De a halál majd szemeinket 45
Szelíd, lágy csókkal zárja be,
S virágkötéllel, selyempárnán
Bocsát le a föld mélyibe.

[1] *In the Name of the People* (*A nép nevében*) (March 1847).
[2] The 'old woe' is the 'envoy from the other world', the awareness of approaching death. The poet longs to die gloriously, even if the poems in his mind remain unwritten.

There's a little inn at the end of the village ...[1]

There's a little inn at the end of the village, it juts out there on to the river Szamos,[2] and it would see itself in the water, if night were not drawing near.

Night draws near, the world grows quiet, the ferry is at rest—it has been moored, the darkness there makes no sound.

But the inn makes plenty of sound! The cimbalom-player is at work, the boys are shouting, the window nearly caves in.

'Bring us your best wine, dear'[3] they say to the innkeeper's wife, 'let it be as old as my grandfather, as fiery as my young sweetheart.

'Play, gipsy, play more, I feel like dancing. I'll dance my money away, I'll dance my soul out of me!'

There is a knock on the window: 'Don't make such a noise. This is a message from his lordship: he's gone to bed and wants to sleep.'

'Devil take your lordship, and you go to hell! Play, gipsy, play, never mind if it costs me my shirt, here and now!'

They come again, and knock: 'Make it quieter, God bless you all, my poor mother's ill.'

Not one of the boys replies; they sip up their drinks, stop the music and go home. (August 1847)

[1]   *Falu végén kurta kocsma ...*

Falu végén kurta kocsma,
Oda rúg ki a Szamosra,
Meg is látná magát benne,
Ha az éj nem közelegne.

Az éjszaka közeledik,   5
A világ lecsendesedik,
Pihen a komp, kikötötték,
Benne hallgat a sötétség.

De a kocsma bezzeg hangos!
Munkálkódik a cimbalmos,   10
A legények kurjogatnak,
Szinte reng belé az ablak.

'Kocsmárosné, aranyvirág,
Ide a legjobbik borát,
Vén legyen, mint a nagyapám,   15
És tüzes, mint ifju babám!

Húzd rá cigány, húzzad jobban,
Táncolni való kedvem van,

Eltáncolom a pénzemet,
Kitáncolom a lelkemet!'   20

Bekopognak az ablakon:
'Ne zúgjatok olyan nagyon,
Azt üzeni az uraság,
Mert lefeküdt, alunni vágy.'

'Ördög bújjék az uradba,   25
Te pedig menj a pokolba! ...
Húzd rá, cigány, csak azért is,
Ha mindjárt az ingemért is!'

Megint jőnek, kopogtatnak:
'Csendesebben vigadjanak,   30
Isten áldja meg kendteket,
Szegény édesanyám beteg.'

Feleletet egyik sem ad,
Kihörpentik boraikat,
Végét vetik a zenének   35
S haza mennek a legények.

[2] A tributary of the Tisza, into which it flows in north-eastern Hungary.
[3] Literally 'flower of gold'.

Yet when Petőfi wrote short stories in prose, the result was heavily didactic. *The Grandfather* (*A nagyapa*) (January 1847), describing the persecution (and its punishment) by a wicked young lord of the lover of a girl on whom he had designs, and *The White Girl and the Chestnut Boy* (*A fakó leány s a pej legény*) (April 1847), illustrating the evils of drunkenness and the cruelty of ostracizing people with physical peculiarities, are in the last resort informed by the same humanity which inspired *There's an inn at the end of the village*; but for Petőfi's prose at its best we must go elsewhere—in fact to the twenty *Traveller's Letters* (*Úti levelek*), which cover the period May–November 1847. These, though sometimes rather obviously written for publication, are entertaining even apart from the special interest attaching to the autobiographical reminiscences[1] and to Petőfi's opinions of other writers, foreign as well as Hungarian: his unbounded admiration for Béranger, the 'greatest apostle of freedom', the 'first poet of the world' (VI), and his dislike of Goethe, especially the 'stupid' Werther (IX).

Of the 160 poems Petőfi wrote in 1847, two are extended narratives. *Szécsi Mária* (August) is an accomplished piece of work—faint praise for Petőfi; the problem presented by the undeniable treachery of the heroine's surrender is solved by showing her as realizing that war is not for women, that a woman can only act the part of a gallant warrior. But *Mad Istók* (*Bolond Istók*) (November–December), a story of a favourite figure of Hungarian folk-lore, is another matter.

It opens with a dramatic monologue by someone in terror at the approach of his enemy. Only in stanza 6 do we learn that the enemy is a rainstorm, only in stanza 13 do we learn that the unfortunate traveller is a philosopher:

The rain can soak all my clothes and strip me; but one thing it cannot strip off, philosophy.[2]

In stanza 24 we learn this philosopher's name, Mad Istók; but he is not so mad, he tells us, as to sleep out in the open on a night like this. 'There is a farm, I will go in.... The chimney is smoking,

---

[1] Cf. p. 229.
[2] Leáztathat rólam
Az eső minden ruhát,
De nem áztathat le egyet, a
Filozófiát. (13)

ergo, there is a fire in the kitchen, *ergo*, I shall warm myself, indeed I may get some dinner. What fortune, what bliss, that I learnt logic . . . long live schools!' (24, 26–7).

The owner of the house receives him hospitably, and a splendid dinner is produced; but Istók's attempts to flavour it with the 'salt of conversation' meet with no response. 'When the tree of your life is beginning to fall,' replies his host, 'and you cannot even say that the bird of happiness once rested on its branches, or sang one song, but torments hang there like men on a gallows, then say what the world is like' (75–76). Not only has his loved one died 'pelted by the mud of slander', but of his three sons he has lost two and is estranged from the third. With much hesitation, Istók rebukes him: despair is the greatest of sins, 'the darkest atheism' (91). The old man drank in the philosopher's discourse 'as a child drinks its mother's milk' (99), and on the following morning, when Istók bade his last farewell, his host asked him to stay on, indefinitely. Istók had just before predicted happiness for the old man, and his prophecy is immediately fulfilled by the arrival of a girl who announces herself as the old man's granddaughter, and begs him to protect her from her father who is forcing her to marry against her will. So when the father comes to fetch his daughter (whom he had forbidden to visit her grandfather) the old man bars his way 'like a column of ice in the Arctic Sea' (142). Now, and again later, Istók takes his leave, but eventually 'he was not so mad as to leave the place where he was so much loved' (170); at the close of the poem

> The young wife spins and sings: her grandfather and husband play with the two boys.—Outside, the winter storm howls . . . there indoors, the spinning-wheel whirls round and the song gaily rings out . . .[1]

Mad Istók glows with the poet's own happiness, and he effortlessly escapes the dangers latent in his story—he avoids being pretentious, by writing in a popular style: avoids being sententious, by making his philosopher a figure of fun, in exactly the right measure, at the outset: also avoids being monotonous, by the irregularity and variety of his verse-forms. If parts of the poem

---

[1] A menyecske fon s dalol: nagyapja
S férje játszik a két fiuval. —
Kinn süvít a tél viharja . . . ott benn
Perg a rokka s vígan zeng a dal . . . — (179)

now seem sentimental, that is just the difference between the nineteenth century and the twentieth.

7

'At last they have grown tired of crawling on the ground . . . help them, God of freedom!' With his poem *Italy* (*Olaszország*) (January 1848) Petőfi greeted the news of the outbreak of revolution in Sicily and its extension to 'the land which Tarquin fled, on which Caesar fell dying'; 'that great, fair age towards which my hopes soar draws nearer, nearer . . . tyranny shall perish.' Louis-Philippe fell in February; on 13 March revolution broke out in Vienna itself, and Petőfi wrote his *National Song*:

National Song[1]

Up, Hungarian, your country is calling! Here is the time, now or never! Shall we be slaves or free? This is the question, answer!—By the God of the Hungarians we swear, we swear to be slaves no more!

Till now we have been slaves, our forebears are damned—they, who lived and died in freedom, cannot rest in enslaved ground. By the God of the Hungarians we swear, we swear to be slaves no more!

A vile vagabond is he who now dare not die if need be, to whom his life of rags is dearer than his country's honour. By the God of the Hungarians we swear, we swear to be slaves no more!

The sword shines more brightly than the chain, adorns the arm more nobly, yet we wear chains! Hither, ancient sword of ours! By the God of the Hungarians we swear, we swear to be slaves no more!

[1] *Nemzeti dal*

Talpra magyar, hí a haza!
Itt az idő, most vagy soha!
Rabok legyünk, vagy szabadok?
Ez a kérdés, válasszatok! —
A magyarok istenére   5
Esküszünk,
Esküszünk, hogy rabok tovább
Nem leszünk!

Rabok voltunk mostanáig,
Kárhozottak ősapáink,   10
Kik szabadon éltek-haltak,
Szolgaföldben nem nyughatnak.
A magyarok istenére
Esküszünk,
Esküszünk, hogy rabok tovább   15
Nem leszünk!

Sehonnai bitang ember,
Ki most, ha kell, halni nem mer,
Kinek drágább rongy élete,
Mint a haza becsülete.   20
A magyarok istenére
Esküszünk,
Esküszünk, hogy rabok tovább
Nem leszünk!

Fényesebb a láncnál a kard,   25
Jobban ékesíti a kart,
És mi mégis láncot hordunk!
Ide veled, régi kardunk!
A magyarok istenére
Esküszünk,   30
Esküszünk, hogy rabok tovább
Nem leszünk!

The name of Hungarian shall again be fair, worthy of its ancient great fame; let us wash away the dishonour with which the centuries have stained it! By the God of the Hungarians we swear, we swear to be slaves no more!

Where our gravestones stand, our grandchildren will fall down and pronounce our sacred names as they pray and bless us. By the God of the Hungarians we swear, we swear to be slaves no more!

The *National Song* had originally been written for a 'reform banquet', on the French model, to be held on 19 March, but now events moved more quickly. 'Logically', wrote Petőfi in his diary, recalling his thoughts on the evening of the 14th, 'to free the Press is the first step, and at the same time the principal obligation of revolution . . . that we shall do! The rest I commit to God and to those who are appointed to continue what has been begun.' So on 15 March the *Song* was recited by the poet to cheering crowds of demonstrators, and printed as the first production of the free Press which those demonstrations had peacefully won; Petőfi became a national hero. Not only the Hungarian people, but all peoples had risen up:

The sea is risen . . .[1]

The sea is risen, the sea of the peoples; terrifying heaven and earth, its dread might casts up wild waves.

Do you see this dance, all of you? Do you hear this music? You who before knew not, now you may learn how the people takes its pleasure.

The sea quakes and howls, ships are storm-tossed, they sink to hell, the mast and sails hang broken and torn.

A magyar név megint szép lesz,
Méltó régi nagy hiréhez;
Mit rákentek a századok,   35
Lemossuk a gyalázatot!
A magyarok istenére
Esküszünk,
Esküszünk, hogy rabok tovább
Nem leszünk!   40

Hol sírjaink domborulnak,
Unokáink leborulnak,
És áldó imádság mellett
Mondják el szent neveinket.
A magyarok istenére   45
Esküszünk,
Esküszünk, hogy rabok tovább
Nem leszünk!

[1]   *Föltámadott a tenger . . .*

Föltámadott a tenger,
A népek tengere;
Ijesztve eget-földet,
Szilaj hullámokat vet
Rémítő ereje.   5

Látjátok ezt a táncot?
Halljátok e zenét?
Akik még nem tudtátok,
Most megtanulhatjátok,
Hogyan mulat a nép.   10

Reng és üvölt a tenger,
Hánykódnak a hajók,
Sűlyednek a pokolra,
Az árboc és vitorla
Megtörve, tépve lóg.   15

Burst forth, flood, burst forth in all your fury, reveal the depths of your bed, and fling to the clouds your frenzied foam!

Write with it on the heavens, as an eternal lesson: though the galley is on top, and the flood of the water is below, nevertheless the water is master! (27–30 March 1848)

As Petőfi was writing *The sea is risen*, a rumour spread that the King was refusing to ratify the appointments to the portfolios of Finance and Defence in the new Hungarian Government; the poet who had exclaimed 'Vive la République' when the news of the fall of Louis-Philippe reached him, now let loose a flood of attacks not on an abstract Tyranny or on the nobility, but on the Throne. As early as 1844 he had addressed Ferdinand V in tones of derisive pity (*To Ferdinand V*) (*V. Ferdinándhoz*) and spoken out *Against Kings* (*A királyok ellen*) in a poem which referred to kings as the dolls with which it was natural for the human race to play in its childhood; but now the storm, of which the blade that severed the head of Louis XVI had been the first flash, would show that 'the world is now no child, but a man!' These poems had of course remained unpublished; but now that Petőfi could express himself freely (*Against Kings* first appeared in print in October 1848) he denounced monarchy both in frenzied frontal attacks and in poems on individual, wicked kings like László V, who treacherously executed *Hunyadi László (*The King's Oath*) (*A király esküje*) (May 1848) or on weak ones like *Ulászló II, whose nickname is the title of *Dobzse László* (June). The former of these poems illustrates particularly well the extreme of passion to which Petőfi's anti-monarchic feelings had risen—he cannot rest content with relating the story, but goes on to tell us what he would have said had he been present. To the young intellectuals the *April Laws were only a beginning, and Petőfi adhered unswervingly to his republicanism, with feelings intensified by his reading of Lamartine, Louis Blanc, and Shelley, and with the Coriolanus in his temperament further hardened by the work of translating Shakespeare's play. So his poem *To Kings* (*A királyokhoz*) (27–30 March), with its refrain 'Whatever shameless flattery says,

Tombold ki, te özönvíz,		Jegyezd vele az égre
Tombold ki magadat,		Örök tanúságúl:
Mutasd mélységes medred,		Habár fölűl a gálya,
S dobáld a fellegekre		S alúl a víznek árja,
Bőszült tajtékodat;	20	Azért a víz az úr!	25

no longer is there any *beloved* king',[1] deeply shocked a wide range of opinion; and when the assumption of office by the *Batthyány Government and the ratification of the *April Laws raised hopes of a peaceful solution, Petőfi's radicalism and attacks on the Government cost him all or nearly all the popularity he had won on 15 March. When in June he offered himself as a candidate for the Diet in his native constituency, his candidature was successfully prevented, and on at least one occasion his personal safety endangered, by a campaign of vilification so unscrupulous that an inquiry was instituted, though nothing came of this, because of the Serbian invasion of southern Hungary. About this time he began his last and longest narrative poem, *The Apostle (Az apostol)* (June–September 1848).

'Dark is the city, night lies on it', begins the poem; then we are taken to a garret where the father of a starving family, when his loved ones have gone to bed, stays up and resolves to serve the whole of humanity: 'he who before belonged to his family, now belongs to the world' (III. 10 f.).[2]

The poet now shows us the earlier life of his hero. As a baby he was left by his mother in a cab and discovered by a lord and lady, who passed him on to the coachman with the words: 'Here is your tip, in your cab, a lovely little baby'. 'Why were you not born a dog?' continues Petőfi, addressing his hero. 'Then you would have been brought up in this lady's lap, ... but because you were a man and not a dog, God knows what fate will be yours' (v. 66 ff.). The coachman deposits the foundling on the doorstep of an inn, and he is adopted first by a drunken thief who brings him up to steal, then (when this foster-father has been hanged) by an old beggar-woman who brings him up to beg; then by a 'surly lord'. The boy's name, given him by his first foster-father, is Szilveszter.

Szilveszter's position in the household of the lord is that of a servant, and he has to endure all the bullying inflicted on him by his young master, the lord's son; only the prospect of receiving an education, not the good food and clothing, restrains him from following his instinctive desire for freedom and leaving. In ability he far surpasses his young master, and their tutor often puts the lord's son to shame by unfavourable comparisons with the foundling, which only aggravates the bullying. This treatment combines

---

[1] Italics in original.
[2] References are to canto and line.

with his education to awaken Szilveszter's democratic consciousness—'"Did God create one man another's superior? ... I will
endure it no more"' (IX. 150–5)—and he leaves the lord's castle,
regardless of the consequences. His tutor goes after him with
a parting gift of money, and urges him to continue his studies:
'"you were not born for yourself, but for the country, for the
world"' (IX. 253 f.). 'This was the first time he [Szilveszter] had
ever met with affection' (IX. 271–2). He was then sixteen.

So Szilveszter goes out into the world, rejoicing in his new-
found freedom. The desire to serve his fellow men grows on him,
as he is struck by the contrast between the beauty of Nature and
human misery; he reads world history, and becomes convinced that
he is 'a ray which helps the earth to ripen' (XI. 94 f.). His conspicuous moral and intellectual stature brings him many attractive
offers of posts from lords; but he rejects them all, choosing instead
to follow the poor men who invite him to become their village
notary. He is loved in every home in the village—except the lord's
castle and the vicarage; but the lord's daughter falls in love with
him so deeply that when the lord and the priest turn the villagers
against him and he leaves for the capital, she follows him and they
live together as man and wife.

But the ease with which the villagers were incited to hatred
against him has not affected his sense of his mission: ' "It will be
different; the people is still a child, easily to be deluded; but it
will grow to maturity, will reach man's estate. Just because it is a
child, it must be tended"' (XIII. 83 ff.). Szilveszter writes a book, but
when he submits it for publication to an editor, the latter replies
' "You are a great man, and also a great fool! ... Have you never
heard of the censorship?"' (XIV. 31 ff.). Szilveszter will not abandon
his principles, even now; but he must live, so he 'copies out the
thoughts of others' (XIV. 107 f.), as Petőfi had done at Pozsony in
1843. In due course two children are born to him; it is at this point
in his life that we saw him at the opening of the poem. But he
cannot support this family, and his younger child dies of starvation
in infancy.

Discovering a clandestine press, he has his works printed there;
they 'cannot die in his head' (XVI. 2). 'What was in these works?
That priests are not men, but devils, and kings are not gods, but
only men; that every man is equally a man, and that it is not only
man's right but his duty to his Creator to be free; for he who

esteems not God's fairest gift, esteems not God Himself!' (XVI. 13–25). 'The thirsty world greedily swallowed this pure, soothing drink . . . but power grew pale' (XVI. 29 ff.) with anger, and the author was arrested, his tearful pleas to be allowed to bid farewell to his family brutally rejected, and imprisoned for ten years. On his release he returns home, to learn that his wife has died of a broken heart—as he had dreamt in prison—and he cannot even trace her grave; his son has left home; he himself is remembered by the old woman whom he questions as a 'godless criminal' (XIX. 31). Then comes the worst blow of all; he finds that while he has been in prison 'human dignity has daily shrunk like a dwarf, tyranny waxed like a giant' (XIX. 92 f.) not only in his country, but in the whole world. He tries to assassinate the king, unsuccessfully, and ends his life on the gallows.

Like *Mad Istók*, *The Apostle* accurately reflects Petőfi's state of mind at the time of its composition. Now, however, we have an idealism whose ultimate nobility is almost totally obscured by the bitterness and uncontrolled vehemence with which it is expressed. The vehemence shows itself in a concern to omit no harrowing detail—in which the poet indeed sometimes overreaches himself; the lack of control, in a desire to infuse the maximum of emotional content into individual episodes, sometimes with little regard for the whole. Not only is the opening in some respects inconsistent with the corresponding part of the main narrative; Petőfi is unable to idealize Szilveszter's dedication to his mission without compromising the attempt to idealize also his devotion to his family.

The poem is not primarily autobiographical, though several passages are unmistakably autobiographical in origin, and the choice of the name Szilveszter, suggested to the foundling's foster-parents in the poem by the fact that they discovered him on New Year's Eve, was doubtless suggested to the poet by the fact that his own birthday was 1 January. In addition, the lord of the village where Szilveszter served as notary, and the lord's daughter, owe their existence to Szendrey and Julia, just as the villagers are recognizably the hostile electorate in Petőfi's constituency. In other respects, however, the Apostle is the Socialist *Táncsics rather than Petőfi. In the village-notary episode he owes something to Tengelyi[1] —for literature as well as life has contributed to his portrait, and foreign literature as well as Hungarian; the account of Szilveszter's

[1] See pp. 175 ff.

early life clearly shows the influence of *Oliver Twist*, and the description of his imprisonment is inspired by *The Prisoner of Chillon*, particularly the bird whose song cheers the prisoner:

Sing, sing, my little bird, sing! . . . From your song I see that I once lived, that even now I live; from your song come thoughts of my youth, the youth that has long, long ago flown past, this fair spring, and the flower of this spring, fair love! Your song arouses my sufferings, but at the same time it comforts me, and pain comforted is perhaps even sweeter than joy itself. Sing, sing, my little bird, sing![1]

The Apostle is international; the village may be unmistakably Hungarian, but we are nowhere told in which country the action takes place. World Freedom was Petőfi's ideal.

In spite of his fanaticism, however, the poet remained able to distinguish principles and persons. When in August Vörösmarty voted with the majority in favour of the proposal that existing Hungarian units should remain within the Austrian Army[2], Petőfi felt obliged to protest, but he began his poem *To Vörösmarty* (*Vörösmartyhoz*) (22 August 1848) with the words 'Shall I be silent, because I love you as my father? Shall I be silent, because my words will never pain you as they pain me?' So powerful was the magnifying glass of youthful ardour that Petőfi could see this incident as reducing the *Szózat*[3] to a 'hieroglyph', and could say, in the refrain of his poem, 'You yourself have torn the laurel from your brow, not I'; but he retained his affection and gratitude to Vörösmarty the man.

Already in July, the Serbs had attacked southern Hungary; and when in September *Jelačić crossed the Drave, the position of those who disbelieved in the possibility of any compromise with Vienna was strengthened, and to that extent Petőfi came into his own again. At the same time it was inevitable that one who had complained so consistently and conspicuously that 'Again we talk, nothing but talk'[4] should now be subjected to derisive pressure

[1] Dalolj, dalolj, kis madaram, dalolj!...
Eszembe jut dalodról,
Hogy egykor éltem, hogy még most
 is élek,
Eszembe jut dalodrul ifjuságom,
A régen régen elszállt ifjuság,   75
E szép tavasz, s ezen tavasznak

Virága, a szép szerelem!
Dalod fölkelti szenvedésimet,
De egyszersmind meg is vigasztal,
S a megvigasztalt fájdalom talán   80
Még édesebb, mint maga az öröm.
Dalolj, dalolj, kis madaram, dalolj!
    (XVIII. 71–82)

[2] See p. 155.   [3] See pp. 142 f.
[4] *Again we talk, nothing but talk* . . . (*Megint beszélünk s csak beszélünk* . . .)
April 1848).

to join up. 'Bullets whistle, swords rattle . . . and you, heroic poet, are still here at home . . . thus does the world fire at me its shafts of mockery. . . . I know very well where my place is.'[1] He volunteered without delay. Julia was expecting a baby in three months.

8

'The song flies forth of itself from our heart', wrote Petőfi in September in one of his replies to his detractors;[2] in such times this meant, inevitably, that most of his poems were political. Their direct connexion with particular events proves the poet's spontaneity as convincingly as do the Julia lyrics of 1846–7. Both the subjects and the treatment in many of the poems he wrote during the revolution often seem unpoetical; but Petőfi had precedents, from Batsányi's lines on the French Revolution[3] onwards, and his spontaneity, as always, made him the antithesis of the fastidious artist who will sing of only a limited range of themes. Besides, literary refinements would be out of place in a poem written, as was the *National Song*, for example, to inspire a large gathering to political action.

Nevertheless Petőfi himself sometimes felt that by concentrating his thoughts on the one subject, events were distorting his art.

Why do you follow . . .[4]

Why do you follow me everywhere, O love that toils to build my country? Why do you show me, day and night, your countenance clouded by care? Ever you are here, here with me; I see you even when I close my eyes.

＊

O let me forget that I am a citizen! Here is the spring, the earth blooms, the scent of the flowers and the song of the birds fill heaven and earth; golden clouds, those kindly spirits, float happily above my head.

---

[1] *Bullets whistle, swords rattle* . . . (*Golyók sivítnak, kardok csengenek* . . .) (September 1848).

[2] *Why are you still singing, pious poets?* . . .' (*Mit daloltok még ti, jámbor költők* . . .) (September 1848). [3] See p. xxi.

[4] *Miért kisérsz* . . .

Miért kisérsz mmden lépten-nyomon,
Te munkás hazaszeretet?
Éjjel-nappal mért mutatod nekem
Gonddal borított képedet?
Örökké itt vagy, itt vagy énvelem,　5
Úgy is látlak, ha behunyom szemem.

Oh hadd feledjem, hogy polgár vagyok!
Itt a tavasz, virít a föld,
Virágillat s a zengő madarak　　15
Dala eget-földet betölt,
Arany felhők, e nyájas szellemek,
Fejem fölött vidáman lengenek.

O let me forget that I am a citizen! The God of poetry is so gracious
to me; shall I fall into ingratitude to him? Shall I leave my lyre to lie
idle till its strings all but break through grief?
O let me forget that I am a citizen! I have my youth, my loved one;
youth and love offer me hours set in pearls, and every hour which I
have failed to take is eternal salvation squandered.
Ah how many fairies, all together: youth, spring, poetry, love! Shall
I let them fly from me? My hand, yearning, reaches towards them . . .
Come to me . . . stretch out your arms, embrace me, I am yours! (May
1848)

So the visionary yearning to die in the final battle for World
Freedom remembered also how he had watched, as a boy, his
'oldest friends', the storks, and the little ones trying their wings;[1]
the prophet who fulminated that Austria would perish like
Jerusalem[2] had not forgotten the games of his childhood;[3] the
republican soldier who proclaimed 'Hang the Kings!'[4] also sang
not only of spring, but of the beauties of autumn, when 'the rays of
the gentle sun look smiling on the earth as a loving mother looks
at her child falling asleep'—at the end of the poem Julia comes
to sit beside her husband: 'when you kiss me,' ends the poet,
'place your lips on my lips slowly; let us not awake Nature from
her slumbers.'[5] We can share, too, his delight when, just before
joining up, he 'stole' a day 'among the hills', leaving his cares 'in
the mist of the blue distance', amid the faraway noise of the city,
bringing with him only the things which give him happiness, his
love and his lyre.[6]

Oh hadd feledjem, hogy polgár
vagyok!
A költészetnek istene   20
Olyan kegyes hozzám; iránta én
Hálátlanságba essem-e?
Ott vesztegelni hagyjam lantomat,
Míg a bútól majd húrja szétszakad?

Oh hadd feledjem, hogy polgár
vagyok!   25
Van ifjuságom s kedvesem,
Gyöngyökbe foglalt órákkal kinál

Az ifjuság s a szerelem,
És minden óra, mit el nem vevék,
Egy elpazarlott örök üdvösség.   30

Hah, mennyi tündér együtt: ifjuság,
Tavasz, költészet, szerelem!
El hagyjam őket tőlem szállani?
Utánok vágyva nyúl kezem . . .
Jertek hozzám . . . nyujtsátok
karotok . . .   35
Öleljetek meg, tietek vagyok!

[1] *The Stork (A gólya)* (June 1847).
[2] *Austria (Ausztria)* (June 1848).
[3] *In my Homeland (Szülőföldemen)* (June 1848).
[4] *Hang the Kings! (Akasszátok föl a királyokat!)* (December 1848).
[5] *Here is Autumn, here again . . . (Itt van az ősz, itt van újra . . .)* (November
1848).   [6] *Among the Hills (A hegyek közt)* (September 1848).

Petőfi was commissioned, with the rank of captain, in October. But he was no ordinary officer, this democrat who on receiving his commission wrote a poem entitled *Honour the Common Soldiers!*,[1] this devoted husband who with little regard for the formalities of military administration remained in Debrecen with his wife to be by her side when she needed him, after his regiment had left that town.

A son was born to Petőfi in December, and a double tragedy only narrowly averted, at a time of 'Lost battles, shameful flights'.[2] True, *Jelačić was ignominiously driven out of Hungary (and the 'good old innkeeper' of 1845[3] was now an 'aged standard-bearer'[4] in that victorious Hungarian army); but elsewhere the picture was grim, and January 1849 saw 'Again a German flag on the fort of Buda';[5] Europe was 'quiet, quiet again'.[6] Petőfi's output in this period exhibits an astonishing range of mood, which he describes in *At the End of the Year* (*Az év végén*) (December 1848), addressing his lyre:

Be a storm, which in its rage tears up ancient oaks; be a breeze, which smilingly rocks into quiet sleep the blades of grass in the meadows.

Be a mirror, from which my whole, my whole life looks out on me, which has as its two fairest flowers mortal youth and immortal love.[7]

In January 1849 Petőfi applied to *Kossuth for transfer to the army of General *Bem in Transylvania—'at present, in my opinion,' he said in his letter, 'only at *Bem's side can a man stand without ignominy.' The request was granted, and the poet set out about the middle of the month; the Vörösmartys, and later the *Aranys, looked after Julia and her baby son. Petőfi became *Bem's aide-de-camp, and the Polish general's loyalty to Hungary inspired in the poet an almost filial devotion, which was returned in

---

[1] (*Tiszteljétek a közkatonákat!*) (October–November 1848).
[2] *Lost battles, shameful flights!* . . . (*Vesztett csaták, csufos futások!* . . .)
(December 1848).   [3] See p. 255.
[4] *Again a German flag on the fort of Buda!* . . . (*Buda várán újra német zászló!* . . .) (January 1849).
[5] *The Aged Standard-Bearer* (*A vén zászlótartó*) (October 1848).
[6] *Europe is quiet, quiet again* . . . (*Európa csendes, újra csendes* . . .) (January 1849).

[7] Légy vihar, mely haragjában   Légy tükör, melyből reám néz
  Ősi tölgyeket szakít,   Egész, egész életem,
  Légy szellő, mely mosolyogva   Melynek legszebb két virága
  Csendes álomba ringatja   A mulandó ifjuság s a
  A mezők fűszálait.   35   Múlhatatlan szerelem.   40

full measure, as is shown by *Bem's moving but useless attempts
to keep Petőfi away from danger-zones, and by his refusal to allow
his faith in his aide to be affected by the latter's clashes with other
(and higher) authority.

Besides acting as *Bem's liaison officer with the Government,
Petőfi was in action several times in the first months of 1849.
The poet's faith in victory was unshakeable; even in *Lost battles,
shameful flights!* . . . (*Vesztett csaták, csúfos futások!* . . .) (December
1848) he had written 'He who is ready for a hero's death will
triumph. March out in hundreds of thousands, in millions, from
the Egypt of slavery into the Canaan of freedom, as did in former
times the people of Moses! We have a God, as they had.' Now
*Bem's remarkable successes further strengthened that faith—
and also the bonds of friendship uniting Hungary and Poland;
'Is there any fate more powerful than these two nations, if they
desire one goal?' he wrote in his poem *The Transylvanian Army*
(*Az erdélyi hadsereg*) towards the end of March.[1] His output in
this period was inevitably small—in March, for instance, only five
poems: a battle-song (*In Battle*) (*Csatában*), two poems expressing
his faith in victory (*I say for certain, the Hungarian will now be
victorious* . . .) (*Bizony mondom, hogy győz most a magyar* . . .) and
The Transylvanian Army, Uncle Peter, to which we shall shortly
revert, and the following:

I hear again the voice of the lark! . . .[2]

I hear again the voice of the lark! I had quite forgotten it. Sing,
herald of spring, sing, dear little bird.

O God, how I love this song after the din of battle, as when a cool
mountain brook bathes a burning wound with its waves.

Sing, sing, dear bird; these songs remind me that I am not only an
instrument of murder, a soldier, but at the same time a poet too.

[1] On Hungarian feeling for Poland cf. Vörösmarty's *The Living Statue* (*Az
élő szobor*) (pp. 145 ff.).

[2] *Pacsírtaszót hallok megint!* . . .

Pacsírtaszót hallok megint!
Egészen elfeledtem már.
Dalolj, tavasznak hírmondója te,
Dalolj, te kedves kis madár.

Oh istenem, mi jólesik   5
A harci zaj után e dal,

Miként ha bérci hűs patak füröszt
Égő sebet hullámival.

Dalolj, dalolj, kedves madár,
Eszembe hozzák e dalok,   10
Hogy nemcsak gyilkos eszköz, katona,
Egyszersmind költő is vagyok.

Your song reminds me of poetry and of love, the many boons which those two goddesses have conferred and will yet confer on me.

Memory and hope, those two rose-trees, bloom again at the sound of your song, and bend their lovely leaves over my enraptured soul, And I dream, and my dreams are so precious, so sweet. . . . Of you I dream, my faithful angel whom I love so faithfully, Of you who are the salvation of my soul, whom God has given me to show that Heaven is not up there but on earth below.

Sing, lark, your sounds bring out the flowers; how bare was my heart, and now how many lovely flowers are bursting forth in it!

The poet who saw himself as an 'instrument of murder' when under arms also saw the tragedy of war from the point of view of others; *Uncle Peter* (*Péter bátya*) portrays the feelings of the older generation whose sons have gone off to fight. Tragic, too, is the ending of an equally vivid picture of the carefree revelry of the soldiers themselves, *What a noise, what a celebration!* . . . (*Milyen lárma, milyen vigadalom!* . . .) (October–November 1848); these young men who will later die in battle are first seen addressing the innkeeper's wife with a gaiety reminiscent of the hero of *The Hortobágy Innkeeper's Wife* (October 1842)[1]—for this is still the same Petőfi who showed us the Hungarian people in his earliest poems. More recently, too (in January 1848, the very month in which the news of the revolution in Sicily came through), *The Winter Evenings* (*A téli esték*) had displayed a panorama of human happiness in a Hungarian cottage, with the past, present, and future, in the persons of the old people talking, two young lovers unaware of their surroundings, and the children playing by the fireside. *The Winter Evenings* is the Hungarian *Cotter's Saturday*

Eszembe jut dalodrul a	Terólad álmodom, hív angyalom,
Költészet és a szerelem,	Kit olyan híven szeretek,
Az a sok jó, mit e két istennő 15	Ki lelkem üdvessége vagy, 25
Tett és még tenni fog velem.	Kit istentől azért nyerék,
	Hogy megmutassa, hogy nem odafönn,
Emlékezet s remény, ez a	De lenn a földön van az ég.
Két rózsafa ismét virít	
Dalodra, és lehajtja mámoros	Dalolj, pacsírta, hangjaid
Lelkem fölé szép lombjait, 20	Kikeltik a virágokat; 30
	Szivem mily puszta volt és benne már
És álmodom, és álmaim	Milyen sok szép virág fakad.
Oly kedvesek, oly édesek . . .	

[1] See p. 232.

Night, though without the patriotic element which forms an important part of Burns' poem.

In March 1849 a typhus epidemic carried away Petőfi's father, but the poet did not learn of his bereavement until May, a week before the death of his mother from the same cause, in the last days of the Hungarian siege of Buda. Petőfi's grief, expressed in *On the Death of my Parents* (*Szüleim halálára*) (May 1849), was soon followed by renewed hope for the fatherland when Buda was recaptured by the Hungarians on 21 May; but a month later the Czar responded to his fellow monarch's request for help. 'Here is the last, the last great test' the poet wrote in *Onward to the Holy War!* (*Föl a szent háborúra!*) (June 1849).

In July Petőfi rejoined *Bem, after first taking Julia and little Zoltán to safety in the care of friends. After a clash with Klapka, the Deputy Minister for War, in May, in which he had been disciplined for alleged insubordination, the poet had resigned from the Army, but now *Bem reinstated him, with the rank of major, and posted him to Headquarters as his adjutant. The two met on 25 July and Petőfi, we are told, 'spoke the whole day in verse'; only one poem, however, was written down in this month, *Dread times . . .* (*Szörnyű idő . . .*).

The Hungarian army went into action at Segesvár,[1] and *Bem saw clearly that against an enemy six times his own numbers his only hope lay in a surprise attack. He scored remarkable initial successes, but then the Russians realized how small was the force opposing them, and caught the Hungarians in a pincer-movement. The poet was last seen alive in the late afternoon of 31 July. He did not grow old, as those that were left grew old.

---

[1] Now Sighişoara in Rumania.

INDEX AND NOTES

(This index includes notes on names and Hungarian words marked with an
asterisk * in the text)

Academy, Hungarian, xxv, 118, 119,
128, 149, 161, 205.
Adrianople, Peace of (1568), xv.
Aeneas, 103.
Aeschylus, 137.
Ahmed III, 63, 78.
Ahriman, 106.
Aix-la-Chapelle, Treaty of (1748),
102.
Alamos de Barrientos, Don Baltasar,
37.
Alan of Lille, 9.
Alcaeus, 118; Alcaic metre, 108 n. 2,
118, and see under Horace.
Alcinous, 245.
Ali, Pasha of Buda, 1.
*alispán: the chief administrative
official of a Hungarian county under
the *főispán, q.v.
Anacreon, xxii.
András III, King of Hungary (reigned
1290–1301), 257.
*Andrássy, Gyula (1823–90), Minister
President of the first Hungarian
Government formed when the
Compromise establishing the dual
Austro-Hungarian Monarchy was
signed in 1867, 224, 227.
Angerianus, xvi.
Anticlaudianus, 9, 40.
Ányos, Pál, xx, xxvi.
Apáczai Csere János, xviii.
*April Laws, the laws passed on
11 April 1848, providing for an
independent Hungarian Govern-
ment within the Monarchy, 279,
280.
*Arany, János (1817–82), one of the
greatest Hungarian poets, especially
in narrative poetry, also a distin-
guished critic and translator, xvi,
30, 123, 273, 286.
Aranyosrákosi Székely Sándor, 104,
106.

Arcadia, xxii.
Argirus, xv, xvi, 113, 124.
Aristotle, 96.
Armenians, 68 ff., 77.
*Árpád, the chieftain who led the
Magyars when they first settled in
Hungary, traditionally in A.D. 896,
45, 103, 142; in Vörösmarty's *The
Flight of Zalán*, 104, 105 ff., 111;
*The Awakening of *Árpád*, 132;
extinction of line (1301), 257.
Athenaeum (Hungarian periodical),
132, 229, 230.
Athos, Mount, 75.
Attila, 114 n. 2.
Auerbach, B., 205.
August II, King of Poland, 78.
Aurora (Hungarian periodical), xxv,
104, 120, 139 n. 2.
Austria, wars of King *Mátyás
against, 44 ff.; reluctance to resist
Turks (16th and 17th cent.), xvii,
1, 2, 3, 25; renews peace with
Turkey (1648), 34; attitude to Zrínyi,
34, 36, 51, 54 ff.; sends Montecuccoli
to Transylvania, 53 ff.; signs Peace
of Vasvár (1664), 59; suspends
Hungarian constitution (1673), 61;
repels Turkish invasion (1683), 61;
rule in Hungary (end of 17th cent.),
62; signs Peace of Passarowitz
(1718), 66; declares *Rákóczi a
traitor and demands his extradition, 66; enters Russo-Turkish
War (1737), 82; attitude to Hungary
in 18th cent., xviii ff.; War of
Austrian Succession, 92; attitude
to Hungarian culture in early 19th
cent., xxv; repressive measures
(1837), 132; grants Hungary responsible government (1848), 196,
280; revolution (1848), 277; treatment of Hungary after 1849, 155,
204; position in 1860, 214 f.;

INDEX OF HUNGARIAN TITLES

TO CH. III (VÖRÖSMARTY) AND CH. V (PETŐFI)

PRINTED IN GREAT BRITAIN
AT THE UNIVERSITY PRESS, OXFORD
BY VIVIAN RIDLER
PRINTER TO THE UNIVERSITY